NORTHWEST
UNIFIED SCHOOL DISTRICT NO. 259
WICHITA, KANSAS

Flush Times and Fever Dreams

Race in the Atlantic World, 1700–1900

*Published in Cooperation with the Library Company of Philadelphia's
Program in African American History*

Flush Times and Fever Dreams

~~~~~~~~~~~~~~~~~~~~~~~~~~~~

*A Story of Capitalism and Slavery
in the Age of Jackson*

JOSHUA D. ROTHMAN

The University of Georgia Press
Athens and London

Parts of chapters 5 and 6 were originally published as
"The Hazards of the Flush Times: Gambling, Mob Violence,
and the Anxieties of America's Market Revolution" in the
Journal of American History 95, no. 3 (2008): 651–77.

© 2012 by the University of Georgia Press
Athens, Georgia 30602
www.ugapress.org
All rights reserved
Set in Adobe Caslon Pro by Graphic Composition, Inc.
Printed and bound by Sheridan Books
The paper in this book meets the guidelines for
permanence and durability of the Committee on
Production Guidelines for Book Longevity of the
Council on Library Resources.

Printed in the United States of America

12 13 14 15 16   C   5 4 3 2 1

Library of Congress Cataloging-in-Publication Data
Rothman, Joshua D.
Flush times and fever dreams : a story of capitalism and slavery in the age of Jackson /
Joshua D. Rothman.
p. cm. — (Race in the Atlantic world, 1700–1900)
ISBN 978-0-8203-3326-7 (hbk. : alk. paper) — ISBN 0-8203-3326-3 (hbk. : alk. paper)
1. Slavery—Southern States—History. 2. Theft—Southern States—History—19th
century. 3. Criminals—Southern States—History—19th century. 4. Vigilance
committee—Southern States—History—19th century. 5. Slave insurrections—
Southern States—History—19th century. 6. Southern States—History—1775–1865.
7. Southern States—Economic conditions—19th century. I. Title.
E441.R82 2012
306.3′620975—dc23   2012030124

British Library Cataloging-in-Publication Data available

A Sarah Mills Hodge Fund Publication

This publication is made possible, in part, through a grant
from the Hodge Foundation in memory of its founder,
Sarah Mills Hodge, who devoted her life to the relief and
education of African Americans in Savannah, Georgia.

For Rebecca

He came here with a horse and two pistols and a name which nobody ever heard before, knew for certain was his own anymore than the horse was his own or even the pistols, seeking some place to hide himself.

—WILLIAM FAULKNER, *Absalom, Absalom!*

We have become the most careless, reckless, headlong people on the face of the earth. "Go ahead" is our maxim and pass-word; and we do go ahead with a vengeance, regardless of consequences and indifferent about the value of human life. What are a few hundred persons, more or less?

—PHILIP HONE, May 22, 1837

CONTENTS

~~~~~~~~~~~~~~~~~~~~~~~~~~~~~~~~~~~~

THE UNITED STATES OF AMERICA, 1835

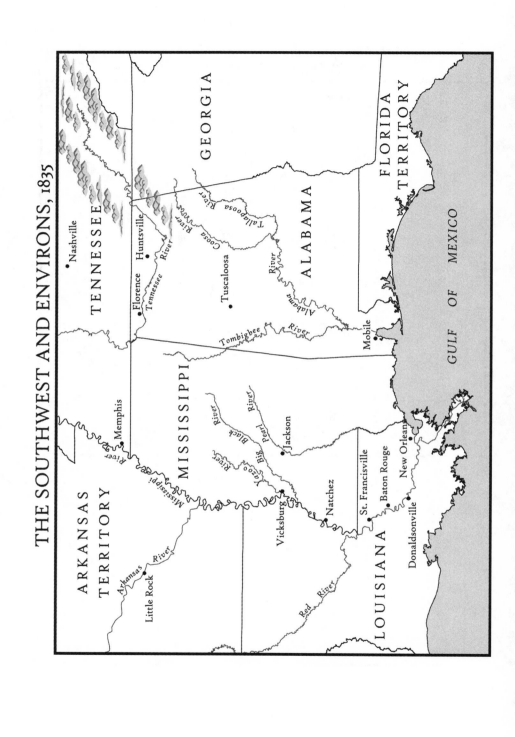

THE SOUTHWEST AND ENVIRONS, 1835

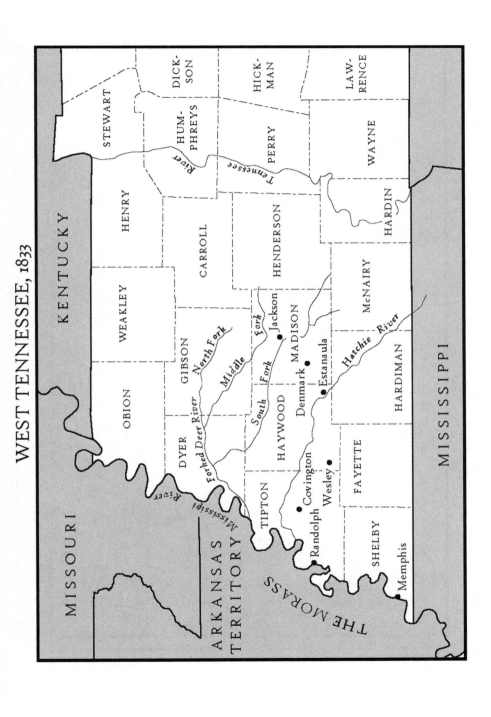

WEST TENNESSEE, 1833

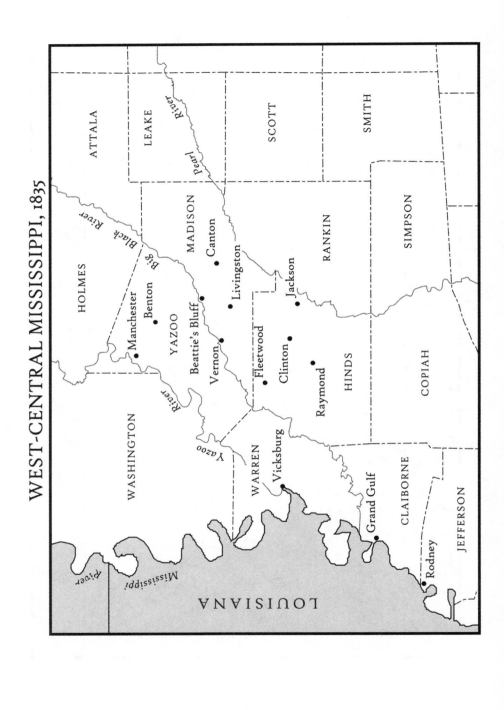

WEST-CENTRAL MISSISSIPPI, 1835

MISSISSIPPI, 1833, SHOWING
CHOCTAW AND CHICKASAW LANDS

MISSISSIPPI, 1835,
SHOWING NEW COUNTIES

TENNESSEE

ARKANSAS
TERRITORY

MONROE

TALLA-
HATCHIE
Tuscahoma

YALO-
BUSHA

Yalobusha   River

Chocchuma

CARROLL

CHOCTAW   River

LOWNDES

OKTIB-
BEHA   Columbus

Mississippi   River

HOLMES

Big   Black   River

ATTALA

WINSTON

NOXUBEE

WASHING-
TON

Manchester

Yazoo   River

YAZOO

MADISON

LEAKE   River

Pearl

KEMPER

NESH-
OBA

LAUDER-
DALE

ALABAMA

Livingston

WARREN
Vicksburg

Jackson

HINDS

RANKIN

SCOTT

SMITH

JASPER

CLARKE

CLAI-
BORNE

COPIAH

SIMPSON

JEFFER-
SON
Natchez

FRANKLIN

LAWRENCE

COV-
INGTON

JONES

WAYNE

ADAMS

WILKIN-
SON   Woodville

AMITE

PIKE

MARION

PERRY

GREENE

JACKSON

LOUISIANA

HANCOCK

GULF   OF
MEXICO

Flush Times and Fever Dreams

~ ~

The Cotton Frontier, United States of America

As he rode from the Choctaw Cession in northern Mississippi toward the plantation districts of western Tennessee, Virgil Stewart likely pondered his future and its possibilities. Possessed of a discontented soul and a firm sense that he was fated for greatness, the twenty-four-year-old Stewart was an impatient and easily frustrated man for whom present circumstances never quite satisfied. His current situation was no exception. It was January 1834, and Stewart had managed to acquire a few small parcels of land and achieve a middling status that many would have considered impressive for someone from beginnings as modest as his. But mostly he peddled furnishings out of a trunk, and he dreamed of doing grander things with his life. His ambitions were no less fierce for their lack of focus, and like many young men of his generation he believed his destiny could be waiting over the next hill. So Virgil Stewart kept on riding.[1]

On arriving in Tennessee's Madison County, Stewart paid a visit to John Henning, a minister and cotton planter with whom he had become acquainted several years earlier. As they talked, Henning mentioned that two of his slaves had recently vanished and that a local farmer and petty criminal named John Murrell had stolen them. Henning had no real evidence that Murrell was the thief. But he was certain, and he asked Stewart if he was willing and had the time to help him corroborate his suspicions. Rumor had it that Murrell would soon be taking a trip to the town of Randolph, and Henning said his son Richard intended to follow him. If all went according to plan, in the course of his travels Murrell would reveal the location of John Henning's slaves, simultaneously exposing his perfidy and enabling the elder Henning to recover his property. Randolph, though, was on the Mississippi River, more than fifty miles from the Henning plantation. John Henning did not want his son to undertake such a long and potentially dangerous mission alone in the middle of winter, so he proposed to Stewart that he join the expedition. Saying yes changed Stewart's life.[2]

Richard Henning never arrived where he and Stewart agreed to meet to begin their journey, so Stewart set off on his own. He located John Murrell, engaged him in conversation, accompanied him on his trip, and acquired information that he claimed confirmed Murrell's theft of John Henning's slaves. On returning to Madison County, Stewart reported his findings to Henning, who gathered a posse, went to Murrell's house, and arrested him. Afterward, sitting in a tavern as Henning and other wealthy citizens showered him with accolades for his bravery and cleverness, Virgil Stewart felt like an important and respected man. His moment to emerge from the anonymous masses and lay claim to an extraordinary future had arrived. He could not have known that his attempt to capitalize on that moment would result in the deaths of dozens of people back in Mississippi, but had he known, he might not have cared. It would not be the first time he had tried to take a shortcut at someone else's expense, and after all, every white man was entitled to make of himself what he could. This is a book about the thrill of that classically American promise and the furious, dark consequences of its pursuit.[3]

THE EARLY 1830S WERE stirring times for many Americans like Virgil Stewart, who lived in a country enjoying material prosperity and expansive growth the likes of which had not been seen since the years right after the end of the War of 1812. As technological advances, infrastructural improvements, and manufacturing innovations converged with the sale of large swaths of expropriated Indian land, a dramatically increased money supply, and government policies that enabled rapidly proliferating state and local banks to unleash a deluge of paper notes and liberal loans, Americans chased unprecedented opportunities in flourishing cities and on burgeoning frontiers. By the middle of the decade, the contours of the economic landscape in the United States were unmistakable. These were flush times, and the sense that nearly anyone might dip into a virtually limitless pool of money and acquire credit with few questions asked made for a heady atmosphere. Countless Americans dreamed that anything was possible for those willing to hustle.[4]

And hustle they did. Indeed, it was common wisdom among many observers that the United States had become a nation of strivers excitedly responsive to the demands and possibilities of market capitalism. Michel Chevalier, for instance, found an irrepressibly kinetic populace when he visited the United States between 1833 and 1835. An engineer on a mission for the French government, Chevalier marveled at the "passion for locomotion" he saw everywhere he went, and despite his ambivalence about Americans' unending obsession with money, he had to concede that he found their "go ahead" attitude invigorating. "If movement and the quick succession of sensations and ideas constitute life," Chevalier thought, "here one lives a hundred fold more than elsewhere." Americans had no interest in idle chatter, no time to digest a meal, no ability even to sit still. Instead, all was "circulation, motion, and boiling agitation." Every man had a scheme for realizing a fast fortune and the collateral conviction that a person of humble origins might soon be a giant among his fellows. Andrew Jackson himself best demonstrated that prospect, his storied rise from frontier wastrel to wealthy squire to the most forceful president the country had ever known having made him the paragon of the self-made man and among the most popular individuals of his age.[5]

No part of the country was more flush in the flush times than what was then its southwestern frontier, because western Georgia, Alabama, Mississippi, and eastern Louisiana possessed some of the most fertile soil on the continent for growing cotton. With the demand for the crop from the domestic and British textile industries practically insatiable and average New Orleans prices for it increasing by 80 percent during the first half of the 1830s, the forced removal of tens of thousands of Native Americans from millions of acres of prime southwestern cotton land dovetailed with federal provisions that set initial prices of public land at just $1.25 an acre to create a frenzy of migration, investment, and agricultural production. Already vital to the American economy by the start of the 1830s, over the course of the decade cotton crops brought to market by southwestern growers swelled capital accumulation that accelerated national economic development, furthered the rising position of the United States as a global power, and cemented cotton's place as the most significant commodity on earth.[6]

In 1831 the United States produced about 350 million pounds of cotton, just under half of the world's raw cotton crop. The bulk of that crop was shipped abroad, and cotton exports in 1831, worth a shade over $25 million, accounted for 35 percent of the value of all the goods exported from the United States. By 1835 the cotton crop had increased to more than 500 million pounds, roughly 70 percent of it grown in Alabama, Mississippi, Georgia, and Louisiana. Cotton exports, now worth nearly $65 million, amounted to more than half the value of all goods America sent overseas, a majority cotton maintained every year until 1841 and for most years prior to the Civil War. Thanks almost entirely to southwestern cotton production, in 1834 New Orleans bypassed New York as the most important export city in the country, and it would hold that position for almost a decade. In 1839 the United States produced more than 800 million pounds of cotton. Its share of worldwide production had become nearly two-thirds, and 80 percent of American cotton came from the Southwest. Of the 86 percent of the crop shipped overseas, two-thirds of it went to England, which relied on the United States for 81 percent of the cotton its mills turned into yarn and cloth.[7]

Little wonder, then, that when Virgil Stewart left his birthplace and sought opportunity in the 1830s, he headed for the Southwest, and even less that he ended up in Mississippi, which boomed like nowhere else in the region. The removal of the Choctaw and Chickasaw Indians between 1830 and 1832 opened the floodgates to white settlement of the northern half of the state, and hopeful purchasers swarmed federal land offices for months on end when they commenced business. The national government sold more than one million acres of public land in Mississippi in 1833 alone, twice as much as it sold in any other state. In 1835 the government sold nearly three million acres, which was more public land than had been sold in the entire country just a few years earlier.[8]

Capital came pouring into Mississippi as well. The number of banks incorporated in the state grew from one in 1829 to thirteen in 1837. Most had multiple branches, and their collective volume of loans bulged from just over one million dollars to more than fifteen million, seemingly with good reason. The nearly seventy-five thousand white people who moved to Mississippi between 1830 and 1836 doubled the state's white population and provided an eager market for that money. Moreover, their ability to pay back what they borrowed appeared beyond question. In 1834 Mississippians produced 85 million pounds of cotton, a more than eightfold increase over the amount they had produced less than fifteen years earlier. In 1836 they brought more than 125 million pounds to market, and by 1839 the Mississippi cotton crop amounted to nearly 200 million pounds, at which point Mississippians grew almost a quarter of America's cotton—more than the residents of any other state in the nation.[9]

Because cotton had the potential to yield returns very quickly and the efflorescence of banks made Mississippi a place where, as one man observed in 1836, "credit is plenty, and he who has no money can do as much business as he who has," nearly anyone able to procure even a small piece of land could indulge the belief that he was on the road to success. It was no coincidence that the 1832 state constitution, which replaced the original 1817 charter crafted when Mississippi achieved statehood, was among the most democratic in the country. Mississippi's growing population and its economic dynamism both reflected and reinforced broader cultural and political trends such that it epitomized the vaunted white male democracy of the age.[10]

Certainly, casual assessments of Mississippi's circumstances made it hard to argue with the results. To Natchez lawyer William Henry Sparks, the 1830s were years when it was as if "a new El Dorado had been discovered; fortunes were made in a day . . . and unexampled prosperity seemed to cover the land as with a golden canopy[;] . . . where yesterday the wilderness darkened over the land with her wild forests, to-day the cotton plantation whitened the earth." Author Joseph Holt Ingraham, who toured Mississippi in 1834, offered a similar observation, considering cotton growing a "mania" that would not pass "till every acre is purchased and cultivated" and the state became "one vast cotton field." Ingraham concluded that "if the satirical maxim, 'man was made to make money,' is true . . . [then] the mint of his operations lies most temptingly" in Mississippi. Burrell Fox, a farmer who migrated to Mississippi in the early 1830s, was not as lettered as Sparks or Ingraham, but no refinement was required to see what cotton made possible. "I like this cuntry," he wrote back to relatives in North Carolina, "better then any cuntry I have evry yet seen for making money."[11]

The dazzling plenty of the flush times, however, could not entirely blind Americans to troubling attendant realities. If the Southwest exemplified the energetic optimism and seemingly limitless potential of the era, it also crystallized the dangerous volatility and unnerving doubts that would ultimately undo Virgil Stewart and leave in shambles the landscape onto which he and so many others projected their fantasies. It was true that Americans everywhere in the 1830s, collectively loaded with cash and credit, enthusiastically engaged in moneymaking ventures of nearly any sort, no matter how questionable. Newspapers by the middle of the decade were filled with reports of "stock jobbers" who persuaded the artless multitudes to make dubious investments they did not understand and with stories of madcap

real estate schemes for land whose skyrocketing prices bore no plausible relation to its actual worth: a township of Maine timberland purchased in the
1820s for $620 that sold for $180,000; a tract of town property in Louisville
bought for $675 in 1815 that brought its owner an offer of $275,000; a remote
river island in northwestern Ohio that cost $1,000 and sold less than two
months later for $3,000; New York village lots along the Erie Canal whose
buyers paid ten times what the land had sold for six months earlier.[12]

But in the Southwest, Americans built a culture of speculation unique
in its abandon. Joseph Baldwin, a young lawyer from Virginia who came
to the region in 1836, recalled literally sensing a shift in the economic environment as he rode into it. Contrasting the "picayune standard" of the
East with "the wild spendthriftism, the impetuous rush and the magnifi-
cent scale of operations" of the Southwest, Baldwin noted that "the new
country seemed to be a reservoir, and every road leading to it a vagrant
stream of enterprise and adventure." With cotton prices continuing to rise
regardless of the volume placed on the market and "marvellous accounts" of
the Southwest's fertile soil circulating nationally, none of the usual rules of
business and finance appeared to apply. "Money, or what passed for money,"
Baldwin remembered, was the "only cheap thing to be had," and real estate
costs "rose like smoke. Lots in obscure villages were held at city prices;
lands, bought at the minimum cost of government, were sold at from thirty
to forty dollars per acre, and considered dirt cheap at that." It barely mattered whether a person even wanted to grow cotton or participate directly
in the land bonanza, as men accumulated "paper fortunes" without ever
girdling a tree or touching a plow and imagined instant riches at "every
cross-road and every avocation."[13]

Baldwin's portrayal of the Southwest in the flush times was not published until years later, and in some measure he intended it as caricature.
But contemporary accounts suggest he exaggerated little about the frenzy
he witnessed. Here too Mississippi led the way. Baldwin's fellow Virginia
lawyer William Gray was thoroughly taken in by the infectious economic
environment he found there. Gray had planned on just passing through
Mississippi en route to Texas, where he was to act as a land agent for some
men from Washington, D.C., but on hearing of "great speculations in lands
in all parts of the State" he stopped to do some business for himself. He
spent days poring over maps and examining settlements where every parcel
had been bought and sold as many as four times in five years at prices that

spiraled higher and higher. Speed was critical, as Gray met men who spent tens of thousands of dollars on plantations without ever seeing the property and others who were disappointed because the land they scouted got snatched out from under them before they could get back to the government land office to purchase it. But Gray was not dissuaded. The energy of the "*new world*" he had stumbled into was intoxicating. "I cannot help feeling the contagion," Gray wrote in his diary, "and want to be dealing in tens and hundreds of thousands."[14]

Given that land companies operating in Mississippi considered short-term profits of 100 percent to be eminently reasonable, Gray's excitement was understandable. Probably he would have concurred with the newspaper editor from his home state who looked to the Southwest in 1835, saw escalating cotton prices and plentiful land, and presumed that prosperity would last indefinitely. "The boundless fields of the South and West will yet take years to explore and settle," asserted the editor of the *Lynchburg Virginian*, "and we know of nothing in the probable course of events likely to throw a damper on the spirit of enterprise which is now impelling thousands to leave the lands which their grandfathers tilled, for new homes and new sources of wealth."[15]

To be sure, there was an unusually large amount of money in Mississippi. The residents of the Natchez District were among the wealthiest in the United States, and they funneled substantial resources into land, banks, internal improvements, and other promising investment opportunities. Moreover, funds streamed into the state from around the country and around the world as nonresident investors from New York, Boston, Philadelphia, London, and other financial centers pumped millions of dollars into land companies, state bonds, and bank stocks. The Second Bank of the United States bloated the state with money further still. In the early 1830s it poured nearly half its business into the Southwest, flooding the region with loans to facilitate and take advantage of the profits produced in the cotton plantation economy. Andrew Jackson's withdrawal of federal deposits from the Bank after his reelection in 1832 threatened to curtail such expansiveness, but the selection of the Planters' Bank of Mississippi as one of the federal depositories that replaced it ultimately kept the deluge of southwestern credit going. By early 1835 it surged at a more frenetic pace than ever. All told, Mississippi's banking capital increased roughly by a factor of ten between 1830 and 1837, at which point bank loans had risen to an average of nearly one hundred dollars per capita, more than triple the national average and almost a sevenfold increase from the start of the decade.[16]

But not everyone was so sanguine about Mississippi's prospects. James Davidson, a lawyer traveling through the state late in 1836, considered the speculative enthusiasms of Mississippians unsustainable, confiding to his diary that there would be "a tremendous failure here some day, and that not far hence." Baldwin, who lived in Mississippi for more than a year, also worried that delusion had supplanted reason and concluded that the craze was an irrational "hell-carnival" where "avarice and hope joined partnership" and everything stood "on its head with its heels in the air." Somewhat more concretely, one newspaper editor devoted nearly a dozen articles in the summer and fall of 1836 to an extended assault on the state's banking system, contending that financial malfeasance and corruption underlay bank operations so profoundly that Mississippi would surely be ruined without reform.[17]

Skepticism about such abundance was not unwarranted. The titanic battle over the Bank of the United States not only highlighted the fragility of credit markets and their vulnerability to shifting political winds, but Jackson's humbling of the Bank also effectively destroyed whatever regulatory influence it had exercised over the broader economy. State and local bankers in Mississippi ran wild with their newfound freedom, so much so that Mississippi's affluence by the middle of the 1830s rested in significant measure on a series of bookkeeping fictions. Often having just a small fraction of their capital in hand, banks counted money stockholders committed as if they had already paid it in, printed notes and issued credit on promised rather than actual holdings, and routinely provided sweetheart loans to institution officers and political cronies who used property purchased with that financing as collateral for still more credit at other banks. Public land sales further distorted bank operations, as purchasers used paper money borrowed from banks to buy cheap land from the federal government, which redeposited the funds back into those same banks, which then loaned that same money out over and over again, creating ever greater speculative momentum.[18]

Indeed, had more Mississippians possessed the expertise to assess financial critiques that appeared in the newspapers, the circumspection to wonder how long the unlikely combination of increasingly high cotton prices and increasingly large cotton crops could possibly continue, or the basic concern that the flush times might suddenly end and leave them in the lurch, the debt-fueled delirium of the era might never have come into being at all. Instead of fearing the possible fallout, however, most came to the Southwest believing, as Virgil Stewart did, that lives of hardscrabble obscurity could be easily transformed into lives of influence and standing, that opportunity was lost to those who hesitated, that great risks yielded great rewards, and that failure always happened to someone else. Still, experience taught all but the most enthusiastic migrants that not everything was as promised on the cotton frontier. They could scoff at the notion that southwestern prosperity was an illusion, but few could deny that disturbing implications accompanied the scramble to turn forests and swamps into plantations and towns nonetheless.

Cultural anxieties nagged as ambition and the pursuit of self-interest shaded into rapacious greed, economic speculation courted fiscal recklessness and resembled the morally questionable practice of gambling, and the sense that staggering wealth might be acquired quickly without much in the way of productive work undermined the notion that success came from diligence and frugality. Politics evolved as an insider game in which jockeying for access to capital and the levers of power often trumped ideological or partisan commitment, and personal recriminations among members of protean cliques could and did descend into bloodshed. The social terrain of the Southwest offered little more psychological mooring. The institutions or customs that might have instilled civility and order were weak or nonexistent, and appearances were often deceptive, allowing the brash, the crafty, the venal, and the predatory to thrive. Fast-talking lawyers manipulated barely functioning courts for their own benefit, surrogates for land speculators bullied settlers to get what they wanted, and swindlers, counterfeiters, horse thieves, and bandits of all stripes worked their own angles. Like all perceptive satirists, Alabama's Johnson Jones Hooper captured an essential truth about the prevailing ethic of the Southwest in the flush times with the maxim that guided his fictional creation, Simon Suggs: "It is good to be shifty in a new country."[19]

Trends like these were hardly confined to the Southwest. Nearly everywhere in the United States, demographic shifts and population movements exposed Americans to unfamiliar people of indeterminate credibility. Engagement in an expanding market economy entailed trusting faceless forces that few thoroughly understood, and the temptations of easy money created epidemics of speculation that leery commentators feared would ruin the minds and finances of those they touched. Making the economic, cultural, and social apprehensions of the era more acute in a place like Virgil Stewart's Mississippi was not merely the stampede created by the availability of so much land from which so much profit might be extracted. It was the fact that everything white Americans envisioned for the future there depended on the successful extension of slavery.[20]

The white population of Mississippi grew fast in the 1830s, but the black population grew even faster. Just over 65,000 in 1830, by 1836 the number of slaves had jumped to more than 164,000, an increase of roughly 250 percent and substantial enough that blacks had come to outnumber whites in the state. Whites brought still another 30,000 slaves into Mississippi before the end of the decade. By 1840 the enslaved population constituted approximately 52 percent of the state's total and was triple what it had been ten years earlier.[21]

Every white man intending to plant cotton in Mississippi aimed to own slaves, and those who already owned some aimed to increase their holdings. Michel Chevalier noted that a cotton plantation was essentially "a sort of agricultural manufactory," and assembling a productive workforce was the key to maximizing output and returns. The more slaves a man owned, the more land he could cultivate and the more cotton he could bring to market. It was no secret that slave labor made everything about the flush times possible. As Joseph Ingraham remarked, "to sell cotton in order to buy negroes—to make more cotton to buy more negroes, 'ad infinitum,' is the aim and direct tendency of all the operations of the thorough-going cotton planter; his whole soul is wrapped up in the pursuit.... [W]ithout slaves there could be no planters.... Without planters there could be no cotton; without cotton no wealth. Without [slaves] Mississippi would be a wilderness, and revert to the aboriginal possessors. Annihilate them to-morrow, and this state and every southern state might be bought for a song."[22]

If cotton was the engine driving the development of American capitalism before the Civil War, the enslaved were the fuel consumed to make that development possible. Moreover, because they were simultaneously laborers who grew the cotton that could make their owners wealthy and relatively liquid assets that could be sold and converted into cash, the enslaved would appear to have been fairly sturdy investments. As regional market prices for field hands rose in conjunction with cotton prices in the early 1830s, the logic behind holding one's capital in human form was ostensibly unassailable.[23]

But the explosive growth of slavery in Mississippi and throughout the Southwest also significantly aggravated the instabilities of the cotton frontier. Thousands of white Mississippians financed slave purchases much as they bought everything else—by borrowing against anticipated cotton production, often to pay professional slave traders who did booming business in the state. Slaveholders also mortgaged slave property bought on credit to provide security for additional loans, and sometimes then used those loans to purchase even more slaves. This was a tremendous piling of debt upon debt, the obligations for which were to be fulfilled by crops that had yet to be planted and worked by coerced laborers who effectively paid with their sweat for their own enslavement.[24]

Had the enslaved been as sound and reliable an investment in practice as they were in theory, such financial leveraging might have been sensible and even shrewd. But Mississippians who bought bondspersons from slave traders had to assess the value of their most crucial assets on the basis of limited information, relying mostly on the assurances of traders that the enslaved people offered as merchandise were healthy and submissive, possessed of solid work habits, and legally acquired. And none of those things was necessarily true. Instead, as white migrants re-created slavery along the frontier, the insalubrious climate and harsh work regime led to high death rates and considerable resistance among immiserated slaves, most of whom had been stolen from their families and communities. Title fraud was widespread, traders sometimes lied about the fitness of the slaves they sold or concealed histories of rebelliousness, and filing suit against deceptive traders could prove a protracted, expensive, or fruitless endeavor. White southerners expressing disdain for slave traders commonly referred to them as "negro speculators." Yet when white Mississippians purchased slaves from traders they were no less profoundly involved in speculation, their collective borrowing of tens of millions of dollars heightening the economic and social contingencies inherent in building a property regime grounded in human chattel.[25]

Southwestern political leaders recognized the problematic nature of the slave trade and tried to control it. Louisiana, Alabama, Georgia, and Mississippi all implemented interdictions against the interstate trade in the early 1830s, with the last putting in its 1832 constitution an outright ban on "the introduction of slaves" to the state "as merchandize, or for sale." Considerations for public safety and economic stability alike were at play here. Really, there was little substantive distinction between the two. By giving force to concerns that devious and unsavory slave traders brought too many slaves from too many places infected with the contagion of rebellion like that which had broken out in southeastern Virginia during the summer of 1831, policymakers in the Southwest hoped to signal to potential immigrants and investors alike that their states remained secure places to live and dependable places to put their money. Slave unrest would neither threaten white lives nor interfere with efficient cotton production.[26]

Had authorities upheld these limitations on the interstate slave trade, it might also have had the salutary and reassuring effect of containing the level of debt citizens of southwestern states owed to nonresidents, thus keeping more capital in the respective states and out of the pockets of slave traders. But whites in the Southwest seldom took paper prohibitions seriously. In Mississippi, the same constitutional clause outlawing the interstate slave trade explicitly protected the right of state residents to purchase slaves anywhere in the country and bring them into Mississippi for their personal use, a guarantee that spurred the increasingly prevalent practice of men buying slaves from traders just across the Mississippi River in Louisiana. Most did not even bother with the technical adherence to the law such a ruse allowed. The ban on the interstate trade was deeply unpopular, and rather than pass enabling legislation clarifying the penalty for violating it, during its 1833 session the state legislature imposed a tax on slave sales, thereby sanctioning a form of commerce that violated the state constitution. Far from having to end or even curb their business, traders in Mississippi sold more slaves in the years after the passage of the constitutional ban than they ever had before.[27]

Thus, while white Mississippians had outwardly clamped down on the potential influx of rebellious slaves and established a method for managed and rational expansion of the slave population, the facts of the situation were nearly the opposite. So the flush times proceeded apace, but an underlying sense of their precariousness lingered, and the social and economic order imperative for the alchemical transformation of the wilderness into money remained an elusive one. Whites on Mississippi's cotton frontier could never be sure that the enslaved who outnumbered them and on whom they depended to lift them out of debt by bringing plantations into being were not also plotting against their lives and livelihoods. They could never even be sure that other white people shared their priorities for securing property rights and racial dominance or whether they were deceitful schemers who reveled in the frontier's very lack of order. An unsteady and unstable amalgam of divergent and contradictory interests, the Southwest in the flush times was defined as much by suspicion, fraud, and extraordinary levels of violence as by opportunity, confidence, and enterprise.

This was not the world Virgil Stewart had expected to find. It was far more dangerous and chaotic than the world in which he had grown up, yet it retained the hierarchies among white people that he had hoped to leave behind. Just about anyone could borrow his way to the top, but slaveholders and other wealthy and politically connected men still held sway and were willing to act ruthlessly should anything or anyone endanger the delicate equilibrium of their surroundings. Those who could not quickly or effectively make their way into their circles or at least their good graces, meanwhile, found themselves in jeopardy of being left behind. People could get cast adrift in this world, whipsawed as they tried to figure out how to proceed, and disillusioned when circumstances forced them to confront their own inadequacies. There were reasons that men in the Southwest became notorious for fighting, drinking, and a seething aggression easily provoked to a boiling rage.

The events that sit at the heart of this book—the collapse of one man's aspirations, the evolution of an imagined conspiracy against the property holders of the Southwest, the eruption of a terrifying slave insurrection scare, the merciless purge of a city carried out by a mob—were linked in time and space, taking place mostly in Mississippi and its environs and mostly between 1833 and 1835, but they were linked too by how they reflected central paradoxes of the social, cultural, and economic changes that came to define the United States in the decades before the Civil War. Most Americans living in the East during the flush times considered the far-flung southwestern frontier exotic and distant from their own experiences. Historians ever since have largely agreed, foregrounding the emergent urban and industrial centers of the Northeast as the quintessential places for understanding the antebellum age, and particularly for understanding the transformations wrought by the ongoing advance of capitalism. We need not deny their significance to ask whether the seductive allure, propulsive power, and cruel disquiet of America's expanding civilization might be seen better instead along its leading edge.

PART ONE

~~~~~~

Self-Made Men and Confidence Men

~~~~~~

CHAPTER ONE

Inventing Virgil Stewart

Virgil Stewart came from a long line of restless men. Their migrations, extended over several generations, typified those of many families of Scottish and Scots-Irish ancestry who sought improved economic circumstances, more fertile land, and higher social status on a series of American frontiers. Stewart's great-grandfather, Lazarus Stewart, acquired property in central Pennsylvania in 1729, only to see three of his sons pick up and move in the 1750s to Rowan County in western North Carolina. One was Virgil's grandfather, James Stewart, who remained in North Carolina for several decades but in time decided that better prospects might await him elsewhere. James and his family moved to northeastern Georgia, probably in the 1780s, and were among the first white settlers of Jackson County when it was established in 1796.[1]

James Stewart had at least seven sons, few of whom stayed in one place for long either. By the 1830s the eldest son, also named James, had moved from northeastern Georgia across the state toward the Alabama border, a demanding journey that nonetheless made him among the more settled of his brothers. His brother Lazarus left Georgia altogether around 1812 for Indiana before moving to Illinois; George moved to Tennessee, also around 1812; David went to Kentucky during the first decade of the nineteenth century before moving to Indiana; and John left Georgia for Florida.[2]

The youngest son of the elder James Stewart was Samuel Stewart, Virgil Stewart's father. Samuel continued his family's evolving journey south and west, taking his wife and children to Amite County in the southwestern part of what was then the Mississippi Territory shortly after Virgil's birth in 1809. That was not the most auspicious time to move to Mississippi, as the federal government had imposed an embargo on trade with England toward the end of 1807, effectively if temporarily crushing a flourishing cotton export market. Local economic stagnation was the least of Samuel Stewart's problems, however. He died just months after arriving in the territory, perhaps from one of the many diseases that plagued European and American settlers of the area. His widow, Virgil's mother, soon took her shattered family back to Jackson County.[3]

Virgil Stewart would later claim that his mother returned to Georgia because she became "dissatisfied" with Mississippi. But given the ambivalence of many southern women toward the dangers and uncertainties of southwestern migration, the disastrous outcome of her husband's decision to move, the likelihood that she knew practically no one in Mississippi after just several months' residence, and the dire economic prospects in the area for a single woman with small children, the question of whether or not to move back to Georgia had only one possible answer.[4]

Samuel Stewart left behind a "slender patrimony" when he died, and his son recalled that in short order much of that "was squandered." Hence, even though Virgil Stewart's "early desire was to receive a liberal education" like the one wealthier young men expected as a matter of course, his financial circumstances enabled him to attend school only until he turned fourteen, at which point he had to find work. Hoping to enter a profession that might further his intellectual development, Stewart apprenticed with a printer. But he soon abandoned that business for a co-partnership in a cotton gin manufacture. Financially the shift was a wise one, as cotton production in the United States took off again after the end of the War of 1812, increasing by approximately 150 percent every five years between 1815 and 1835. So long as crop yields continued to proliferate, a subsidiary enterprise like gin manufacturing was bound to make at least some money. Over the course of the late 1820s the business both improved Stewart's finances and helped establish him, at least in his own eyes, as a man of "industry, decision of character, and much moral worth, among his fellow-citizens."[5]

But that was not enough for him. Whatever modicum of social and economic standing Virgil Stewart had achieved in Georgia, he still felt like the undistinguished son of an undistinguished man, and he was sure he deserved more. He too was "dissatisfied." So when he turned twenty he decided, as many Stewarts before him had done, to seek his fortune elsewhere. Joining tens of thousands of other white American migrants who fled the Eastern Seaboard in the 1820s and 1830s for the bounteous cotton lands they had heard about in the interior, Stewart headed out to see what he might make of himself "amid the newer regions of the western country." But Stewart discovered that despite the economic possibilities and the chance for personal reinvention the frontier supposedly offered, there too the footing was unequal. There too the choices a person made could follow him wherever he went. Even on the frontier, the past was not easily left behind.[6]

I.

Virgil Stewart's first "western country" residence lay in Madison County, Tennessee, more than four hundred miles from his Georgia home. Created by the Tennessee legislature in 1821, Madison was a perfect square carved from the center of the state's Western District, a block of territory between the Tennessee and Mississippi rivers that the Chickasaw Indians had ceded to the United States in 1818. By the time the legislature drew boundaries for the county, however, surveyors, speculators, and settlers had already begun hungrily evaluating the land's prospects. They wasted little time divvying up forested Chickasaw hunting grounds and turning them into the cleared farms, plantations, and towns that most Americans of the age envisioned when they heard the word "civilization."[7]

White settlers may have been relatively new to Madison County when Virgil Stewart arrived in the fall of 1830, but more than seven thousand of them had already poured in by horseback, wagon, keelboat, and flatboat, bringing with them more than four thousand slaves to grow the corn, tend the livestock, and especially produce the cotton that promised to make them rich. The South Fork of the Forked Deer River wended its way across the county toward the Mississippi diagonally from southeast to northwest, and the burgeoning county seat of Jackson grew up rapidly at a crossroads along its banks. In 1830 nearly seven hundred people lived in Jackson and almost five thousand bales of cotton shipped from its landings, headed eventually to New Orleans and from there to international markets and the noisy machinery of the early Industrial Revolution. With an observer describing Madison as having "a fertility [even] in its poorest soil that I have seen nowhere else," one can see how the editor of the local *Jackson Gazette* could report that the county was still "swimming with land hunters" nearly a decade after settlers started rushing there in the 1820s. It was only appropriate that Madison's congressional representative was none other than the archetypal frontiersman himself, David Crockett.[8]

Although Virgil Stewart arrived in western Tennessee at a seemingly propitious moment for someone in search of social and economic opportunity, the outlook there ultimately was not what he had in mind. During the time he lived in Madison County he worked a small farm about six miles west of Jackson. By his own account, he did reasonably well and had "by industry and economy, increased the little estate left him by his father to a respectable competency." Nonetheless, after a little more than two years he resolved to move to Mississippi "and invest his whole property in land" in the Choctaw Cession instead.[9]

Virgil Stewart had probably never worked regularly as a farmer before moving to Tennessee, and inexperienced settlers could find growing cotton more challenging than regional boosters made it sound. Stewart was also not one for difficult physical labor, but we need not necessarily chalk up to indolence his determination to exchange one frontier for another, as he was hardly the only western migrant to make such a decision. Obviously, Americans who moved to western frontiers would not have assumed the risks of migration at all had they not tended toward inconstancy to begin with. But many sought not merely a place where they might make a better life. They sought the place where they might make the best of all possible lives. And in nineteenth-century America, the best place was always someplace else. Every new territory that opened for American settlement in the 1820s and 1830s seemed more promising and productive than the last. There, not here, the most fertile land could be had at the cheapest prices. There, not here, crops grew most bountifully. There, not here, men could strive for success freed from the burdens of the past and the hierarchies of the East. There, not here, individual and national destinies would be fulfilled.[10]

When Virgil Stewart decided to sell his holdings in Tennessee, Mississippi was that place. Perhaps more than for any other impending land sale in recent memory, Americans itched for the moment when the national government would auction more than ten million acres of territory that had been pried away from the Choctaw by the Treaty of Dancing Rabbit Creek in 1830. Land companies, individual speculators, and their agents looked at the enormous, roughly boot-shaped tract stretching across northwestern, central, and southeastern Mississippi and saw opportunities to acquire enormous wealth by buying and hoarding property to sell when prices became their most inflated. But less financially endowed men like Stewart looked at Mississippi and thought they saw democracy in its finest and purest form—a spot where an entirely new society would be built from scratch and any white man, no matter his background or history, could transform himself into whatever he wished to be. Virgil Stewart, who was insecure about his upbringing but resolved to show that it made him no worse than any other person, imagined that Mississippi was better than Tennessee because it was fresher than Tennessee, free of even the elementary social and economic ranks that had already begun to emerge in Madison County by the time he arrived. In Mississippi, Stewart thought, he could become a man of standing more easily and more rapidly than anywhere else in the United States.[11]

But he had to move quickly. No one was sure when the Choctaw lands would be auctioned, but President Jackson had made clear that he wanted it to happen soon. In the latter months of 1831, government surveyors had begun drawing the grid of rectangular townships, ranges, and sections that would describe the land available for purchase. Administrative and bureaucratic obstacles might cause brief delays, but once the surveyors completed their task it was just a matter of time before the General Land Office declared the sale imminent. Moreover, given how fast land values were bound to rise once public auctions gave way to private deals, a man had to know what he wanted and be ready to buy it the instant it was offered. If Virgil Stewart wanted to turn his "respectable competency" into something more, if he wanted to transform what remained of the "little estate" his father had left him into the abundance his father had been denied by early death, he had to go now.[12]

Late in 1832 Stewart liquidated his assets. He used most of the cash he realized to purchase an array of household goods, farm implements, medicines, cloth, and additional items that he planned to sell to those in need of basic supplies in Mississippi. He knew that being able to demonstrate a reputation for integrity could help him acquire the credit used by most people who bought land, and the people who knew him best lived in Georgia. So he made a brief trip back there to procure a certificate signed by nearly forty men who had known him in his youth and were willing to testify that he had "always supported a respectable and honorable character." Back in Tennessee on June 1, 1833, Stewart boarded a boat bound for Tuscahoma, Mississippi. A new village along a short tributary of the Yazoo River known as the Yalobusha in the north-central part of the state, Tuscahoma sat just a few miles northeast of where the U.S. Land Office had been established at a place called Chocchuma. The boat ran aground in the Yalobusha's shallow summertime waters around twelve miles from its destination, but Stewart was undaunted. Equipped with a large trunk and a chest full of merchandise, a letter vouching for his worthiness, and a conviction that his prospects were bright, Virgil Stewart was ready to begin the next phase of his life.[13]

II.

After disembarking on the banks of the Yalobusha, Stewart hired a wagon to haul his things to the home of Duncan McIver, whom he had known back in Tennessee and who had since settled a mile from Tuscahoma. Stewart quickly sold most of the items he had brought with him and spent much of the time he boarded with McIver "examining the country" for land he might wish to purchase. By September 1833, when the federal government announced that sales at Chocchuma would commence the following month, Stewart was living about ten miles east of McIver's residence with yet another associate from his time in Tennessee, a man named Matthew Clanton.[14]

Born in Virginia around 1798, Clanton had made his way by 1830 to Perry County, Tennessee, before moving farther west the following year to the small but growing Madison County village of Denmark, located southwest of Jackson on the former site of a Chickasaw settlement. Clanton stayed in Denmark long enough to achieve some degree of social standing and became a trustee for one of the village's schools late in 1831. Even so, in 1832 he left behind his wife, Eliza Ann, his four-year-old son James, and his infant son Joseph while he headed into the Choctaw Cession to look for a more promising future. Clanton established a little store on the northern bank of the Yalobusha River to sell provisions to settlers. But that business offered uncertain expectations, so Clanton spent the ensuing months traveling back and forth between his store in Mississippi and his family in Tennessee as he pondered his next step.[15]

Though Matthew Clanton and Virgil Stewart had met mostly in passing during the brief period both lived in Madison County, they took an immediate liking to one another on becoming reacquainted by happenstance in Mississippi. Ten years older than Stewart, Clanton saw himself as a sort of mentor to the younger man. He may not have known Stewart well, but they had traveled similar paths, and Clanton claimed he "felt a much deeper interest in [Stewart's] welfare than the same degree of acquaintance would have produced towards a man from a country different to the one [from which] I had myself come." Thinking Stewart "an honest young man," Clanton let him sleep at his store and trusted him enough that when Clanton decided in October 1833 to relocate his family to Mississippi, he asked Stewart to attend to his business while he went to Tennessee to fetch them.[16]

When Clanton returned in early December, Stewart gave him a quick tally of the store's accounts and assured him that everything had gone smoothly in his absence. Clanton was so pleased that he offered Stewart the chance to become his business partner. Stewart declined, telling Clanton that he and a neighbor, William Vess, had decided to form a partnership in Stewart's old trade manufacturing cotton gins and hoped to build their shop nearby. Stewart liked the fellowship and knew that Clanton anticipated starting a small town on the land surrounding his store, so opening a shop right where he was seemed to Stewart both personally agreeable and commercially savvy. Grateful for how Stewart had minded his affairs while he was away and thinking that a cotton-gin business could only improve the outlook for his prospective town, Clanton gave Stewart a small plot of land adjacent to his store as a token of his appreciation.[17]

Events turned even more favorable for Stewart in the weeks after Clanton's return. In mid-December, having spent months looking at land and making innumerable trips to the public auctions that had been taking place at Chocchuma since October, Stewart finally purchased property from the federal government. At the minimum price of $1.25 an acre, Stewart bought one forty-acre plot roughly three miles northwest of Clanton's store and another of the same size about five miles almost due north. The latter parcel indicates how close his relations had become with his new neighbors despite their relative brevity, as it was surrounded on three sides by property Clanton owned. William Vess bought several plots bordering Clanton's territory as well.[18]

Also buying property contiguous with that of Stewart, Clanton, and Vess was a forty-six-year-old farmer named George Saunders who had come to Mississippi from Tipton County, Tennessee, just a few months earlier. Saunders settled in the vicinity of Clanton's store and in short order had joined Stewart, Clanton, and Vess in a situation that bred a very intense familiarity. All four men—along with Eliza Clanton, her two children, and Ann Vess, William's wife—lived within a few hundred yards of one another and saw each other daily. Stewart had moved his personal effects into the Vess household after Matthew Clanton brought his family back from Tennessee, but with comfortable living space at a premium on the frontier and privacy hard to come by, he still sometimes spent the night in Clanton's store. It was fortunate that Stewart and Vess had decided to become business partners, that Saunders "thought well" of Stewart, that Stewart could claim he "loved" Clanton, and that Clanton treated Stewart with what he believed to be "the kindness and friendship of a brother," because theirs was a living arrangement Saunders aptly described as "very intimate."[19]

On the surface, everything seemed to be falling into place for Virgil Stewart during the six months after his arrival in Mississippi. He had avoided the misfortunes and mistakes that turned golden aspirations into stinging disappointments for thousands of other migrants, and he was in the right place at the right time to invest in some of the finest untilled cotton land in the United States. Moreover, he got there early enough to be among the first residents of a brand-new county. Less than two weeks after Stewart bought his land, the Mississippi legislature divided much of the Choctaw Cession into sixteen new counties. Stewart's land lay in the southwestern part of one called Yalobusha that had enormous potential. Early population totals are hard to find, but by 1837 Yalobusha County already housed more than forty-three hundred white people and more than forty-two hundred slaves. The total population jumped to more than twelve thousand by the end of the decade.[20]

Stewart had also begun building a network of personal relationships—in part by capitalizing on those he had created in Tennessee—and forging useful connections to men who might become powerful and influential in the place he now considered home. George Saunders had brought at least eight slaves with him to Mississippi and intended on becoming a cotton planter, and Matthew Clanton was considering running for probate judge when Yalobusha's first elections took place in February 1834, a position that would make him the most important magistrate in the county. Stewart even felt he had started acquiring some local regard in his own right. He floated the idea of running for county clerk and joined a neighborhood company of regulators, a group of local vigilantes like those that appeared on many frontiers in the United States to enforce order and morality on those they believed criminals and reprobates. Self-appointed, capable of tremendous violence, and interested in the security of private property as much as the public good, regulator companies nonetheless often comprised estimable members of their young communities.[21]

But Virgil Stewart had also encountered things in Mississippi that bothered him. On the one hand, as a relatively young man with no family and little in the way of social or financial privilege, he recognized that in-gratiating himself with older men who had some of those advantages was a way of building his own reputation. And he was good at it. Stewart was un-remarkable in appearance aside from a shock of red hair, but many people took a shine to him on meeting him for the first time. He seemed earnest, sincere, and eager to help, and one man who claimed to have known him well recalled thinking Stewart "one of the most sagacious and insinuating persons" he had ever met. At the same time, however, Stewart resented feeling that he had to prove himself to people like Matthew Clanton and George Saunders at all. Among the lures of the southwestern frontier was that doing well there supposedly required no such solicitousness. Joseph Baldwin, for example, claimed that in the Southwest there was "no *prestige* of rank, or ancestry, or wealth, or past reputation—and no family influence, or dependants, or patrons." The "stranger of yesterday," he went on, "is the man of mark to-day." Stewart found the reshuffling of selfhood and status that accompanied reinventing one's life in the Southwest a more frustrat-ing and ambiguous experience. With an ego matched in size only by its brittleness, Stewart was caught between his desire to exploit the anonymity offered by frontier migration for the sake of creating a new identity and the sense that he could never truly consider himself successful without recogni-tion from men conventionally considered his betters.[22]

Further rankling Stewart and making his conundrum all the more dispir-iting was that despite commonplace assertions like Baldwin's, rank, wealth, and influence obviously *did* matter in Mississippi. Nothing demonstrated that reality better than the public land auctions at Chocchuma. Hundreds of people crowded the tiny village during the fall of 1833 in hopes of acquir-ing title to some of the nearly 250,000 acres of land the government sold there, but only a small fraction of the land was actually sold directly to farmers and planters who planned to work and live on it. Instead, an entity known as the Chocchuma Land Company purchased some three-quarters of the total.[23]

Founded in a tavern after the second day of land sales, the company en-compassed three groups of speculators from Alabama, Tennessee, and Mis-sissippi who pooled financial resources and information about desirable real estate rather than compete with one another and drive up prices for land they all wanted to purchase. Ultimately composed of around 150 men, the consortium authorized four agents to bid on its behalf for land, the profits from which would then be apportioned to individual investors based on the amount they had contributed to the company purse. To prevent the mass of settlers from bidding against them, representatives of the company met with representatives of the settlers and assured them their only concern was keeping prices low for everyone. All a settler had to do was submit to the company a description of the land he was currently working or had an interest in buying. So long as the parcel did not exceed 160 acres and the settler agreed to bid on no other property, the company would purchase the described land for the minimum price on his behalf and then sell it to him privately at cost.[24]

In some ways the agents of the Chocchuma Land Company shrewdly manipulated the workings of a federal land auction to the advantage of company shareholders and ordinary settlers alike. Company agents only rarely found competitive bidding situations at Chocchuma, as most settlers and other small purchasers determined that the easiest way to get the land they wanted at the lowest possible price was to accept the conditions laid out by the consortium. For their part, even after transferring the parcels agreed on in advance, company investors not only held the interest-bearing promissory notes that many of the settlers and other small purchasers used to buy those parcels, and which themselves were negotiable instruments. They also collectively held tens of thousands of acres of prime real estate that could be sold later for a sizable return. In the end, the company's share-holders earned about thirty cents for every dollar they invested, a payoff that did not even include potential profits from reselling land that many of them bought through the company for themselves as individuals.[25]

Still, what transpired at Chocchuma prompted a fraud investigation by the Senate Committee for Public Lands, and even though that investiga-tion concluded no laws had been broken, the activities of the Chocchuma Land Company clearly circumvented the spirit behind the auctions. For one thing, company investors effectively hijacked for their own gain sales whose benefits were supposed to accrue to the federal government, and by extension to the American people. Every transaction in which prices remained artificially low because the company short-circuited the bidding process represented the loss of money that should have entered the national coffers. Furthermore, it all happened with the knowledge if not the complicity of the land office register at Chocchuma, Samuel Gwin. Every evening at a tavern just yards from Gwin's office the Chocchuma Land Company held private sales of the land its agents had purchased during the day. Gwin could not have failed to grasp what was happening, and among the questions that dominated the Senate investigation was whether Gwin lined his own pockets by colluding with company agents.[26]

Moreover, there is no doubt that the company stifled the ambitions of some prospective buyers and bullied others into submission with its sheer financial might. When company agents originally presented their terms to the settlers' representatives, several balked, arguing that individuals ought to be allowed to purchase more than 160 acres of land. That demand was flatly rejected, and as the auctions progressed, those who tried either to buy more acreage than the company sanctioned or to challenge the company in a bidding war found the price of land they sought run up by as much as ten dollars per acre. The company represented its actions as benefiting the majority of the settlers and facilitating the efficient and democratic sale of public lands. In reality, those who belonged to the company got almost exactly what they wanted while hundreds of settlers got an "arrangement" that was, in the words of one of their representatives, "the best that we could form."[27]

Virgil Stewart was not opposed to land speculation. He never intended to work the property he bought at Chocchuma, and while both Matthew Clanton and George Saunders purchased some of their land through agents of the Chocchuma Land Company, Stewart got his directly from the land office, his parcels apparently being among those in which the company lacked interest. But he wondered why the benefits of a process purportedly designed for the good of ordinary citizens redounded so systematically to those who already had financial and political connections. Just holding the Chocchuma auctions in October, in fact, disadvantaged small buyers. Purchasers of public lands had to make a down payment in cash. But southwestern farmers were at their cash poorest in the early fall, and despite plentiful credit options generally in the region there were no banks or large mercantile firms in the immediate area of the Choctaw Cession, which presented a problem for those who needed money without delay. As one man told the Senate Committee for Public Lands, when the government announced in September that land sales would begin a mere six weeks hence, "the general sentiment among the common class of people was, that the lands would go into the hands of wealthy men, who could raise large sums of money on short notice, and that the season of the year, together with the shortness of the notice, gave such men almost entire control of the sales."[28]

A perusal of the stockholders in the Chocchuma Land Company supports that contention. The company's lead bidder from Mississippi, for example, was Robert Walker, a Pennsylvania-born lawyer who moved to Natchez in the 1820s, joined his brother's already established law practice there, became a leader of the state's nascent Democratic Party, and quickly created what his biographer terms "an empire of plantations and slaves founded on credit." When the Chocchuma land sales were announced, Walker's influential position enabled him to borrow more than ten thousand dollars on extremely generous terms from the Planters' Bank of Mississippi—from a fund that had been set aside to pay interest on state bonds. Surely it helped that the group of speculators Walker put together included other wealthy and politically powerful Mississippi insiders, among them plantation owner and congressman Franklin Plummer; John Quitman, a planter and the state chancellor; William Gwin, federal court marshal in the state, former private secretary to Andrew Jackson, and younger brother of the register at Chocchuma; Natchez-born planter James Girault, who was also receiver of the public monies at Chocchuma and thus perfectly placed to know the location of the best land being sold; and the governor of Mississippi himself, Hiram Runnels. Robert Walker alone purchased more than seventy-five thousand acres of land at Chocchuma. He immediately transferred about a third of it to individuals who had entered into agreements with the company and kept the other fifty thousand acres for himself.[29]

Thus, by the time Virgil Stewart left Mississippi in January 1834 for a visit to Tennessee, having promised Matthew Clanton he would try to encourage people there to move to Yalobusha County and settle near the site of the town Clanton hoped to build, he understood who got the bulk of what the frontier had to offer and how they got it. He had always suspected that only a few people rose rapidly to prominence through hard work alone. Already having money or pull on arriving in the Southwest was ideal, but a man who got a little luck, had some guile, became well thought of by the right people, and was willing to resort to just enough chicanery not to get caught might claw his way right to the top. Maybe that was unfair. Maybe character and effort and seriousness of purpose should have been enough to demonstrate one was of singular worth. But the Southwest was not an entirely fair place. To the contrary, when Stewart got to Tennessee and John Henning asked him to help track down John Murrell, he already knew that the pursuit of self-interest in the Southwest sometimes required a bit of deceit.

III.

Like Virgil Stewart's parents, the parents of John Murrell decided to move west when their son was just an infant. Murrell was born in Lunenburg County, Virginia, in 1806, the third child of Jeffrey and Zilpah Murrell. That same year, Jeffrey and his brother Drury left Lunenberg to take up farming in Tennessee's Williamson County, just south of Davidson County and the city of Nashville. The Murrell brothers purchased 146 acres of land on the headwaters of the West Harpeth River bordering the property of Zilpah Murrell's father, Mark Andrews, who had relocated to Tennessee from Virginia several years earlier. By 1810 several of Mark Andrews's children and their families lived near one another in middle Tennessee, and for their part, Jeffrey and Zilpah Murrell were reasonably prosperous. By the early 1820s Jeffrey owned three slaves and Zilpah had given birth to five more children. On the surface the Murrells appeared to be models of the sturdy yeomen whose success Thomas Jefferson imagined the American West would nurture.[30]

Below the surface, though, things were significantly less placid. The male children of southwestern migrants generally developed a reputation for wildness and for lacking the sense of responsibility men of the Revolutionary generation possessed, but the generational differences within the Murrell family were striking nonetheless. Four of Jeffrey Murrell's eight children were boys, and all routinely ran afoul of the law in Tennessee from an early age. By the early 1830s, the oldest Murrell brother, William, had been hauled into court for debt, indicted for forgery, arrested for larceny, and divorced by his wife for abandoning her before he finally left the state altogether for Arkansas. William proved such a source of grief, in fact, that Jeffrey Murrell disinherited him. The next oldest brother, James, was indicted for perjury and tried for counterfeiting before he too left the state, probably for South Carolina. A county grand jury charged the youngest Murrell brother, Jeffrey, and a woman named Polly Staggs with fornication and running a house of prostitution. Several years later, Jeffrey Murrell the son was also indicted for larceny. He eventually left Tennessee as well. Taking up a different sort of illicit flesh trade, he turned to stealing horses in Kentucky and taking them to other states for resale.[31]

The early criminal escapades of John Murrell were similar in scale to those of his siblings. A handsome young man just under six feet tall with blue eyes and black hair, Murrell found his first legal troubles in January 1823 at the age of sixteen when he and his older brothers were indicted, convicted, and fined fifty dollars apiece in Williamson County on the misdemeanor charge of "riot" for having forced their way into the home of Thomas Merritt and terrorized him and his wife, Rebecca. Why the Murrells attacked Merritt's home is unclear, though one historian has plausibly suggested that Merritt owed John Murrell money and refused to pay. Merritt did not even file charges against the brothers until John Murrell filed a civil suit against him nearly a month after the incident, suggesting that Merritt had preferred to keep his conflict with Murrell private. Whatever the precise reason for their dispute, John Murrell and Thomas Merritt dropped their mutual suits in July 1823, and the fines against the Murrell brothers were reduced on appeal from fifty dollars to just fifty cents.[32]

Even as his legal conflict with Thomas Merritt made its way through the courts, however, John Murrell created bigger problems for himself. In February 1823 he was arraigned for stealing a horse belonging to a neighbor, William Shumate, a crime for which he was determined to avoid punishment. After being indicted by a Williamson grand jury, Murrell failed to show for his August 1823 court date. He was found, arrested, and committed to jail a few days later, only to break out of prison in October, prompting frustrated Williamson County deputy sheriff W. B. McClellan to place a newspaper advertisement offering a twenty-dollar reward for the apprehension of the "monstrous rascal." Murrell managed to elude detection for nearly five months before being recaptured several counties away, whereupon he asked for and received a change of venue on the grounds that he could not receive a fair trial in Williamson. In May 1826, more than three years after being arraigned, John Murrell was finally tried in Davidson

County and convicted of horse theft. He was sentenced to twelve months in prison, thirty lashes at the public whipping post, and six hours in the pillory, and to have the letters HT (for "horse thief") branded on his left thumb.[33]

Guilty or not, one can understand why a man would go to great lengths to sidestep such painful and humiliating punishments. Nonetheless, John Murrell's evasiveness also caused his family a great deal of distress. His father and uncle had posted one thousand dollars' bond for his release when he was originally arraigned, even though Jeffrey Murrell claimed that John had "always been an expence to him" and contributed almost nothing to help support his family. Though far from indigent, Jeffrey and Drury Murrell were not especially rich either, and when John failed to appear in court and then escaped from custody, they stood to forfeit the entire amount. William Shumate, meanwhile, was none too pleased about having to wait several years to see John Murrell pay for his crime, and he seems to have suspected him of stealing more than just his horse. Both before and several times after Murrell was recaptured, more than a dozen of Shumate's male friends and relatives showed up at the Murrell home, broke down the door, assaulted its inhabitants, and searched the house and outbuildings for unnamed items.[34]

When John Murrell got out of prison in 1827, his family was in dire straits. Jeffrey Murrell had died in 1824, leaving behind a modest but debt-free estate to his wife and children. As much as economic sustenance, though, John Murrell's father seems to have provided stability and cohesion for his troubled family, and his death marked the onset of a precipitous decline. Sons who preferred stealing to working did not promise the widowed Zilpah Murrell a great deal of economic assistance or security, and she had had to borrow money while John served his jail sentence. When she then found it impossible to repay the loan, a court ordered that the family's land, slaves, livestock, farm equipment, and household goods be auctioned for cash to cover the debt.[35]

Thus, within three years of Jeffrey Murrell's death his family had practically nothing left. Once able to count themselves among the ranks of independent farmers, the Murrells instead became landless wanderers. Shortly after John Murrell was released from jail in 1827, he and his entire family moved to rented land in Wayne County, southwest of Williamson along Tennessee's border with Alabama. In 1829 Murrell married Elizabeth Mangham, and the couple lived near Murrell's mother, who headed a large household of fourteen people, including nearly half a dozen children under the age of five.[36]

But the Murrells would not find permanence in Wayne County either. Between late 1831 and early 1832 the extended Murrell family moved yet again. Heading northwest out of Wayne and into Tennessee's Western District, they stopped south of Jackson near Denmark in Madison County, where they probably rented land once more. Zilpah and John Murrell combined their households into a single very large one, and John nominally began working as a farmer. Elizabeth Murrell either had or was about to give birth to a child, and perhaps having become a husband and a father since his release from jail encouraged John Murrell to try and amass something more substantial than the clothes on his back, a gun, and a few tools, which had been the sum total of his recorded worth when he was tried for horse theft six years earlier. He was not entirely unsuccessful. An inventory of his possessions performed early in 1833 revealed that he and Elizabeth managed to accumulate two horses and forty hogs in addition to some household items and furniture. Unfortunately, that inventory was performed because the Murrells were about to lose practically all of their property to pay debts they owed to several merchants. By the middle of 1833, a Madison County court determined that John Murrell was "not worth lands goods or chattels to any amount whatever."[37]

Even this circumstance, however, did not mark Murrell's legal and financial low point in the years before he encountered Virgil Stewart. One moment in his criminal career had yet to unfold, and it was perhaps the most critical of all in determining the path his life would take. In the early summer of 1833, three slaves belonging to a Madison County planter named William Long went missing and were accounted runaways. When one of the slaves reappeared on Long's plantation to retrieve some clothing, Long's overseer spotted and interrogated him, whereupon the enslaved man admitted that he and his fellows had secreted themselves in some woods near the Murrell homestead. Long became convinced that John Murrell had lured his slaves to the location and was helping conceal them with the intention of eventually removing them from the county and reselling them. Long gathered a small company of men, followed his slave back to the hiding place, and confronted Murrell when he arrived there with provisions. Forced to explain himself, Murrell claimed he had been feeding Long's slaves clandestinely so as to keep them in one place until he could inform Long of their whereabouts.[38]

Long found this unlikely excuse thoroughly unbelievable, as did the members of a jury impaneled by the Madison County Circuit Court. They did not see enough evidence to convict Murrell of the felony charge of slave theft for which Long and the county solicitor general wanted to prosecute him, but they could not disagree that Murrell had done something illegal with another man's property. On July 10, 1833, they found him guilty of the misdemeanor charge of harboring runaway slaves. The impoverished Murrell could not pay even the smallest fine that might be levied against him, so as an alternative the judge sentenced him to labor for William Long for five years as a servant.[39]

Murrell immediately appealed the judgment and the inventive sentence to the Tennessee Supreme Court, an appeal that was still pending when John Henning's slaves vanished six months later. It is not surprising that Henning looked to Murrell when that happened, despite having no material proof that Murrell was the thief or even that a theft had taken place. Plantation owners saw poor whites like John Murrell and his family as inherently untrustworthy characters who deserved neither respect nor even, as the widely used epithet "trash" suggests, basic human dignity. Given his poverty, his itinerancy, the stories about his knavish past that had followed him west from Williamson County, and his recent conviction in connection with the slaves who left William Long's plantation, by early 1834 John Murrell had become one of the usual suspects for property crimes in his part of Madison County whether he committed them or not.[40]

It is surprising, though, that Henning or anyone else would think that Murrell was more than that, as Murrell had never in his life perpetrated a crime signaling that he was a particularly dangerous man. Which is not to say he was an innocent man. Horse theft, after all, was considered a serious offense, and slave stealing even more so. Punishable in Tennessee by up to fifteen years in the state penitentiary, kidnapping or enticing the enslaved to flee their owners was a capital crime in several other states. Because slaves could be moved and resold without documentation to less than scrupulous buyers, to steal a slave was to appropriate chattel illegally, to introduce uncertainties into regional labor markets, and to unsettle the security of titles to the most valuable form of personal property in the United States.

Equally if not more alarming, because slave stealers frequently got the enslaved to accompany them voluntarily by pledging to grant them freedom, their "tampering" with the slave population also called mastery into question and encouraged slaves generally to be discontented and insubordinate. By making it difficult for slaveholders to feel entirely sure about either their wealth or their authority, slave stealers compromised the very foundations of profit and power on which the entire system of slavery rested.[41]

Jurors in Madison County had only been comfortable concluding that John Murrell had concealed some runaways and not that he had intentionally stolen William Long's slaves. Given the Murrell family's desperate economic circumstances in 1833, though, Long may well have been right about Murrell's intentions. Murrell needed the money, and poor men did not normally feed runaway slaves for days or weeks without an ulterior motive. Moreover, Madison County was a perfect location for slave stealing. It was in a plantation district with a sizable slave population and it sat just a few days' ride from Tennessee's borders with both Alabama and Mississippi, enabling thieves to move relatively quickly outside the jurisdiction of often-ineffective authorities.

Madison was almost equally close to the Mississippi River and the swampy eastern Arkansas Territory that lay on its far side, a sparsely populated region known colloquially as "the Morass" that networks of horse thieves, counterfeiters, slave stealers, highwaymen, and other lawbreakers who worked both sides of the river from Illinois and Missouri all the way down to New Orleans found especially useful. One editor in western Tennessee warned about "lawless freebooters, infesting the Arkansas shore of the Mississippi for some hundred miles" who harassed and stole from travelers and people living on the east side of the river alike. "Horses, negroes, cattle, and every species of property is their prey," he continued, "and such is their adroitness, and so impregnable their marshy skulking places, as to make their detection almost impossible, burying themselves when pursued, in the almost impervious canebrakes." An Arkansas editor likewise wrote about "a lawless gang of villains" hiding in the area "who make a regular business of kidnapping negroes and stealing horses, and running them off to the lower country and selling them."[42]

Doubtless John Murrell knew some members of this criminal underworld. His brother William had become at least a part-time counterfeiter after leaving Tennessee for Arkansas, his brother Jeffrey was a horse thief, and John himself sometimes traveled in the early 1830s to the river counties of both Tennessee and Arkansas. But if John Murrell's connections to desperadoes who used the Morass to hide themselves and their pilfered property ran particularly strong or deep, he managed to conceal them well. When Murrell was arrested late in 1831 for illegal gambling in Tipton County, north of Memphis, for example, the county solicitor general thought him so innocuous that he did not even bother pursuing the charge. Moreover, nothing suggests John Murrell ever engaged in the kind of murderous violence for which southwestern outlaws became notorious. Regional newspaper editors liked to fill their pages with ghoulish stories of men waylaid and killed along secluded roads, decapitated bodies discovered floating in rivers, and corpses mangled so severely that they could barely be identified. But even presuming such stories were true, the only act of violence to which John Murrell can be tied definitively took place when he was sixteen and he and his brothers threatened Thomas Merritt and his wife.[43]

Ultimately, if Murrell devoted a great deal of time and energy to committing crimes, one would be hard-pressed to conclude that he gained any material benefits from doing so. When Virgil Stewart tracked him down on January 26, 1834, near the Hatchie River about eight miles southwest of Denmark at a place called Estanaula, John Murrell had no money and no property, and he was just a shadow of his younger self. When Deputy Sheriff W. B. McClellan had offered a reward for Murrell the "monstrous rascal" in 1823, he was pursuing a "free spoken" teenager "tolerably well made" with a "very good countenance" who was all in all "quite a nice looking fellow." Ten years later, Murrell's hair was still black and his eyes were still blue, but he also had a back disfigured from a public whipping and a face described as "much pitted with the small pox," and he had spent the better part of a decade living the nomadic and debased life of the destitute. Stewart would certainly make Murrell out to be "free spoken," and perhaps he was. Describing him as anything other than a local pest, however, and a rather sad one at that, would have taken a vivid imagination. But Stewart had one of those.[44]

IV.

To begin with, Virgil Stewart found John Murrell largely by accident. Stewart was supposed to meet Richard Henning in Denmark, and from there the two were to proceed together in pursuit of Murrell. But by the time Stewart decided that Henning was not going to show, he presumed Murrell had already left for Randolph and that he ought to head there directly. In the event, Murrell and Stewart arrived at a tollhouse on the road near Estanaula almost simultaneously. Shortly after ascertaining from the toll taker that the man who had passed on horseback just ahead of him was in fact Murrell, Stewart sidled alongside and started a conversation. Presenting himself as someone hunting for a lost horse, Stewart intimated that he disliked traveling alone and—when Murrell suggested that perhaps his horse had been stolen—that he found a great deal to admire in men who refused to let the law keep them from taking the things they wanted.[45]

Stewart's well-practiced skills of insinuation paid off on the road with John Murrell no less than they had in the Choctaw Cession. Murrell liked Stewart right away, and the two kept company for the rest of the day and through the damp and frigid evening, traveling almost twenty miles from Estanaula before completing their journey close to midnight at the home of a friend of Murrell's. Murrell indicated that he would be going on in the morning toward Randolph but that his real destination lay across the Mississippi in Arkansas, and he suggested that Stewart should continue riding with him and forget about the lost horse, as he might steal one every bit as good on the other side of the river. Stewart was nervous about prolonging the time he spent alone with a man John Henning considered too dangerous for his son to follow by himself. But Henning's slaves were still nowhere in sight, and Stewart still hoped to find them. Thinking that sticking close to Murrell would eventually bring him right to Henning's stolen property, Stewart decided to take Murrell up on his offer.[46]

When the sun rose the next day, Murrell already had his and Stewart's horses saddled. As they set off, Murrell realized that he had not yet asked Stewart his name. Having already told Murrell when they first met that he was from Yalobusha County, and concerned that Murrell might recognize his real name given that for more than a year they had lived within a few miles of one another in Madison County, Stewart said his name was Adam Hues. Either unconcerned or oblivious to the possibility that his traveling companion might be lying about his identity, Murrell unhesitatingly accepted the alias and began excitedly bragging about the women they would find in Arkansas, who were "as plump as ever came over" and among whom the two of them would be "right in town."[47]

The wet, cold west Tennessee winter made the journey to Arkansas more arduous than either man had anticipated. It took them two more days to get to the Mississippi River, only to discover that high water prevented them from crossing at the spot Murrell preferred. Heading upriver to find another crossing point, they eventually had to dismount and work their way on foot through several miles of swamp, hoping to find someone with a boat that could take them to the Arkansas side. When they finally located a means of transportation, a snowstorm delayed them yet again. Ultimately, it took six days for Stewart and Murrell to travel to Arkansas from Murrell's friend's house, a trip of less than forty miles.[48]

Meanwhile, as they plodded and stalled, Murrell continued to be as careless about concealing his criminality from Stewart as he had been in suggesting that Stewart steal a horse before he even bothered asking Stewart his name. Regarding John Henning's slaves in particular, Stewart would later claim that Murrell admitted to having been involved in their theft, that he had arranged for someone to bring them from Tennessee to Arkansas, and that the primary purpose of his trip was to take possession of them in preparation for resale. Moreover, Stewart would assert that Murrell became increasingly aggravated with each delay the weather imposed. Henning's suspicions had already put Murrell behind schedule, because once Murrell had discovered them, he had felt forced to craft a ruse about his actual travel plans so as to misdirect Richard Henning in his attempt to follow him. To then encounter such dreadful conditions, including snow so blinding as to prevent a river crossing, finally led the exasperated Murrell to exclaim "that the devil had quit cutting his cards for him, and that the damned old preacher's negroes had cost him more trouble and perplexity of mind, than any he had ever stolen in his life."[49]

Murrell did in fact send a letter to Richard Henning designed to throw him off the trail, and he may well have been as unabashed about his part in stealing John Henning's slaves as Stewart said he was. It would have been consistent with his other behavior during his and Stewart's travels, as he made no effort to keep Stewart from seeing him act the swindler. After being stymied in their first attempt to cross the Mississippi, Murrell and Stewart stopped at the riverside home of a man named John Champion. Pretending to be a slave trader from Williamson County with the last name "Merel," Murrell told Champion he was heading to Arkansas to collect some debts and proceeded to engage him in conversation about horse theft, slave stealing, counterfeiting, and other sorts of scams. Finding that Champion disdained banditry, Murrell let the subject drop. He had better luck with the same spiel the next day. After he and Stewart left their horses at Champion's home and tramped through muck and mire for several hours, they arrived at the home of Matthew Erwin, who agreed to buy three slaves with which Murrell arranged to return in a few weeks.[50]

For his part, if Virgil Stewart had been nervous about agreeing to travel with Murrell and questioned himself for even striking up their initial conversation, his unease turned into outright fear as the days passed. Because Stewart had never met up with Richard Henning in Denmark, no one even knew he was following Murrell, much less riding with him. He had given Murrell a fake name, but Stewart's red hair made him easy to recognize, and he worried about running into someone who would accidentally expose his real identity. At the very least, he had spent enough time at John Henning's home during his residence in Madison County that if Murrell led him to Henning's missing slaves, they would almost certainly remember him. Most troubling of all, Stewart had no plan for what he would do if Murrell really did lead him to Henning's slaves. Stewart had brought a gun, but he had also been told that Murrell was not a man to trifle with and that he had equally forbidding friends. None of them would be cheered to discover that Stewart was acting at Henning's behest and intended to have them taken into custody.[51]

Accordingly, Stewart took precautions. He rode behind Murrell whenever possible so he could keep an eye on him. When he and Murrell passed through the village of Wesley on their first full day riding together, Stewart contrived to speak privately with a friend there who loaned him a second pistol and understood to act in Murrell's presence as if Stewart was a stranger. Several days later, shortly after he and Murrell left the home of John Champion, Stewart pretended he needed to go back to retrieve his gloves, whereupon he told Champion his real name and his purpose in following Murrell. Champion agreed to help, giving Stewart yet another gun and promising that he would gather fifty men to help him arrest Murrell and any of his compatriots should Stewart manage to discover the location of Henning's slaves. Stewart liked the plan, but he was afraid that he would never be able to escape from Murrell unharmed after finding Henning's slaves. So Stewart told Champion that if Murrell returned alone for his horse, Champion should arrest him on the spot as it almost surely meant Stewart had been murdered. Finally, before heading into Arkansas, Stewart managed to have a private conversation with Matthew Erwin. Realizing that the plan he had designed with Champion might miscarry, Stewart arranged with Erwin to have Murrell arrested when he showed up with the three slaves he had promised, as all of them would certainly be stolen.[52]

Stewart had three weapons concealed beneath his heavy overcoat by the time he and John Murrell at last crossed the Mississippi into Arkansas, but they did little to alleviate his sense of dread. For three hours Murrell led him, partially on foot and partially in a series of skiffs, through sluggish bayous, deep marshes, and thick canebrakes where the only sign of human habitation was the occasional hut, cabin, or primitive campground. They arrived at a small house where Murrell was to meet the man who had John Henning's slaves, only to be told that they were no longer there, as Murrell's significantly delayed arrival had persuaded his associates it was best to move the slaves on to market for resale. Unfazed, Murrell introduced Stewart to the other dozen or so men in the house, and the two then moved on to spend the night at the home of Jehu Barney, with whom, Stewart claimed, Murrell made plans to deliver and then resteal the slaves he had agreed to sell to Matthew Erwin.[53]

This was about as far as Virgil Stewart was willing to go. Realizing that he would never be able to find John Henning's slaves in Arkansas, he decided it was time for him to get back to Tennessee and as far away from John Murrell as possible. It had taken the two men a week to travel to the west side of the Mississippi River, but Stewart spent less than twenty-four hours there. In the morning he told Murrell that he wished to return to Matthew Erwin's house to flirt with a woman he had seen, and Murrell reluctantly agreed to escort him back through the Morass. At Erwin's, Murrell took the opportunity to finalize the terms and timing of the upcoming delivery of the slaves he had promised. He and Stewart then retrieved their horses from John Champion and proceeded back in the direction whence they had come.[54]

Two days' ride returned them to Wesley. There they parted ways, with Stewart extracting from Murrell the information that Henning's slaves had been sent for sale to the western Mississippi town of Manchester and Murrell extracting from Stewart a promise that he would visit Murrell at his home so that they could bring Matthew Erwin his slaves together. Stewart headed off in the direction of Yalobusha County, waited until Murrell was out of sight, and then doubled back toward John Henning's house, arriving there on the morning of February 6, 1834. He had been gone for nearly two weeks.[55]

Henning acted more precipitously on the information Stewart brought him than Stewart would have preferred. Stewart told Henning that Murrell had admitted to stealing his slaves, but he also cautioned that without any substantiating evidence other than his own word, it might be best to catch Murrell red-handed when he and Stewart presented the slaves Murrell had promised to Matthew Erwin. Henning would have none of it. He and many other slaveholders living in his vicinity had been suspicious of Murrell ever since he moved to Madison County, and they were furious that he was still free despite having been convicted of harboring William Long's slaves the previous summer. They might have a better case to present against Murrell in court if they waited, but then again, Murrell might abandon the sale at Erwin's or disappear altogether. Murrell did not deserve even a few days, and he would certainly not get a few weeks. Stewart's story was good enough. Henning spent the thirty-six hours after Stewart's return quietly assembling as many men as he could find. On the evening of February 7 they all rode to Murrell's house and arrested him.[56]

V.

The months that followed Murrell's arrest should have been good ones for Virgil Stewart. It had been gratifying to have prominent men celebrate him as a hero, and rewarding to see the color drain from Murrell's face when he saw Stewart accompanying the party arresting him. Many posses had shown up on Murrell's doorstep over the years, and he was cocksure and even a bit amused when this one appeared until he realized that the man he knew as Adam Hues had deceived him so thoroughly.[57]

Cockiness, in fact, may have been a trait of Murrell's that Stewart found worth emulating. He swaggered into the spring, delighting in his newfound renown. Between February and April 1834 Stewart traveled back and forth between Tennessee and Mississippi, bragging to nearly anyone who would listen about his adventure with John Murrell and elaborating significantly on what he had told John Henning. Henning had been interested mostly in what Stewart could tell him about his own missing slaves. But in the aftermath of Murrell's arrest Stewart began saying that Murrell had told him about a lengthy catalog of crimes he had committed over the years and that he had professed to being the leader of a criminal syndicate of horse thieves, slave stealers, counterfeiters, and murderers. Moreover, Stewart told people he had been introduced in Arkansas to several members of the syndicate and that he knew the names of many others.[58]

Stewart's tale was improbable, but the Southwest was a place where men inflated their own achievements as a matter of course and where bluster was practically an art form. That Stewart in particular might engage in some puffery is hardly surprising. Insecurity about his own status had long been a salient theme in his life, and the more extraordinary a bandit John Murrell was, the more extraordinary was the man who brought him to heel. Matthew Clanton, for one, was sympathetic to Stewart's need to crow about his ride with Murrell. After Murrell was apprehended, the first thing Stewart did was accompany one of John Henning's sons to Manchester, Mississippi, in the hope of recovering Henning's property and obtaining some external corroboration for his story. Passing through Yalobusha County on the way, Stewart stopped at Clanton's and told him about his experiences, whereupon Clanton "expressed much astonishment at the intelligence, and manifested much concern on the occasion."[59]

Clanton appears to have understood that Stewart was probably embellishing his story, and he thought Stewart went a bit far when he claimed that the men he had met while in Murrell's company were members of a criminal confederacy. Such unsupported accusations were best kept quiet, and Clanton consequently told Stewart he would give "the strictest secrecy as to the names given." Whether or not he swallowed Stewart's story whole, though, Clanton was willing to indulge him because he knew that Stewart viewed him "in the light of a particular friend." Moreover, Clanton was genuinely "much pleased" to see that Stewart had returned from Tennessee, and that affinity was no small thing for Stewart because Clanton would win his election to the position of probate judge less than two weeks later. Thus, in the first three weeks of February alone Virgil Stewart had become a respected ally of the newly elected top judicial official in a thriving Mississippi county and someone to whom the property holders of western Tennessee owed a debt of gratitude. Basking in what grit and fortune had provided, he seemed poised on the brink of a promising future.[60]

Yet no matter how buoyant Stewart's outlook in the days and weeks after John Murrell's arrest, discouragement and disappointment could not be kept at bay. For starters, on arriving at Manchester, Stewart and John Henning's son learned that the water route Murrell had said his associates intended to follow there from the Morass had been impassable by boat for weeks. Henning's slaves had never made it to Manchester at all. They probably had been sent somewhere farther down the Mississippi River instead.[61]

Stewart's failure to acquire tangible evidence supporting his story about Murrell was disheartening, but more so was the realization that many people wondered whether they ought to believe it in the first place. In some measure that was Stewart's own doing, because even as he told his story again and again he could not keep it straight. Arousing particular skepticism was his assertion that he knew the names of men belonging to Murrell's criminal collective, because what he meant by that changed with the telling. Sometimes he said that Murrell had simply told him "of some men who were concerned with him." Sometimes he said Murrell had promised to provide a list of the organization's members when Stewart returned to Tennessee to help deliver Matthew Erwin's slaves. Sometimes Stewart said he already had an actual list with seventy names on it, and sometimes he said he had no list at all.[62]

No matter which version of the story he told, though, no one ever heard any names or saw any list, and in short order Stewart found the public reputation he had barely started establishing for himself called into question, sometimes by estimable men of the very sort he most wanted to impress. In Yalobusha County, among those expressing doubt that Stewart was worth listening to were Robert Malone, a physician who had won the office of county treasurer at the same election in which Matthew Clanton became probate judge, and Thomas McMackin, a hotelkeeper and merchant who had been elected to Yalobusha's board of police, an administrative body comparable to a modern board of supervisors. Though voters could not have known them well, Malone and McMackin had gained enough local regard to acquire positions of public trust. To the extent anyone's opinions carried weight in Yalobusha, theirs did.[63]

Equally bad for Stewart was the situation in Tennessee, where he returned early in March to find out how John Henning wanted to deal with the fact that his slaves remained unrecovered. Stewart was able to get Henning, William Long, and half a dozen other men to sign a certificate swearing that Stewart had "supported a character of firmness and unsullied honor" for as long as they had known him. Yet when Stewart told others in Madison County his story, he refused to provide any details about the members of Murrell's gang and evaded inquiries about whether or when he intended to be more specific. Stewart may have thought his vagueness imparted an air of mystery to his tale, but his listeners mostly found it irritating, and it disinclined them to trust him. Instead, what Stewart considered a "spirit of detraction and abuse of his character" like the one that had begun to gather in Mississippi started to spread in Tennessee as well.[64]

By the first of April John Henning had abandoned the prospect of finding his missing slaves anytime soon, and Virgil Stewart decided to leave. After promising Henning he would return in July to testify at John Murrell's trial, Stewart went back to Mississippi, began erecting some buildings on the land Clanton had given him to establish a gin shop, and generally picked up his life where he had left it off nearly three months earlier. Even so, the wounds inflicted by those who had dismissed and slighted him did not heal easily. Stewart believed he had earned public distinction, and instead he met raised eyebrows and belittling insults nearly everywhere he turned. Never especially thick-skinned to begin with, such criticism made him a little paranoid and more than a little angry.

He told almost no one when he was leaving Tennessee, and he carefully avoided indicating the route he intended to take to Mississippi for fear that he might be followed. In Yalobusha, the preparations he was making to open his own business did not stop Stewart from trying to leverage whatever standing he had managed to acquire to settle some scores. He lacked enough clout to avenge himself against Robert Malone or Thomas Mc-Mackin, but they were not the only ones whom he felt deserved his scorn. Stewart mobilized the regulator company to which he belonged and proposed that the body roust from the neighborhood "all suspicious characters, and such whose business was either unknown or disreputable, and loungers who appeared to have none." The things he had seen and heard on his ride with John Murrell had convinced him, he said, that such persons "might be much less harmless than appearances seemed to indicate." In truth, Stewart wanted retribution.[65]

But his efforts to rally "the better class of his neighbours" mostly demonstrated how little influence he was capable of exerting. Several men told Stewart plainly that they were uninterested in the undertaking, and while those willing to ride with him beat up and chased away a man named Tucker whom Stewart claimed had threatened to kill him, that was about all the appetite for violence members of the regulator company had. Stewart tried to convince them that their next target ought to be a man named Glen, a "notoriously base character" and someone whom Stewart asserted was an affiliate of Murrell. But after riding to Glen's house and asking him a few questions, the regulators decided to leave him be. Then they all went home.[66]

Virgil Stewart roiled inside, his emotional state about as low by April as it had been high in February. Had he not performed a great public service in taking down John Murrell? He had received no monetary reward. Did he not deserve at least the esteem of his fellow settlers? So he had boasted about his achievements and perhaps stretched the truth. Were there not men whose fame and fortune rested on falsehoods far larger and more significant? None of it made any sense. Drawn to the frontier in part by the prospect of remaking himself into someone entirely new, Stewart discovered he had gained no purchase at all. For a man whose outward self-assurance barely disguised his internal diffidence, this was a terrifying feeling. The only place where he found some support was the tiny townsite he, Matthew Clanton, George Saunders, William Vess, and their families were developing. There, at least, he could feel comfortable among a circle of friends that was as close to a family as he had in the region. Clanton, in fact, asked Stewart toward the end of April if he would carry eight hundred dollars to Memphis and purchase a boatload of goods to restock Clanton's store, a demonstration of the older man's continued faith in Stewart that revived his flagging spirits somewhat. And then the already fragile world of Virgil Stewart utterly shattered.[67]

VI.

One evening around the first of May, as Stewart was preparing to leave for Memphis, William and Ann Vess approached Matthew Clanton and told him there was something he needed to know. When Stewart had first left Yalobusha County for Tennessee in January, he had told the Vesses that he anticipated being gone about two weeks. He left his possessions in their care and asked Ann Vess to go into his trunk and lay his coat and vest in the sun should the trip take longer than he expected lest the clothes mold and rot. Diverted by his travels with John Murrell and the ensuing events, Stewart did not return for the better part of six weeks. By the time Ann

Vess opened his trunk, Stewart's garments appeared in pretty bad shape, so she thought she would look in the chest holding the rest of his personal items to see if its contents needed sunning as well. Inside, under a few pieces of old clothing, she found the chest packed with a collection of items that seemed to have come from Clanton's store: calico and cambric cloth, scissors, saltcellars and pepperboxes, a vinegar cruet, bars of soap, saltpeter and sulfur, and an array of spices.[68]

That was curious. Ann Vess had known Stewart for only a few months, but she thought him "miserly" and unlikely to have purchased such an assortment of goods for his personal use. She told her husband of her discovery and her misgivings, but he cautioned her not to leap to conclusions. He suggested instead that they wait and see if Stewart used or wore anything from the chest, as a man who came by the items honestly would have no reason to conceal them. In the weeks since Stewart's arrival back in Mississippi, however, the Vesses had watched him carefully, and if their monitoring of Stewart contributed to his sense of persecution in the spring of 1834 it did nothing to allay their suspicions. So far as they could tell, Stewart would not even open the chest if either of them was present. The Vesses had no concrete proof of anything, but if Clanton was going to trust Stewart with eight hundred dollars, they felt he should be cognizant of the situation.[69]

Matthew Clanton was not a particularly careful businessman. He kept no inventory of his store, and while he maintained a ledger listing those to whom he sold goods on credit and the amounts they owed him, when people bought things with cash he simply put the money in a drawer without recording the purchase at all. Stewart, meanwhile, had had the full run of the store for weeks the previous fall when Clanton was preoccupied with relocating his family, buying land at Chocchuma, and campaigning to become probate judge. Still, Clanton was stunned by the Vesses' information. Stewart had neither taken out a line of credit in his own name nor indicated that any of the cash he received in Clanton's absence had come from his own pocket. So far as Clanton knew, Stewart had never bought or taken anything from the store for his own use, and his apparently honest attendance to the business had been a central reason why Clanton still continued to have confidence in Stewart when other people did not. There had to be some explanation for what the Vesses were telling him.[70]

The next morning Clanton told George Saunders what the Vesses had said. Saunders was no more ready to believe the story than Clanton. That Stewart had stolen from Clanton "could not be so," Saunders said, for "Stewart was certainly an honest man." Clanton concurred and insisted that "no man had respected" Stewart more than he did. But the only way to resolve the matter was to present Stewart with the claims made by William and Ann Vess. If they were untrue, Clanton said to Saunders, "he could easily satisfy us by opening his chest and showing us what he had and telling us how he got them." Saunders agreed to accompany Clanton on the potentially uncomfortable errand.[71]

They found Stewart splitting a tree that had fallen in the Vesses' yard. Clanton told Stewart what the Vesses said they had seen in his chest, asked whether it was true, and if so, how Stewart came to have so many things from the store. Stewart blanched, dropped his ax, and slumped down onto the log he had been working. Unable to speak, he sputtered and swallowed. Saunders thought Stewart might faint. Finally, after several minutes, Stewart acknowledged that "he had a good many goods he had taken from Mr. Clanton's store" while minding it in the fall, but said he had put money in the cash drawer to pay for them. Openly skeptical, Clanton asked why Stewart had never told him he had bought any merchandise. Stewart responded that "he had forgotten it, or did not think it worth while" to account for his personal purchases. Clanton was not convinced. He wanted to see what was in the chest.[72]

With obvious reluctance Stewart led Clanton and Saunders into the Vesses' house. Pulling out the chest, he turned and opened it such that the lid blocked the view Clanton and Saunders might have of its contents and began rummaging around inside. Neither Clanton nor Saunders appreciated such stalling. "Act like a man, Stewart," Saunders said. "Haul out your chest here, and let us see what you have in it." Responding that everything in the chest belonged to him, Stewart began lifting things out one at a time, replacing each item before showing another. After holding up several articles, he told Clanton and Saunders that was all there was. When a dubious Clanton asked whether Stewart had "a piece of coarse calico" and Stewart said he had never had such a thing, Clanton had had enough shenanigans.[73]

Walking around to Stewart's side of the chest, he could see the calico. "There it is now, Stewart; haul it out," Clanton demanded. Taking out the cloth, Stewart said "he had entirely forgotten it." Clanton asked about the saltcellar, the pepperbox, and the vinegar cruet Ann Vess had mentioned.

Stewart denied having these too. But the increasingly annoyed Clanton had already spied them as he looked down at the contents of the chest, and when he said as much it further riled him to hear Stewart again claim that "he had entirely forgotten getting them out of the store." Clanton could plainly see that the "chest contained something of every kind there was in the store, and nothing that was not in the store." Many of the items, in fact, "were of women's wear, for which a young man had no use." Stewart tried to explain that he had brought some of the things in the chest with him when he moved from Tennessee and that he had gotten some others in Tuscahoma. Whether or not that was true hardly mattered now. Clanton did not need a detailed list of his stock to conclude what he had been unable to imagine possible a day earlier: Virgil Stewart was a thief.[74]

Stewart tried desperately to salvage the situation. With the Vesses already convinced of his culpability and Clanton inclined to agree, Stewart turned to George Saunders for counsel. But when Stewart spoke with Saunders later in the day, Saunders advised him to pay for the items he had taken from the store. Stewart said he could not do that, as it would practically be admitting his guilt. Stewart tried to talk with Clanton directly, but Clanton refused to listen and told him flatly that he believed Stewart had stolen most if not all the items in the chest from the store. Still, Clanton regretted the situation and did not want to disgrace Stewart by bringing him up on charges, so he offered him a proposition. Clanton was willing to present the circumstances to three of their neighbors, including William Minter, a newly elected member of the board of police. If Minter and the other men found Stewart's account convincing, Clanton would forget the whole thing ever happened and "would never again accuse" Stewart of theft. Stewart could not accede to that proposal. As things stood, he was profoundly embarrassed and had lost the trust and regard of his patron, probably irrevocably, no matter what his neighbors said. Keeping the affair completely private was his only hope for staving off public humiliation as well. Stewart recognized that Clanton and Saunders "would judge as charitably of his conduct as any body else." If they thought he was a thief, everyone else would too. Out of options, Stewart told Clanton he was sorry for what he had done. He promised to reform. Then he began to cry.[75]

Virgil Stewart saw now that the life he had imagined for himself in Yalobusha County would almost certainly never be his. Too many who barely knew him considered him a braggart if not a fool, and those he had once thought confidants considered him a liar and a thief. Reputations were easy to make but hard to redeem, and Stewart understood that he ought to leave before things got any worse. But he could not bring himself simply to ride away. He might not be able to undo entirely the damage he had done, but he had to make one last effort to contain it.[76]

About thirty-six hours after abasing himself before Clanton, Stewart solicited Saunders to persuade Clanton and the Vesses "to say nothing about his taking the goods." When Saunders refused to intercede, Stewart asked if he would at least accompany him back to Clanton's while Stewart spoke for himself. Saunders thought Stewart was wasting his time, but he had business with Clanton anyway and told Stewart he might come along. They found Clanton in his garden, and Stewart "commenced talking to him about the charge against himself." He assured Clanton that he had put money in the store's cash drawer for the items he had taken. Seeing that Clanton did not believe him, he changed his story and said that he had given customers change from his own pocket when they paid for merchandise and had taken items from the store in lieu of cash reimbursement. At that point Clanton cut him off, "telling him he did not wish to hear any thing more from him to extenuate his conduct." If anything, the more Stewart talked, the more obvious his guilt became. Stewart "had told so many contradictory tales," Clanton said, "that all could not be and perhaps none of them were true." There was nothing left to talk about. Tears again began streaming down Stewart's face. After shaking Clanton's hand, he bid Saunders farewell, mounted his horse, and left Yalobusha County.[77]

Several days later Stewart arrived back in Madison County, Tennessee. It made sense he would go there, as it was just about the only spot where there was anyone left he might consider a friend. At the very least there were people there who needed him if they wanted to see John Murrell committed to prison. In Tennessee, however, Stewart received the worst news he could have possibly imagined. John Murrell had escaped from jail and was nowhere to be found.[78]

Dejected though Stewart was when he departed Yalobusha County, Murrell's disappearance plunged him into near-total despondency. He had spent nearly four years on the southwestern frontier, and it had yielded just a few small pieces of land in a county he could not even live in without the suffocating feeling that people ridiculed or condemned him. He had risked his life for men like John Henning, but now he "looked on his labors as lost," Murrell's flight leaving him "nothing for his dangerous adventures" but the questionable story of the adventures itself. By his own account, Stewart "was no company for his friends, neither were there enjoyments in those objects around him with which he was once delighted."[79]

Stewart soon left with vague plans of heading to Kentucky, where he had a notion he might write and publish an account of his ride with Murrell. But he never got there. In late May, when George Saunders went to visit relatives in his old Tipton County neighborhood, he came across a troubled and practically distraught Virgil Stewart. Regardless of whether he still trusted Stewart, Saunders could see that he needed someplace to rest and collect himself, and he invited Stewart to stay with his family. Keeping a close eye on his guest, Saunders noticed that he "seemed much concerned about religion," "prayed much at night," and generally "seemed greatly distressed." Stewart, moreover, seems to have been somewhat at a loss about his future. He may have intended on going to Kentucky when he left Madison County, but he apparently had changed his mind, telling Saunders "he was on his way to Texas, to engage in the mule trade."[80]

Around the same time, Matthew Clanton received a letter from Stewart "couched in the most humble, penitent terms." Stewart, Clanton said, wrote that "he had had recourse to traveling" since leaving Mississippi, "hoping a change of company and scenery might better reconcile him to life." But it had done no good. Rather, he feared that "his Creator had given him up to hardness of heart and reprobacy of mind." He wrote that he yearned for God's forgiveness and he begged Clanton "to look on his conduct with as much charity" as he could. Stewart knew how things appeared, but "he did not think he could long survive the loss of his character" and wanted Clanton to know that "he was not so degraded and base a man" as "circumstances might appear against him." Only absolution from God and from Clanton, Stewart wrote, would allow him to "die in peace."[81]

Few places would have been more appropriate than Texas for Virgil Stewart to make another attempt to recast himself. Though still nearly two years from declaring its independence from Mexico, by 1834 Texas had entered America's imagination as the continent's next promising frontier, it sat at the forefront of the imperial designs of the United States, and it was a common refuge for scoundrels. So too, of course, was prayer, and while Stewart had never before been especially inclined to look for divine guidance, he knew that his own transgressions were at least partly to blame for his feeling that nearly everyone and everything had turned against him. God probably seemed like the only source of solace and mercy left in the world.[82]

And Stewart could not be blamed if he thought God was listening, because early in June 1834 Richard Henning arrived in Tipton County with the message that John Murrell had been recaptured near the northern Alabama town of Florence, that he was on his way back to Tennessee, and that Stewart was needed in Madison County to testify at Murrell's trial, which would take place after all. Miraculously, Virgil Stewart had been given one more chance. So far, his desire to transform himself into a person of standing and substance had clashed badly with his inclination to exploit for personal gain or self-aggrandizement every opportunity that presented itself. He had considered poorly the possible consequences of his actions, and they had gone so horribly awry that he had mentally prepared himself to move on. But this time he was determined not to blow it. A courtroom was a public theater, and his chance to play a starring role was literally the answer to his prayers. This time, Virgil Stewart would not be denied.[83]

~ ~

CHAPTER TWO

Inventing John Murrell

Theoverflow crowd of spectators gathered in and around the two-story brick courthouse in Jackson, Tennessee, on July 24, 1834, had come to see Virgil Stewart as much as they had to see John Murrell. The reputation Murrell had developed during his residence in Madison County, the seriousness of the crime for which he was to be tried, the audaciousness of his jailbreak, and the elusiveness that enabled him to spend two months at large might have been enough by themselves to attract a sizable audience. But it was the promise of hearing Virgil Stewart describe his travels with Murrell that, in the words of the editor of the *Jackson Truth Teller*, "imparted an interest to the trial seldom if ever before witnessed in this community." It was not every day that a person could be present at the prosecution of a criminal "master spirit," and while the crimes may have been Murrell's, it was the rumors about the stories Stewart had been telling that had made their supposed perpetrator a "far famed personage" whose "very name was associated with all that was bold and desperate in villany."[1]

Indeed, John Murrell sorely disappointed those who expected him to evince the brazenness and brilliance the editor of the *Truth Teller* suggested he possessed. Old for his twenty-eight years, the pock-faced Murrell barely spoke during his trial, instead telling Judge Joshua Haskell "that by reason of his poverty he was unable to employ counsel" and leaving his defense to four court-appointed lawyers. Stewart, on the other hand, delivered testimony every bit as riveting and thrilling as anticipated. But Murrell's trial neither redeemed nor vindicated Stewart. The jury convicted Murrell of stealing John Henning's slaves, but throughout the trial and in its aftermath Stewart felt beset by critics who whispered about his past and questioned his honesty and motives. At the very moment he had hoped to establish his courage and integrity before a rapt audience, Virgil Stewart instead discovered skepticism and distrust.[2]

Ultimately, instead of garnering Stewart admiration and the laurels of a grateful populace, Murrell's trial proved the occasion for his accumulated resentment, frustration, and sense of persecution to coalesce into a venomous rage. When he was not ambling about the Southwest wallowing in despair, Stewart spent the months following the trial writing a pamphlet that relayed an even more fantastical account of his travels with Murrell than any he had recounted before. In this version of the story, John Murrell was a merciless killer with hundreds of henchmen at his command, and Virgil Stewart was an intrepid and self-sacrificing soul slandered and victimized by Murrell's omnipresent confederates for his role in exposing them and bringing their leader to justice.

To read Stewart's pamphlet merely as an attempt to inflate his own importance and assail his detractors, however, is to miss the richer story it reveals about how Stewart had come finally to understand the socioeconomic realities of the southwestern frontier. Embedded in Stewart's semidelusional yarn about John Murrell, his devious collaborators, and their dastardly criminal conspiracies is a deeply cynical commentary on the very notion of self-fashioning that was purportedly one of the frontier's great appeals. Rather than a place where men achieved success and prominence through hard work and virtuous deeds, Virgil Stewart's frontier was a place where the so-called best men amassed power, status, and wealth selfishly and unjustly. It was a place where the most promising opportunities for common men to distinguish themselves and take their share of the spoils lay less in modeling their behavior after those at the top of the social and economic order than in mocking and undoing that order through trickery, deception, and theft.

Stewart's pamphlet unmistakably reflects its author's bitterness about his own failures and his unwillingness to assume responsibility for them. But it also reflects his broader disillusionment with the moral value of the path followed by most who rose to renown on the frontier. It is telling that in the pamphlet, Stewart claimed Murrell had revealed to him a plot to provoke the largest slave insurrection the United States had ever seen, during which Murrell and his associates would pillage the southern countryside. If part of Virgil Stewart still craved public approval for vanquishing the man he claimed was the greatest threat to property the Southwest had ever seen, part of him also thought the whole regime deserved to come crashing down.

I.

Although no transcript of John Murrell's trial survives, the report of the proceedings published in the *Truth Teller*, the information about the trial in surviving court records, and the description of events later provided by Virgil Stewart enable a rough reconstruction of what transpired. There is no doubt, for example, that Stewart's testimony was virtually the only substantive evidence the state of Tennessee offered against Murrell. Responding to the questions of Alexander Bradford, solicitor general for Tennessee's Fourteenth District, Stewart spent five or six hours over the course of two days relaying what the editor of the *Truth Teller* described as "incidents of a most romantic adventure, by which he had wound himself into the confidence of Murrell, and obtained from him a confession of his guilt." Stewart detailed how he had set out looking for the slaves who had gone missing from John Henning, had crossed paths with Murrell, and had given Murrell the impression that he might be interested in casting his lot with criminals who worked the banks of the Mississippi River. Murrell, Stewart testified, responded positively to such overtures, invited Stewart to accompany him across western Tennessee and into Arkansas, and proceeded to tell Stewart not only that he had engineered the theft of Henning's slaves but also that he had crafted "a splendid scheme of organized villainy [by] which he and others expected to amass a fortune."[3]

Essentially, Stewart said that Murrell had described a large and well-coordinated slave-stealing ring. Murrell bragged about how simple it was to steal and resell the enslaved, how he had put together a network of several hundred thieves whose workings could never be detected and whose participants could never successfully be prosecuted, and how his singular talents would bring him tremendous wealth and the high regard of his outlaw colleagues. Murrell, Stewart attested, said "he thought negro stealing when properly directed entirely safe, and the sure road to fortune."[4]

If all Stewart had to offer on the witness stand were the vague albeit extravagant boasts of a thief, his testimony would not have been nearly so arresting. But Stewart also related a series of anecdotes that he said Murrell shared with him, through which Murrell described how he had made himself so nettlesome to the slaveholders of Madison County and how his experience stealing slaves and committing other crimes had convinced him that the broader project he had conceived would work. According to

Stewart, for example, Murrell gloated about avoiding imprisonment for his dealings with William Long's slaves. Where Long and many others felt certain Murrell would go to jail for slave stealing, Stewart said Murrell told him he never worried for a moment. He was equally certain his bogus claim to have been securing Long's slaves until Long could retrieve them would raise enough doubt that the judge in the case would impose no punishment more serious than a fine. The actual sentence of servitude, though unforeseen, hardly discomfited Murrell. On the contrary, he told Stewart, he was so confident that he would triumph on appeal that he responded to the verdict by winking at Long and sarcastically addressing him as "master Billy."[5]

Stewart said that Murrell told him he recognized that even as asserting his innocence had gotten his more credulous neighbors to believe he was the victim of a vendetta by Long, his smugness in court had also aroused the ire of many local property holders. Determined to send him to jail, in the aftermath of the William Long affair they came to consider Murrell a likely perpetrator whenever anything in the area disappeared. John Henning, who lived two miles from Murrell, was especially vocal in his opinion that the entire Murrell family was a nuisance, a sentiment that made John Murrell angry enough to orchestrate the theft of Henning's slaves and Henning angry enough to try and track Murrell down once and for all.[6]

Yet Murrell remained unconcerned that Henning would have any better luck than Long had had in incarcerating him, an attitude of indifference Stewart said Murrell explained by way of another story. Several months before stealing Henning's slaves, Murrell said, he had come across an enslaved man named Sam while traveling in northern Alabama. Murrell knew Sam, who had once belonged to someone in Madison County but recently had been sold to an Alabamian named Eason. Murrell asked Sam how he liked his new home and his new owner and, when Sam responded that he disliked both, offered to ensure his safety if he ran away. Sam soon showed up on Murrell's doorstep in Tennessee, and Murrell kept him hidden until Eason advertised Sam in the newspaper as a runaway. At that point, Murrell got one of his brothers and another man to take Sam to Mississippi. There, they sold Sam to one Thomas Hudnall, instructed him to run away, met him at a prearranged location, moved on, and sold him again. After running this scam multiple times over the course of seven weeks, Murrell's brother and his accomplice finally returned to Tennessee with twenty-eight hundred dollars in cash, goods, and promissory notes. They left Sam in

Texas with another criminal acquaintance and intended to carry out the con again sometime in the future.[7]

Concluding the story, Murrell told Stewart that even had Sam's owner in Alabama managed to locate Sam and track down Murrell's brother and his accomplice, the legal consequences would have been negligible for them and nonexistent for himself. In part, that was because he never personally stole anything. Rather, he acted primarily as a spotter and a manager of criminal ventures. Frequently masquerading in a black frock coat and broad-brimmed hat and pretending to be a Methodist minister, Murrell would scout for likely horses and slaves, delegate their thefts to someone else, and then share in the resale profits. Stewart said Murrell told him that sometimes he even delivered sermons in his disguise and had confederates steal horses belonging to audience members while he preached. In disguise or out, Murrell touted to Stewart a facility for getting other people to do his bidding that made him practically immune to prosecution.[8]

In any case, Stewart claimed, Murrell insisted he had found a loophole in the criminal law as it related to the chattel status of slaves that made schemes like the one involving Sam effectively foolproof. The key to stealing a slave successfully, Murrell told Stewart, was concealing the slave until the slave's owner placed a newspaper advertisement describing his property as a runaway and offering a reward for the slave's return. Murrell explained to Stewart that the advertisement amounted to a virtual power of attorney enabling whoever took up the runaway to act in a limited capacity as the slave's owner. Should that person choose to treat the slave in his possession as a saleable asset rather than return the slave to the original owner, then the owner might file a civil lawsuit for breach of trust, but he would never be able to prosecute as a slave stealer the person who carried out the sale.[9]

Slave stealing could be a dangerous business, though, and conducting it in the "entirely safe" fashion that Stewart claimed Murrell argued it could be entailed more than using clever tricks, relying on intermediaries, and resorting to legal technicalities. Real caution called for disposing of incriminating evidence, and if the most tangible physical evidence of a slave theft was the slave himself, then covering one's tracks required action more pitiless and depraved than that of a mere trickster. Stewart averred that Murrell told him he had let Sam live after he had allowed himself to be repeatedly sold largely because of their personal acquaintance and Sam's willingness to participate in Murrell's operations for as long as Murrell wished him to. But Murrell also said Sam's was an unusual case.[10]

More typical was the fate that befell another enslaved man Stewart claimed that Murrell had told him about. Murrell persuaded the man to run away from his master in Tipton County and arranged for associates to meet him and conduct him down the Mississippi River. Murrell then traveled to Natchez, took possession of the slave, brought him to New Orleans via steamboat, and sold the man for eight hundred dollars. Days later, the man ran away again and some of Murrell's comrades took him into a parish northwest of the city. There, Murrell donned his Methodist outfit, preached a sermon in which he proclaimed his desire to divest himself of slavery, and sold the man for seven hundred dollars to a Louisiana slaveholder named Higginbotham. The enslaved man then escaped from Higginbotham and traveled in the custody of some of Murrell's collaborators northwest into Arkansas, where he was sold yet again, this time for five hundred dollars. Finally, after the man escaped a fourth time, Murrell's partners killed him and tossed his body in a swamp.[11]

All of this was sensational testimony. The editor of the *Truth Teller*, unwittingly anticipating (and perhaps inspiring) Stewart's later course of action, wrote that the tale of Stewart's adventure, "if well written out and properly embellished, would form a legend in real life unsurpassed by any thing produced by fiction." More astonishing still was Stewart's assertion that Murrell started telling him these stories within hours of their meeting and hardly stopped talking during their time together. By Stewart's reckoning, Murrell had told him about everything from his clash with William Long to the murder of the slave from Tipton County before the two had even reached Wesley, at which point they had been riding together for perhaps thirty-six hours.[12]

But if Murrell was garrulous he was not so indiscreet as to begin confessing his misdeeds immediately to a total stranger, or even to tell Stewart his name. Rather, Stewart claimed that once he had expressed his sympathy with those who flouted the law, Murrell started telling him about his illicit activities in the third person, pretending that they were the acts of a pair of especially clever brothers. Much as Murrell would broach the subject of thievery with John Champion and Matthew Erwin, he initially felt out Stewart obliquely, gauging his reaction to discussions of criminality as a way of figuring how much he could trust him. Only during their second day traveling together, just outside Wesley, did Murrell finally reveal to Stewart that the brothers in question were named Murrell, that he was the older and more designing of the duo, that he was on his way to rendezvous with those who were holding John Henning's slaves on his behalf, that he was the leader of a gang of bandits, and that he had decided Stewart ought to join them.[13]

As Virgil Stewart described him, John Murrell was deeply impressed with himself, so much so that keeping him talking was mostly a matter of periodically expressing admiration for the "brothers" and their ingenuity. Nonetheless, even as Murrell filled Stewart's head with stories of devilish deeds and daring plans, he had yet to explain how he stole slaves in the first place. From what Murrell had already told Stewart, his methods differed from those of a kidnapper who slipped away with an enslaved person like he might rustle a horse. Rather, for Murrell it was essential that slaves flee their masters of their own volition, because the repeated act of reselling necessary for maximizing profits required convincing performances before a series of buyers that no person abducted against his will could be relied on to deliver. Stewart had not wondered at Murrell's success in luring away Sam, with whom he had a personal relationship, but how Murrell pulled off the crucial aspect of his larger scheme, which entailed prevailing on slaves to whom he was just another strange white man, remained a mystery.

But Stewart asserted that it was a mystery on which Murrell shed some light. He claimed that as he and Murrell left Wesley behind and continued on their way to Arkansas, Murrell offered to illustrate just how easy slave stealing was by cajoling the very next slave they came across into leaving his master. Soon enough, Stewart said, he and Murrell encountered an elderly enslaved man working by a roadside corncrib and Murrell struck up a conversation. After expressing his sympathy that the man had to labor outdoors on such a cold day, Murrell elicited the man's admission that his owner was cruel and asked him whether he would not rather be free and wealthy than enslaved. The man responded enthusiastically, whereupon Murrell offered to steal him, sell him four or five times, give him half the money, and leave him in a free state. Once the man consented to the deal, Murrell told him to listen for pistol fire in the night. That would be the signal for him to come, along with several of his fellow slaves, to the end of the road, where they would find Murrell waiting with horses. Vowing to return soon, Murrell bid the man farewell. The entire exchange had taken less than fifteen minutes.[14]

None of the stories Virgil Stewart told on the witness stand was wholly implausible. Central elements of some of them can even be corroborated and likely did originate with Murrell. The story about Murrell mocking William Long in court could have been common knowledge locally or something Stewart heard about from John Henning or Long himself rather than from Murrell.[15] But Thomas Hudnall actually was a planter in Mississippi who really did buy an enslaved man from an Alabamian named William Eason, and that slave really did disappear from Hudnall's plantation just days afterward. Similarly, a slaveholder in Louisiana's East Feliciana Parish named Willis Higginbotham did buy a slave from someone who gave the impression "that he was a professor of religion," only to have the slave vanish two days later. Hudnall lived more than 100 miles from Virgil Stewart's home in Yalobusha County, Higginbotham's residence was more than 250 miles away, and neither of their misadventures in the domestic slave trade was a matter of especial public notice until after Stewart testified and then wrote about them in his pamphlet. It was only Stewart who said that the slave who left Hudnall's plantation made his way to Texas and was named Sam, and it was only Stewart who claimed that the slave who absconded from Higginbotham's possession ended up dead at the bottom of a swamp. Still, it is hard to imagine how he could have known any of the particularities of these frauds unless Murrell told him about them.[16]

Perhaps the least believable of Stewart's stories was that Murrell had picked a slave at random and convinced him in a matter of minutes that a white man he had never seen before would deliver on promises of money and freedom. But Orville Shelby, a man who lived near John Champion on the Mississippi River, later reported that his wife had seen Stewart and Murrell when they passed through the neighborhood and told him that the two "had been among our negroes tampering with them, [and] offering to take them to a free state," which suggests that Stewart may have exaggerated Murrell's facility but accurately depicted his methods. Moreover, Murrell's idea of exploiting the legal ambiguities of slavery to turn slave stealing from a criminal to a civil offense was ingenious. It was surely neither a coincidence nor solely Tennesseans' concerns about abolitionism that moved the Tennessee legislature in the session following Murrell's trial to make it a felony punishable by up to ten years in jail to "directly or indirectly tempt or persuade any slave or slaves, to leave his, her or their master or mistress's service, with an intent or design to carry him, her or them out of this state, or with the intent or design to deprive the true owner thereof, or . . . harbor or conceal such slave or slaves for that intent or purpose."[17]

Whether or not Virgil Stewart told the truth, John Murrell's lawyers knew that they had to impeach Stewart's testimony if they had any hope of getting their client acquitted. Rules of evidence were looser in antebellum southern courtrooms than they are in contemporary ones, and Judge Haskell would not peremptorily toss out Stewart's information even though much of it was hearsay. But Henning's slaves were still missing, and the prosecution had submitted no evidence that a crime had even been committed other than Stewart's claim that Murrell had confessed to stealing them, which meant oppugning Stewart's word was the soundest strategy Murrell's counsel had at their disposal. Stewart's testimony was damning, but if they could get the jury to question his credibility Murrell might walk out of the courtroom a free man.

Virgil Stewart, though, was not a man who liked having his word challenged. After four confusing, blundering, and rancorous years in the Southwest, the value of that word was uncertain at best, but Stewart knew that without it he would have practically nothing to show for his sojourn on the frontier. Defensive under the best of circumstances, Stewart could probably already feel the anger rising within him as Murrell's lead attorney, Milton Brown, rose to conduct his cross-examination.

II.

However Stewart felt when Milton Brown started asking him questions, he was furious by the time Brown finished. Only thirty years old, Brown was already a lawyer of significant ability and local renown when he agreed to help defend John Murrell. Born in 1804 and raised in Ohio, Brown moved to Nashville at the age of nineteen and studied law with Felix Grundy, a member of the Tennessee legislature who had already served multiple terms in Congress and who would later become a U.S. senator and attorney general under Martin Van Buren. In 1832 Brown moved to Jackson, where he opened a law office, involved himself in the town's temperance society, and attracted notice as a talented orator. While Brown would eventually be elected to Congress in his own right in addition to serving as a chancery court judge and as president of two different railroads, in 1834 he was still building his reputation. Some of Brown's descendants would claim that he engaged in Murrell's defense despite the warnings of friends and fellow lawyers that doing so would damage his future prospects. In truth, it was a good career move, and there were probably others who wanted the case besides Brown and the three additional attorneys Judge Haskell appointed. Win or lose, playing a prominent role in the widely noted trial of a nefarious criminal could only help an ambitious man like Brown establish a name for himself even beyond central and western Tennessee.[18]

Brown certainly took his job seriously. He spared no effort to cast doubt on Stewart's testimony, attacking it from numerous angles. Brown tried using the convolutions of Stewart's own story against him, suggesting that some of the things Stewart claimed Murrell said showed that Murrell knew Stewart was following him and would therefore never have divulged so much incriminating information. Bringing the implication that Stewart was a liar right to the surface, Brown pointed out that Stewart admitted to deceiving Murrell into thinking he was hunting for a lost horse and that he was interested in becoming an outlaw. A person willing to act so falsely, Brown proposed, would also be willing to speak falsely under oath. When he was not arguing that Stewart simply invented Murrell's supposed disclosures, Brown tried making the case that Stewart and Murrell actually had been friends before John Henning's slaves ever disappeared. Regardless of what Stewart may or may not have known about Murrell, Brown reckoned Stewart's testimony a betrayal of friendship that marked him as untrustworthy.[19]

From a certain perspective, Milton Brown's cross-examination need not have bothered Stewart. Brown's arguments, after all, relied in some measure on suppositions that were mutually exclusive. Stewart could not both know Murrell well and lie to Murrell about his identity, nor could he both wholly invent stories and at the same time give away the secrets of a friend. Moreover, while the case against Murrell depended primarily on Stewart's testimony, the prosecution did call other witnesses to testify to Stewart's character. Ideally, their word would bolster the strength of his claims and allay the doubts Brown endeavored to raise in jurors' minds.[20]

Its internal inconsistencies notwithstanding, however, Brown's questioning stung. A few people in Tennessee knew about Stewart's falling out with Matthew Clanton, but not many. Milton Brown was surely ignorant of the affair else he would have used it to gainsay Stewart's testimony. Still, Stewart knew the ignominious feeling of being discovered acting duplicitously, and the fresh memory of that shame easily shaded into prickliness. Stewart later claimed, in fact, that only the intercession of several other men dissuaded him from giving Brown a beating in the street for having treated Stewart in what Stewart considered "an unwarrantable and dishonorable manner" on the witness stand.[21]

Moreover, Milton Brown was not the first person to speculate about the nature of Stewart's personal association with John Murrell. Stewart would write in his pamphlet that he had seen Murrell only once in his life (and that from a distance) before following him on John Henning's behalf, but even those eager to see Murrell in jail wondered otherwise. Members of the guard that took Murrell into custody repeatedly asked Murrell how he knew Stewart and under what circumstances. Murrell told them that he had never met Stewart before running into him near Estanaula and knew him only as Adam Hues. The guardsmen, including two of John Henning's sons, believed Murrell. But that did not end skepticism from other Tennesseans about how Murrell and Stewart really knew each other. Madison County sheriff Mathias Deberry remembered that many people came out of curiosity to see Murrell while he was in custody, that they peppered Murrell with questions, and that "one of the most common topics of conversation" was Murrell's relationship with Stewart.[22]

Deberry too believed Murrell when he said that the man calling himself Hues had been unknown to him before their travels together, and insisted as well that any number of "other respectable citizens who conversed with Murrell on the subject . . . were as firmly convinced of the fact that Murrell and Stewart were strangers." Nevertheless, Stewart could not have been pleased that the very people he had hoped to impress by bringing Murrell to justice wondered for weeks whether Stewart was himself a criminal. If anything, they seemed to believe Murrell's claims to have been unfamiliar with Stewart more readily than they believed Stewart himself. For Milton Brown still to be trying to tar Murrell and Stewart with the same brush months after Murrell's arrest may speak merely to a strategic decision on Brown's part to defend his client with every possible argument at his disposal. But it may also speak to the fact that Brown could tell that not everyone was convinced that Murrell and Stewart had been unacquainted before January 1834.[23]

The persistence of questions about Stewart's relationship with Murrell is understandable. Stewart's residence in Madison County had overlapped with Murrell's by about a year. They had lived only a few miles apart, and while Murrell's nearly unprompted blabbing to Stewart about his crimes might seem almost mindlessly imprudent, it would be somewhat less so if the two at least had been acquaintances before they met up near Estanaula. The suggestion that Stewart was a turncoat raised the question of motivation, of course, but Murrell's defense had a ready answer for that. After the prosecution rested its case, Murrell's lawyers called one of their only witnesses, a man named Reuben McVey, who swore that Stewart told him John Henning had offered him money to track down Murrell and bring about his conviction for slave stealing.[24]

By the time John Murrell's defense rested on July 25, 1834, Virgil Stewart had delivered a story that entertained nearly everyone who heard it. But he had also endured an uncomfortable grilling by a skilled attorney and had been vilified publicly as a liar, a traitor, and a mercenary. One can only imagine Stewart's bafflement and outrage when it became apparent how much damage Milton Brown had inflicted. Before the afternoon was even out it was clear that things were not proceeding as Stewart might have supposed, as the jury deliberated for several hours before informing Judge Haskell that they could not agree on a verdict.[25]

Haskell, not about to let Murrell get away so easily, sequestered the jurors and insisted that they try again the next day to reach a unanimous decision. This they managed to do, but Stewart could take little satisfaction in it. The original indictment against Murrell had contained eight criminal counts, and while the surviving record does not disclose what most of them were, it does indicate that the jury dismissed six of them. They found Murrell guilty of just two counts of slave stealing and recommended him to ten years' hard labor in the Tennessee state penitentiary in Nashville, a prison term five years short of the maximum.[26]

The implication of such an outcome was obvious. Joseph Snodgrass, a juror for Murrell's trial, commented privately once the proceedings ended "that it was the opinion of every man on the jury that Stewart had perjured himself." Other jurors surely talked about the group's deliberations after the fact as well, but even if Stewart never heard remarks like Snodgrass's, lingering misgivings about his testimony were manifest. Despite acknowledging that Stewart's story was "finely told," for example, the editor of the

Truth Teller also virtually admitted to thinking there was no way all of it was true, writing that Stewart "made too much effort at display." And he was not the only doubter. Stewart's testimony may have been lively, the editor continued, but in Jackson there plainly existed "difference[s] of opinion . . . as to the merit of the witness."[27]

Stewart was not wholly without defenders. In late September nearly four dozen men from Madison County's "most honorable and respectable class of citizens" decided to give Stewart some money as a "token of gratitude" for "the important and dangerous services" he rendered in capturing Murrell. Whether or not Stewart had ever sought a reward, these men believed him entitled to compensation "for the loss of time and expenses which were necessarily incurred by Mr. Stewart for the public good." Even these supporters, however, conceded they had been moved to act not merely by a desire to recognize Stewart for "his courage" but also because two months after Murrell's trial they still felt the need to "discountenance the odium which has been attempted at his character."[28]

Though they never said as much, the men who pooled their financial resources for Stewart probably did so partially in the hope that a cash payment would make him go away. As soon as Murrell's trial ended, Stewart had started telling a few of those he considered "his most intimate friends" that he intended to write and publish "a detailed history of this whole affair." But none of them thought that was a good idea. Some tried deterring Stewart by claiming it was unwise and perhaps even dangerous for him to provoke John Murrell's criminal colleagues any more than he already had by testifying against one of their own in court. That argument was disingenuous, though, and Stewart knew it, because he could tell that those who made it did not believe his story in the first place. "It was peculiarly mortifying," Stewart recalled, "to meet with much incredulity from even those in whose faith and integrity he reposed the most entire confidence."[29]

The fact was that John Murrell had not been convicted as a result of Virgil Stewart's testimony at all. Murrell went to jail because property holders in his part of Madison County were so frustrated by his slipperiness that they were willing to use any convenient pretense to imprison him. As Joseph Snodgrass reported, even though he and his fellow jurors thought Stewart fabricated much of his testimony, they found Murrell guilty because "they were convinced if [he] had not committed the offence charged in the indictment, that he had committed many others for which he merited punishment, and that they should not be inflicting punishment on an innocent man."[30]

Murrell also had the misfortune to be tried at a moment when residents of western Tennessee were particularly peeved by the kinds of banditry in which they were certain he was involved. In June 1834, just a month before Murrell's trial, some fifteen armed men stole nearly everything off a flatboat "laden with flour and whiskey" that had run aground on a sandbar on the Arkansas side of the Mississippi River a few miles south of Randolph. It was at least the second flatboat robbery committed at that spot in the previous year and a half, and it prompted irate Tennesseans to try and clear out the Arkansas canebrakes where they believed the robbers headquartered. About thirty men from Randolph raided a settlement called Shawnee Village, where they burned down some ramshackle cabins and arrested eight or ten people. The following day, forty or fifty armed men from Covington, just east of Randolph, embarked on a similar expedition. Over the course of the next week groups of west Tennesseans repeatedly traveled back and forth across the Mississippi, often carried free of charge by sympathetic steamboat captains. They took nearly two dozen men into custody, tied several others to trees and whipped them, and retrieved property they claimed had been stolen over the preceding years. John Murrell, sitting in jail waiting for his day in court, could not have participated in the flatboat plundering that touched off this series of assaults. But for anyone even thought connected to the "band of villains" that carried it out, the summer of 1834 was an especially bad time to be under indictment.[31]

Virgil Stewart had been extremely useful to those who wanted to see John Murrell in prison because his testimony attached Murrell, however tenuously, to a particular criminal act. But once the trial ended, no one had any further need for him. When he was still around months later and still insisting that he was going to publish his whole ridiculous and potentially embarrassing story, something had to be done. If he needed money that badly, it was easier just to give it to him. Those who took up contributions for Stewart failed to realize, however, that he could not be deterred by money. For Stewart, moving to the frontier had always been about achieving personal prominence as much as gaining financial security, and perhaps more so. Reuben McVey was right that John Henning had offered Stewart money for his pursuit of Murrell. In fact, after Murrell had been arrested Henning offered Stewart a gift of new clothes to replace the ratty ones he had worn every day for several weeks while riding with Murrell. But Stewart had refused it all, and the cash bounty Henning's fellows in the "respectable class" were now trying to give him reeked of a payoff. He took the money. But he could tell he had been used, and he saw now for the second time that Madison was no better place to make his destiny than Yalobusha had been. He left the next day. County residents would hear from him again, though. And they would know that Virgil Stewart would not tolerate being cast aside.[32]

III.

Some psychological turmoil already plagued Virgil Stewart as he headed out of Madison County, but his mental condition declined precipitously during the ensuing months, even compared with its dismal state when he had left the county after John Murrell's jailbreak. Then, George Saunders had found a disconsolate Stewart praying for forgiveness and divine guidance. Now Stewart was wretched, and he became increasingly erratic and unstable. First he rode east into Perry County, where he spent several days at the home of someone who had expressed interest in buying Stewart's land in Mississippi. Stewart planned to continue northeast from there through Nashville and on to Lexington, Kentucky. But he changed his mind and went south instead to Columbus, Mississippi, where he hoped to find boat passage to Mobile. Failing to find transportation, he then headed west across the state toward the Mississippi River, intending to get to Natchez and eventually to New Orleans.[33]

Somewhere along the way he fell ill, and by his own account he became so delirious that he lost track of time or even exactly where he was. In late October, however, he was in west-central Mississippi staying at the home of a farmer named James Moore. Stewart told Moore he planned on leaving the United States altogether for Europe, most probably for France, but apparently he altered his plans yet again, because he never even got to New Orleans. Instead, when he reached Natchez sometime during the last few days of October, he arranged for the commission merchant firm of Arthur, Fulton, and Company to receive any items sent to him and forward them to a spot where he aimed to settle on the Red River in northwestern Louisiana. By November 1 he had moved south about seventy miles down the Mississippi to the Louisiana town of St. Francisville, from which he wrote a letter to Saunders asking his former neighbor to ship anything he had left behind in Yalobusha County to Natchez. It is unclear whether Saunders ever followed through on Stewart's instructions. If he did, the packages could not have been delivered to Stewart anyway. Rather than go to northwestern Louisiana, he boarded a steamboat and rode fifteen hundred miles up the Mississippi and Ohio rivers to Cincinnati, where he stayed until March 1835.[34]

Perhaps the illness Stewart claimed to have contracted accounts for the "fits of delirium" he reported enduring. The frenzied pace of his travels about the Southwest, however, and the wild careening of his plans for the future from expatriation to Europe to settlement in Louisiana to steamboat voyage to Cincinnati suggests less a man who was physically unwell than one who had been overtaken by a sort of mania. Not only did Stewart evidence remarkable vigor. He also never stopped thinking about and working on the manuscript describing his experiences with John Murrell, and he began both publicly and privately to demonstrate the kinds of grandiosity, delusions, and unalloyed fabulism that would characterize the story that manuscript told.[35]

In the middle of November the *Randolph Recorder* received a curious letter describing "a bold attempt to assassinate" Stewart that had taken place more than a month earlier. According to the letter, which the paper described as written in a "cramped and prolix" script and signed by "John G. Brown," Stewart had ridden only about fifty miles from Madison County when three armed men rushed from the woods and ordered him to dismount. Stewart refused and discharged his pistol at one man who raised his shotgun to fire, killing him. A second man shot at Stewart with a rifle but missed, while the third man trained his weapon on Stewart only to lose his aim when Stewart flung his pistol and hit the man in the forehead. Stewart, the letter continued, then jumped from his horse intending to stab the third man with a dagger, but the second man struck Stewart in the back of the head with his rifle before Stewart was able to do so. Stewart managed to stumble back to his horse and escape through the trees, taking a rifle shot to the left arm as he rode away. Concluding the letter, "John G. Brown" wrote that he had last seen Stewart in Louisiana "confined in all probability to his death bed" from the lingering effects of his wounds.[36]

The injuries described by "John G. Brown" could explain the discomfort and indisposition Stewart said he experienced during the final months of

1834. But that presumes he actually incurred them. In fact, it is impossible to believe that this assassination attempt ever took place or that anyone other than Stewart himself wrote the letter to the *Recorder*. For one thing, the author of the letter claimed to have written it "on board a steamboat among a dense crowd," which is precisely where Stewart, miraculously improved and on his way to Cincinnati, would have been at the time it was penned. Moreover, the style and the phrasing of the letter closely parallel the somewhat more elaborate version of the story that would appear in Stewart's pamphlet, with the wording matching precisely in numerous instances. For his part, the editor of the *Recorder*, F. S. Latham, found the story implausible, writing that he was "disinclined to believe a word of it." Similarly, about a year later, nearly four dozen people who lived on or near the road where the attack supposedly occurred signed a statement saying that no one in the area had even heard of a fight like the one the letter described until Stewart published his account of it. Concluding that the entire affair was a product of Stewart's imagination, the statement asserted that "no unprejudiced man . . . could read the story without feeling satisfied of its utter want of truth."[37]

The letter to the *Recorder* was the first time Stewart trotted out the attempted assassination story in print, but it was not the first time he experimented with telling it. James Moore would later sign a statement saying that Stewart had told him "of his rencounter with three assassins near Tennessee river" as he "lay sick" at Moore's home just weeks before the story appeared in the newspaper. Moreover, Stewart told Moore that the assailants had belonged to "the band of villains whom his adventure and trip with Murrell to Arkansas had exposed, and which they were trying to prevent being published." As he was both ill and being pursued by these "banditti," Stewart said he had decided to "put his papers into the hands of a friend to be made public." In the meantime, he intended to disappear until the danger had passed and the public was "sufficiently aroused to a sense of the extent and designs of" Murrell's men.[38]

The story Virgil Stewart told James Moore was no more probable than the contents of the letter from "John G. Brown." Indeed, Moore's statement drew attention to holes in Stewart's story, as Moore mentioned Stewart's being sick and his saying he had been ambushed, yet he neglected to mention a gunshot wound, head trauma, or specific injury of any kind at all. But the things Stewart said to Moore did suggest how far Stewart had advanced in his thinking about his pamphlet because they pointed clearly, if in broad strokes, toward what would appear in the final product: the story of Stewart's travels with Murrell and their aftermath, including details about the reach and plans of Murrell and his confederates more explosive than anything Stewart had mentioned at Murrell's trial; the displacement of ultimate authorship onto a third party who would make Stewart as significant a character in the adventure as Murrell himself; and the framing of the entire series of events such that Stewart simultaneously could be hero and victim, bravely and single-handedly exposing Murrell as a menace to society even as Murrell's agents lurked everywhere to destroy him.

Though Stewart's story became increasingly unlikely, he himself had not become completely irrational. On the contrary, his attempt to compile the last few years of his life into pamphlet form was perfectly explicable. For one thing, he needed the money. Nothing indicates that Stewart had managed to sell any of his Yalobusha land by the end of 1834. He had not held any particular job for several years before that, and the cash he had been insulted to take when he left Tennessee could only have gone so far.[39] Selling things was the one kind of work for which Stewart had shown any aptitude, and the appetite of American consumers for sensational literature, especially stories about crime and criminals, was voracious in the early nineteenth century. Given how little else he had going for him, Stewart would have been foolish not to try hawking his story in print.[40]

Also impelling Stewart to publish his story were the concerns about character and status that had preoccupied him from his first days in the Southwest. Stewart had been raised in a southern society that placed a premium on a code of honor in which a white man's standing and self-regard depended largely on his public reputation. Yet the defining signifiers of honorable masculinity eluded Stewart, as he had neither the property holdings that indicated autonomous wealth, the household in which to act the patriarch, nor the slaves over whom to exercise mastery.[41]

On the turbulent frontier where thousands of ambitious men jockeyed to demonstrate their independence and boldness, the aggressive and visible displays of manhood entailed by honor were all the more important. In particular, a man could compensate for material uncertainty with verbal combativeness and a hair-trigger willingness to respond violently to slights and insults. Stewart's ineptitude showed here as well, as he reacted to Matthew Clanton's accusations of theft with self-abasement and to Milton Brown's intimations that he was a liar with spluttering indignation. Insofar as he had made a name for himself, Stewart had become known as a man who deserved pity more than respect and who had a habit of slinking away like a coward when confronted with questions about his integrity.[42]

But Stewart had come to understand that establishing a reputation as an honorable man mostly meant presenting a convincing appearance as one and that by writing his pamphlet he could publicly recast his entire life as he chose. In this version he could make himself into the boundlessly courageous and morally principled man of his imagination, and his critics into connivers and criminals who deserved contempt if not reprisals. Whether the story was entirely true was less important than whether he could convince readers to believe it. By successfully reframing his every action and decision, Stewart could persuade doubters that they had been wrong about him. And he would finally receive his due.

Honor was hardly the only value system informing the lives of southern men, however.[43] Understanding Virgil Stewart's pamphlet solely or even primarily within that regionally distinctive framework overlooks both the complexities of experience in the Southwest and the ways many young strivers in the United States would have recognized Stewart's vexed state of mind. Worries about identity, reputation, and appearances were conspicuous throughout antebellum America, as the increasingly fluid and individualistic socioeconomic environment was confusing and alienating even as it could be exciting and rewarding. With traditional mores of questionable application, certain knowledge of whom to trust impossible to acquire, and the fear of failure looming everywhere as the marketplace coldly determined a man's worth, intense scrutiny defined social interactions, and self-consciousness dominated the psyche. The risks of losing oneself in this world were great.[44]

The story Virgil Stewart would tell was a product of these sorts of tensions and ambiguities. The very act of writing was a way of rooting himself, projecting a stable sense of his own identity, and grounding his vertiginous experience on the frontier such that his authoritative narrative account of that experience was its own virtue. No one who credited the tale of his travels with John Murrell would deny that Stewart had earned the right to be renowned and that respectable men in the Southwest ought to be showering him with praise, fame, and fortune. At the same time, though, it did not take an especially careful reader to see the current of bile and ill will flowing just beneath the surface of Stewart's pamphlet. Discouraged about his life, envious of others' accomplishments, and ready to blame anyone but himself for his troubles, Stewart had reached the conclusion that none of those who had achieved success in the Southwest really deserved the rewards they had reaped. Perhaps the difference between the slave stealer who acted a confidence man and the slaveholder who acted a self-made man was not so great after all.[45]

IV.

In the early spring of 1835, copies of *A History of the Detection, Conviction, Life and Designs of John A. Murel, the Great Western Land Pirate* began appearing in western Tennessee, eastern Arkansas, and elsewhere in the lower Mississippi Valley. Eighty-four pages long and printed in Cincinnati, the pamphlet was written ostensibly by someone named Augustus Q. Walton. But Virgil Stewart himself was almost surely the actual author. Walton was merely a pseudonym.[46]

After a short preface promising that the story of John Murrell's villainy and capture would "amuse and entertain the reader," Stewart began *The Western Land Pirate* (as the title commonly came to be abbreviated) by establishing some context for those unfamiliar with the Southwest or its criminals. He described an epidemic of horse and slave thefts in the region that had "become a matter of the greatest concern to persons whose capital is invested in property of that kind, there being no security of its safety," and wrote that the members of a "mysterious banditti" who bore responsibility for a "great number of outrages" had managed to elude punishment for years. But, he continued, the disappearance of the slaves belonging to John Henning would prove their undoing, leading as it did to the apprehension of Murrell, their "leader and master spirit," and to the exposure of their "awful deeds" and "their more awful plans and designs."[47]

To a certain extent, the body of the text that followed these "introductory remarks" trod the same ground Stewart had covered at Murrell's trial. Stewart detailed his pursuit of Murrell on Henning's behalf, delineated the path he and Murrell traveled together, described their interactions with other people along the way, and recounted the anecdotes that Murrell allegedly had relayed to him on their ride. Stewart made clear that Murrell had admitted to stealing Henning's slaves, and he included an account of Murrell's prosecution and sentencing for that crime.

Yet a great deal set *The Western Land Pirate* apart from even the fanciful testimony Stewart had provided nearly a year earlier. For starters, Stewart's language and writing style in *The Western Land Pirate* made his appearance on the witness stand seem tranquilizing by comparison. Stewart employed prose so melodramatic and bombastic that its sheer silliness would make most modern readers laugh out loud. But it neatly captured the inflated tone of romantic adventures and dark criminal biographies that were immensely popular in the antebellum era.

In Stewart's telling, John Murrell was no small-time irritation to his neighbors or even an unusually dangerous and pesky crook. He was, rather, a "destroyer of the lives and happiness of man" whose "villainous feats have never been surpassed by any who have preceded him." A "depraved" person who "knew no law but his rapacious will" and who reveled in the "splendor of his horrid crimes," Murrell had "steeled his heart against all of the human family, except those who will consent to be as vile as himself."[48] By contrast, Stewart himself was not merely someone willing to do John Henning a favor by following Murrell, nor even merely a singularly brave man. He was also a person of "untiring perseverance" and "possessed of an inordinate share of public spirit." Equipped with "nobleness of heart" and "a firm nerve," Stewart was "respected and esteemed in every country where he has lived by its best citizens," "governed by high and honorable motives," and "one of those young men who is devoted in his friendship, generous in his sentiments, and true to his country." Even Murrell himself could sense that his companion was "a young man of splendid abilities."[49]

The Western Land Pirate nodded to conventional moralism. Murrell was a man who "cared for neither God nor devil" and assumed a clerical costume for the sake of committing robberies. Stewart, in contrast, asserted that his own survival showed "the power and protection of our Creator to those who look to him for support and defence." But pious lessons were not the primary appeal of sensational adventure and crime literature, and Stewart was not stingy with graphic details and spooky atmospherics that shocked readers and stirred their emotions. The Murrell of *The Western Land Pirate* swore profusely and bragged about swamp animals eating the corpses of slaves he and his partners murdered, and Stewart frequently called attention to the eeriness that seemed to suffuse his surroundings. Recalling the day he met and began traveling with Murrell, Stewart noted how the smoke rising from the cabins of the small settlement of Estanaula mixed among the trees "and seemed to wrap all nature in deep mourning." Later, as evening approached, Murrell and Stewart rode through a cluster of poplars in which "the mingled rays of light and darkness ... were highly calculated to produce superstitious notions." Stewart "began to feel as though he was on enchanted ground," his mind filled with "strange phantoms." Finally, after the sun had set, Murrell suggested they stop and rest "until the queen of the night blesses us with her silver beams," he and Stewart remounting their horses only "when the moon began to make the sleet glisten on the surrounding trees."[50]

It was less style than content, however, that distinguished *The Western Land Pirate* from Stewart's previous versions of his story. Stewart had altered and amplified the story almost constantly from the first time he told it such that it evolved from Murrell's stealing two slaves to his leading a sizable organization of slave stealers. But the account in *The Western Land Pirate* transcended the imaginative into the realm of the bizarre. Here, Murrell's organization, which he referred to as his "clan" and which Stewart sometimes referred to as the "mystic clan" or the "mystic conspiracy," had more than one thousand members and a formal structure designed to preclude revelation of its existence. The majority of the clan comprised individuals whose jobs consisted mostly of moving stolen horses and slaves from place to place. Known as "strikers," they ran the greatest risk of getting caught but would do just about anything for a few dollars. A smaller number of clan members composed the "grand council." These men were more valuable than the strikers, in part because they could be trusted to "keep all their designs and the extent of their plans to themselves," and in part because Murrell claimed at least half of them were "men of high standing; and many of them in honorable and lucrative offices." If anything about the existence of the clan should "leak out by chance," the grand councilors could "crush it at once, by ridiculing the idea," their presumed respectability settling the matter for fearful members of their communities.[51]

Virgil Stewart lacked the high standing or lucrative office many grand councilors held, but he claimed Murrell wanted to make him one nonetheless. In *The Western Land Pirate*, Murrell promised to put Stewart "on the high road to fortune," and when he and Stewart crossed the Mississippi River, they made their way to the "council house" of the clan located at the base of an enormous cottonwood that towered above every tree in the forest. Once there, Murrell presented Stewart to his fellows, announcing that he had brought "a counsellor of my own making," whereupon Stewart learned the secret hand signals he would need to identify himself to fellow clan members in the future.[52]

And Stewart learned so much more. When reading *The Western Land Pirate*, in fact, one wonders what Murrell chose *not* to reveal to Stewart, for he seems literally to have offered his entire life story. He told Stewart that although his father "was an honest man I expect, and tried to raise me honest," his mother encouraged her children to steal. Murrell said he committed his first theft at the age of ten and by the age of twenty had begun associating with more experienced criminals. In their company he ranged ever farther from home, stealing horses and slaves, passing counterfeit money, learning how to impersonate a preacher, and robbing and killing travelers on the road. He also became "a considerable libertine," gambling, drinking, and "rioting in all the luxuries of forbidden pleasures" with many different women.[53]

In time, Murrell told Stewart, he traveled the entire southern portion of the United States committing crimes and meeting a variety of highwaymen and thieves. During those travels he was struck by the notion of forging these associates into what would become the "mystic clan." Soon after completing this "grand circuit," he gathered about a dozen of his closest allies together in New Orleans. Over the course of three days they gave life to the clan and agreed to recruit men to carry out a "grand object" that would provide "an inexhaustible fortune to all who would engage in the expedition." On December 25, 1835, Murrell told Stewart, the clan would "excite a rebellion among the negroes throughout the slaveholding states." As Murrell explained the plan, he and his men would coordinate the activities of the slaves enlisted for the rebellion such that it would begin everywhere at precisely the same time. Then, "while all is confusion and dismay," strategically stationed clan members would "fire the towns and rob the banks" all across the South. By the time the rebellion had been quelled, they would be gone, their "pockets replenished from the banks, and the desks of rich merchants' houses."[54]

Ever since that meeting in New Orleans, Murrell told Stewart, he had spent the bulk of his time making yet another tour of the South, laying the groundwork for the operation and establishing "emissaries over the country in every direction." He said he thought the clan would have more than two thousand members by the time of the insurrection, and before the end of his and Stewart's ride together Murrell provided the names and states of

residence of nearly five hundred of them. Stewart had been hinting for
more than a year that he had a list of those affiliated with Murrell. In *The
Western Land Pirate* he finally delivered it, publishing every name he said
Murrell gave him.[55]

Long before he did that, though, Virgil Stewart obviously had become
the repository of a great deal of information about a massive criminal conspiracy, and he claimed that once clan members became aware that John
Murrell's latest recruit was a spy, they endeavored to kill him and to sully
his reputation so severely that no one would believe a word he said. Accordingly, while the bulk of *The Western Land Pirate* centers on Stewart's
ride with Murrell, most of the last twenty pages turn instead toward "the
efforts of John A. Murel and his friends, for the destruction of the life
and character of Mr. Virgil A. Stewart." Those efforts culminated with the
assassination attempt in the woods of Perry County, but Stewart wrote
that they began soon after Murrell's arrest. Stewart claimed, for instance,
that when he first returned to Yalobusha County after Murrell's capture, he
heard "rumors" about armed and "rather suspicious characters" who were
"passing through the country" looking for him. Weeks later, he recalled, he
became violently ill after drinking a cup of coffee Ann Vess prepared for
him, making him wonder whether she had tried to poison him.[56]

But he discovered the full scope of the forces arrayed against him only
on the following day. Stewart claimed that as he rode home after scouting
some land he encountered a man named George Aker, who flashed one
of the secret hand signals of the clan. Immediately on his guard, Stewart
returned the gesture and gave Aker to believe his name was Tom Goodin.
At that point, Aker informed him that the grand council had settled on a
plan to assassinate Stewart and "disgrace him too," which would result both
in Murrell's release from prison and in suspicion falling away from clan
members whose names Stewart possessed. Aker said that a clan member
had paid "an old man and his wife" one hundred dollars to poison Stewart,
but their lack of success had prompted an impatient council to give Aker
two hundred dollars "to despatch the d———d traitor." If he failed, Aker
continued, the council intended to have some Arkansans accuse Stewart
of passing them counterfeit money, whereupon Stewart would be extra-
dited and susceptible to kidnap and execution in the Morass. Finally, no
matter who managed to kill Stewart, the council had agreed to give "the
fellow with whom [Stewart] lives . . . one thousand dollars to raise a charge

against" him. Aker never mentioned the man's name, saying only that he was a "confidential friend of Stewart's," "that they have frequently done business for each other," and that he was "a good friend to some of our clan." But he was "a big fish" and "any thing he says will be believed."[57]

Thinking quickly, Stewart told Aker he had been unaware of the council's plans but that he had met Stewart and needed only an opportunity to get him alone to carry out the murder himself. An excited Aker gave Stewart one hundred dollars "to help me get his scalp," and the two parted ways. As he rode away Stewart "began to reflect on the dangerous condition he was in; he saw himself surrounded by enemies who were plotting against his life." He wrote that Aker's information convinced him that Ann Vess had indeed poisoned him, and even though Aker had not said the "confidential friend" bribed to malign Stewart was Matthew Clanton, Stewart suspected it had to be. For days afterward he fell into a "deep melancholy," "thought of the devoted friendship which he had borne to Clanton and his interest," and resisted "believing that Clanton would be hired for so base a purpose." When Clanton accused him of theft, however, Stewart knew for certain he "was the man whom George Aker had alluded to, for the matter had then been fairly demonstrated by the charge made."[58]

Stewart wrote that he then left Yalobusha County because he thought it necessary to "go out of the influence and power of his enemies" and that before he left he told Clanton "that whenever he was convinced that he had acted dishonorably towards him, to publish it to the world; but cautioned him of the bad consequences of being too premature in his conclusions and engagements." Stewart discovered, however, that he could not escape the hounding of Murrell's clansmen and realized that the knowledge that he might reveal their names did not intimidate them. Instead, when he returned to Tennessee he felt himself "surrounded with a legion of devils and slanderers, whose fate depended on his destruction." During and after Murrell's trial, clan members and sympathizers were everywhere. They might have been too afraid to testify on Murrell's behalf "now that their names were on a list." But Milton Brown, Stewart wrote, was "nothing more than the organ through which the venom of a detestable and piratical clan of villains were vented," while those who later discouraged him from publishing *The Western Land Pirate* were "private agents of the clan, who came in the garb of friends." Yet Stewart could not be put off. Writing his pamphlet was "the performance of what he conceived to be his duty, undaunted by all the fictions of horror and death which they were capable of presenting to his imagination."[59]

V.

The Western Land Pirate is a document that resists a straightforward reading. Strictly from a literary perspective, Stewart modeled his story primarily on lurid tales whose popularity rested in large measure on their bloodiness and the wickedness of their protagonists. One needs to read only so much about John Murrell's cavalier and remorseless attitude toward murder, his penchant for disemboweling his victims and replacing their entrails with stones so that they would disappear beneath the waters into which they were tossed, and his desire to see the "cities and towns" of the Southwest "one common scene of devastation, smoked walls and fragments" to take the point. Yet clichés and conventions of other genres with appeal to ante-bellum readers shaped *The Western Land Pirate* as well.[60]

Stewart drew in part, for example, on stereotypes from middle-class advice literature. Though not nearly so didactic as the etiquette guides and sentimental fiction geared mostly to young men and women in American cities, the tale of Murrell's departure as a young man from an honest path of industry and frugality leading inevitably to imprisonment and a life wasted might be read as homiletic nonetheless. Stewart said as much, contending in *The Western Land Pirate* that Murrell's fate ought to serve as a "warning to others who may be posting the road which leads to misery and degradation, and convince them of the final justice of their Creator, before their consciences are for ever steeled to his reproofs by progressive crimes."[61]

Also influencing *The Western Land Pirate* was the emerging genre of southwestern satirical writing. Stewart's Murrell may have been a scoundrel and even a sociopath, but he was not without a roguish sense of humor that calls to mind the comic sensibilities of the many frontier authors who contributed to William T. Porter's popular newspaper, *Spirit of the Times*. Murrell disguised himself and deceived people as much for sport as for profit, he found just about anyone wealthy or respectable to be fair game, and his schemes could be in the service of his own amusement rather than his greed. He liked an ironic turn of phrase, such as when he told Stewart how he had acted the minister and "preached like hell for a neighborhood of Methodists," and the juxtaposition of brutal and random violence with lighthearted gaiety, such as when he described how he and a friend "frol-icked" and acted "the highest larks you ever saw" with money stolen from a man whose body they threw off a cliff.[62]

It is hard to say how many readers would have laughed at the stories Stewart told, some of which were disturbing even by frontier standards. But the fact that his narrative used a hodgepodge of literary formulas raises the question of whether the tales *The Western Land Pirate* comprises were even true. There is indeterminacy here too, as one cannot separate fact from fiction with total precision. This is particularly so regarding the obscene number of crimes Murrell supposedly confessed, most of which were com-mitted against anonymous men in unnamed and lonely places. Nonethe-less, if Stewart encrusted some essential facts with an overlay of hyperbole and improbable flourishes when he testified at John Murrell's trial, much of the material making its debut in *The Western Land Pirate* was almost certainly a succession of outright lies.

For someone who claimed Murrell gave him "a short history of his life," Stewart knew remarkably little about the basic details of Murrell's biogra-phy. Stewart wrote that Murrell said he "was born in Middle Tennessee," when in fact he was born in Virginia. Stewart wrote that Murrell told him he had spent most of the five years before their meeting making two sepa-rate circuits of the entire South, covering thousands of miles as he traveled the East Coast from Maryland to Florida, ranged the interior from Ken-tucky to Texas, and even headed down into Mexico before going back to Tennessee. Moreover, on the rare occasions he was at home, Stewart's Mur-rell liked to spend weeks at a time "among the girls of my acquaintance, in all the enjoyments that money could afford." Putting aside the grueling toll so much travel would have taken on him, one wonders what Murrell's wife made of his near-constant absence and his philandering. But there is no indication that Stewart knew Murrell even had a wife. Nor does he appear to have known that Murrell had two children by 1834 or that he had been totally bankrupt as recently as 1833.[63]

Turning from Murrell's past to his present and his plans for the future, it is not merely odd that Stewart would say nothing for more than a year about the "mystic clan" or the plans of its leader to launch a slave insurrec-tion. It is absurd. Stewart wrote that he withheld "the horrid confessions, designs, and life of Murel ... from even his best friends" and that he had divulged only information that "was connected in some way" to the theft of John Henning's slaves because he wanted to be sure Murrell would get "a fair trial before the legal representatives of his country." Thus, if Stewart is to be believed, he brooked a rhetorical pummeling on the witness stand, a false accusation of theft, multiple attempts on his life, and the derision of nearly everyone he talked to because he did not want "the minds of the people ... [to] be prejudiced to unreasonableness against Murel." Moreover, he considered the administration of "law and justice" so vital that he kept his mouth shut about a confederacy of more than one thousand criminals plotting to spark an uprising that would result in millions of dollars of property damage and the deaths of hundreds of people, and did so for a man "he knew to be of the basest and most corrupt principles." In Stewart's telling, these choices demonstrated his "nobleness of heart, and magnanimous feelings." They also demonstrated that he thought his readers extremely gullible.[64]

There was no "mystic clan" headed by John Murrell, or by anyone else, for that matter. Some of the names on Stewart's list of clan members did belong to actual criminals. Among clansmen from Missouri was one "Col. S. W. Foreman." This was Stephen W. Foreman, a counterfeiter who had escaped from a St. Louis jail only to be captured in Arkansas on suspicion of involvement in the flatboat robbery that had prompted Tennesseans to try and clear out the Morass in the spring of 1834. Among "transienters" in the clan who lived in no particular state was "Soril Phelpes," a reference to Alonzo Phelps, who had been convicted and sentenced to hang in Mississippi for murder, also in the spring of 1834. "R. Tims" of Tennessee was probably Reuben Tims, who would be arrested for horse theft in 1835, and clansmen from Arkansas included members of the Barney, Bunch, and Lloyd families, around all of whom swirled accusations of robbery, counterfeiting, slave stealing, and general disreputableness.[65]

But Stephen Foreman was regionally notorious, and Alonzo Phelps was so famous that he had acquired a popular sobriquet, "the Rob Roy of the Mississippi." Anyone who picked up a newspaper would have known their names, and anyone who listened to local gossip would have been familiar with the others. As the editor of the *Arkansas Gazette* noted after reading *The Western Land Pirate*, Stewart's list of clan members included a number of "known and long suspected rascals." That Stewart invented out of whole cloth most of the hundreds of names on the list is nearly self-evident. With the exceptions of Foreman, Phelps, and a few others, Stewart enumerated clan members almost solely by last name. He added a first initial about half the time but was never more specific than that, and many of the surnames were so generic as to be found practically anywhere in the United States. His roster of Kentucky clansmen, for example, comprised "three Forrows, four Wards, two Forsythes, D. Clayton, R. Williamson, H. Haley, H. Potter, D. Mugit, two Pattersons, S. Goin, Q. Drantley, L. Potts, four Reeses, [and] two Carters."[66]

Stewart would later account for the list's skimpiness by claiming that he did not have enough paper to transcribe it in greater detail, having used most of the notebook he carried to surreptitiously record the things Murrell said in a kind of journal whose pages Stewart stuffed into his hat for safekeeping. Although this excuse provides the amusing image of Virgil Stewart trying to keep Murrell from noticing that Stewart's hat teetered atop a growing pile of crumpled papers, it was too convenient. In any case, it was not just the imprecision of his catalog of names that suggests Stewart invented the mystic clan. It was that to the extent an organization of southwestern criminals actually existed in the 1830s, it only dimly matched Stewart's description.[67]

Newspaper editors liked to refer to southwestern bandits as forming themselves into "gangs," but in fact they seem to have been affiliated with one another loosely and provisionally and without any singular or hierarchical leadership. The confession of Willis Watson opens a rare window onto the workings of the southwestern underworld. Arrested for counterfeiting in Missouri in the fall of 1834, Watson provided information about nearly twenty men who he claimed were engaged in criminal activities in the region. "The counterfeit money," Watson disclosed, was made in Arkansas by John and William "Merrill," by whom he surely meant John Murrell and his older brother. Ten other men were "co-partners" with the Murrells, and Watson believed one had also stolen several slaves and horses. Another man who had "always received and befriended" the Murrells and their partners "and received money of them" sometimes "shows and tells what negroes will go with them, and where to get horses." Among four others who were "friendly also," one knew how to counterfeit and a second had passed some phony bills. At least three other men, meanwhile, had "had an interest in the business, but quit it," and a fourth had "been a grand villain, but has quit."[68]

Watson's confession indicates that networks of criminals in the Southwest could be geographically extensive. The men he described moved slaves, horses, and counterfeit money from western Tennessee and eastern Arkansas down to the Gulf of Mexico. But their range basically followed the Mississippi River and was not nearly so far-reaching as to cover the whole South. In addition, Watson detailed circumstances in which criminals were related less in terms of relative degrees of authority and power in a syndicate than with regard to the different skills and specialties they possessed, and he explained that a life of crime could be a temporary one that men might and not uncommonly did abandon at some point. In short, John Murrell probably did steal slaves and horses, make and pass counterfeit money, and associate with others who did the same. It is even likely that he did so regularly and for long enough that he might be said to have been part of a "gang." But he was no mastermind, and he led no clan.

Without the thread of the "mystic clan" holding them together, other significant elements of *The Western Land Pirate* unravel. No plot to steal the wealth of the South existed, and no criminal cabal was coordinating a diversionary slave rebellion. In the wake of Murrell's trial, people in Tennessee began asking questions about Virgil Stewart, and as reports of why he really had left Mississippi became more widespread, Stewart became progressively more mortified, more desperate to turn threats to his reputation back on those who he felt threatened it, and more inclined toward vindictiveness. But Matthew Clanton had not been given a thousand dollars to spread lies about Stewart, and Ann Vess had not tried to poison him. Milton Brown was not an operative retained by Stewart's enemies, and no one was trying to assassinate him.[69]

Sometimes Stewart hinted in the text that all was not as it seemed in *The Western Land Pirate*. When he described introducing himself into Murrell's company by pretending to be a horse hunter as "ventur[ing] a trick," an astute reader might wonder whether the portrayal of Murrell as one of the most vicious men in the world was the more extensive hoax. When Stewart noted how traveling with Murrell reminded him of "all the old superstitious stories that he had heard or read in his whole life," he intimated that what lay before the reader itself comprised fable as much as fact. And when Stewart wrote of telling Murrell that he would "look back to the hour of our meeting, as the fortunate era when my importance and victories were to commence," he gestured toward the streak of opportunism running through his life that never let reality stand in the way of his expectations.[70]

Perhaps the only clear truth to be found amid the hackneyed convolutions of *The Western Land Pirate* is the puzzlement and anger of its author at how things worked on the frontier and how dismally his ventures there had turned out for him. Virgil Stewart had come to the Southwest thinking he could make himself into the person he wished to be, only to find that he had no firm idea who that person was. He had tried living in several places and earning money at several occupations, but nothing translated into anything steady or particularly promising. He wrote *The Western Land Pirate* in an effort to give his story shape and coherence, but the fact that he had become a drifter with no family and few friends was unavoidable. It was no wonder he tried on many selves. Virgil Stewart was also Adam Hues and Tom Goodin and Augustus Walton, and he was probably John G. Brown too. One moniker was no better or worse than any other, and there was some sorrow mixed in with the dissembling when Stewart replied to John Murrell's asking how he called himself by saying "I seldom ever have a name."[71]

In Stewart's own mind, at least, he had tried hard to show himself worthy of something better than his background. Personally lacking resources and social prestige, he sought out those who had them in the hope that they would see his potential and escort him toward the station he believed he ought to inhabit. Yet his time in the Southwest had taught him that what you had was not only more important than who you were but that it made you who you were; that it was pointless to curry favor with others because they would do nothing for you; and that selfish disregard was the only reasonable approach to surviving in an environment without room for sentiment. As Stewart explained his personal philosophy to Murrell in *The Western Land Pirate*, "we are placed here, and we must act for ourselves, or we feel the chilling blasts of charity's cold region; and we feel worse than that, we feel the power of opulent wealth, and the sneer of pompous show; and, sir, what is it that constitutes character, popularity and power in the United States? Sir, it is property; strip a man of his property in this country, and he is a ruined man indeed—you see his friends forsake him; and he may have been raised in the highest circles of society, yet he is neglected and treated with contempt. Sir, my doctrine is, let the hardest fend off."[72]

Throughout *The Western Land Pirate* Virgil Stewart expressed great admiration for John Murrell when in his company, claiming that "his vanity was his accessible point" and that flattery helped persuade Murrell to reveal his secrets. But Stewart's fawning reflected his personal preoccupations so consistently that it cannot be accounted for merely as palaver to gain Murrell's confidence. Stewart's hostility toward the privilege bestowed on elites by virtue of their wealth surfaced again and again. He applauded Murrell's boasting that he and his "company of rogues" stole without repercussions, saying that "if they have sense enough to evade the laws of their country, which are made by the wisest men of the nation, let them do it. . . . It is just as honorable for them to gain property by their superior powers, as it is for a long-faced hypocrite to take the advantage of the necessities of his fellow-beings." To Stewart's way of thinking, the men who merited admiration were those whose cunning was more striking than their riches, and he told Murrell he considered him among them, pronouncing that if Murrell were "placed in a situation to make a display of his talents, [he] would soon render the name and remembrance of an Alexander, or a Jackson, little and inconsiderable, when compared with him: he is great from the force of his own mental powers, and they are great, from their station in the world; in which fortune, more than powers, have placed them."[73]

Virgil Stewart would never have acknowledged genuinely esteeming John Murrell. But that he saw the appeal of men like him—who took what they wanted, thrived thanks to their wits rather than their money, inverted the laws designed to protect the propertied, and undid the supposed assurance of appearances—seems undeniable. In keeping with his tendency to try and win the approval of older men who might guide his path, Stewart repeatedly spoke of his desire to be molded in Murrell's image. Agreeing to follow Murrell into Arkansas, Stewart said that he had "no doubt but I should learn many things under so able a teacher as I expect you are." The following day he said that he wanted Murrell to "make a man" of him and that he imagined Murrell as "the genius of some master spirit of ancient days" who was "sent as a guide to protect and defend me before all which may oppose."[74]

That the John Murrell of *The Western Land Pirate* served as a mouthpiece for the disdain Stewart had come to feel toward everything he had seen and everyone he had met in the Southwest is most plainly indicated in the speech Stewart claimed he gave to the grand council of the mystic clan.

Asked by the clansmen in Arkansas to whom Murrell introduced him "to give them his opinion concerning their negro war, and what he conceived to be their faith," Stewart began humbly and with deference to Murrell, saying that he felt himself ill-equipped to speak "as all my ideas have been received from our honorable dictator, and I should deem it presumption in me to offer any amendments to the present deep and well arranged plans and purposes of his majesty." But Stewart warmed to his subject, telling those gathered that he believed the members of the mystic clan to be "absolved from every other power or obligation to either God or man." It made no sense for them to be "surrounded with every thing needful for our comfort and enjoyment" and to "stand supinely by and see others enjoy and make no provision for ourselves, because an established religion and moral custom, which we neither believe nor respect, forbids us from choosing the mode of providing." By Stewart's reckoning, every living creature on earth, including man, was "falling a victim to each other." The only realistic thing to do was "live the lords of our own wills, rioting in all the luxuries which the spoils of our enemies and opposers will afford." The world was a harsh place, and only hard-heartedness paid off. "If I live in hell," Stewart told Murrell, "I will fight for the devil."[75]

It is easy to criticize Virgil Stewart for his attitude. He never succeeded as he might have wished, but he also never put in any sustained effort that might have brought success. Instead, he expected that things would just happen for him, and he abandoned one place and one plan after another when they did not happen fast enough. He cut corners by stealing from and lying to those who otherwise liked and might have been willing to help him and then begrudged them for the odium he had brought on himself. Stewart's response to ignominy might be explained as a product of living in a society that placed a high value on honor, but that would be too exculpatory. In truth, Stewart was a narcissist whose insecurities bred an overblown sense of his own importance and an eagerness to be appreciated that left him vulnerable to coming undone and lashing out when criticized. Such a constellation of personality traits lent itself well to the atmosphere of paranoia that ran through Stewart's life and the pamphlet alike. In *The Western Land Pirate* John Murrell proclaimed that the desire for vengeance ultimately motivated his slave insurrection plot. "I look on the American people as my common enemy," Stewart wrote that Murrell told him. "They have disgraced me, and they can do no more; my life is nothing to me, and it shall be spent as their devoted enemy." But little in Murrell's experience, either in reality or as detailed in the pamphlet, justified the intensity or the scope of such animosity. Virgil Stewart, on the other hand, had nothing but rancor for a nation he felt had turned its back on him.[76]

Stewart lacked the reflective capacity to see that many of his wounds were self-inflicted, but he was not entirely wrong about the Southwest. Economic status and identity were easily conflated, wealth did go a long way toward dictating a person's reputation, and the affluent condescended to the impoverished and even to those of more moderate means in ways that ran against the grain of the frontier's promise of white male equality. Moreover, Stewart saw the flimsiness and hypocrisy of the foundation on which the entire social and economic edifice of southwestern expansion rested. There was a reason why he fantasized about a wholesale slave insurrection as the greatest plot a bandit might ever engineer. All the region's potential riches and the standing of its most prosperous people depended on slave laborers. They produced the cotton that made the land valuable. They were chattel more treasured even than cash. And their bodies underwrote the elite pomp and presumption that Stewart coveted and loathed all at once. Were the enslaved to revolt, all would be chaos, all would be worthless, and the high and mighty would be laid very, very low.[77]

VI.

Virgil Stewart was not well educated and gave few signs that he was particularly bright. He sold some copies of *The Western Land Pirate* in the spring of 1835, but if he truly thought the pamphlet would revive his reputation or that people would take it seriously, he experienced yet another letdown. In Tennessee, the editor of the *Jackson Truth Teller* thought Stewart's work had a "rawhead and bloody bones character" that was "well calculated to excite popular interest and give it a wide circulation." He hesitated to doubt Stewart's "veracity and honest intentions," particularly with regard to "the historical part of the pamphlet" that substantially duplicated Stewart's testimony at John Murrell's trial. But on the whole he thought *The Western Land Pirate* a badly written "miserable affair," considered "the extraordinary disclosures made by Murrell" beyond what Stewart recounted on the witness stand to be "too incredible in themselves to be believed," and concluded "that the leading motive of the author of this edifying history, is to speculate upon the natural love of the marvellous, which has ever characterized mankind." Believing that "no good" could come of that, "but on the contrary much harm," the editor felt obliged to state his "decided disapprobation of the pamphlet."[78]

Others were even less kind. In Mississippi, a Vicksburg editor saw no reason to "give credit to the 'Land Pirate.'" In Louisiana, a writer from Baton Rouge thought the pamphlet to be of a "most preposterous style" that "was of itself sufficient to destroy all pretensions to credibility." And in Arkansas, the editor of the *Gazette* managed to read only "some ten or a dozen pages" before he "threw it down as a catchpenny affair and a bait to catch gulls with." Comparing the language of the pamphlet to "that which we generally find used in gallows confessions," he failed to see why he ought to waste his time on the rest.[79]

Matthew Clanton, of course, had a more personal stake in the reception of *The Western Land Pirate*. Accused of venality and collusion with criminals, Clanton feared that his own reputation would suffer if Stewart's narrative went unchallenged. As significantly, Clanton had mostly stayed silent about his dealings with Stewart for nearly a year only to have Stewart defame and spread falsehoods about him. It was galling and it was infuriating. It so gratuitously compounded Stewart's original betrayal that Clanton now saw his erstwhile friend and neighbor for the petty and malicious spirit that he was. And Clanton was not going to stand for it. In May 1835 thirty-seven men from Yalobusha County signed and published a statement in Clanton's defense, certifying that he was "a gentleman of high standing in society, esteemed among us as an honest, correct, high-minded man, incapable of the baseness with which he is charged." Not content to stop there, they attested that they knew Stewart too and shared "the deepest conviction that he is a base young man, whose word is entitled to no credit, entirely unworthy of the countenance and respect of honest men." Finally, the signers revealed Stewart's motive for vilifying Clanton, explaining that Clanton had charged Stewart "with stealing money and goods from him, while attending to his business . . . in the fall of 1833, the truth of which charge none of us entertain a doubt."[80]

Less than a month later, in June 1835, a grand jury in Yalobusha County indicted Stewart for larceny and Clanton filed a libel suit against him. The final volley of Clanton's counterattack, however, came in early July when he published a pamphlet of his own titled *A Refutation of the Charges Made in the* Western Land Pirate, *against* Matthew Clanton; *together with an exposition of the character of* Virgil A. Stewart, *its author*. In it Clanton described what had transpired between the two men from the moment they met until Stewart left Yalobusha County, and he enclosed affidavits from George Saunders and others supporting his version of events. He systematically dismantled the claims Stewart levied against him in *The Western Land Pirate* by pointing out inconsistencies and impossibilities, accused Stewart of trying "to raise his character . . . by blackening mine," and absolutely eviscerated Stewart personally.[81]

Clanton called Stewart a "rogue," a "calumniator," and a "liar." He asserted that "a man of his character would just as soon say one thing as another," claimed that in Yalobusha he had "heard of no man base enough to avow himself" Stewart's friend, and suggested that if Stewart really believed the things he wrote, he "ought to be sent to a mad house." Clanton dared Stewart to sue him for slander if he took exception to his charges or assertions and openly doubted Stewart's courage to do so. In the end, Clanton regretted ever having pitied Stewart. With hindsight, he wrote, he should have given Stewart the "good flogging" he deserved. Now he hoped only that Stewart might "go forth into the great desert of human infamy, to perish and die by the stench created by his own offences."[82]

Clanton was right that Stewart lacked the nerve to file a lawsuit against him, but after being granted a change of venue for his larceny trial because of the "prejudice that exists against him in the public mind" in Yalobusha, Stewart did sue for libel sixteen of the men who signed the statement supporting Clanton. Then he wrote a letter "to the public" that appeared in several newspapers conceding that he could "never expect to obtain" hard evidence proving that Murrell's clansmen had bribed Clanton but asking his "fellow-citizens of the South" to withhold judgment while he marshaled circumstantial evidence that would show he was telling the truth.[83]

In a different place and at a different time, the entire affair might have come to nothing. Virgil Stewart's pamphlet and Matthew Clanton's reply might have been a peculiar but ultimately insignificant exchange involving two men at loggerheads about who took what from whom, who told the truth, who lied, and whose character warranted a reputation for soundness. John Murrell might have faded from the memory of all except the most devoted chroniclers of local history and gone down as a small-time legend men told stories about in their dotage. But somewhere in the Southwest there were people who believed Virgil Stewart's pamphlet. They believed John Murrell's men had not abandoned their plan for inciting a slave rebellion, and they believed they would be under siege at any moment. As Stewart started gathering materials to sustain himself yet again before a skeptical audience, even he never would have guessed that Murrell was about to enter the ranks of the most famous outlaws in pre–Civil War America, or that *The Western Land Pirate* was about to catalyze one of the deadliest incidents of extralegal violence and mass hysteria the antebellum South would ever see.

PART TWO

~~~~~~

Settlers and Insurrectionists

~ ~

CHAPTER THREE

Exposing the Plot

A t first, what was happening near Beattie's Bluff, Mississippi, did not seem to have anything to do with John Murrell, Virgil Stewart, or his pamphlet. Rumors passed of strange goings on, but no one could determine their source, and in any case they were too airy and uncertain to pay much mind. But the widow had a bad feeling. The young enslaved women who worked in her house seemed less inclined to listen to her than they normally were. Sometimes they spoke to her downright disrespectfully, and she often found them whispering among themselves when they should have been working. As the last weeks of June ushered in the summer of 1835, the widow decided she ought to pay closer attention and perhaps try to overhear their conversations.[1]

The widow was careful not to reveal herself, and it was disconcerting when she heard one slave tell another that "she wished to God it was all over and done with, that she was tired of waiting on the *white folks*, and wanted to be her own mistress the balance of her days, and clean up her own house." It was mysterious too. She wished *what* would be over and done with? A few days later the widow overheard the woman again, this time in conversation with an enslaved man owned by a neighboring farmer named David Landfair. They spoke in hushed tones and the widow could not make out everything, but what she did hear was chilling enough. "Is it not a pity to kill such ———," the woman asked as she held the widow's young grandchild in her arms. Landfair's slave replied that "it was, but it must be done, and that it would be doing a great favor, as it would go to heaven and escape the troubles of this world."[2]

The widow still did not know exactly what they were talking about, but it hardly mattered. When slaves used the word "kill" in the context of white people, someone needed to investigate. That evening the widow told her son, Lorenzo Latham, what she had heard. Latham wasted no time. He asked another neighbor named James Lee to assist him in questioning the woman, and the men confronted her. Latham and Lee informed the woman that her conversation had been overheard and demanded she tell them everything that had passed between her and her fellow bondspersons. Intimidated by the two white men, the woman disclosed what she knew. If the fragmented exchange Latham's mother had heard was troubling, what she had missed was absolutely terrifying. "The negro man," the enslaved woman told Latham and Lee, "had informed her that there was to be a rising of the black people soon, and that they intended killing all the whites."[3]

Latham and Lee knew what to do next. Early the following morning they began reporting their discovery to other white people in the vicinity, and given the vigilance with which white southerners monitored the enslaved population for signs of rebelliousness, it might seem odd that not much happened for a few days. But if rumors that slaves were planning an insurrection were nothing to take lightly, they were also nothing new in the South. Whites quickly circulated the details from the Latham plantation well beyond the neighborhood of Beattie's Bluff, and initially they pursued them with relative composure. Systematically gathering additional information while stepping up their general watchfulness, they appeared to exemplify self-assured American settlers confident in their ability to overcome any obstacles before them as they expanded the realm of the southwestern cotton kingdom.[4]

The social and economic ground of the cotton frontier was always less solid than it looked, however, and such imperturbability would not last. Some people thought they knew what was happening among the slaves and who was responsible for it, and as more intelligence materialized in murmured bits and fragmentary pieces they became more convinced in that knowledge. Acquiring absolute certainty might require techniques more forceful than simply asking questions, but in the hands of those already inclined to think it could be true, Virgil Stewart's pamphlet would become a self-fulfilling prophecy. And a lot of innocent people were going to die.

I.

Though it was only a coincidence that Beattie's Bluff sat in a county called Madison, like the one in Tennessee where John Murrell had been tried and convicted of slave stealing, it was no coincidence that Virgil Stewart's pamphlet circulated and gained currency there. Stewart had spent time in

Madison County, in west-central Mississippi, on at least two occasions during the year and a half before Lorenzo Latham's mother started worrying about the behavior of her slaves. Thomas Hudnall, to whom John Murrell told Stewart he had sold and then absconded with a stolen slave named Sam, lived in this Madison County, and in February 1834, after failing to find John Henning's slaves in the Mississippi town of Manchester where Murrell's Arkansas associates had supposedly sent them, Stewart paid a visit to Hudnall in an attempt to verify whether any of Murrell's stories actually were true. James Moore, with whom Stewart stayed in October 1834 as he recuperated from injuries he allegedly incurred while fighting off assassins on the road, lived in Madison County, Mississippi, too. Given the mutual acquaintance between Stewart and at least some of the county's planters, surely it was among the places where he personally distributed his account of Murrell's "mystic clan" and its machinations after publishing it in the spring of 1835.[5]

The notion that a connection might exist between what transpired on the Latham plantation and the insurrection plot described by Stewart, however, did not immediately gain purchase. It certainly did not cross the mind of anyone living near Beattie's Bluff, because it is unlikely that anyone there had read or even heard about *The Western Land Pirate*. Situated on a bend in the Big Black River, Beattie's Bluff sat close to the northeastern edge of white settlement in Mississippi when it was established in the early 1820s and for a time looked poised to become an important place. It served as the first seat of Yazoo County in 1823, became the first seat of Madison County when it was carved out of Yazoo in 1828, and was a popular spot for farmers to load their cotton onto flatboats for transport south and west toward the Mississippi River. But places stayed popular in Mississippi only as long as they stayed profitable, and the steamboats becoming increasingly common for moving goods to markets could ascend the Big Black only about as far as Vernon, a village several miles downriver from Beattie's Bluff, and then only at certain times of year. The land surrounding Beattie's Bluff still yielded fine cotton crops, but by 1834 the settlement itself had become so insignificant that a newspaper correspondent describing Madison County did not even mention it. It was hardly a place Virgil Stewart would have thought to peddle his pamphlet, presuming he knew it existed at all.[6]

One place Stewart likely would have thought to go was Livingston, which was situated about ten miles south of Beattie's Bluff. Thomas Hudnall's plantation was located nearby, so Stewart had probably been to Livingston before. But Livingston was also a trade center with about two hundred residents, it had become the seat of government for Madison in 1829, and it sat at the intersection of three major roads, all of which combined to make it arguably the most important place in the county. The residents of Beattie's Bluff understood that. When they "thought it advisable to invite the attention of the citizens of the county" to what Lorenzo Latham and James Lee had elicited from the enslaved woman overheard by Latham's mother, they went to Livingston.[7]

Few people there were completely surprised by the report from Beattie's Bluff. What one man referred to as indistinct "floating rumours" that slaves in the area might be plotting something had been circulating for some time. But now, with something specific on which to fix their attention, the white residents of Livingston decided to act. On June 27 they called a public meeting at which they voted to create committees of investigation to gather more information from across the county. They created patrols to monitor the roads and plantations for suspicious activity among the slave population and scheduled another meeting for June 30 to see what the committees and patrols had managed to uncover.[8]

They did not uncover much. When the residents of Livingston reconvened, the only substantive news they heard came from William Johnson, a planter who lived close to the village. Johnson knew that most of the slaves on his plantation would never willingly tell him anything about an uprising, so he had asked a slave he trusted and used as a driver to look into things and report whatever he was able to find. According to Johnson, the driver spoke to an elderly male slave who told him that another slave named Peter had told him there was going to be "a rising of the blacks soon." That, however, was about all the man knew. He told the driver he had no idea when exactly this "rising" was supposed to take place. The only real item he had to add was that Peter, who belonged to a Livingston man named Ruel Blake, had said that in preparation he intended to break into a village store and steal several kegs of gunpowder.[9]

This was pretty weak stuff. There were hundreds of farms and plantations with slaves in the area, and several days of probing them had revealed little beyond the generic scattered rumblings of insurrection that whites living in the county had already heard. True, both the woman at Beattie's Bluff and Johnson's elderly slave had indicated that the insurrection was going to take place "soon," so whites would have been fools not to find that detail disturbing and more than a little frightening. But there would not seem to be much to do other than stay alert and make further inquiries. The committee of men running the meeting in Livingston asked William Johnson to bring his driver's informant to them for interrogation, which Johnson readily agreed to do, and they sent some people to take Peter, Ruel Blake's slave, into custody.[10]

The committee then started questioning a white man named William Saunders, a drifter known to keep company with other white men whose character many in Livingston judged "none of the best." Spotted near the village on the day of the meeting, Saunders was taken in to "see if he could give any account of himself." He had little to say about the insurrection rumors. Really, it did not sound like he knew much about them. But he conceded that an associate of his named Albe Dean was a "great rascal," and that another, Joshua Cotton, "was in the habit of trading with negroes" and "would buy any thing they would steal and bring to him." Saunders also said he believed Cotton and a man named Andrew Boyd had stolen several slaves belonging to a man from a neighboring county.[11]

The decision to question William Saunders might seem strange. None of the slaves who had provided information about the supposed uprising had said that Saunders was involved, or for that matter that any white people were. But Virgil Stewart had made clear that members of John Murrell's "mystic clan" worked among the enslaved to inspire rebellion, and that sufficed for some in Livingston to start imagining the possibilities. As the sun went down on June 30, white men in Livingston returned to their homes and shored up their defenses. They gathered and readied every weapon they could find, and some families huddled together seeking strength and security in numbers. And they prepared notices to be sent with fast riders to villages and towns throughout central and western Mississippi urging residents to be on their guard. By the end of the next day, one of those warnings had traveled nearly seventy-five miles southwest to the town of Rodney. Signed by one Israel Spencer, it stated "that an insurrection was expected in th[is] county on the 4th July, and that with some evidence and strong suspicion, several negroes and several suspicious white men have been imprisoned, supposed to belong to Murel's clan."[12]

Given how little the investigations in Madison County had actually uncovered, Spencer's warning was quite a leap. Thanks to Stewart, after all,

John Murrell was in a Tennessee prison, and the conspiracy he allegedly had hoped to put into action across the South on Christmas Day lay in shambles. But Stewart never said the scheme had been abandoned altogether, and those who believed his story had no reason to think there were not still hundreds of Murrell's clansmen skulking about the Southwest at that very moment ready to implement it. Moreover, slaves in the county had indicated an insurrection was coming soon, so why not the Fourth of July? No one had said the uprising was planned for then. But like Christmas, July 4 was a day when masters did not force slaves to work and the enslaved were "permitted to assemble together from the different plantations, and enjoy themselves in uninterrupted feasting and festivity." Logistically, at least, the date made sense, and being Independence Day, it carried symbolic weight too. Among whites in Livingston, that was sufficient to establish a "general impression" of what was about to happen.[13]

Hushed wisps of a conversation, a fourth-hand rumor, some criminal activity carried out by a few shady white men. Nothing amounted to anything concrete. But whites in Livingston thought they had a lot more. They thought the pieces were starting to fall into place. They had Virgil Stewart's pamphlet, which outlined the insurrection plan. They had a date for its execution. And they had some names. Peter, who belonged to Ruel Blake. William Johnson's elderly slave. William Saunders. Joshua Cotton. Andrew Boyd. Albe Dean. It all still did not quite connect, but as the information made its way back out of Livingston and circulated around Madison County, some at Beattie's Bluff thought it a good idea to revisit their initial investigation and to start asking the enslaved some more questions. Maybe showing them that the white people knew all about the plot, and even knew the names of some of those involved, would draw forth something more than the woman on the Latham plantation had confessed. There were many ways to make slaves start talking, and once they did, things in Madison County took a very rapid turn toward the very nasty.

II.

By themselves, neither Virgil Stewart's travels through Madison County nor the dissemination of his pamphlet there can sufficiently explain why the hazy scuttlebutt heard from a few slaves convinced whites in the area that they were about to face the uprising supposedly conceived by John

Murrell. Arguably there were few places where the optimism about the future of the United States bred by the flush times was more justified than Madison County, which exemplified many of the broader trends that made Mississippi an exhilarating destination for the era's white migrants.

With rich loess soil the result of centuries of accumulated hardwood forest leaf mold and dust deposited by Great Plains winds, Madison bore out one man's observation in 1834 that "no other county in the State contains as large bodies of fertile lands, adapted to the culture of cotton." In addition, Madison's landscape of gentle hills was bounded by the Big Black River to the northwest and the Pearl River to the southeast, effectively situating it between two natural commercial highways. The white population grew by nearly 50 percent during the 1830s, from around twenty-eight hundred to almost four thousand, and real estate values jumped more than tenfold during the first half of the decade alone. Politically, though Andrew Jackson was very popular in Mississippi—indeed, the state capital was named for him—many county settlers gravitated toward the emerging opposition Whigs, who embraced the modern market economy that enabled the area's blossoming prosperity. Part of the domain of the Choctaw until it was ceded to the United States in 1820, less than two decades later Madison County had been thoroughly colonized by forward-looking white American fortune seekers.[14]

Establishing plantations and cotton farms in Madison County or any other part of the Southwest, however, was not a simple matter of neatly lifting up an existing socioeconomic system from the East and transplanting it in perfectly replicated form. On the contrary, the expansion of the cotton frontier was an arduous, chaotic, and frequently ignoble process. Even when a place had moved past the scramble for federal land that Virgil Stewart observed in Yalobusha and settlers had dedicated themselves more earnestly to cotton cultivation, as they had in Madison, the Southwest was a rugged, filthy, disease-ridden place. On budding farms and plantations scattered widely and haphazardly amidst miles of canopied woods, dense thickets, and swampy muck, most lived crudely, their energies devoted to wrenching fields out of forests, bayous, and canebrakes rather than to material niceties. No one liked living that way, but comfort could wait. "Planters are not destitute of taste," one man noted, but "it is their principle to make it yield to interest."[15]

Though aspirants to wealth envisioned a future life of ease, building a mansion or buying fancy furnishings diverted attention and resources from potential profits lying in the ground, and making money quickly was about the only way to keep up with the rapidly escalating prices engendered by easy credit and rampant speculation. Most settlers preferred to believe the boom years would never end, that the worth and size of their crops would outpace inflation, and that their land values would continue to rise. But there were always contrary indicators. Late in 1833, for example, Andrew Jackson's assault on the Second Bank of the United States had prompted the Bank's director, Nicholas Biddle, to cut back the institution's loans by millions of dollars. Credit markets all over the country seized up, threatening to touch off a financial panic and sending cotton prices into free fall for months. Voters in places like Madison County, which had flourished under Biddle's administration, blamed Jackson for the upheaval and inclined even more toward the Whig Party, and white Mississippians everywhere were reminded that their prosperity was especially tenuous and could vanish in a flash.[16]

More broadly problematic, the richness of Mississippi's soil was not matched by its depth. After several years of cotton planting, lush fields generally had eroded down to the underlying clay, rendering them useless and forcing their owners to clear fresh land or hunt for new holdings altogether. Such chronic soil degradation compounded the already relentless pressure and pace of southwestern economic development, and even those who anticipated it had to find it worrisome.[17]

The harsh landscape and the rapacious but flimsy economic environment, combined with the notoriously pugnacious personalities of driven and impatient prospective cotton planters, already imparted a measure of jitteriness to Mississippi in the flush times before Virgil Stewart ever set foot in Madison County. Fortunes could be gained there, but they might be lost just as quickly, and anything that presaged a possible setback was cause for alarm. Even the weather could underline the frangibility of the cotton frontier, and the fact that it rained nearly every day in the summer of 1835, leading to cotton rot and dire predictions about that year's crop, helped establish a context for the reception of *The Western Land Pirate* in which white people in the county were highly attuned to their economic insecurity.[18]

But by suggesting that planters' control over their slaves was not nearly so strong as they liked to think, Stewart touched on their greatest vulnerability of all, and whites in Madison County were more vulnerable than most. Because if Madison held out to white settlers all the promise of the flush times, it also presented its perils in exaggerated forms. In 1830 the enslaved population of Madison County stood at 2,167. By 1840 it was nearly 11,500, an astonishing increase of more than 400 percent. Where blacks had constituted less than half the county's population in 1830, in 1840 they outnumbered whites by a margin of three to one, far outstripping the slight majority the enslaved population held that year in Mississippi as a whole.[19]

Making matters even more volatile, as of 1835 settlers in Madison County had failed to establish reliable mechanisms of law and order or even an organized militia system, realities that could be attributed only in part to the county's newness. Instead of providing for their own collective safety or the protection of their property, settlers had dedicated themselves singlemindedly to growing cotton, so much so that large sections of the county barely had any white people living in them at all. Many plantations had absentee owners who lived in more established parts of Mississippi or in other states altogether and left only a lone white overseer to supervise operations worked by scores of slaves. Beattie's Bluff and Livingston were surrounded by neighborhoods where blacks outnumbered whites by at least fifty to one, and the county possessed almost no schools, no churches, and no materials for building what one newspaper correspondent called "an interesting state of society." Madison County had a few villages and some stores, but mostly it was a series of cotton production facilities.[20]

Thus, even as rising prices for slaves and the debts assumed to pay for them reminded Madison County slaveholders how much they had riding financially on the output of a disciplined and productive labor force, they crafted circumstances that undermined that imperative and potentially imperiled their lives. Extorting the infamously grueling work of clearing land and growing cotton from enslaved people who vastly outnumbered them, most of whom they barely knew as individuals and many of whom had been wrested by the slave trade away from established families and communities, slaveholders ultimately found violence their only reliable mechanism for enforcing control. The enslaved hardly needed incentives to resist enslavement, but slaveholders in Madison County had managed to concoct an especially toxic brew of restive blacks, apprehensive whites, and tremendous brutality. It was whites' own greed that crowded out institutional development and created racial demographics that endangered their own families and threatened the very abundance they believed slave labor made possible. Nonetheless, Virgil Stewart's pamphlet landed in just the right place at just the right time. Given their situation, it is not hard to see why whites in Madison would react vigilantly to the threat of a slave insurrection if they had any tangible reason to think one might break out.[21]

Jesse Mabry was certainly taking no chances, because no white man in Madison County stood to lose more from a slave insurrection than he did. Born in South Carolina in 1791 or 1792, Mabry came of age in that state's Union County just as cotton was beginning to emerge as a cash crop. But Union was a piedmont county near the limits of where cotton could be profitably grown, and if Mabry tried participating in the cotton economy as a young man he had little at first to show for it. By 1810 Mabry had married a woman named Nancy and the couple had established an independent household for themselves. They did not own much and likely brought in at least some income by selling cloth that Nancy wove herself. But Jesse Mabry had an enterprising spirit, and he and Nancy amassed some wealth slowly and steadily over time. Around 1820 they left South Carolina to pursue new economic opportunities in Mississippi, and by 1830 Mabry had become a moderately prosperous man. Living in Wilkinson County below Natchez in the extreme southwestern corner of the state, Mabry was the father of three children, the owner of eleven slaves, and a partner in the newly founded mercantile firm of Ware and Mabry.[22]

Being a merchant was a decent way to make a living in Mississippi, but serious money came from cotton planting, and in the spring of 1832 Jesse Mabry showed his aspirations when he made his first foray into that world. He used seven slaves as collateral for a fifteen-hundred-dollar loan from the Bank of Mississippi, took about five thousand dollars already in his possession, and pooled the money with the funds of a partner named Mason Saunders. The two bought 225 acres of land near the town of Pinckneyville, close to Mississippi's border with Louisiana not far from the Mississippi River, along with four slaves and all the livestock and farming utensils belonging to the land's previous owner. Mabry and Saunders then went to Natchez and purchased sixteen more slaves from Isaac Franklin, a partner in the largest slave-trading firm in the South. By the end of April 1832 Mabry and Saunders had a fully stocked cotton plantation and more than twenty-five bound laborers to work it.[23]

But Mabry aborted this initial attempt to launch himself into the planter class. Perhaps he and Saunders reaped less of a profit than they had anticipated. Perhaps they fought and decided to dissolve their partnership, or perhaps they had never intended their arrangement to last more than one season. Whatever the case, in January 1833 the two sold their land and all the slaves they had purchased from Isaac Franklin and went their separate ways. Mabry returned to the mercantile business in the Wilkinson County town of Woodville, partnering this time with a man named Austin. The new firm did quite well, selling thirty thousand dollars' worth of merchandise in 1834. Mabry owned no land, but he still owned a number of slaves and was a trusted enough businessman that several individuals in nearby Louisiana parishes asked him to serve as their Mississippi agent on some economic dealings.[24]

By the middle of the 1830s, then, Jesse Mabry was almost forty-five years old and over the course of nearly fifteen years in Mississippi had followed a relatively careful path to some economic success. He had flirted with planting, but something about it had not been right, so he withdrew. In 1835, though, he finally saw his big chance to make his ambitions beyond the retail world into reality, and he was going all in. In January the mercantile firm of Mabry and Austin dissolved. A few months later Mabry went to Madison County, which was around 150 miles northeast of his Woodville home. If the $30,000 he brought with him was not all the money he had in the world, it must have been nearly so. When he got to Madison, he put down that $30,000, took out a mortgage for another $180,000 from a planter named Mark Cockrill, and bought Cockrill's entire plantation—more than seventeen hundred acres of land near the Big Black River in the neighborhood of Beattie's Bluff—along with 127 slaves and every horse, mule, cow, farming utensil, and piece of furniture Cockrill owned.[25]

This was an exorbitant price for a cotton plantation, and assuming so much debt to pay it was out of character for someone like Mabry, who owed what financial standing he had achieved largely to privileging prudence over extravagance. But the flush times had a way of tempting even cautious and responsible men to adventurism, and owning Mark Cockrill's plantation made Jesse Mabry the man he wanted to be. Given the size of his mortgage, it would be more accurate to say that he indebted himself into ascendance than that he worked his way there. Still, he had come far from his yeoman beginnings in South Carolina. He had gone to Mississippi because it promised riches, and when his moment came, Mississippi delivered. In a matter of months and with a single economic transaction Jesse Mabry had transformed himself from a successful though middling merchant into the second-largest slaveholder in Madison County.[26]

Having leveraged his finances to a ludicrous degree and risked everything he owned to get his cotton plantation and its slaves, Mabry was not about to let it all disappear before he even reaped his first harvest. He had been away from Madison County when the news from the Latham plantation began circulating, but he was told about it when he returned home a few days later. And although he was new to the area, being one of the wealthiest men around brought status and clout. So when whites living near Beattie's Bluff heard what had transpired at Livingston on June 30 and decided to dig a little deeper, they looked to Mabry to assume a leading role.[27]

The next day, July 1, a small number of white people gathered and asked Mabry to question the two enslaved women whose conversation had initially aroused the concern of Lorenzo Latham's mother. Mabry later recalled that they could add nothing to what he had already been told, namely that an enslaved man belonging to David Landfair "had informed them that the negroes intended rising and slaying all the whites." Like everyone else, Mabry badly wanted to know more, but Landfair's man had since run away, doubtless aware that there could be deadly consequences when whites suspected a slave of being involved in a conspiracy to rebel. Seemingly without any additional leads, Mabry and the other whites at Beattie's Bluff might have let things lie, remaining vigilant while awaiting more news from Livingston. But then James Lee spoke up, and he gave Jesse Mabry the grounds on which to show that he would do whatever it took to stay in the planter class.[28]

III.

Himself the owner of fifteen slaves and three hundred acres on the Big Black River, James Lee had never dropped his guard after helping Lorenzo Latham first acquire information from his mother's slave. Lee had spent the ensuing days and nights prowling about and trying to eavesdrop on conversations of any slaves he could find. After Mabry had finished talking with the enslaved women from the Latham plantation, Lee told the meeting what he had been up to and reported that several slaves in particular were making him uneasy. Joe and Weaver, both of whom belonged to a man named Sansberry, had said some things that troubled him, and Lee had also heard Weaver and a third slave named Russell talking in ways that made him think they were up to something. Those gathered at the meeting thought Lee's hunches worth pursuing, and they chose Jesse Mabry along with two other planters named James Smith and Andrew Beattie to follow up on them.[29]

The three men proceeded to the Sansberry plantation to interrogate Joe, who worked as a blacksmith. They began by asking Joe if he knew who they were. Joe replied that he knew Beattie and Smith but not Mabry, which was probably true given that Mabry had lived in the area for only a few months. True or not, it was the wrong answer. With his purchase of Mark Cockrill's plantation Mabry had acquired instant wealth, and he expected with it an instant reputation. Enslaved people especially were going to give him the respect he deserved. If Joe did not know who Mabry was, he was about to find out. Insisting that in fact Joe did know him, Mabry "continued to look him full in the face for some minutes, until he began to tremble." Whether or not Mabry's stare clarified his identity, it told Joe the one thing that mattered: this was not a white man he ought to trifle with. Once Mabry had Joe good and scared, he asked him if he knew a slave named Sam. Joe replied that he did and said that Sam had come to his shop twice recently. That was the right answer. Sam was one of Mabry's own slaves, and Mabry himself had sent him to Joe's shop several times. But Mabry also considered Sam "a great scoundrel." He was sure that if Joe knew anything about the impending insurrection, then "Sam was also in the scrape," so he asked Joe what he and Sam had talked about. Joe replied that they had discussed nothing out of the ordinary, only "what was usual when fellow servants met."[30]

Once again, if that was an honest answer it was the wrong one. But this time the cost would be more than a browbeating. Mabry, Smith, and Beattie got a rope, bound Joe's hands, and started striking him, going on for "some time" until finally Joe "said that he knew what [the men] wanted" and that if they "would not punish him that he would tell all that he could recollect." According to Mabry, Joe proceeded to say that he had nothing personally to do with the insurrection plot but that "*Sam* had told him that the negroes were going to rise and kill all the whites on the 4th, and that they had a number of white men at their head."[31]

Joe said he knew most of the white conspirators only by face, but Mabry claimed that he offered the names of Ruel Blake, Joshua Cotton, and William Saunders. Further, Joe said that along with Sam, Weaver and Russell—the other slaves James Lee had reported were acting suspiciously— were "ringleaders in the business" and "Captains under those white men." Finally, Mabry said Joe provided the details of the plot, asserting that on July 4 the slaves on plantations near Beattie's Bluff would use axes and hoes to murder the white people in their homes. They would then break into storehouses and collect all the guns and ammunition they could find before heading to Livingston and then to Vernon, gaining strength as they gathered more recruits from plantations along the way. After pillaging Vernon the rebels planned to march south to Clinton, a town in neighboring Hinds County, by which point Joe said the plotters calculated their forces would be strong enough to face down any opposition. From Clinton they would move toward Natchez, and "after killing all the citizens of that place, and plundering the banks," they would head finally to a place called the Devil's Punch Bowl. A natural depression north of Natchez near the Mississippi River fabled as a spot where pirates and outlaws hid themselves, their treasure, and corpses of people they murdered, the Devil's Punch Bowl was where the rebels would "make a stand."[32]

Joe did indeed know what Mabry, Smith, and Beattie wanted to know— because they told him what they wanted to know, and they beat him until he repeated it back to them. It beggars belief that Joe, without prompting, told the three white men exactly and only the names of slaves they already believed involved in the conspiracy, exactly and only the names of several of the white men that had already emerged from the June 30 meeting at Livingston, and the details of a plot that effectively fleshed out with local landmarks the one outlined by Virgil Stewart in his pamphlet. What Joe gave Mabry, Smith, and Beattie was less a "confession" than a parroted narrative the white men had put together themselves based on what they had been told transpired at Livingston the previous day.[33]

It is nonetheless a revealing narrative. For one thing, it shows how information could mutate and become dangerously distorted as it spread through the Mississippi countryside. Ruel Blake, for example, did own Peter, who had been accused of being involved in the insurrection, and consequently Blake's name surely traveled back to Beattie's Bluff. That Blake had not been named in Livingston as a conspirator in his own right, of course, was the most important thing Mabry, Smith, and Beattie needed to know about him. But that distinction either disappeared as the news passed from person to person, as in the children's game of telephone, or was lost on men intent on vigilance and unlikely to be acquainted with Blake personally. In addition, the plot Joe described demonstrates the kind of event whites in Madison County feared far more than it demonstrates anything slaves in Madison County might have actually wanted to carry off, unless all they wanted was vengeance. Never did Joe mention the possibility of slaves achieving freedom. Instead, they would kill every white person they could find and create indiscriminate mayhem on plantations and towns, all in the service of white criminals interested in robbing banks and general despoilment.

Regardless of the dubious means they had used to extract it, Joe's "confirmation" of the information Mabry, Smith, and Beattie wanted to hear convinced them that they were getting closer to the truth, which made their subsequent engagement with Weaver all the more frustrating. No matter what they did to him, Weaver refused to admit his involvement in the insurrection plot. When Mabry, Smith, and Beattie told Weaver what Joe had said, Weaver replied "that Joe had told lies on him, and that he did not know any thing about the matter at all." A beating had gotten Joe talking, but that approach failed with Weaver. The white men whipped him, yet he said nothing. James Lee arrived on the scene and told Weaver that he had heard him and Russell "pledge themselves to each other that they would never confess any thing, either on themselves or any others." Weaver said nothing. As the blows continued to rain down on Weaver's back, Lee repeated to Weaver what he said he had heard, again and again, waiting for Weaver to break under the pain and the bullying. And still he said nothing.[34]

Initially, the white men had little better luck with Russell. Abandoning for the moment their effort to force Weaver to disclose what they were sure he knew, Mabry, Smith, and Beattie headed to the plantation where Russell lived and began whipping him as well. But where Weaver had been defiant, Russell was baffled. "All was as mystery with him," Jesse Mabry later recalled. "He knew nothing, nor could he conceive what we were punishing him for." At that point, Mabry, Smith, and Beattie were about ready to stop their questioning. If physical torment had failed to get Weaver and Russell to divulge anything, for now the two could be confined and kept under guard while the whites pursued the information Joe had given them. With the insurrection plot scheduled to come off in a matter of days, there was little time to squander.[35]

James Lee, however, was not ready to let matters end there. He had told other whites that he had heard Weaver and Russell talking, and he was not about to have the enslaved men make him seem a liar. Just as Mabry, Smith, and Beattie decided to "hand [Russell] over for safe keeping," Lee rode up and began himself beating Russell anew, demanding all the while that he tell the contents of his conversation with Weaver. Whatever Russell and Weaver may or may not have discussed, Mabry, Smith, and Beattie had told Russell what they wanted to hear when they had whipped him the first time, and one beating was enough. They could have whatever they wanted. Russell implored Lee to stop hitting him, promising "that he would tell him all about the business." Unsurprisingly, "his statement was, in all particulars, precisely like the one made by Joe."[36]

The next morning, July 2, a number of white people convened at Beattie's Bluff again. Jesse Mabry probably shared with those gathered everything that he and the others had uncovered the previous day on their visits to various plantations. Then the investigations continued, as this time a number of farmers and planters had brought slaves directly to the meeting for questioning. Mabry, assuming control of the interrogations once more, started with an enslaved man named Jim, beating him "at length" until he agreed to "make a full confession" so long as Mabry did "not punish him any more." Jim's statement was in many ways like Joe's. He implicated Ruel Blake, William Saunders, and Joshua Cotton, and he said that the slaves intended to kill every white person they could. Jim also claimed that the white ringleaders of the plot had told the enslaved that they could spare "some of the most beautiful" white women and keep them "as wives," that he had already picked out one such woman for himself, and that he and his own wife had quarreled when he told her what he intended.[37]

It is hard to know what to make of this embellishment. On the one hand, it is obvious that Jesse Mabry wanted the slaves he questioned to confess what he told them to confess. While the fear among whites that black men harbored secret desires to rape white women would not reach hysterical levels until the post–Civil War period, it did emerge sometimes in the antebellum era as well, particularly at moments when whites felt threatened and less than certain of their control over the enslaved. Undeniably this was such a moment, and it is possible that Jim's elaboration on what Mabry got Joe and Russell to say came in some way at Mabry's behest.[38]

On the other hand, eavesdropping could go in both directions, and blacks paid attention to white conversations far more commonly than the other way around. Given the power whites had over slaves' lives, they had to. So if whites in Madison County had been sharing rumors about an insurrection and talking about Virgil Stewart's pamphlet since at least the spring, surely blacks had been as well. What the widow Latham overheard on her plantation, in fact, may well have been just that sort of gossip, with David Landfair's slave saying that he had heard talk of an impending uprising in which white people were going to die, and Latham's enslaved woman responding that the death of white children during such a hypothetical event would be unfortunate. That both Landfair's man and Ruel Blake's Peter had never claimed to know the date of the supposed uprising similarly may indicate that it was all just something heard through the grapevine. With regard to Jim's comment about plans for preying on white women, it is conceivable that under the duress of a beating that would stop only when he relayed everything he knew, he recounted literally everything he could think of, including what amounted to big talk, coarse humor, or crass chatter shared among members of the enslaved population.

It seems more likely that Jim's inflammatory claim originated with him rather than with Mabry only because Mabry was relatively uninterested in whether the slaves of Madison County intended to sexually assault his wife or those of his neighbors. What he really wanted to know were the identities of others involved in the insurrection plot. In fact, mostly he wanted to know the identities of any white men who were involved. When Mabry a few months later relayed what he considered the important information from his interrogation of Jim, he mentioned without comment Jim's assertion about taking white women as wives, and he noted almost offhandedly and without elaboration that Jim had added the names of "some more slaves" to the list of enslaved conspirators divulged by Joe.[39]

Instead, Mabry stressed that Jim had said that a white man named Angus Donovan, who was "present on the ground" at the meeting at Beattie's Bluff, was "deeply implicated" in the plot along with Saunders, Cotton, and Blake. Jim had also said that another white man named Elisha Moss, along with his sons, provided shelter for "bad white men" at his house and was "very friendly to the slaves," buying stolen goods from them and providing them with whiskey. Mabry thought this information significant even though Jim said explicitly that he did not know whether Moss "intended to take any part with them in the intended insurrection."[40]

Mabry interrogated a number of other slaves in addition to Jim on July 2, including a man named Bachus, who "stated, in substance, all that Jim stated." Bachus added the name of one more white man to those Jim had provided—a peddler named Sliver, to whom Bachus said he had given six dollars after the man told him he "was making up money to buy arms." But Bachus said he had not seen Sliver since giving him the money, and Mabry later said that attempts to locate him were unsuccessful.[41]

At this point the meeting at Beattie's Bluff began to wind down. There were no more slaves whom whites at the meeting thought worth interrogating, and those who had been interrogated were providing essentially the same information. Meanwhile, July 4 was drawing nearer by the hour. Whites throughout the county and beyond needed to know that the suspicions first aroused at the Latham plantation and then enlarged at Livingston had been confirmed in detail at Beattie's Bluff and that they were in grave danger. There were just a few things left to do first. The whites gathered at Beattie's Bluff placed Angus Donovan under arrest. They took Jim, Bachus, Weaver, Russell, and Sam, and unceremoniously hanged all five. Then they began to spread the word about what they had uncovered and what they had done about it.[42]

IV.

Even as Jesse Mabry and other whites at Beattie's Bluff were convincing themselves that they had been infiltrated by fiends with designs on their property and their lives, Livingston residents had been following their own leads. To a certain degree, matters proceeded there much as they had at Beattie's Bluff, with attempts to wring confessions out of enslaved suspects. The committee of investigation operating in Livingston had asked at the June 30 meeting for William Johnson's elderly slave and Ruel Blake's Peter to be brought to them for further questioning. On July 1 both men appeared before the committee. The enslaved man belonging to Johnson denied ever having any conversation with Johnson's driver, least of all one in which he had discussed rumors of a slave insurrection. So the committee ordered him whipped. Only "after receiving a most severe chastisement" did he say that he had told the driver there was going to be an uprising, adding that he had no knowledge of when it was supposed to take place but that Peter had said "he would let him know in a few days."[43]

Peter, however, was not forthcoming. Brought forward for questioning, he was told that the whites were already aware "that a conspiracy of the negroes to rebel against their masters was on foot, and that they wished to know if he had any knowledge of it." But even after being "severely whipped" and ordered to talk Peter refused to confess his knowledge of anything. In fact, he challenged his tormenters, insisting that "if you *are* whipping me to make me tell *what my master told me*, you may whip on till I die, for I promised him I never would tell."[44]

That was a cryptic thing to say, and it was not the only peculiar aspect of Peter's examination. When Peter refused to confess, the committee of investigation asked Ruel Blake to whip Peter himself "and *make* him tell what he knew about the conspiracy." The request made a certain sense, as the committee had no actual legal authority and Peter was Ruel Blake's personal property. But Blake seemed to lack the conviction those in attendance wanted him to bring to the task. Before he started whipping Peter, he practically apologized for doing it, explaining what the punishment was for and requesting, rather than demanding, that Peter tell whatever he knew about the conspiracy. When Peter refused, Blake began whipping him but, as one witness recalled, "in such a manner as to convince every one present that he did not wish to hurt him, occasionally striking a hard lick to keep up appearances." Whether Blake had a bit too much concern for Peter as a person or just did not want to damage his property, this was no way to get a man to talk. Those gathered asked Blake to step aside and let someone else administer the punishment instead.[45]

Blake complied, but he did not like what he saw. He paced nervously at the edge of the throng before finally rushing forward and insisting that if Peter was struck one more time the crowd would have to whip him as well. Around thirty-five years old, six feet tall, and "well made and athletic," Blake was probably someone who could hold his own in a fistfight. And he got one. The man who had been given responsibility for whipping Peter was displeased at having his newly granted authority questioned and probably disgusted with Blake to begin with given the lameness of his performance as a torturer. He drew back with the whip and set his sights now on Blake instead, touching off a brawl between the two men.[46]

At this point we might easily suppose that Ruel Blake was in serious trouble. Whites in Livingston had found "alarming" the information they had sent around the county and the state after the June 30 meeting, and a number of men and their families had spent that night armed and crowded together for safety. Few probably had slept very well, and when everyone came back together on July 1 they were "under increased apprehensions and excitement." They already believed that Peter was a conspirator, and now Blake had become so upset at the sight of his slave being beaten that he was willing to fight a fellow white man to stop it.[47]

Sympathy of this sort for an enslaved suspect had proved disastrous for Angus Donovan at Beattie's Bluff. Donovan's troubles there began when he stepped forward and tried to untie Jim as Jesse Mabry was still examining him, because by interfering with Mabry's interrogation Donovan called himself into question. Jim soon implicated him, surely at Mabry's behest once Donovan had been pulled away. What kind of white man, after all, would help a slave rather than expose an impending insurrection? In Livingston, Blake's intervention, along with Peter's mysterious reference to the things Blake told him being so valuable that he would rather go to the grave than reveal them, would seem likely to make Blake a target for the crowd's suspicions as well.[48]

But here the course of events in Livingston departed for the moment from that at Beattie's Bluff, because Blake did not straightaway become the target that Donovan did. Blake did flee Livingston on July 1, but only because the man who had been whipping Peter took Blake's attempt to stop him as a personal insult, leading a number of bystanders to urge Blake to run lest the man kill him. Far from suspecting that Blake was involved in the insurrection plot, in fact, one man later recalled that because Blake was a slaveholder, no one "supposed, or had the most distant idea, that he was connected with the conspiracy, but attributed his conduct to sympathy for his negro." This same eyewitness said that Blake had been allowed to leave Livingston because Peter's interrogation took place "before it was *known* or *suspected* any white men were engaged in the conspiracy." But that was not the case. If it had been, there would have been no reason to issue warnings about disreputable white men in John Murrell's clan and no reason to ask

William Saunders to provide information about himself and his associates, both of which happened before Peter's interrogation. There would also have been no reason to arrest and examine one of those associates, Joshua Cotton, on the very same day that Ruel Blake left the village.[49]

Blake successfully got out of Livingston in part because he had a very prominent patron in Thomas Hudnall, who not only owned several thousand acres of land but was also the single largest slaveholder in Madison County, with somewhere between 130 and 175 slaves on his several plantations. Blake was a cotton gin maker, wheelwright, and carpenter who often worked for Hudnall, and he had borrowed money from him on several occasions in the years leading up to 1835, even using Peter as collateral on the loans. Hudnall was powerful, widely respected, and considered by many other wealthy men in and around Livingston to be deeply interested in the economic future of the village. Just six months earlier, for example, they had asked Hudnall to chair a meeting at which he and fellow planters pledged nearly two hundred thousand dollars to extend to Livingston a railroad being contemplated that would connect Natchez to the Mississippi interior. In a place as unformed as Madison County, Thomas Hudnall was one of the few steady sources of authority. Moreover, he had spoken with Virgil Stewart personally. If Hudnall did not think Ruel Blake likely to be involved in the plot Stewart had described, that was enough to buy Blake time to disappear. Hudnall liked Blake and was willing to use his influence to protect him, going so far as to give him a horse and some money to help him leave Livingston and telling him "to stay away until the excitement should subside." Blake, grateful and not wanting Hudnall to seem stupid for helping him, promised that when he returned he would "make the necessary apologies."[50]

As significant for Blake as Hudnall's protection, however, was that unlike the people out at Beattie's Bluff, as of July 1 not everyone in Livingston was convinced that any particular white men ought to be suspected of involvement with the rumored insurrection. Israel Spencer's warning implied that whites in Madison County were in accord that they were up against the criminal confederates of John Murrell, but events in Livingston suggested ambivalence. Though the members of the committee of investigation in the village thought William Saunders a shifty fellow, they had released him after they questioned him on June 30. They examined Joshua Cotton on July 1, but as Saunders had provided the only evidence against him and had left the area, Cotton was released as well. Peter had admitted nothing, and while a whipping had gotten William Johnson's slave to say that one of Hudnall's slaves was involved in the conspiracy, he had implicated no white men as accomplices.[51]

All in all, some in Livingston started wondering whether their initial fears were overblown. Perhaps the rumors inflated reality. Perhaps the conversations overheard on the Latham plantation spoke to isolated problems, or perhaps the scheme Stewart's pamphlet described was either too incredible to be true or no longer operational in light of Murrell's incarceration. Where the committee of investigation in Livingston had thought it likely on June 30 that members of Murrell's clan had made inroads among Madison County slaves, by the end of the day on July 1 they determined instead "that the conspiracy was confined to the negroes of a few plantations, and to be principally within the knowledge of *negro preachers.*" Members of the committee considered black religious leaders "the greatest scoundrels among negroes" and "the originators" of "all negro conspiracies heretofore detected in the slave-holding States," and the fact that Weaver and Russell had been known as preachers among the enslaved near Beattie's Bluff lent credence to the idea. In any event, the committee suspected that based on what had been disclosed so far in Livingston, there was probably "little system or concert" in the plans of the conspirators. Whites needed to stay alert, of course, and once they ascertained exactly who the leaders were they could "make examples of them immediately by hanging, which would strike terror among the rest, and by that means crush all hopes of their freedom." Having reached this tentative agreement, the committee ensured that Peter and William Johnson's slave would be kept in custody pending some sort of trial, and then it adjourned.[52]

Given the suffering they had endured, neither Peter nor William Johnson's slave would have characterized whites' actions in Livingston as either deliberate or calm. Considering the hasty brutality exhibited at Beattie's Bluff, however, the people in Livingston responded to the imminent uprising they expected with far greater equanimity. Tensions were high in the village while the committee of investigation met, but no one died. In part, whites in Livingston seemed more self-possessed than whites at Beattie's Bluff because they felt somewhat safer. Livingston comprised just nine blocks of land laid out in three rows. Eight were divided into smaller individual lots, and a center square contained a small two-story brick courthouse. It was not much of a place, less than a square mile in size, but it was among the few spots in Madison County where white people lived in any concentrated numbers. Beattie's Bluff, meanwhile, was entirely a plantation district where blacks composed the bulk of the population. Most white people in the area lived in relative isolation and probably went for days without seeing any other white person aside from family members or perhaps their nearest neighbors.[53]

The differing degrees of social organization in the two places ramified through the ways whites in them conducted their investigations. Beginning with the first meeting called there on June 27, white people in Livingston arranged themselves into a semblance of structured if extralegal order as they sought and shared information. They voted for committees with chairmen who oversaw proceedings, and they passed resolutions to determine their courses of action. In Livingston, someone seemed to be in charge. By contrast, things at Beattie's Bluff proceeded haphazardly. The small number of white people there did come together on multiple occasions, and they did ask men like Jesse Mabry to assume leadership roles. But interrogations at Beattie's Bluff were more decentralized than they were at Livingston. Mabry, James Smith, and Andrew Beattie traveled from plantation to plantation to find information, and James Lee shadowed them on his own accord and periodically decided to inflict punishment and ask questions himself. Even when whites at Beattie's Bluff met as a group on July 2, they kept the slaves they examined several hundred yards apart from one another, presumably to keep any individual slave from influencing what others said. But that made it impossible for any one person to be certain about what was happening. Just as important, it was impossible to feel that anyone else knew either.[54]

Whatever control the Livingston committee of investigation was able to maintain over meetings in the village, though, was imperfect and shaky at best. Its authority was improvised, and members exercised it over people who, over the course of twenty-four hours, had gone from thinking they and their families might be slaughtered to being told that there was probably little to worry about. With emotions veering so wildly, it would not take much for them to go careening in unpredictable directions, and regardless of what the committee concluded on the afternoon of July 1, the initial fear lingered that the conspiracy went beyond a few plantations. Not everyone was convinced that Peter and William Johnson's slave had told all they knew.

During the night of July 1, it seems that Peter and William Johnson's slave were visited in jail and beaten anew, because by the time people in Livingston woke up on July 2 the two had "acknowledged their participation in the conspiracy, and confessed that they had been drawn into it by white men." When word from Beattie's Bluff then arrived early in the evening that five slaves had been hanged and that before dying they had implicated some of the very same white men those in Livingston had been eying all along, there was no way any committee could have convinced people that they were not in danger, and there was nothing any committee could have done to contain their rage. There would be no vote. There would be no meeting. There would be no deliberation. Instead, a mob of whites seized the two enslaved men and hanged them on the spot.[55]

Hanging Peter and William's Johnson's slave, however, did not solve anything. The white people of Livingston remained in an "unsettled and fearful condition" and wanted desperately "to be relieved from the intensity of their concern about the state of things." They had focused most of their attention thus far on rooting out enslaved conspirators, but the confessions extracted from the slaves executed at Livingston and Beattie's Bluff revived the notion that John Murrell's clan was about to wreak havoc on the Mississippi countryside and beyond. By the night of July 2 the conviction had again become widespread among whites in Madison County "that a general disaffection and the plan of an insurrection had been spread among the negroes, by a band of desperadoes that infested not only that section of the United States, but the whole country from Maryland to Louisiana." The Fourth of July was less than two days away, and hanging a few slaves was not going to dissuade men as depraved as Murrell's from carrying out their plans. Indeed, however scared white Mississippians were of rebellion among the black population, from this moment forward it was less fear of the enslaved than their suspicions of one another that drove what transpired.[56]

But what was to be done? Clearly, William Saunders and Joshua Cotton had to be apprehended again. Saunders had mentioned Albe Dean and Andrew Boyd at his initial interrogation, so they were worth tracking down as well. Angus Donovan had already been arrested, and if the slaves at Beattie's Bluff had said Ruel Blake was a conspirator, suddenly his behavior appeared in a very different light than it had at first. He had to be brought back to Livingston too. But then what? The hanging of Peter and William Johnson's slave had not slaked the bloodlust of those milling about Livingston. Many in the crowd, which amounted to several hundred people, wanted the white suspects brought to the village and hanged directly as well.[57]

Down the vigilante road, however, lay ethical and legal perils. Executing slaves without trial was one thing, but the proper course of action regarding white men accused of crimes, even in a place where legal and judicial institutions were as poorly established as Madison County, was to hand them over to legitimately constituted authorities. Moreover, killing those men immediately could be counterproductive. Virgil Stewart claimed there were hundreds in Murrell's clan, and his sketchy list of names notwithstanding, the only people likely to provide conclusive information about the identities of those in Mississippi were individuals like Joshua Cotton and William Saunders. If they died, that knowledge would die with them and the plot might remain intact. Finally, there were broader issues of social order to consider. To the extent that mobs could be said to act consciously, they tended to lash out irrationally and impulsively until their energies were spent. At least one witness to the scene saw the potential for disaster if men like Cotton and Saunders were handed over to the crowd. Not only would the crowd "have massacred them instantly," but "perhaps, in the natural fury excited by facts so atrocious, [it] would have plunged into the wildest excesses." If the white people of Madison County devolved into anarchy in their efforts to eliminate John Murrell's clan, they would only be advancing the clan's aims.[58]

Holding Cotton, Saunders, and the others for the sake of delivering them to a regular court of law seemed unacceptable for a variety of reasons, though, even to those disinclined to let the mob in Livingston have its way. Given what had happened to Peter and William Johnson's slave, who themselves had been held in anticipation of trial, there was good reason to believe that white men similarly placed in Livingston's ramshackle jail would never survive to see a courtroom. Moreover, the only real evidence against them came from enslaved witnesses whose testimony against white men was inadmissible in Mississippi courts—and dead ones, at that, because whites in both Livingston and Beattie's Bluff had already hanged them. In addition, Stewart had warned in his pamphlet that Murrell's men escaped whenever they got in trouble with the law because their confederates lied on the witness stand to protect them or sprung them from prison. Most significant, placing these men on trial would take too long. With the time planned for the insurrection fast approaching, something had to be done now.[59]

As the agitation of the crowd in Livingston swelled, a physician named Joseph Pugh managed to get its attention. "Haranguing the multitude," he proposed a sort of compromise, namely "that a Committee of Safety be immediately organized, composed of thirteen citizens, upon the responsibility of the rest, vested with ample authority, to devise means of defence, to try, acquit, condemn, and punish white or black, who should be charged before them." Pugh suggested that everyone discuss among themselves who ought to serve on such a body and gather again first thing in the morning to choose its members. The people of Livingston had been confronting their anxieties through the vehicle of ad hoc committees for nearly a week already, and if there was grumbling from the crowd about continuing to do so in a more lasting manner, there is no record of it. Instead, Pugh's call for order met generally with approval, as it seemed a reasonable way "to arrest the progress of the impending danger, to extend to the parties implicated something like a *trial*, if not *formal* at least *substantial*, and to save them from the inevitable fate of a speedy and condign punishment."[60]

The crowd dispersed. Patrols effectively locked down the village of Livingston and continued to monitor it all night long. Other groups of riders, meanwhile, set out in all directions, and they too remained "on duty the whole night, vigilantly scouring the surrounding country." They pursued Joshua Cotton, William Saunders, and other suspicious white men. They checked plantations to be sure the enslaved were where they were supposed to be when the sun went down, and they arrested any slaves they thought might still know something. Severe though it was, order would seem to have prevailed in Madison County. Once the decision had been made to create a committee of safety that would operate for the duration of the crisis, the proceedings in Livingston and those at Beattie's Bluff converged, and the committee provided social organization that brought at least some disparate parts of the county together in a single unit.[61]

But form and content are easily confused. To be sure, in light of what would transpire in Mississippi while the Livingston Committee of Safety met, it is hard to dispute entirely that its existence probably helped save some people's lives. That was certainly what the white residents of Madison County told themselves. After the insurrection scare finally subsided, the members and backers of the committee asked a young lawyer named

Thomas Shackelford to compile a report describing what had happened in the county, explaining why its white residents had felt compelled to act as they did, and detailing the proceedings of the committee itself. Published early in 1836, the report was written with an eye toward justifying the committee's actions, and Shackelford unsurprisingly presented the efforts of its members as necessary, democratic, and fair under the circumstances. Shackelford would claim that the committee provided suspects with a kind of judicial process that allowed for distinguishing the innocent from the guilty, and he would argue that it saved innumerable people from makeshift justice by channeling the anger and fear of the populace, thus "wresting and restraining those wild sallies of passion and not unfrequently of private revenge, which mark the devastating career of an excited and enraged people."[62]

Still, critics of "democracy" in antebellum America routinely sneered that its advocates really supported little more than a "mobocracy" in which men chosen to enact the caprices of the ignorant ran roughshod over established principles of law and justice. Such critics were often motivated by their own elitism or conservatism, or by a desire to protect their own interests. But they were not always wrong. Moreover, it is debatable, to say the least, how well the committee actually separated the innocent from the guilty. The committee showed some limited ability to keep Madison County from exploding into outright chaos in July 1835, but it soon became clear that the settlers of Madison, with the help of Virgil Stewart, had called forth their own bogeymen. They were white, and they could be anywhere. No committee could completely contain the fear that everything Americans were trying to build in the Southwest would be subverted and destroyed from within. The Livingston Committee of Safety did provide some framework for white migrants who hardly knew each other to act in concert, and under tremendous pressure the committee chiseled the rough outline of a community. But as it did so, the pieces that fell away became expendable. Ultimately, more than anything else the proceedings of the committee revealed just what sorts of white men could and could not be trusted to sustain the cotton frontier.

~ ~

CHAPTER FOUR

Hanging the Conspirators

For men who knew they might be suspected of helping plot the largest slave insurrection the United States had ever seen, Joshua Cotton and William Saunders were surprisingly easy to find. When Cotton had been summoned to Livingston on July 1, he had probably been at the home of his father-in-law in Hinds County, just south of Madison, and that was exactly where a company of men on horseback found him again on the night of July 2. Saunders was not much more of a challenge. He had had two full days and nights to disappear since being released in Livingston on June 30, but he neither went very far nor tried especially hard to conceal his whereabouts. The same group of riders that took Cotton into custody captured Saunders the same night. Perhaps Cotton and Saunders had concluded or been led to believe they had nothing to worry about once they were told they could go after being questioned in Livingston the first time. If so, it was the biggest mistake of their lives, and among their last.[1]

People started trickling back into Livingston early on July 3. They came not only from varying parts of Madison County but from Hinds County as well, and by nine in the morning "a vast concourse" more than 160 strong picked up where they had left off the previous evening. Some decisions had obviously been made during the night, as it took just an hour for the crowd both to choose thirteen men to constitute a standing Committee of Safety and to affix their names to a series of resolutions defining the powers of the committee and how it would function.[2]

The committee's members were men one would imagine as authority figures in a frontier plantation society. Seven owned more than six hundred acres of land apiece, and all owned slaves. Four were among the twelve largest slaveholders in the county, including Thomas Hudnall and Jesse Mabry, and ten owned more than twenty slaves, holdings that put them across the threshold historians have traditionally defined as constituting the planter class. The only member of the committee who owned fewer than fifteen slaves was, ironically, its chair, a physician named Marmaduke Mitchell, who had also chaired the provisional committee that had been meeting in the village since June 30.[3]

Of committee members whose ages can be determined, all were over thirty years old, most were at least forty, and a few were over fifty, making them collectively somewhat older than the average man in the county. The man with the most widely recognizable name was probably Hardin Runnels, whose younger brother Hiram was governor of Mississippi. In fact, given the newness of Madison County, most committee members probably were not especially well known even to those who chose them, particularly given that some who chose them did not live within the county's borders. But if there was to be a slave uprising, planters, in the words of one observer, were "more exposed than others to the dangers" and thus had the keenest desire to stop it before it began. Moreover, being "conspicuous for wealth" was considered a good signifier of a man's character in frontier Mississippi. At the very least, rich men could be counted on to do what was necessary to protect their property. The committee members' reputation for possessing "intelligence" and being "distinguished for integrity and energy" was a bonus, though it flowed at least in part from their affluence.[4]

The task before the committee was undeniably challenging. Its members were expected to act on behalf of people under enormous stress, and they were expected to act quickly. The Fourth of July would be upon them in less than twenty-four hours, and patrols had rounded up for questioning not only Cotton and Saunders but between half a dozen and a dozen other men suspected of involvement in the conspiracy. The committee, however, was also expected to act deliberately, without the undue haste of a mob and in ways resembling a judicial body. And members took seriously what they considered their responsibilities. After their selection the men retired to a room. They posted a sentry outside to keep anyone from hearing or interfering with their proceedings, and they crafted rules designed to give accused individuals a semblance of the legal privileges and protections to which they would be entitled in an actual courtroom. Committee members determined, for example, "to take no cognizance of any crime which was not directly connected with the contemplated insurrection." They mandated that every witness had to testify under oath, that no one would be convicted except by unanimous decision, and that accused persons would have the opportunity "to prove their good character, or any thing that would go to establish their innocence."[5]

Still, the Livingston Committee of Safety was vested with power so overarching as to be practically total. Its members assumed the authority to summon for trial anyone they chose, and outside the room in which they met stood dozens of men waiting to act on those arrest orders. Committee members, moreover, acted together quite literally as judge, jury, and executioner. They and only they examined evidence, listened to testimony, reached a verdict, and determined punishments. There was no appealing their decisions, and while a set of principles governed how trials would proceed, those principles contained a great deal of leeway.[6]

The resolutions creating the committee, for example, provided that its proceedings would be "always governed by the *Laws* of the *Land*." Unless those laws were inconvenient, because they were to apply "so far only as it shall be applicable to the case in question." Otherwise, committee members were empowered "to act as in their discretion shall seem best for the benefit of the country, and in protection of its citizens." Similarly, the rules the committee created for itself provided that no one would be convicted and punished "without strong circumstantial evidence, in addition to the dying confessions of those previously executed." If there wasn't some suggestive evidence to supplement information extracted under torture from dead men, though, so long as there was "such other evidence as should seem convincing," a man could hang for that too.[7]

From the committee's very first hearings, it was evident not only that the trials in Livingston would be highly irregular by actual American legal standards but also that the committee would not even abide by its own rules. At ten in the morning the committee began the trial of Joshua Cotton after charging him "with inciting the negroes in Mississippi to insurrection, and aiding and abetting other white men in the same." Despite stating explicitly that they would contemplate only criminal activity directly related to the insurrection plan, committee members thought it relevant that Cotton had been considered suspicious well before he was ever brought before them.[8]

I.

Originally from New England, by 1830 Joshua Cotton had made his way to Henry County, Tennessee, along the border with Kentucky near the Tennessee River. Exactly what he did in Tennessee is unclear, but he did not stay there especially long. In the spring of 1834 he moved to Mississippi, where he initially established residence in Hinds County. After what must have been a brief courtship, he married a woman named Clarey Johnson and then moved to Livingston. Cotton managed to acquire at least one slave, a fifty-year-old woman named Dilsey, but he owned no land. He probably rented space in the village instead, where he began advertising his services as a practitioner of Thomsonian medicine, known colloquially as a "steam doctor."[9]

Developed early in the nineteenth century by a New Hampshire farmer named Samuel Thomson, the Thomsonian system of medicine treated nearly any kind of illness with a therapeutic regimen that combined steam baths with the administration of herbal emetics and other botanical remedies. Thomson was hardly the first to make claims for the curative powers of botanical medicine, and his ideas about how the body worked drew on humoral theories thousands of years old. But amid the wide array of popular healing methods that could be found in the antebellum United States, Thomsonianism was by far the most widely used alternative to "regular" medicine.[10]

In part, Thomsonianism owed its vogue to an underlying philosophy about medical expertise that accorded neatly with the spirit of the age, as the self-educated Thomson insisted that ordinary Americans needed only common sense and familiarity with a few simple and inexpensive natural ingredients to heal themselves. Physicians formally educated in American medical schools might claim unique authority rooted in years of study, but Thomson argued that they were elitists more interested in their own social privilege than in the health of their patients. Worse, the treatments and services they offered were unnecessarily costly and did more harm than good. In this last, Thomson had a point. Through the first half of the nineteenth century, American physicians of orthodox training relied heavily on harsh and aggressive remedies. Bloodletting, blistering, opiates, and massive doses of a mercury-based medicine called calomel were especially prevalent and especially painful, severely debilitating if not poisoning people already weakened by illness.[11]

Thomson tapped a vein of skepticism toward specialized expertise generally and distrust of medical training specifically, but he succeeded too because he built an effective business model for marketing and disseminating his regimen. Thomson began sharing his ideas as a traveling healer, working a circuit that took him across New England. In the 1810s, however, he patented his system, wrote the first of several books detailing how it worked, and oversaw the appointment of agents and subagents who dispersed across the United States peddling the Thomsonian method and prepared medicines for profit. By the early 1830s more than one million Americans relied on Thomsonian medicine, and by the middle of the decade a Thomsonian periodical claimed that one in six did so. That was probably an exaggeration, but Thomson's *New Guide to Health*, first published in 1822, sold more than 100,000 copies within less than twenty years.[12]

Southern states proved especially fertile ground for Thomsonianism because it allowed slaveholders to save money on medical care for their slaves. They could also act as their own medical authorities, which bolstered the patriarchal ideal they sought to cultivate. Thomsonian medicine flourished on western frontiers too. Whether or not in locations where slavery was legal, these were predominantly rural places where regular physicians might be few and far between, and they were filling with people whose resources could be scarce and who considered themselves particularly self-reliant.[13]

Thus, when Joshua Cotton set up shop in Livingston with a wagonload of lobelia, cayenne, lady slipper, and the panoply of other roots, plants, and herbs comprising the standard inventory of a Thomsonian, he knew exactly what he was doing. Both southern and a frontier, Mississippi was a great place to be a steam doctor. William H. Thomson, a North Carolina native who received a medical degree from Kentucky's Transylvania University and moved to Hinds County in the 1830s, saw that the medical field in the state was a competitive one. No relation to Samuel, William Thomson gained renown and a growing practice by successfully treating wealthy patients but conceded in a letter to his wife that continued growth would not be easy. "The *steamers*," he told her, "will likely interfere with me. One has located within a mile and will get a part of the practice, as it is a new thing here and some are in favor of the system." More than "some" favored it, actually. In 1835 the editor of the *Mississippi Free Trader* estimated that a third of the state's population followed Thomsonian prescriptions. Governor Runnels thought the proportion closer to a full half.[14]

Popular though it was, Thomsonianism was also controversial. Formally trained doctors like William Thomson attacked Thomsonians as uneducated frauds who took advantage of the ignorant and endangered their health, and by 1830 their anti-Thomsonian campaigns had led thirteen states to pass restrictive medical licensing laws. Most of those laws were short-lived, and Mississippi's was no exception. Just months before Joshua

Cotton's trial, in fact, the state supreme court ruled an effort to bar Thomsonians from practicing medicine in the state to be unconstitutional. Nevertheless, "steam doctor" was itself a pejorative term, as were other names commonly applied to Thomsonians such as "steamer" and "puker." Items appearing in successive issues of the *Woodville Republican* underscored Thomsonians' ambiguous position in Mississippi. On May 23, 1835, the paper ran an editorial asserting that Thomsonians were "quacks and imposters" who were "not entitled to the name of physician," while on May 30 it ran a full-column advertisement from a Thomsonian doctor offering a wide range of books and medicines for sale and crowing about the "patronage so liberally bestowed upon me since the commencement of my agency."[15]

That the editorial in the *Republican* referred to Thomsonians as "imposters" begins to explain why Joshua Cotton's neighbors in Livingston eyed him warily. Few in Livingston ever particularly cared for Cotton. He had almost no social interaction with anyone in the village, and while being reserved was no crime, it was easily taken for secretiveness. Not helping his local reputation was that Cotton supposedly "had been detected in many low tricks, and attempts to swindle" his customers. Neither did being from New England, a region whose residents many native southerners stereotyped as commercial cheats and opponents of slavery. Cotton owned a slave, and maybe he was just a man selling medicinal herbal compounds. But he barely ever talked to anyone, he sometimes tried to defraud people, and his ostensible profession entailed itinerancy and peddling on plantations where he could talk to slaves without arousing suspicion. So who could say who he really was and what he was really up to?[16]

William Saunders could, or so people in Livingston believed. Originally from Sumner County, Tennessee, northeast of Nashville, in the fall of 1834 Saunders had moved to Mississippi and found work near Livingston as a plantation overseer. Soon after being fired from that job Saunders became acquainted with Cotton, who persuaded him to go into the steam-doctoring business. It probably seemed like a good idea at the time. Saunders lacked the money to buy land and the skills necessary to do anything other than farm labor, which explains why he had taken work as an overseer, a job typically held by nonslaveholders who saw it as a way to begin climbing the agricultural ladder toward property ownership. Having lost that position, Saunders likely saw steam doctoring as a way to provide some income while he figured out what to do next.[17]

No one ever accused Saunders of being unfriendly or a swindler, and he was a native southerner, but selling Thomsonian medicines exposed him to the same distrust Joshua Cotton faced anyway. Saunders initially based his operations in Hinds County to expand the range of his and Cotton's enterprise. But the man from whom Saunders rented a room in Hinds did not like having a steam doctor under his roof. That Saunders was often seen in remote parts of the countryside could be accounted for by the desire to sell his products to as many customers as possible. That sometimes he did not return home at night could be attributed to being what amounted to a traveling salesman in a place where going from one residence to the next could take hours. Whatever the reasons for Saunders's behavior, his land-lord never found his explanations "satisfactory" and thought his answers to questions "equivocal." He asked Saunders to leave, and Saunders returned to the area around Livingston, which is where he just happened to be on June 30 when villagers met to discuss the insurrection rumors from Beat-tie's Bluff.[18]

There is a certain irony in someone as peripatetic as William Saun-ders being in so precisely the wrong place at so precisely the wrong time. Given how little had gone right for Saunders in Mississippi since he moved there, there would almost be something comic in it had his haplessness not brought such serious consequences. As it was, though, people in Livings-ton knew of Saunders's association with Joshua Cotton, which led them to ask about his business partner and any other white men he knew who might be engaged in illegal or subversive activities with the enslaved. That first interrogation put Saunders's name on tongues throughout the county and eventually in the mouths of tortured slaves at Beattie's Bluff, whose "confessions" led to Saunders being taken back into custody and brought before the Livingston Committee of Safety. The committee then tried him for his life, essentially concurrently with Cotton, as committee members decided that because Saunders and Cotton had such a "close connexion" and because most of the evidence against one applied to the other, time could be saved by having both men present in the room and question-ing witnesses for information about both of them simultaneously. William Saunders could see that he might get out of this mess only by creating some distance between himself and Joshua Cotton. And the only way to do that was to testify against Cotton and tell the members of the committee what-ever they wanted to know.[19]

II.

Saunders was the only white witness to offer significant testimony at Cotton's trial, and much of what he told the committee members confirmed their impression that Cotton was a cold and devious man. Saunders told them, for example, about a scheme Cotton had for abandoning his wife, claiming that Cotton had proposed that Saunders travel with her to Arkansas and leave her there on the false pretense that Cotton intended to join her after settling his business affairs in Mississippi. Committee members already suspected that Cotton had done something similar, if not worse, to a wife and child they somehow discovered he had had in Tennessee, as he had arrived in Mississippi alone and quickly remarried, and his first family was *"never afterwards heard from."* At the very least, Saunders's accusation suggested that Cotton treated women and children as tools to be discarded when he no longer found them useful.[20]

Saunders also elaborated on what he had said at the June 30 meeting in Livingston about Cotton's involvement in the theft of slaves. Cotton, Andrew Boyd, and some other men were "extensively engaged in negro stealing," he asserted, and had crafted a clever scam. As a steam doctor Cotton could roam the countryside, note the layouts of plantations, get a sense of how many slaves lived on them, and sometimes speak to the enslaved. But a person needed only so much lobelia and cayenne, and because inducing an enslaved person to risk running away with an unfamiliar white man usually took even a persuasive person multiple visits, Cotton needed a plausible explanation for appearing repeatedly in the same places. Accordingly, Saunders testified, Cotton had arranged to buy some horses from a man who lived near Livingston and had then turned the animals loose. That gave Cotton the cover he needed to return to plantations, talk to slaves, "and, by that means, seduce them from their allegiance to their owners, by instilling rebellious notions among them, and to form plans and make converts to his propositions." If anyone ever asked him what he was doing, Cotton could say that he was "hunting horses."[21]

Nothing Saunders said about Cotton spoke well for him, and committee members already knew that slaves at Beattie's Bluff had identified Cotton as one of the insurrection plot's ringleaders. Moreover, at Cotton's trial the committee acquired damning testimony about him from a slave who was still alive. Somewhere near Beattie's Bluff, after executing most of the

slaves they had originally questioned, whites had found yet another enslaved man who said he knew something about the conspiracy, or at least
one convinced that his well-being depended on knowing something. Several months earlier, the man said, he had been looking for some missing
horses and had encountered a white man who said he was doing the same.
The white man, the slave claimed, proceeded to ask him whether his master "was a bad man," whether the slaves on his plantation were "whipped
much," and whether "he would like to be free." He then offered the slave a
drink, told him he had a plan for "liberating the negroes," and promised to
tell him when the insurrection was going to begin if the man would come
to see him in Livingston. The slave said that he never got the white man's
name but would know his face if he saw it. Brought to Livingston on July 3,
the slave fingered Joshua Cotton.[22]

Cotton had been on trial for just a few hours, but he knew was in trouble.
Saunders had done him no favors, and when the slave from Beattie's Bluff
pointed him out as the man who had told him there was to be an insurrection, Cotton "looked thunder-struck, and came near fainting." Yet Saunders
had said nothing necessarily implicating Cotton in the insurrection scheme
or indicating that Cotton was involved with John Murrell's clan, and the
members of the Livingston Committee of Safety do not seem to have been
wholly comfortable with convicting Cotton of inciting insurrection based
on the testimony of the enslaved alone. As Joshua Cotton's trial dragged
into the afternoon on July 3, however, the committee found itself without
white witness testimony unambiguously tying Cotton to the impending
uprising.[23]

So they invented some, got William Saunders to say it came from
him, and then contrived a backstory to explain how they had gotten it.
If Thomas Shackelford's account of the committee's proceedings is to be
believed, Saunders actually confessed everything he knew about the insurrection plan voluntarily before he was ever arrested. Shackelford wrote that
after Saunders had been examined on June 30, he had taken to the road intending to go to Texas but had not gotten far from Livingston when he encountered someone Shackelford identified only as a "gentleman." Saunders
purportedly told the "gentleman" that a conspiracy had been discovered in
Madison County, described in detail how the conspiracy was supposed to
unfold, asserted that Joshua Cotton and Ruel Blake were among its leaders,
and acknowledged that Cotton had asked him to help carry out the plot

but said that he had refused. The "gentleman," suspecting that Saunders was more deeply involved than he let on, detained him and turned him over to a patrol from Livingston on July 2. Cotton, Shackelford contended, had then been arrested that same day on the basis of Saunders's admissions.[24]

Shackelford took special pains to stress that Saunders and Cotton "were arrested and in custody ... before the disclosures of the negroes at Beatties Bluff were known," and he seems to have included the story about the "gentleman" in his report partially to conceal how much the members of the Livingston Committee of Safety—and many white people in Madison County—let information extracted from slaves who had been tortured and then murdered drive their actions. But that chronology was a total lie, and Shackelford himself carelessly betrayed the deception. He noted that the man Saunders supposedly met on the road delivered Saunders to a patrol that was out "in search of" him. Unless whites in Livingston had already received the information from Beattie's Bluff, though, there was no reason to be looking for Saunders. Nothing else that would impel such a search had transpired between the time Saunders was questioned and released on June 30 and the time he was taken into custody on July 2. Moreover, if Cotton and Saunders were already in custody when the news came from Beattie's Bluff, one wonders why and how the mob in Livingston calibrated its fury so as to hang the two enslaved men then in jail but not the white men they believed had ultimately orchestrated the insurrection plot.[25]

Indeed, the whole story about Saunders's encounter with the man on the road was patently fictitious. The "gentleman" who supposedly detained Saunders was the committee's only white witness who was not accused of being involved in the conspiracy and who could tie Saunders and Cotton directly to it, yet he did not testify at their trials, and Shackelford did not name him in his account. In addition, believing that this "gentleman" existed and conversed with Saunders would require believing that Saunders offered him inside information about the conspiracy and the people involved in it despite having seemed to know nothing about it when he was questioned hours earlier in Livingston. One can understand why Saunders would have lied about such knowledge if he had had any. It is somewhat harder to understand why he would think possession of that knowledge important enough to conceal initially and incriminating enough that he decided to try and leave the state but also that he would then reveal it without solicitation to a complete stranger.[26]

Still, even if there was no "gentleman," Shackelford may not have completely invented the notion that Saunders admitted something about the conspiracy before the patrol brought him back to Livingston. Nothing indicates that the men who took Saunders into custody beat, tortured, or otherwise physically mistreated him to extract information, but surely they did not arrest Saunders and return to Livingston in total silence. The patrollers knew what the slaves at Beattie's Bluff had said, and it is not hard to imagine them telling Saunders the particulars of the allegations against him. Neither is it hard to imagine Saunders, surrounded by armed men on horseback who thought he was plotting with slaves to kill them and their families, trying to save his own skin by telling the patrol that Cotton and Blake were involved in the plot just as they said but that he personally had refused to participate.

The way the Livingston Committee of Safety introduced Saunders's "confession" at Joshua Cotton's trial strengthens the suggestion that the information originated with the members of the patrol rather than with Saunders himself. The committee never actually asked Saunders to describe the particulars of the insurrection plot at all. Instead, it put into evidence a "statement" that purportedly reproduced what Saunders had told the "gentleman" on the road and that read almost exactly like the description of the plot that Jesse Mabry, James Smith, and Andrew Beattie had beaten out of Joe at Beattie's Bluff two days earlier. Asked if the statement accurately reflected what he had admitted, Saunders "could not nor did deny" it. Why bother? What mattered to Saunders was that committee members understand he was not involved and that he knew what he knew because "Cotton told him all when he requested him to join the clan."[27]

If Saunders really had known as much about the planned uprising as the members of the committee seemed to think, they could simply have asked him to repeat his description of it himself. Telling what they knew, after all, was what witnesses did. But William Saunders was not really a witness. He was a patsy who found himself alone and at the mercy of very scared and very angry people who were going to kill him unless he could convince them he was not who they thought he was. If that meant Joshua Cotton and Ruel Blake hanged instead of him, so be it. It was every man for himself.[28]

Saunders, however, faced several hurdles in getting the Livingston Committee of Safety to believe that he was not involved in the conspiracy. One was that few of its members thought Saunders entirely trustworthy in the first place. They were willing to accept Saunders's stories about Cotton wanting to abandon his wife and being involved with slave stealing. But consistency was not the committee's strong suit, and crediting Saunders's assertions about Cotton did not keep it from entering into evidence that Saunders himself had previously been convicted of theft in Tennessee, had spent some time in the state penitentiary, and possessed a "general bad character."[29]

An even bigger problem for Saunders was that he had trapped himself by ever allowing patrollers and committee members to believe that he knew anything about the insurrection plot. He had already testified that, excepting his own role in it, the details of the plot were as the patrollers and committee members had described. But that concession only prompted committee members to ask him how he knew so much about the conspiracy without being a conspirator. The truthful answer was that he did not know anything about the plot other than what the residents of Livingston had told him. But because he had admitted that he did, he had no choice but to stick with the only exculpatory strategy he had been able to devise. He asserted, again, that Cotton had told him about the plot when he had asked Saunders to join Murrell's clan, but that when Cotton "made the proposition to him he positively refused." Saunders even amplified the claim, saying that he had "attempted to dissuade Cotton from the attempt, and henceforth he determined to cease all intercourse with Cotton, which determination he had adhered to."[30]

With that amplification Saunders dug himself a deeper hole, because he had not cut his ties with Cotton. On the contrary, there is no reason to believe the two had ever ended their business partnership. They probably never thought they needed to. The committee of safety had little trouble finding witnesses to testify that in fact, Saunders remained "on very intimate terms with Cotton" and that the two had been seen "together, in Livingston, but a few days before the developments at Beattie's Bluff." Pursuing him through the labyrinth of his lies, committee members then asked Saunders why he had not revealed what he knew about the conspiracy when he was first questioned in Livingston on June 30. The truthful answer, again, was that he had said nothing because he had known nothing.

But now Saunders had talked himself completely into a corner, and there was no escape. He had no plausible answer for the question, and made no serious attempt to provide one. All he had was silence.[31]

III.

Despite the contortions and contradictions of Saunders's testimony and their doubts about his character and Joshua Cotton's, the members of the Livingston Committee of Safety were not quite ready to say that either man was guilty of inciting the slaves of Madison County to insurrection. When the committee adjourned for the day on the afternoon of July 3, William Saunders, Joshua Cotton, and the other prisoners brought in by patrols over the preceding days were taken back to jail, where they spent what must have been an excruciating night awaiting knowledge of their fates. Midnight would bring Independence Day, and the tension in Livingston was exquisite. Most committee members thought Saunders especially had dug his own grave, but they had not reached a unanimous decision and thus remained unwilling to pass judgment on him, Cotton, or anyone else.[32]

On the morning of July 4, however, they appeared prepared to make some pronouncements. The committee introduced into evidence the confessions of the slaves who had been hanged at Beattie's Bluff, listened to brief testimony from a few more witnesses, and then removed Joshua Cotton from the room so that they might deliberate on his case. Cotton entertained no delusions that he might be acquitted. The case against him may have been one lie set down in front of another, but he could see where the trail led. As he was escorted away, Cotton implored the men guarding him not to leave his body hanging for long after he died and to give him a decent burial. He had said little at his trial, and his guards, sensing his despondency and vulnerability, encouraged him to tell everything he knew and especially to provide the names of his accomplices. Doing so, they said, "would be some atonement for his guilt" and would help sort the innocent from the guilty among the others in custody. That suggestion seems to have given Joshua Cotton an idea. He told his guards that he would confess everything about the conspiracy if the committee would promise not to hang him immediately.[33]

Cotton saw a glimmer of hope in exchanging a confession for more time. If he could manage to stay alive until July 4 had passed, the residents of

Livingston might see that the conspiracy they feared was a figment of their imagination, and cooler heads might prevail. But by the time the guards relayed Cotton's offer to the committee, it was too late. The members had reached a verdict, and Marmaduke Mitchell emerged from the hearing room to tell Cotton that they "would not pledge themselves to extend any favor to him whatever." They were satisfied of his guilt. Mitchell told Cotton he "might confess or not." He was going to hang either way.[34]

At that point Joshua Cotton's mindset turned from gloomy desperation to calculated spite. He had listened helplessly as William Saunders effectively put his head in a noose, but he was not going down alone. If the members of the committee wanted names, they could have William Saunders. In fact, they could have more than just Saunders. Anyone could see that the white people of Madison County were scared. If they were going to execute him for involvement in this so-called conspiracy, then Cotton would give them something to be scared about. They could hang him, but he was going to make them pay for it after he was gone. He thought for a moment. Then he told his guards to tell the committee that he was ready to make a full confession.[35]

Cotton began by admitting that he was a member of John Murrell's clan. In fact, he professed that he was among its most important members and had twice attended meetings of the clan's "grand council," including a gathering near Columbus, Mississippi, a few months past. He asserted that the clan intended to carry out Murrell's insurrection scheme just as Virgil Stewart's pamphlet described it: incitement of the slaves of the southern states to rebellion, wholesale slaughter of the white population, and destruction of the countryside so that clan members might plunder the region amid the chaos. He claimed that he had spent two years spreading disaffection on every plantation he visited and that he and his fellow clansmen had managed to engage the involvement of slaves on nearly every large plantation in Mississippi. He conceded that the insurrection originally was to begin on Christmas Day but said that Stewart's exposure of Murrell and his clan had forced a change of plans, that the operation had been moved up to the Fourth of July instead, and that guns and ammunition had been cached in numerous locations in preparation.[36]

Then Cotton named names. He made a special point of saying that only those who had already agreed to participate in the conspiracy were allowed to know its details and that William Saunders was one of its leading organizers. He insisted that Andrew Boyd, Albe Dean, and Ruel Blake were all involved, and that two men from Hinds County named Rawson had a list of about 150 Mississippi members of Murrell's clan and another of the 51 white men under Cotton's direct control. He claimed not to remember the names of all the conspirators with whom he was connected directly, but he provided the identities of eight other men in four different counties. For the most part, there is little information indicating who they were, how exactly Cotton knew them, or whether or how any of them knew each other. John Rogers had acted as witness to Cotton's wedding to Clarey Johnson in Hinds County. Lee Smith was originally from Tennessee and owned a few slaves, also in Hinds County, and may have been selling some Thomsonian medicines acquired from Cotton to supplement his income. John Ivy owned a small lot in Vernon and had as late as 1834 owned a couple of slaves. James Leach was a butcher and tanner of some substance who lived near Woodville in Wilkinson County. William and John Earl owned about 160 acres of land and a slave in Warren County close to the city of Vicksburg. About Lunsford Barnes and Thomas Anderson the public record tells us nothing at all. Some of these men may have been customers of Cotton's. Perhaps they were just acquaintances, though if so they were acquaintances Cotton cared little about given that he understood what might happen to them once he told the residents of Livingston they were associated with the planned insurrection.[37]

Whoever these men were, their names were just about the only information Joshua Cotton provided that the Livingston Committee of Safety did not already know. Everything else—about Murrell's clan, Stewart's pamphlet, and the details of the insurrection plot—had become common knowledge and popular wisdom in and around the village over the last several days. Cotton needed only to have been paying attention to the "evidence" presented at his trial to provide an account of his supposed involvement that accorded with what whites in Livingston already believed to be true. Some accounts of Cotton's confession indicate that he even said that attractive white women would be spared during the uprising, a detail Jim had provided at Beattie's Bluff that was surely introduced along with the rest of Jim's confession at Cotton's trial earlier that morning.[38]

Providing additional names on top of those of Saunders, Boyd, Dean, and Blake and saying that lists containing dozens more existed was bound to achieve Cotton's goal of spreading panic even after he died. But Cotton was not quite finished. He signed his confession, which someone had transcribed as Cotton offered it, and the committee sentenced him to be hanged within the hour, hoping that word of the execution would circulate before nightfall and deter Cotton's accomplices from carrying out their plan. The committee quickly sentenced William Saunders to hang as well, as Cotton's description of the depth of Saunders's involvement removed the last remaining doubts about his guilt. The two were then marched back to the jail. Ropes were attached to a window grate of one of the cells and two rails leaned against the jailhouse wall. Cotton and Saunders were walked up the rails, and the ropes were tied around their necks. Cotton made one last attempt to stall the proceedings, claiming that he could provide more information if he was given more time. When that request was refused, he faced the crowd that had gathered, acknowledged his guilt, swore that every word of his confession was true, and offered a final warning, shouting to the assembled to "beware of to-night and to-morrow night." Then the rails were pulled from the jailhouse wall, leaving Joshua Cotton and William Saunders dangling and dead.[39]

IV.

The corpses of Cotton and Saunders, swaying alongside the Livingston jail when the sun rose on the morning of July 5, bore gruesome testimony to the events of the previous afternoon. But white residents of Madison County took no solace from the fact that the pandemonium, destruction, and mass murder they had anticipated on Independence Day failed to materialize. If anything, they grew more apprehensive, their fears now unanchored to a particular date on which to focus them. Joshua Cotton had told the people of Livingston that he had scores of accomplices in Mississippi and that the uprising might begin on July 4 or July 5. But maybe it could start on July 6 or July 7 or July 8. Or anytime. No one could really say, leaving those who believed the plot was real with little recourse but to keep worrying and keep hunting for John Murrell and his confederates.[40]

Which is exactly what they did. Angus Donovan was already in custody. So was Albe Dean, who had been arrested by the same patrol that brought Cotton and Saunders back to Livingston. Riders from Livingston were dispatched with a pack of dogs to chase down Andrew Boyd, who had been spotted near the village on the afternoon of July 4. But Boyd fled north and managed to stay ahead of his pursuers in the bogs, canebrakes, and forests near the Big Black River for more than thirty-six hours before he disappeared on a horse he found in the woods. Ruel Blake, though, was still at large. So were the Rawsons, Lee Smith, and the other men Joshua Cotton had implicated, and they were not the only supposed conspirators who might be out there. The Livingston Committee of Safety did not meet on July 5. It was a Sunday, though the committee stayed adjourned less for the sake of prayer and contemplation than to give posses from the village time to arrest additional prisoners. Clusters of men on horseback showed up in Livingston almost hourly over the course of the day and throughout the night, bringing in people individually and in groups of two or three. Soon enough, Livingston's jail, designed for six or eight prisoners, was packed with nearly twenty white men and an untold number of slaves.[41]

As committee members reconvened on Monday morning, July 6, and began dealing with the ever-growing number of captives in the Livingston jail, they had become relatively uninterested in acquiring more information about the supposed conspiracy. Instead, they were simply doling out punishment to those they believed might be involved in it. The committee had taken the better part of two days to examine, convict, and hang Joshua Cotton and William Saunders, but that relatively measured pace picked up dramatically thereafter. Moreover, while it would be hard to argue that any judgment could be harsher than execution, the committee sentenced several individuals to suffer ordeals astonishing in their ferocity, almost as if its members hoped that Murrell's clansmen would be overawed by their sheer savageness.

On July 6, for example, the committee ordered two white men to be flogged and banished from the state of Mississippi, though the word "flogging" practically euphemizes what seventy-two-year-old John Gregory and another man, age fifty, actually endured. Both received something called "slicking," a gory and humiliating torment in which the victim was stripped naked and laid facedown with each of his four limbs tied to a peg in the ground while several men alternated lashing him with whips. Perhaps because of his advanced age, Gregory received just 50 lashes. The younger man was sentenced to 150 blows, and after they had been administered "his back was literally flayed."[42]

Committee members had not completely lost the desire to discriminate between those they thought innocent and those they thought guilty. They seem to have recognized that some of the people caught in the sweeps during the first week of July had probably done little more than make the acquaintance of the wrong people or say things that perhaps they should not have said. In some instances the committee decided that such people were untrustworthy and needed to disappear anyway. Joshua Cotton had named Lee Smith, for example, as a conspirator. The posse that showed up on the morning of July 6 at Smith's home in Hinds County, just over the border from Madison, found him heavily armed and demanding to know whether Cotton had implicated him. At Smith's trial later that day, witnesses testified that Smith and Cotton knew each other well and were in the steam-doctoring business together. But other witnesses attested to Smith's "good character," and Smith himself claimed he had met Cotton only twice. Committee members did not believe that, but they were uncertain enough about Smith's guilt to release him on the condition that he get out of Mississippi within forty-eight hours.[43]

Cotton had also identified Lunsford Barnes as a member of John Murrell's clan, and witnesses at Barnes's trial on July 7 testified that they had seen him with Cotton and Saunders, and that Barnes had agreed to go to Texas with Cotton to sell stolen slaves. But Barnes was very young and was known in Madison County as a "good, honest, hard-working boy" who "was very ignorant and uneducated." Taking into consideration his youth and perhaps his ingenuousness, the committee gave Barnes the option of receiving five hundred lashes or leaving the state.[44]

It offered the same choice to William Benson, a day laborer from New York who had been working for Ruel Blake when the insurrection scare began and who was arrested when he tried to flee the county after Cotton and Saunders were hanged. At Benson's trial, also held on July 7, the committee heard evidence that Blake's slave, Peter, had asserted before his death that Benson had said he thought slavery was a "hard case," that the enslaved ought to be free, and that he believed slaves so outnumbered white people that they might successfully procure their freedom if armed "with *sticks* alone." Benson, however, seems to have had a mental disability that mitigated the judgment against him, as Shackelford noted that "he was considered by the committee a great fool, little above an idiot." That he may have been, but he, like Barnes, had enough sense to prefer exile to five hundred lashes. So did two other men the committee tried on July 7, both of whom were allowed to leave Mississippi, taking with them the admonition that they would be hanged if they returned.[45]

In a few cases, the Livingston Committee of Safety decided that those on trial were altogether innocent. A man named Holden was acquitted on July 7, for instance, as was James Mitchell. No evidence exists to tell us much about who these men were, why they became suspects, or why the committee determined they had nothing to do with the supposed conspiracy while an old man like John Gregory had earned a vicious thrashing. Mitchell's good fortune, though, might be attributed simply to the fact that other whites in Livingston found him useful. He was a blacksmith, and with companies of riders galloping through the countryside and bringing in prisoners around the clock, horses needed shoeing and chains needed forging. After Mitchell was discharged the committee requisitioned his services, and in the words of one witness, "he seemed the happiest man on the hill, rendering every service required, with the utmost promptness and cheerfulness."[46]

No doubt, given that the committee was not finished hanging people. Albe Dean went on trial on July 6, and he had almost nothing going for him. William Saunders had named Dean as an associate the very first time he was questioned in Livingston, and Joshua Cotton had named him as a conspirator in his confession several days later. Moreover, many had thought Dean disreputable even prior to the insurrection scare. Originally from Connecticut, Dean had migrated to Mississippi in 1833. He tried to make some money near Livingston by building and selling "washing machines," but as Shackelford noted, his "general character, before the disclosure of the conspiracy, was not good," and "he was considered a lazy, indolent man, having very little *pretensions* to honesty." Dean soon moved to Hinds County, went into business with Cotton and Saunders selling Thomsonian medicines, and exhibited the same kinds of behaviors that got his partners into trouble. Witnesses testified that Dean could sometimes be found "prowling about the plantations in the neighborhoods of Vernon, Beatties Bluff, and Livingston, ostensibly for the purpose of inquiring for runaway horses." But few believed that was his real interest. Rather, members of the committee concluded, "he was reconnoitering the country and seeking opportunities to converse with the negroes."[47]

Supposedly, Dean not only spent an inordinate amount of time with the enslaved but would also "often come to the owners of runaways and intercede with their masters, to save them from a whipping." Whether or not any of that was true, Dean, like William Saunders, had little sense of when to keep his mouth shut. One of the patrollers who arrested him testified that Dean had asked whether the slaves of some particular white men, including William Johnson and Ruel Blake, were accused of participation in the conspiracy. Johnson's enslaved man and Blake's Peter had been interrogated and jailed on July 1. Dean could have heard rumors to that effect before he was taken into custody the next day, and he might well have asked his captors about those rumors, if only to assess his own situation. But the members of the committee of safety found it hard to believe he would or could have heard anything, deciding instead that Dean's question about those particular slaves confirmed both his and their involvement in the conspiracy.[48]

One thing Dean was unlikely to have known before he was taken into custody was that Peter had already been hanged, as that execution had taken place only hours before Dean's arrest. But when the patrollers told him of Peter's death, Dean proceeded to make things worse for himself by asking whether Peter "had made any disclosures about him." Again, Dean might have asked this sort of question simply because he was wondering how and why he had ended up in such a fix. The members of the Livingston Committee of Safety did not see it that way. Instead, by unanimous vote, they found Dean "guilty of aiding and exciting the negroes to insurrection" and sentenced him to be hanged.[49]

V.

By the time the committee convicted Albe Dean, whites in Livingston and its environs had spent a week and a half thinking they were in imminent danger. But they also believed they understood the threat they faced and how to respond to it. White Mississippians dreaded nothing more than that slaves might rise up en masse, and the language they used to describe the likely results of the insurrection they had convinced themselves was gathering speaks vividly to the grisliness of the antebellum white southern imagination. One man wrote that he and his neighbors expected "every moment to be burned up or have our throats cut by the Negroes." Another thought the "whole country . . . was to be ravaged and inundated with the blood of men, women, and children." The macabre scene a slave revolt conjured in the minds of white southerners, though, is suggested best by the expression Mississippians used most commonly. Were there to be an uprising, several people wrote, it would undoubtedly be characterized by "indiscriminate butchery."[50]

Some members of the enslaved population of Mississippi paid a horrible price for the sanguinary fears of those who kept them in bondage. On July 2 five slaves were hanged at Beattie's Bluff, and two were executed in Livingston. Of the unknown number of slaves rounded up and jailed in the days after that, none seems to have received a trial before the Livingston Committee of Safety. But witness accounts make clear that with or without the committee's sanction, perhaps a dozen slaves, in addition to the first seven who died, were executed during the first week of July. We will likely never know how many others were beaten or murdered without publicity on remote plantations that were the private fiefdoms of their owners.[51]

Even many slaves who never came near a noose or a whip spent the insurrection scare wondering whether the fury of the white people of Mississippi would settle on their heads, as the patrols riding through the nights of early July 1835 terrorized the enslaved wherever they encountered them. Israel Campbell provided a rare glimpse of such a confrontation from an African American perspective. Born into slavery in Kentucky early in the nineteenth century, in the middle of the 1830s Campbell lived on a plantation about fifty miles southwest of Livingston near the Mississippi River. In his 1861 autobiography Campbell recalled having been awakened in the middle of the night several decades earlier by the shouts of two white men ordering him to open the door of his cabin. Groggily getting to his feet, Campbell had barely gotten dressed when one of the men grabbed him by the collar. Threatening Campbell with the bowie knife he held in his other hand, the white man swore at Campbell and asked him what he knew "about Doctor Cotton's scrape." When Campbell replied that he knew nothing, the man called him a liar and demanded to know if Campbell knew an enslaved preacher named Dave and whether there had been talk at the last church service Dave had held "about getting free and killing the white people." Campbell admitted that he knew Dave but insisted he had heard nothing about an uprising. Campbell was fortunate that the white men eventually concluded that his ignorance was genuine. Offering Campbell a swig of brandy that he surely needed, they ordered him not to leave his plantation or speak to any unfamiliar slaves or white men else he would be shot.[52]

In his memoir, Campbell further recalled that whites assailed all the slave quarters in the area over the next several days, scaring some people "so badly, that they told lies of every description, and suffered for it." In particular, Campbell claimed that whites arrested all the black preachers they could find, decapitated them, put their heads on poles, "and placed them along the road, where they remained until they were bleached." Campbell claimed to have seen a number of the preachers' skulls on display several months later in an apothecary shop.[53]

That some of the enslaved, in their fright, told patrollers whatever they wanted to hear accords entirely with what transpired at Beattie's Bluff and in Livingston, and Campbell's recollection that slaves believed to be preachers were special targets of white wrath fits with Shackelford's claim that white Mississippians categorically believed black preachers to be forces for unrest. The hideous spectacle of heads impaled and left to putrefy may never have happened. Contemporary sources describing the insurrection scare of 1835 record many instances of brutality but nothing that hints at violence quite so purposefully grotesque being unleashed on the enslaved population. True or not, that Campbell would either imagine or falsely remember such a scene speaks graphically to the trauma inflicted on the slaves of Mississippi that summer.

While patrollers harassed, beat, killed, and otherwise menaced the enslaved, however, they were looking above all else for other white people. Similarly, as white residents of Mississippi crafted editorials, wrote letters, and sent reports to friends and relatives about what was happening, they recognized the dangers slaves presented but stressed that diabolical white men were more dangerous because they had initiated the whole affair. The editor of a newspaper in Columbus, more than one hundred miles northeast of Livingston, wrote that "an organized band of ruffians" had "conceived the plan of instigating a general insurrection" and had "induced a number of slaves to believe that they could rise and murder the whites." The editor of another Columbus paper was equally convinced, if shocked, that at the head of the conspiracy were "individuals enjoying all the privileges of free citizens." People like these, who had "instigated the ignorant and generally contented Africans to rise against their fellow-citizens," were "fiends, for men they can hardly be called—they must be devoid of all the common attributes of human nature."[54]

A Hinds County man agreed, expressing outrage in a letter to a Nashville merchant that the insurrection plot had "been traced to the unwarranted interference of the whites." He could understand why a slave might revolt, and even claimed that one "who strikes for his freedom is perhaps rather an object of compassion than anger." But a white man who could foment such unrest, "the first step of which is taken in blood, and the object of which is lust and slaughter, must be a fiend incarnate." In Livingston itself, meanwhile, the committee of safety focused its attentions from its very first meeting on finding the white men its members believed had been trying to incite the revolt, and Shackelford would assert baldly that there was "no doubt" that "the plot was headed by a daring band of villainous white men." Even as the scare was still ongoing, one man wrote from Livingston that whatever their initial fears, village residents quickly came to "apprehend no danger from the blacks." Instead, they directed their energies toward "tracing out the [white] conspirators."[55]

It was wishful thinking, of course, to believe that the enslaved were too ignorant or contented to organize a rebellion. Particularly in a place where the workforce was treated as pitilessly as it was on the cotton frontier, white southerners knew better, though for the sake of being able to sleep with both eyes closed they liked to tell themselves that racial superiority and their own generosity would keep slaves placid and under control. Moreover, whites in Madison County believed that white men were behind the supposed insurrection plot because Virgil Stewart's pamphlet told them it was so. But the only indication Stewart provided of exactly who was in John Murrell's clan came from the list of names he claimed Murrell gave him while the two men traveled together in 1834, and there was no Joshua Cotton on that list. Neither was there a William Saunders, an Albe Dean, a Ruel Blake, a Lee Smith, or any of the other white men who came under suspicion and sometimes lost their lives in 1835. Yet when the white residents of Livingston gathered on June 30 to discuss the plot, among their first instincts was to ask William Saunders to account for himself. They then sought Cotton in part because Saunders provided his name, and others because Cotton provided theirs, and so on. But the links in that chain of accusations were also held together by a broader context. There was something about Saunders, Cotton, Dean, and many of the rest that convinced other whites they were subversive and dangerous.[56]

VI.

Israel Campbell recalled that the patrollers who came to his door were not looking just for black preachers. They were also looking for steam doctors, and several witness accounts of the insurrection scare indicate that many in Mississippi came to believe that Thomsonians, or men pretending to be Thomsonians, formed the core of Murrell's clan in the region. A man from Hinds County wrote to the editor of the *Jackson Mississippian* under the assumption that the plot had been organized by "steam doctors slipping about amongst negroes" and telling them "fine tales of freedom." A Vicksburg man, writing to a friend in Kentucky, similarly concluded that "the character of steam doctor was a fine cloak for these villains to assume. They had no books to read—no time or pence to lose in preparing, and it introduced them among families and negroes."[57]

Even a casual examination of the men who came under suspicion in Madison County, however, demonstrates that they fit no pattern so straightforward or singular as that. Joshua Cotton and William Saunders were selling Thomsonian medicines, and Albe Dean and Lee Smith may have been doing so as well. But no one accused Ruel Blake, Angus Donovan, or anyone else of steam doctoring. Other conspicuous characteristics that might have brought these individuals before the Livingston Committee of Safety also applied imperfectly. That Joshua Cotton was from a free state, for example, did not work in his favor, and Blake, Dean, and William Benson were all northerners too. But there were other northerners among the white settlers of Madison County, and patrollers and committees never thought twice about most of them. Moreover, Saunders and Smith were from Tennessee, and Angus Donovan was from Kentucky.

Whether or not a man owned slaves was certainly a significant factor shaping how other white people viewed him, his position, and his intentions in frontier Mississippi, as someone invested financially in enslaved property would presumably be unlikely to instigate a revolt. That presumption helped Ruel Blake get out of Livingston on July 1 despite his going too easy on Peter, and there is no indication that Albe Dean, Angus Donovan, William Saunders, or most of the other men brought before the Livingston Committee of Safety owned slaves. Most do not appear in the tax and property records of Madison or nearby counties at all. But Joshua Cotton owned a slave. Lee Smith owned at least four, and Peter was not the only person Ruel Blake owned. In fact, Blake held six people in bondage.[58]

Owning a few slaves did not necessarily indicate absolute dedication to the institution of slavery, of course, and it is not unreasonable to ask whether whites in Madison County looked askance at some of the men who fell under suspicion in the summer of 1835 because the relative brevity of their residence had provided insufficient time to assess their allegiance. Joshua Cotton had lived in Mississippi for only about a year, after all, and William Saunders had been in the state for only about nine months. There does seem to have been some general skepticism of those who lived transient lives, even when they were not steam doctors. Recall that William Benson was a day laborer and that Jesse Mabry, reporting the information wrung from a slave at Beattie's Bluff, had raised the specter of a traveling peddler known only as Sliver. For his part, Angus Donovan arrived in Mississippi just weeks before the insurrection scare broke.[59]

If impermanence and the brief time these men had been in Mississippi made them "strangers" and thus untrustworthy in the eyes of those who had lived there longer, however, one wonders what to make of Lee Smith, who owned his own land and had been in the state for more than a decade. Smith lived in a different county than the residents of Livingston, and members of the committee of safety did have to rely on witnesses to vouch for Smith's character, but his land nearly bordered Madison County and he lived several miles closer to Livingston than the residents of Beattie's Bluff did. Even stretching the definition of "stranger" to include Smith, though, would not account for the suspicions that attached to Albe Dean, who had been familiar to residents of Livingston for two years. Nor would it explain the doubts about Ruel Blake. He owned land, had a regular occupation, and had resided in Madison since around 1829, which made him practically an original settler of the county. Certainly Dean and Blake were less "strangers" than, say, Jesse Mabry. He had owned his plantation for just three months before the Livingston Committee of Safety was formed but was believed so steadfast that he was asked to join that body nonetheless.[60]

That Mabry owned a plantation was clearly crucial, and it is impossible to deny that class played a significant role in determining which white men served on the Livingston Committee of Safety and which white men were judged by it. Nearly every member of the committee was a planter, and all those who became its targets stood relatively low on the economic ladder. Even Ruel Blake, with his half a dozen slaves, small piece of land, and business building and repairing cotton gins and doing other sorts of carpentry, occupied at best the status of a yeoman. He participated in and benefited from the plantation world, but he was no plantation owner.

Ultimately, though, whether a person became a suspect in the summer of 1835 was not merely a matter of whether he was rich, middling, or poor either. The issue was more abstract and multifaceted than that. Life in Madison County was precarious for white settlers not least of all because the enslaved on whom they depended for their economic success and who embodied invested capital both resented and outnumbered them. Given that some racial turbulence was inevitable, aspiring farmers and planters needed a socioeconomic order that functioned smoothly and predictably and in which at least other whites were known quantities—people who could be relied on to stick together for the sake of everyone's safety and who seemed honestly dedicated to making possible the profits promised by the market production of cotton.

Those accused of involvement in the supposed insurrection plot, however, were all men of whose racial or economic commitment other whites just could not be sure. No single factor inherently made someone questionable. But when a man's circumstances, behavior, and attitudes combined to suggest an ambiguous or ambivalent relationship to the project of building the cotton kingdom, he was vulnerable to accusations of being involved in an organization like the one John Murrell purportedly headed and a scheme like the one Virgil Stewart described. Far from being considered strangers, in a way the problem for the white men targeted during the insurrection scare of 1835 was that other white men thought they understood exactly who they were.[61]

Joshua Cotton, for example, may have owned a slave, but he was also a northerner. His occupation entailed no necessary involvement in the agricultural economy, and at least some who did business with him thought him a chiseler. He moved his residence from place to place too frequently, he spent a lot of time wandering about and trying to talk to slaves who did not belong to him, and William Saunders claimed he stole slaves and acted as a fence in the illegal interracial underground economy. And, not insignificantly, instead of trying to forge connections with his fellow frontier migrants, Cotton just seemed distant and unfriendly. As Thomas Shackelford wrote, he "was not liked by the citizens of Livingston" and "had no social intercourse" with them.[62]

Having undue sympathy for or social associations with slaves was obviously important in determining who got singled out in Madison County. The circumstances, after all, called particularly for locating white men considered to be less than vigilant in their support of slavery and close enough to the enslaved to be able to convince them to rebel. But there was a subtler element at play, namely whether those who knew a man believed he was or was likely to become well integrated into the broader social order and emerging economic community of the Southwest. Shackelford repeatedly made a point of noting the quality of a man's "character" when explaining why individuals were brought before the Livingston Committee of Safety and how its members decided what to do with them. And character in frontier Mississippi was more than a matter of whether a person was too friendly with the enslaved.

Take the case of Ruel Blake. Of those in and around Livingston thought to be dodgy sorts, he might appear the least likely to promote a slave rebellion. He owned half a dozen slaves and made and repaired equipment vital for the cotton economy. He had lived in Madison County for a relatively long time, and one witness to the insurrection scare reported that he "was remarkable for industry and perseverance." But that witness also noted that Blake merely "assumed an honest appearance" while in reality he "was totally destitute of principle or morality." Similarly, Shackelford asserted that Blake's "character, as known to the citizens, was one of the darkest die."[63]

Blake's racial loyalties were one concern. He was "oftener seen among negroes" than among white people, and his work as a gin wright often meant going where the machinery was, which gave him "opportunities of becoming acquainted with the negroes on most of the large plantations in Madison." But whites in Livingston had difficulties with Blake that predated even the hint of an insurrection. Shackelford claimed that despite having lived in Livingston for years, Blake "could claim but few or none [of its residents] as his friends." People thought he possessed "a cold phlegmatic temperament, with a forbidding countenance," and he stayed "aloof from white society." Shackelford even asserted that Blake, who told people he was a "sea-faring man in his youth," might have been "a pirate" before coming to Mississippi, and that he was noted for "insatiable avarice, and unnatural cruelty."[64]

That last was ironic coming from opportunist planters who wanted to put Blake on trial partially because he had lacked the requisite cruelty to interrogate a slave. But greed and callousness were acceptable and even praiseworthy when they came at the expense of the enslaved. The problem with Blake was that he had supposedly "been detected in several attempts to swindle his fellow-citizens, who (if they exposed his rascality,) were ever after the objects of his deadly hatred." The meaning of that accusation is unclear, and that a man as rich and reputable as Thomas Hudnall repeatedly loaned Blake money may suggest that the claim overstated things at best. But Blake had clashed with at least one customer who failed to pay him for building a gin house, and it is not inconceivable that he was in fact a personally and commercially challenging man to deal with. Whatever the realities of Ruel Blake's personality, it is telling that Shackelford chose to frame the uneasiness other whites had long felt around him less in terms of his racial associations than in terms of his ability to attract personal enmity and create economic friction.[65]

Standoffishness and having economic disputes with other white people were thus two ways a man could gain a reputation for having a questionable "character." But if some of those who ended up before the Livingston Committee of Safety were relatively established men like Blake whose neighbors disliked and distrusted them, others were people who floated in an economic environment whose hazards demanded fixity. The case of Angus Donovan best demonstrates the point. Donovan had arrived in Madison County sometime in the spring of 1835, and he never intended to stay. He was in Mississippi only because he had brought a boatload of corn down from Kentucky to sell. Having sold the boat along with the corn, he was slowly making his way back home to the Ohio River city of Maysville when he came across some keelboats half-sunk in the Big Black River near Beattie's Bluff. Donovan was poor, but he was not without industry. Wood could be salvaged and sold, so he decided to stop and scavenge what he could.[66]

Like Ruel Blake, Donovan chose racial associations other white people thought doubtful. People around Beattie's Bluff noticed his "intimacy with the negroes in the neighborhood" and suspected he illegally traded with them. Donovan rented a room in a private home, but his behavior so troubled the owner that the man asked him to leave, whereupon Donovan went to live in the house of Elisha Moss, who had a local reputation for entertaining slaves and generally being a "great scoundrel." Whites in the area began watching Donovan extremely closely, and after "he was repeatedly found in the negro cabins, enjoying himself in negro society," they told him he ought to get out of Beattie's Bluff altogether.[67]

Donovan refused to leave, and if the way he acted when the insurrection scare broke out a short time later was even remotely as Thomas Shackelford described it in his report, he had not grasped the dangers he courted by keeping close company with slaves. With whites at Beattie's Bluff becoming convinced the enslaved were about to rebel, Donovan had the opportunity to turn people's impressions of him around by helping to investigate and trying to prevent it. But "instead of using his exertions to ferret out the ringleaders and to assist the citizens in their efforts of detection, he would be found sneaking about the negro quarters, seeking opportunities to converse with them." When Donovan stepped forward during the interrogations of slaves believed to have knowledge of the plot and tried to undo the ropes holding Jim in place as Jesse Mabry alternately questioned and beat him, he finally went too far.[68]

Donovan was pulled away and ordered to keep his distance. Only then did he realize his peril. As the interrogations and the torture went on, Donovan "evinced considerable uneasiness, and kept walking to and fro, in view of the negroes under examination." Shackelford claimed Donovan's nervousness could be explained by the fact that the enslaved started providing information about the conspiracy once Donovan had been removed from the scene, which other whites took as a sign of Donovan's involvement. A more likely explanation for Donovan's consternation, other than disgust, was that he could hear Mabry and the other interrogators start asking the slaves to give up his name along with those of Cotton, Saunders, and the others. Sure enough, in their anguish the slaves at Beattie's Bluff soon began mentioning Angus Donovan as a leader of the conspiracy as well.[69]

When the Livingston Committee of Safety tried Donovan on July 7, its members heard evidence that three slaves had admitted that Donovan actively had been trying to engage their participation in the planned rebellion. None of those slaves was still alive, but one purportedly claimed Donovan had told him that "nothing was easier, than for [slaves] to get their freedom, that the negroes could kill all the white people—and if they should be pushed that he would take them to a free state." Another supposedly asserted that Donovan was to be one of the white "captains" directing the uprising in the area of Beattie's Bluff, and a third said before being executed that Donovan had "persuaded him to enter into the conspiracy" and "encouraged him to go on, and get as many negroes to join as possible."[70]

Angus Donovan may well have enjoyed the company of the enslaved. He may have sincerely sympathized with them in their suffering and had a personal distaste for the institution of slavery. Back in Kentucky, Donovan's father owned several slaves, but only genuine compassion really explains Donovan's courageous if unwise decision to interpose himself between Jim and the punishing blows Jesse Mabry was raining down on him. Yet whites in Madison County considered his displays of fellowship and mercy thin disguises for malevolence, and not merely because his behavior had led them to coerce some of the enslaved to say he belonged to "a band of cut throats and robbers" trying to recruit them for a revolt. When Donovan was arrested at Beattie's Bluff, his person and meager possessions were searched, and among his effects was a letter, nearly a year old and written by Donovan's wife, Mary. If Donovan's preference for spending time with black people and his efforts to alleviate their pain made whites in Madison suspicious, the letter clinched the case in their minds that he was a man "of a dissolute and abandoned character . . . and ripe for every rash enterprise."[71]

Whether or not the letter really demonstrated that is something we can judge for ourselves, as Thomas Shackelford thought it so self-evidently incriminatory that he included it as an appendix to his report. Dated August 24, 1834, it begins with a profession of devotion. "You say you have not heard from me since you left here," Mary Donovan wrote, but she insisted that she had "answered every letter since you left this place." Surprised that Angus had written in his most recent letter that he had "little hopes of receiving an answer," Mary wondered how he could "think that woman's heart is so hard, or that she could forget the one she once loved?" Mary conceded that caring so much for Angus was not easy and that "your conduct has grieved me more than you have any idea of," but she was pleased to hear that he had "come to a full determination to break off from all bad habits, and to study yourself and try to become a useful member of society."[72]

Recognizing the challenge Angus faced in trying to turn his life around, Mary wrote that she had prayed he would do so and urged him also to "pray to God that he may change your heart and give you grace to put those good resolutions into practice." Straightening himself out was the most important thing in the world, because Mary could not bring herself to come and live with Angus until she was "fully convinced that you will not return to your former ways." She believed, however, that time would prove him capable of reform, and she encouraged him to study "geography and grammar," which might enable him to run a school. Meanwhile, she pressed him to settle down and "lay up something to commence house-keeping with," which she was convinced he had yet to do as he had been gone for a year but had not sent her any money. Closing her letter, Mary exhorted Angus "to be on your guard, and never give way to those evils you have so fully determined to forsake; for it is a great consolation for me to think of seeing you again, and once more enjoying your company." Informing him that his family was well and asking him to write, she signed herself "yours, affectionately, Mary A. S. Donovan."[73]

Mary Donovan's letter reveals that Angus Donovan was far from a perfect man. He had his share of failings, he had deeply hurt a woman who cherished him, he had problems finding a place in the world, and he lacked wealth and formal education. So severe were his troubles that he had spent months away from his family with hopes of rehabilitating himself. But Mary Donovan had written that letter almost a year earlier, and if Angus Donovan is to be believed, by the summer of 1835 he had made significant progress. At his trial he claimed to have a family and a home in Kentucky. He admitted that he was not a man of means but said he worked as a boatman to make money to feed his loved ones. That meant he traveled a lot, but he insisted, despite what the letter said, that he had sent home practically every cent he had managed to earn.[74]

Though the residents of Beattie's Bluff, Thomas Shackelford, and the members of the Livingston Committee of Safety believed the letter decisively proved Angus Donovan to be the sort of man liable to conspire against the lives and the wealth of white Mississippians, in reality it proved only that Donovan had once lived a sad and aimless life. It is impossible to say what Mary Donovan meant when she begged him to cease his "bad habits" and make himself a "useful member of society." Perhaps he had been a drunk or a profligate. Perhaps he had committed a crime. But that was his past, and if the fact that he had kept the letter suggests that he found sticking to the path of rectitude a constant challenge, it also suggests how badly he wanted to do so. If he ever needed a reminder of his purpose, his goal, and the costs of failure, it was right there in his pocket. Entirely righteous, Angus Donovan was not. But to judge him irretrievably "dissolute and abandoned" seems bitterly unfair.

The American frontier is often mythologized as a place of second chances where a person's past did not matter and new identities could be crafted. Angus Donovan found the opposite to be true. When he arrived in Beattie's Bluff, whites in the area knew almost nothing about him or what he was doing in Mississippi. What they did know was that he had no particular occupation and no apparent interest in joining whatever established white society there was in Madison County. Instead, he hovered at the edges, and the only signals he gave of his intentions suggested he could not be trusted, especially around the enslaved. When the residents of Beattie's Bluff then became afraid that white villains among them were rousing the slaves to rebellion, he was the kind of person they were bound to see as suspicious. Ruel Blake's racial and economic behaviors may have fit awkwardly in Madison County, but Angus Donovan's did not fit at all. His attempt to protect a defenseless man from a vicious beating and his possession of a document that hinted at his once having a questionable "character" were perhaps the two most important pieces of the puzzle whites in the area put together about him, but they already thought they had a sense of what it would look like when it was completed. It looked like one of John Murrell's men. Sometime on the afternoon of July 7 the Livingston Committee of Safety sentenced Angus Donovan to hang.[75]

VII.

The most thorough firsthand accounts of the trials in Livingston generally come from the pen of Thomas Shackelford himself, with supplementary material enabling some cross-checking of Shackelford's information appearing in letters from other witnesses that were published in newspapers and that helped disseminate awareness of events beyond Madison County and beyond Mississippi. Angus Donovan's trial is an exception, thanks to Henry Stuart Foote. Born in Virginia in 1804, Foote graduated from college at fifteen, was admitted to the bar in Richmond in 1823, and soon thereafter moved to Alabama and then, in 1826, to Mississippi. He practiced law in a number of Mississippi cities and towns, founded several newspapers, and would go on to serve in the state legislature, the U.S. Senate, and as governor of Mississippi. In 1835 he was living in the Hinds County town of Clinton, and on July 6 he received a note from Angus Donovan asking him to serve as Donovan's legal advocate before the Livingston Committee of Safety, which would hear his case the next day.[76]

How exactly Donovan found Foote is unclear, given that Donovan knew almost no one in the state and certainly no one with the stature of Foote, who was already beginning to make a name for himself in state political circles. For Foote's part, he recalled in an 1874 memoir that he was not sure he would be able to help. He had heard about the proceedings of the committee and had witnessed the "extravagant and even maddening excitement" that was beginning to spread throughout west-central Mississippi by the end of the first week of July. Under the circumstances he thought Donovan gravely mistaken "to have imagined that it was a real court that was about to examine into his case, and that a lawyer would be allowed to defend him before it." But sympathetic to Donovan's plight and wishing to see the committee in action for himself, Foote went to Madison County anyway.[77]

Clinton was about eighteen miles from Livingston, and Donovan's trial had already begun by the time Foote rode into the village on July 7. Foote "saw a large multitude convened, composed almost altogether of excited white citizens." Many recognized him, but Foote was afraid to tell anyone why he was there. This was not a forgiving or understanding crowd, and Foote determined immediately that he ought to keep his business to himself. Henry Foote was not a timid man. He had left Alabama in part because he broke that state's antidueling law, he would duel in Mississippi on at least four occasions, and later in his life he engaged in numerous fistfights, including once on the floor of the Senate and once during a debate with a political opponent. But Foote knew his pugnacity would be of no avail in Livingston. If people discovered he had come at Angus Donovan's behest, Foote believed "there was not much probability that I should have ever returned to my own home again."[78]

Instead, he tied his horse to a post and quietly made his way to the room where Donovan's trial was being held. Going inside, Foote decided not to reveal his identity to Donovan, "deeming it prudent" simply to watch the proceedings. What he saw appalled him. "The examination was conducted in a very rapid and informal manner," Foote remembered, "and without the least regard to the established principles of the law of evidence." Foote thought it fairly clear that Donovan was just a poor boatman trying to support his family, and he saw "not a particle of evidence implicating him in the guilt alleged, except that of two or three ignorant negroes in the vicinage, who had been seen once or twice near his boat, and from whose reluctant lips certain disclosures had been coerced under the severest infliction of the lash."[79]

It did not take long for the committee to finish its task, and Foote saw that it was about to convict Donovan. Thinking there was little he could do to help, Foote said nothing. But Hardin Runnels had seen him enter the room and, noticing that Foote paid an unusual amount of attention to Donovan's case, asked him if he wished to question Donovan himself. Foote said he did, and he remembered of Donovan that he never saw "a more honest and benign face than this man presented." He decided to ask Donovan the one question he thought might make committee members think twice about what they were doing while simultaneously giving Donovan the chance to state conclusively where he stood when it came to race, slavery, and the plantation economy. "You are a *white* man," Foote began. "You say that you have a wife and children at home whom you love dearly; you say, also, that you are very poor, and that you came down here on a trading expedition, in order to get the means of saving that loved family from starvation; you declare, in addition, that you have written to some member of your family whenever you could, and have sent them nearly all the money you have been able to earn; now tell me, I beseech you, were you to witness a bloody conflict between the slaves of this country and the white people, on which side would you be?" Foote could see that Donovan understood the importance of the question and the possibility it held. His eyes lighting up and his voice "marked with all the emphasis of deep and manly feeling," Donovan responded: "Certainly, sir, I should be on the side of my own color." Foote asked him no further questions. It did not matter. Twenty minutes later the Livingston Committee of Safety sentenced Donovan to death.[80]

Foote recalled that after Donovan was dead, the newspapers in Kentucky were filled with love letters he had sent to Mary and that no one who read them, even in Mississippi, doubted that Angus Donovan had been an innocent man. At least one of the letters, published initially in Donovan's hometown *Maysville Eagle,* was reprinted in newspapers across the country. Writing just after his conviction, Donovan informed his wife that "this is the last you may ever expect to receive or hear from me. I am doomed to die on to-morrow, at 12 o'clock, on a charge of having been concerned in a negro insurrection in this State, among many other whites." But Donovan insisted there was some peace to be found in knowing "what few can say, that I can meet my God innocently. By the false accusation of both black and white, and some particularly who have come forward and sworn falsely to my prejudice, I have been condemned unjustly by their oaths." Hoping "that the God of the widow and fatherless will give you a grace to bear this most awful sentence," Donovan bid his wife farewell. At noon on July 8 Angus Donovan and Albe Dean were hanged together on a makeshift gallows erected in the center of the village of Livingston.[81]

The Livingston Committee of Safety was not finished holding hearings. There were still men in jail, there were still patrols riding the countryside, and a few days earlier the residents of Madison County had pooled their resources and offered a five-hundred-dollar reward for the arrest of Ruel Blake, who remained at large. So far as the members of the committee were concerned, they were going to see things through until they considered their task complete.[82]

But as Henry Foote's horrified recollections suggest, by the time Angus Donovan and Albe Dean died the seeds of a backlash had already been sown. In part that was true because the Livingston Committee of Safety, while created to channel and curb the impulses of men who believed themselves facing an existential threat, had mostly lent those men a veneer of institutional legitimacy that licensed them to act on those impulses. The longer the insurrection scare went on, the more fear edged its way past paranoia and into delusion that became increasingly uncontrollable as it reached beyond Madison County.

In part, though, the reaction against vigilantism acquired momentum because it became clear by the end of the first week of July that a prospective slave insurrection was not the only thing that could trigger its outbreak. Anxieties about the solidity of slavery bore special resonance in the Southwest because it was the social and economic foundation on which the cotton frontier rested. Anxieties about the freewheeling financial speculation that laid that foundation, however, transcended slavery and spoke to dilemmas confronting Americans everywhere who struggled to find stability and meaning in the flush times. That resolving those dilemmas might require violence too did not occur solely to Mississippians, but as that violence converged with the response to the threat of John Murrell's clan it portended the utter dissolution of the state and helped provoke an effort to save white Mississippians from themselves. One imagines that would have been small consolation to Mary Donovan and her children.

A Slave Plantation.   Page 94.

Woodcut from abolitionist George Bourne's *Picture of Slavery in the United States of America* (1834) depicting a coffle of African Americans being driven from Virginia to the southwestern frontier, where most would serve as slaves in the region's cotton fields. (Courtesy Library of Congress, Rare Book and Special Collections Division)

PORTRAIT OF MUREL.

Taken in the Tennessee State Prison at Nashville

Frontispiece from an early edition of Virgil Stewart's *A History of the Detection, Conviction, Life and Designs of John A. Murel, the Great Western Land Pirate* purporting to depict John Murrell as he appeared in prison in 1835. (Courtesy American Antiquarian Society)

MUREL AND STEWART, AT THE ROAD SIDE.

Illustration from *The Western Land Pirate* depicting John Murrell and Virgil Stewart pausing to get warm by the roadside on a frigid winter night in western Tennessee en route to Arkansas. (Courtesy American Antiquarian Society)

MUREL ENTICING AWAY CLITTO.

Illustration from *The Western Land Pirate* depicting John Murrell convincing an enslaved man to run away and allow himself to be "stolen." (Courtesy American Antiquarian Society)

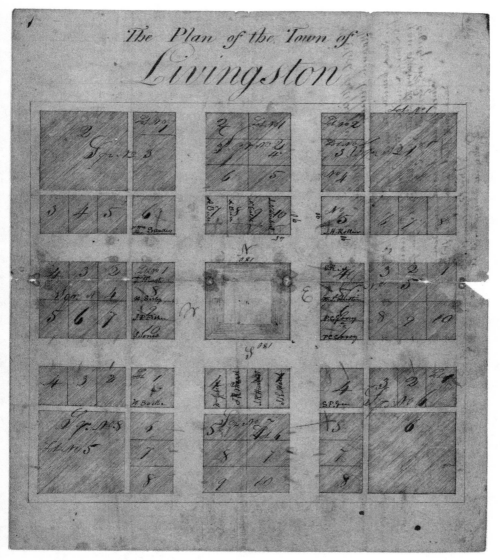

Livingston, Mississippi, in 1836. Founded in the late 1820s, Livingston was the seat of Madison County and the meeting place for the primary committee of safety created to investigate rumors of slave insurrection in the summer of 1835. (Courtesy Mississippi Department of Archives and History)

Senator Henry S. Foote in 1849 (daguerreotype by Matthew Brady). Foote provided detailed eyewitness accounts of the violence perpetrated in west-central Mississippi during the summer of 1835. (Courtesy Beinecke Rare Book and Manuscript Library, Yale University)

Advertisement for botanical medicines necessary for administering the curative regimen devised by Samuel Thomson. Largely consisting of purgatives and emetics to be taken in conjunction with a series of steam baths and designed to eliminate impurities from the body, Thomsonianism was an extraordinarily popular though controversial form of alternative medicine in the antebellum era. (Courtesy U.S. National Library of Medicine)

MEYER, THOMSON & CO.

WHOLESALE & RETAIL
THOMSONIAN
BOTANIC MEDICINE STORE.

The subscribers have the largest and most valuable collection of

BOTANIC MEDICINES

in the United States, comprising all the compounds and crude articles recommended by Dr. Samuel Thomson, part of which is as follows:

African Cayenne	Lobelia,—do. Seed
Balmony	Nerve Ointment
Barberry	Nerve Powder
Butter Nut Syrup	Pond Lily
Cancer Plaster	Poplar Bark. coarse and fine
Clivers	Prickly Ash
Composition	Raspberry Leaves
Conserve of Hollyhock	Slippery Elm
Cough Powder	Woman's Friend or Females'
Ginger	Bitters
Golden Seal	Unicorn Root
Gum Myrrh	Wake Robin. &c. &c. &c.

Notice.

AT a meeting of the citizens of Vicksburg on Saturday the 4th day of July, it was

Resolved, That a notice be given to all *professional* GAMBLERS, that the citizens of Vicksburg are resolved to exclude them from this place and its vicinity, and that *twenty-four hours* notice be given them to leave the place.

Resolved, That all persons permitting Faro dealing in their houses, be also notified, that they will be prosecuted therefor.

Resolved, That one hundred copies of the foregoing resolutions be printed and stuck up at the corners of the streets, and the publication be deemed notice.

Vicksburg, July 5, 1835.

Broadside posted at intersections throughout Vicksburg on July 5, 1835. The next morning, a crowd led by the local militia unit walked the city's streets destroying gambling equipment and hunting for supposed gamblers. Armed resistance to the mob at one house prompted an assault on the building and the execution of five men without trial. (Courtesy Mississippi Department of Archives and History)

IN MEMORY
OF
DR. HUGH
S. BODLEY
Killed in the fight to
rid Vicksburg of
vicious gamblers
JULY 6. 1835

Governor Hiram Runnels, 1833. The subject of intense criticism for his inaction during the insurrection scare that swept Mississippi during the summer of 1835, Runnels was defeated in his bid for reelection that fall. (Courtesy Mississippi Department of Archives and History)

Facing page: Memorial to Dr. Hugh Bodley. This obelisk, which still stands in the city of Vicksburg, was erected in the aftermath of the gambling riot. Part of the mob that carried out the riot, Bodley, according to the inscription at the obelisk's base, was "murdered by the gamblers . . . while defending the morals of Vicksburg." (Courtesy of the author)

Facing page, inset: View of the base of the Bodley memorial depicting a woman weeping and standing next to a tree whose crown has fractured, symbolizing the felt loss to the community of a young physician of Bodley's promise. In truth, the memorial helped create Bodley's legacy as much as commemorate it. (Courtesy of the author)

"*Our Peculiar Domestic Institutions.*"

Illustration published in the *Anti-Slavery Almanac for 1840*. The drawing demonstrates how abolitionists folded the gambling riot, insurrection scare, and general violence prevalent in Mississippi during the summer of 1835 into their larger attacks on slavery and the South. (Courtesy Library of Congress, Rare Book and Special Collections Division)

"On either side of me were ten men, dressed like Monks, in black gowns, each face concealed under a black mask. Above each head, on a rough shelf which ran entirely around the cave, to my horror I beheld a row of human skulls! their whitened faces, sightless sockets, and bare teeth grinning in the sickly light with a ghastly horrible effect.'—P. 17.

One of several illustrations in *The Female Land Pirate; or Awful, Mysterious, and Horrible Disclosures of Amanda Bannoris*. Purporting to be the story of a woman married and accomplice to one of John Murrell's clansmen, *The Female Land Pirate* was typical of the more sensational and macabre efforts many authors made in the nineteenth century to capitalize on fascination with Murrell and the tales of his criminality. (Courtesy American Antiquarian Society)

Poster advertising *Natchez Trace*, a 1960 film that, like many iterations of the John Murrell story in popular culture by the middle of the twentieth century, attempted to fit Murrell within the rubric of the western genre. (Courtesy of the author)

PART THREE

~~~~~~

Speculators and Gamblers

~ ~

CHAPTER FIVE

Purging a City

The Fourth of July began peacefully enough in Vicksburg. White residents of the city, located on the Mississippi River around fifty miles southwest of Livingston, had received word the previous day about the insurrection fears convulsing Madison County, and they had been urged to be alert. But they were not going to let anything spoil their commemoration of the nation's founding, which they planned to celebrate much as cities elsewhere in the United States did in 1835. In conjunction with a muster of the local militia unit known as the Vicksburg Volunteers, participants in the organized public festivities gathered just outside the city for a barbecue to be followed by speeches, a reading of the Declaration of Independence, and a series of patriotic toasts extolling the virtues of the nation and recalling the glories and heroes of the Revolution. The Volunteers would then conclude the day's events in Vicksburg's public square with a parade and a display of military maneuvers.[1]

For a while the program proceeded smoothly. William Benton and John Chilton lauded the bravery and sacrifice of the colonists who rebelled against English tyranny while reminding their audience that Americans needed to remain virtuous and deserving of the legacy bequeathed by their patriotic ancestors. Lawyers well suited to their oratorical tasks, Benton had been born in Connecticut and Chilton in Virginia, but both swelled with nationalistic pride as they vaunted what Chilton referred to as "Freedom's natal day." So rousing, in fact, were Chilton's remarks that the buzz and cheering among the crowd drowned out the toasts that began in their aftermath, prompting a militia officer to call for order and quiet so they might be heard.[2]

Francis Cabler was not inclined to accede to that request. Arrested a year earlier for disorderly conduct after he and several other men brandished knives and sword canes while verbally abusing some steamboat passengers, Cabler had a reputation in Vicksburg as a ruffian and a professional gambler. Probably drunk and apparently feeling that the occasion of the day's events entitled him to an especially vigorous interpretation of individual liberty, Cabler took umbrage at being silenced, insulted the militia officer, began breaking dishes, and struck another man who stepped forward to help quell the disturbance. A sketchy character at best, Cabler had never been entirely welcome at the barbecue and was tolerated only so long as he behaved himself. His refusal to do that incensed some of the other celebrants, and only the interference of the commander of the Vicksburg Volunteers and the threat of a sound thrashing convinced Cabler to leave.[3]

Cabler stumbled away from the scene, but he was determined to have his revenge. As the militia paraded in front of the county courthouse later in the afternoon, word began to spread that Cabler had armed himself and was vowing to kill one of the men who had expelled him from the gathering earlier in the day. Cabler never found that man, but he did find the limits of the assembly's indulgence. Several of the Volunteers took him into custody and found in his possession a pistol, a dagger, and a large knife. Certain that releasing him would only postpone Cabler's quest for vengeance and equally certain that no court would convict him for a crime he had not yet committed, Vicksburgers considered suitable punishments for Cabler. They settled on lynching.[4]

The term "lynching" had yet to acquire the connotation of deadliness or the common association with white supremacy that it would assume later in the nineteenth century. First appearing in the Revolutionary era, by the 1830s the word simply referred to any incident of extralegal violence seemingly sponsored or sanctioned by a community. No matter what it meant, though, a lynching was plenty rough. Guards marched Cabler to some nearby woods where "a crowd of respectable citizens" watched as he was tied to a tree, whipped, tarred and feathered, and ordered to get out of town within forty-eight hours.[5]

As night fell the residents of Vicksburg held a meeting at the courthouse. Sure that professional gamblers were malicious hoodlums who watched out for one another and that the entire lot had likely been provoked by Francis Cabler's treatment, the meeting's attendees determined that rather than wait for retaliation they would take the offensive and rid their city of men like Cabler once and for all. They resolved to give professional gamblers twenty-four hours to evacuate Vicksburg and to notify all those dealing in the popular game of faro that they would be prosecuted for doing so. They ordered one hundred copies of the warnings to be printed and posted at intersections throughout the city and then adjourned.[6]

Exactly what happened next would become a matter of significant controversy. It is indisputable that in their efforts to eliminate what they considered a scourge the residents of Vicksburg instead saddled themselves and their city with a reputation for bloodthirstiness that would take decades to live down. But that may have been undeserved. Though what transpired in Vicksburg was undeniably drastic and uniquely grim, underpinning those events were apprehensions and ambivalence about the economic energies unleashed by the flush times that could be seen beyond Vicksburg and beyond the Southwest. They were shared across the United States.

I.

For his part, William Mills saw explaining and defending what happened to Vicksburg's professional gamblers as his job and his responsibility, but he also embraced the undertaking. Thirty-five years old and a native of South Carolina, Mills had moved to Vicksburg in the late 1820s and had done well for himself there. A lawyer by training, Mills had become the first editor of the city's newspaper, the *Register*, on its establishment in 1830. He bought a valuable city lot, acquired eighteen slaves, and in the spring of 1835 had wed Virginia-born Minerva Elliott. Increasingly prosperous, proud of himself, and looking toward starting a family, Mills believed in Vicksburg, had a lot riding on the city's success, and held an occupational position that gave him one of its most prominent public voices.[7]

Many would have agreed that Vicksburg merited Mills's devotion, for in the 1830s it appeared to be a brilliant example of how white Americans saw themselves extending civilization to the wilderness and creating opportunities for thousands of southwestern settlers in the process. Vicksburg was first established in 1819 on cotton fields that had been part of the plantation of Newit Vick, but long before a town ever existed there observers commented that the land seemed like a good place for one. Situated several hundred feet atop a bluff amidst a ridge known as the Walnut Hills, Vicksburg overlooked the Mississippi River from a spot just below its confluence with the Yazoo. It was extraordinarily scenic, and many even thought it romantic. It was also well protected from flooding and an ideal location for a commercial river port. Travelers heading north past Vicksburg would not see high ground on the east bank of the Mississippi again for hundreds of miles.[8]

The timing of Vicksburg's founding proved fortuitous. As Native Americans were expelled from the northern half of Mississippi over the course of the next decade or so, much of the cotton grown on the farms and plantations rapidly springing up in the state's interior as a consequence found its way to the thriving city. Named the seat of Warren County in 1825, by the middle of the 1830s Vicksburg was the retail center for products desired by farmers and planters in the surrounding countryside, and more than forty thousand bales of cotton came to its docks annually, enabling it to rival Natchez as the premier commercial hub in the state.[9]

A branch of the Planters' Bank of Mississippi opened in Vicksburg in 1832, and a second bank opened in 1834. A railroad company had been chartered to build a line connecting the city to the interior of the state, and the population had grown from practically nothing to more than two thousand people. So small in 1822 that a traveler passing the Walnut Hills by flatboat could not even see it from the river, Vicksburg less than fifteen years later bustled with dozens of mercantile firms, cotton warehouses, law offices, and other businesses. Migrants packed its streets and wharves, horses drew carts laden with goods from docked vessels in a constant stream, and hotels were so crowded that guests had to draw chalk marks on the floors to designate their sleeping spaces. "The noise of the saw and the hammer" erecting new buildings filled the air, and a correspondent for one Mississippi newspaper reported that "mechanics who are steady, temperate and industrious, accumulate money very fast, and in a few years you will either find them at the head of a large mercantile house, or the owner of a plantation with from 50 to 100 negroes." Author Joseph Holt Ingraham may not have been far off the mark when he wrote in 1835 that there was "no town in the south-west more flourishing than Vicksburg."[10]

According to William Mills, however, the presence of professional gamblers in Vicksburg was extraordinarily troublesome. The city might be burgeoning economically, but as Mills saw it, professional gamblers so severely compromised virtue, honor, and the rule of law that public decency, moral integrity, and proper order could be achieved only by expunging them from Vicksburg altogether. He regarded the problem as one that well predated the lynching of Francis Cabler, and he argued in a lengthy article for the *Register* that what happened on the Fourth of July and in the days that followed had to be seen against the backdrop of the city's recent history to be understood.

Portraying a constant battle between upstanding "citizens" and a vicious band of "desperadoes," Mills wrote that professional gamblers had been gathering in Vicksburg "for years past," making the city a base for their "vile and lawless machinations." Selfish and motivated entirely by greed, gamblers were formidable enemies to what Mills referred to as "society." As he did with the word "citizen," Mills repeatedly used "society" as a conceptual foil for the noxious environment gamblers supposedly created wherever they traveled. In just a few lines Mills claimed that professional gamblers "poisoned the springs of morality, and interrupted the relations of society," that they were "unconnected with society by any of its ordinary ties," and that they hatched nefarious schemes "in the very bosom of our society." To Mills, the "citizens" of Vicksburg "society" were quiet, industrious, orderly, and law-abiding. They felt responsible for nurturing the character of future generations and contributed to a convivial public sphere where everyone might feel secure. Professional gamblers, by contrast, were loud, drunken, unprincipled, and criminal. They defrauded and corrupted the young and made the streets unsafe and unsavory. "Citizens" of Vicksburg saw their fellow residents as friends and neighbors. Gamblers saw them as prey.[11]

Making matters worse was that more gamblers flocked to Vicksburg all the time and there seemed to be little anyone could do to stop them. There were laws against gambling and other sorts of objectionable and disruptive behavior, of course, but Mills argued that no matter how strict the laws or how severe the punishment for breaking them, nothing had been proven "sufficient to correct a vice which must be established by positive proof, and cannot, like others, be shown from circumstantial testimony." For all their wickedness, gamblers were also clever and careful "to violate the law in such a manner as to evade its punishment." Even when brought to trial, Mills wrote, gamblers found people to lie on their behalf, "secret confederates to swear them out of their difficulties, whose oaths cannot be impeached for any specific cause."[12]

Mills thus accused professional gamblers simultaneously of being driven entirely by individual self-interest and also of bearing such strong allegiances to one another that none of them could be prosecuted successfully for their crimes. If Mills was conscious of such an apparent contradiction he never betrayed it. Overall, gamblers as he described them were redoubtable foes. United in defense of their own cravenness, professional gamblers stood as a threat to any class of persons but themselves, a collection of villains so powerful in their collaboration and so evil in their intent that they were ultimately "the secret or open authors of all the disturbances and crimes that distract the community."[13]

Situated in such a context, the outrage with which the residents of Vicksburg responded to Francis Cabler's unruliness on Independence Day was not only understandable, it was long overdue. Moreover, if the antipathy William Mills evinced for gamblers even remotely represented how others in Vicksburg felt about them, it is no wonder that over the course of the twenty-four hours following the posting of the warning notices on the morning of Sunday, July 5, most of them fled the city, "terrified," in Mills's telling, "by the threats of the citizens." Perhaps they were not so tough as Mills made them out to be. But only the passing of the deadline established at the courthouse meeting would truly test the resolve of both the citizens of Vicksburg and their treacherous opponents.[14]

On the morning of July 6 the Vicksburg Volunteers convened again to finish the job of cleansing the city that they had begun two days earlier. Followed by a throng that Mills claimed numbered several hundred people, militia members began marching through the streets, sending into homes representatives who tossed out faro tables and any other gambling apparatus they discovered on the premises. The real target of the soldiers against fortune, however, was a house owned by a man named North, where "it was understood that a garrison of armed men" had barricaded themselves, defying the warning to evacuate the city. The crowd surrounded the house, and Mills wrote that everyone gathered hoped that the men inside would surrender rather than mount "a desperate defence."[15]

But impatience and anger overwhelmed restraint. Someone kicked down the back door of the house, and the men inside opened fire. Situated in the open doorway was a "citizen universally beloved and respected," a physician named Hugh Bodley, who took the brunt of the volley. Hit flush, probably with a load of buckshot, he was killed instantly. Members of the mob, guided by the muzzle flashes of the weapons used by those defending North's house, returned fire into the dark building and severely wounded one man, who cried out in pain. Despite being led by a militia unit, a firefight was not exactly what the Vicksburg assailants had in mind, especially after seeing the impact of gunshots on Hugh Bodley. Sensing that the cry of the wounded man gave them an opening, the crowd rushed the house and overwhelmed the "garrison" of four men inside.[16]

North, the owner of the house, was not one of the four. But he was believed to be "the ringleader" who had foolishly "contrived this desperate plot" to resist the militia, and the members of the mob were not about to let him disappear. When he was apprehended nearby while attempting to make his escape from Vicksburg, his fate was sealed along with those of the men extracted from his house. All five were conducted "in silence" to a nearby gallows and hanged. Mills claimed that no one present objected, as any "sympathy for the wretches was completely merged in detestation and horror of their crime." The faro tables and other gambling equipment the mob had confiscated were piled and burned after the executions, and the bodies of the five executed men were left on the gallows until the following day, when they were cut down and buried without ceremony in a ditch.[17]

Concluding his description of the riot, William Mills explained that the citizens of Vicksburg really had no choice but to behave as they did. Charitable impulses had no claim on people as brutalized as they had been, and for them to tolerate professional gamblers in their city even after the actions of Francis Cabler and the death of Hugh Bodley would have proved them not only "destitute of every manly sentiment, but would also have implicated us in the guilt of accessories" to the gamblers' crimes. Perhaps weaker men susceptible to "sickly sensibility and mawkish philanthropy" would have followed a different path to ridding Vicksburg of gamblers, but Mills was certain there was only one way. "Society," he wrote, "may be compared to the elements, which, although 'order is their first law,' can sometimes be purified only by a storm."[18]

Moreover, Mills claimed that every decent person in Vicksburg agreed. "The Revolution," as he called it, was a collective project "conducted here by the most respectable citizens, heads of families, members of all classes, professions, and pursuits. None have been heard to utter a syllable of censure against either the act or the manner in which it was performed." In case anyone doubted that the effort of "exterminating" the "deep-rooted vice" of gambling was a truly democratic project sanctioned by "society," Mills noted that an antigambling society had been founded in Vicksburg, the members of which, in a manner and language appropriate for declaring liberation from the bane of their city, "pledged their lives, fortunes, and sacred honors, for the suppression of gambling, and the punishment and expulsion of gamblers."[19]

II.

Though offering no apologies for what the residents of Vicksburg had done, William Mills anticipated criticism. There was some defensiveness to the tone of his report, and he asserted plainly his understanding that a mob hanging five men without trial would surely receive "censure from those who had not an opportunity of knowing and feeling the dire necessity out of which it originated." He was right. Newspaper editors across the United States wrote blistering condemnations of Vicksburg and the people who lived there, with headlines describing the hangings as a "tragedy" and an "outrage," as "murders" and "butchery."[20]

Running through the commentary was the notion that Vicksburgers had crossed a fundamental line into barbarism. In Baltimore, an editor asserted that "the annals of no civilized nation are blotted with a darker stain than that which is fixed upon this country by the late doings at Vicksburg." A Raleigh editor wrote that events in Vicksburg "must be denounced by every reflecting man as one of the most wantonly cruel outrages ever perpetrated in a civilized community." A commentator in Hartford thundered that the "horrid transactions" in the city had "scarce a parallel in the most barbarous ages and amongst the most savage people." A writer for a national religious journal insisted that contrary to their pretenses of rectitude, those responsible for the executions in Vicksburg were in fact moral inferiors to those they executed, and that it was "a most awful burlesque upon all truth and decorum to call such men any thing else but banditti of the most ferocious turpitude." In an age of highly partisan journalism when almost no important issue or event saw complete agreement among the nation's editors, it was remarkable that the editor of the *New York Evening Post* could observe without exaggeration that "the Vicksburgh outrage is commented upon in terms of suitable indignation and reprobation in almost every mail paper which we open."[21]

In part, most of the nation's editors found the Vicksburg riot troubling because they argued the United States was supposed to be a country governed by laws. They insisted that gamblers—no matter how much William

Mills tried depicting them otherwise—were citizens entitled to the protection of those laws, that the occupants of North's house had acted in self-defense when they killed Hugh Bodley, and that even if they were guilty of murdering Bodley in cold blood, executing Americans without even the pretense of a trial was itself a serious and dangerous crime. As the editor of the *New Orleans True American* wrote, when it came to gamblers, the "unpopularity (and where it is the case) the illegality of their profession, furnishes no warrant to Tom, Dick and Harry to deprive them of liberty or life at their pleasure—they are as much as any other citizens, entitled to the privileges secured by the Constitution, to the protection of the laws of the land and the right when illegally assailed, to a practical resort to the first principle of nature—*self defence.*"[22]

The editor of the *Hartford Times* was still more forceful. "Are persons to be butchered like wild beasts," he asked, "because they are guilty of vicious propensities and immoral practices? If so, wretched indeed is our country. The laws must be supreme, or we are a ruined people. It is wicked to attempt glossing over the Mississippi murders. They are a reproach to our country, a disgrace on the American name." That Vicksburg had embarrassed the entire United States in the eyes of the world was a common sentiment in the aftermath of the riot. For a young nation that saw its global responsibility to be demonstrating the possibilities of republican government and democratic institutions, this was no small matter. The hanging of the Vicksburg gamblers was infuriating not merely because, as the editor of the *Baltimore Gazette* asserted, it was "a detestable mockery of justice," but also because it seemed to call into question America's very character and viability as a free country whose people could govern themselves without collapsing into anarchy.[23]

One editor felt forced by events at Vicksburg to make the "melancholy confession" that "our laws are too ineffectual to protect us, without the commission of illegal violence and murder," a humiliating admission he felt "must degrade us in the eyes of Europe." Another maintained that the hangings indicated the failure of Americans to "appreciate universally the responsibilities which rest upon them," as "the cause of liberty and free institutions, not merely in our own land, but throughout the world, is deeply wounded, by every instance of lawless outrage." Still another found himself nearly in despair and wondering what "the nations of Europe [must] think of us and of our country?—of us who boast that our land is the home of the free and the asylum of the oppressed. . . . Can we longer boast that ours is the land of liberty? No, rather must we say; and we do it with shame, 'tis a land of anarchy and licentiousness, where liberty and law are trampled in the dust, and the arm of the civil authority is paralyzed and nerveless."[24]

Though it is tempting to conclude that such rhetoric inflated the importance of the riot and the American national experiment alike, events in Vicksburg did in fact become fodder for skeptics of democracy abroad, especially in England. A Virginia newspaper, for example, noted that the "Vicksburg Affair is eagerly seized by the Tory Press and Tory Orators of England as an unfavorable illustration of the effect of Republican institutions, and of their tendency to degenerate into licentiousness." Many papers published excerpts of a speech delivered in the fall of 1835 by Sir Robert Peel, a former prime minister and the leading Tory in England, who scoffed at American democracy and at "the vaunted happiness of the inhabitants of the United States." Having read in American newspapers about recent outbreaks of mob violence, Peel pointed particularly to the hanging of gamblers in Vicksburg and suggested to his audience that if they "only bear in mind what has been the issue of similar experiments," they would "not very much indulge in a popular Government."[25]

Few Americans concurred with Peel that the Vicksburg riot actually signified the shortcomings of democracy itself. Yet William Mills's attempt to defend what had taken place in his city did fall decidedly flat. James Burns Wallace, a New Hampshire native visiting the Southwest early in 1836, accurately predicted in his diary that the "rash & bloody transactions" that had occurred in Vicksburg the previous summer would "long be remembered." But instead of making Vicksburg a place Americans thought of as peaceful, safe, and filled with upright citizens, the hangings of professional gamblers gave the city's very name an association with danger and menace that it would not quickly shed. Within weeks of the hangings, newspapers were referring to extralegal punishments as being "on the Vicksburg plan," "in the Vicksburg fashion," or simply as "*Vicksburg* law," and for years afterward, foreign and domestic travelers to the Southwest who stopped in Vicksburg mentioned the notoriety the mob assault had given the city. Until the Civil War siege brought a different kind of fame and a different kind of misery to Vicksburg, Americans outside the Southwest considered it, as Virginia lawyer James Davidson did in 1836, "the famous Vicksburg of Lynching memory."[26]

III.

Editorial condemnation of the hangings in Vicksburg was not just a matter of principle or public relations, however. Part of the problem with William Mills's version of events was that it did not seem particularly believable. Mills assured readers that he had witnessed the acts his story described and that they could rely on "the correctness of the account." But several editors were so skeptical that they essentially accused him of fabricating an extended lie to disguise the depravity of the people in Vicksburg. Thomas Ritchie, editor of the *Richmond Enquirer*, suggested that Mills had put the best face possible on "the horrors" of the hangings but that his story did "not carry conviction with it." Hezekiah Niles, whose *Niles' Weekly Register* had a national readership and one of the largest circulations in the United States, was even more openly incredulous. Mills's story might "be considered an 'official' account of the hanging of five gamblers at Vicksburg," Niles wrote, but it was of a "specious character."[27]

It is easy to see why some observers had doubts. William Mills's story of the violence in Vicksburg was reprinted in dozens if not hundreds of newspapers all over the country. But that was only his version, and the story was not solely his to tell. The same roads, rivers, canals, and rail lines that carried his report in the *Vicksburg Register* through the increasingly interconnected information networks of the United States moved competing narratives of the hangings as well. One element of Mills's account was assuredly true—many people had seen what happened in Vicksburg during and after the Fourth of July celebration in 1835. But as some of those people described what they witnessed, it was clear that not everyone saw what Mills claimed to have seen. Instead of a display of bravery and valor, they had seen something ghastly.

A few of the other eyewitness accounts differed from Mills's version mostly in supplementary details, leaving the substance of his story basically intact. The *Natchez Courier*, for example, which got its information "from individuals, who left Vicksburg since this affair took place," reported that North's house doubled as an establishment known as the Vicksburg Coffee House, that the men hanged alongside North included two barkeepers and two "others (gamblers)," and that the gallows on which all five were hanged was situated in some nearby woods. "Several gentlemen" who arrived in Little Rock by steamboat told the *Arkansas Gazette* that the militia and the attendant mob paraded to North's property with musical accompaniment, that Hugh Bodley was shot through the heart, that more than four men had barricaded themselves inside North's house but most escaped as the mob rushed the building, and that the gallows was roughly one mile from the city.[28]

Even small details like these hint at how William Mills carefully constructed his story to place the actions of his neighbors in the best possible light. Failing to mention the name of North's business denied him and it legitimacy that Mills obviously decided neither deserved. Making a point, meanwhile, as Mills did, of claiming that the accused gamblers had been conducted silently to the gallows created a mental image for readers of deliberation and solemnity. Such an image sat jarringly alongside the more sinister frivolity he neglected to note of a musical procession by hundreds of men to a house where they intended, at the very least, to beat the occupants into submission and make them into social pariahs with a coating of liquefied tar.

If these seemingly minor items hinted to careful readers that the riot in Vicksburg had a darker side than William Mills allowed, the account of it that appeared in the *New Orleans Louisiana Advertiser* made the darkness visible. Other than Mills's report, no extensive version of the story was published in more newspapers than that of the *Advertiser*, and the picture its author painted was not a pretty one. Claiming to have received its information from "two gentlemen" who had just arrived in New Orleans from Vicksburg, where they had been "eye witnesses to most of the transactions" they described, the *Advertiser* immediately struck a different tone than Mills had in the *Register*. Vicksburg was indeed a place in turmoil. But where Mills presented it as a city plagued for years with disorder caused by professional gamblers, the witnesses for the *Advertiser* described it as a "hitherto tranquil place" that the rioters themselves had so disturbed that "almost all the women have left it, to avoid any future commotion."[29]

The *Advertiser* and the *Register* agreed that the proximate stimulus for what happened was a dispute between Francis Cabler and a militia officer at a Fourth of July celebration. But other than in the broadest of strokes, that was where the two parted ways. The *Advertiser* noted that Independence Day festivities were often boisterous occasions where arguments and fights were common. It was thus unfortunate but hardly unusual when

Cabler and a militia member named Alexander Fisher began quarreling and exchanging blows, or even when Cabler pulled a knife. What was unusual was the way the other members of the Vicksburg Volunteers responded to Cabler's assault on "their comrade." They grabbed Cabler, tied him to a tree, and "inflicted thirty two lashes on his person." Then, "not considering this sufficient" and "alleging that he was a gambler," they decided to tar and feather him, even as "he entreated them to shoot him rather than disgrace him in that manner." As they prepared to pour a bucket of tar over his head, Cabler begged that they at least keep the tar from falling into his eyes, a plea that was met "violently with a stick across the eyes" instead. When the militia had finished, they ordered Cabler to get out of Vicksburg.[30]

The next day, according to the *Advertiser*, "in order to appear consistent, and continue their work of civilization (as they called it)," thirty to forty men under the command of militia captain George Brungard armed themselves and marched through the city determined to destroy "every thing appertaining to gambling" and warning that they would tar and feather anyone who tried to stop them. As the mob made its way from house to house, several terrified men sought sanctuary in North's establishment. They found none. Hugh Bodley, the *Advertiser* wrote, kicked down one of the building's doors, and shots were exchanged, resulting in Bodley's death and in critical injuries to one of the men inside the house. The mob promptly dragged the man outside, bleeding and unconscious, along with three others. They tracked down the fleeing North about a mile away and brought him back to Vicksburg, where he and the three captured men who could still walk were bound with their hands behind their backs. Ropes were placed around their necks and used to drag all four to a scaffold.[31]

As the *Advertiser* described the scene, North and his compatriots "claimed to the last the privilege of AMERICAN CITIZENS." They asserted their right to a jury trial and professed their willingness to submit to any legal punishment that might result. The mob would have none of it, instead ordering a company of black musicians to drown out the prisoners' voices with music. The cashier of the Planters' Bank, a man named Robert Riddle, asked the band to play "Yankee Doodle," perhaps feeling that the song added a bit of patriotic and holiday-appropriate levity to the spectacle. The *Advertiser* did not see the charm of it, writing that the tune had "never been so prostituted." Finally, after the prisoners had been denied even their repeated requests for water, North realized their cause was hopeless. He asked a friend to look after his family, and he and the three other captives mounted the scaffold and waited to die.[32]

In the *Advertiser*'s telling, this entire series of events did not go unchallenged. Few people had stood up to the mob as it went about its business looking for gambling equipment to destroy, and even those who wanted to protect their personal property quailed "when they saw the state of excitement of the volunteers." But destroying faro tables was a far cry from executing people without any legal proceeding, and not everyone in Vicksburg had the stomach for the latter. As the prisoners were hauled to the gallows, the *Advertiser* wrote, they "presented such a horrible appearance, that the passers by were moved even to tears" and "some of them endeavored to interfere, but were threatened with a similar punishment, and obliged to desist." Some local magistrates tried to step in as well, but they too "were cautioned at their peril not to intermeddle in the affair."[33]

In the end, North and three other men stood on a platform, noosed and unhooded. Hugh Bodley's brother-in-law, a lawyer named William Henry Hurst, cut the rope that held up the platform under the men's feet, and all four dropped and swung by their necks until they died. The fifth prisoner never regained consciousness. Covered in blood, he was driven to the scaffold in a wagon, carried up the stairs, noosed, and thrown into open space alongside the four dead men. The *Advertiser* wrote that the wife of one of the five victims tearfully "begged permission to inter her husband's body." She was refused, and the executioners warned that anyone attempting to lower the bodies before a twenty-four-hour period had expired would be hanged too. The next morning at eleven the corpses "were cut down and thrown together into a hole which had been dug near the gallows."[34]

The accounts of William Mills and the *Louisiana Advertiser* described the same events in entirely different terms. One described hundreds of upstanding men in Vicksburg acting with moral righteousness and the official sanction of a militia to eliminate dangerous criminals lacking a sense of civic responsibility or basic human decency. The other described a significantly smaller gang of sadistic thugs, driven by rage, hijacking what should have been an impartial protective force to enact personal retribution on people who had friends and families. One described a community united for the common purpose of locating and removing sources of disorder in its

midst and unwavering in its determination to take the harshest steps necessary in pursuit of that goal. The other described a city population divided
about the wisdom of a lynch mob and dissenters bullied into submission
and silent witness. One described justice. The other described vengeance.

Eyewitness reports that departed from the narrative he had crafted irritated William Mills, and he did what he could to undermine their credibility. Soon after publishing his initial story in the *Register*, Mills insisted
that other papers allow their readers to hear his voice, asserting that "in
consequence of the gross mis-statements made by some newspapers, of the
occurrences which took place in this city on the 6th inst., it is the earnest
request of the citizens, that all papers having made any remarks concerning them, will do them the justice to publish the account of the transaction
from the Vicksburg Register ... which is a correct and impartial statement." He deemed the *Louisiana Advertiser*'s story especially pernicious and
lashed out, calling that paper's reports "so distorted and detestable,—so
different from the truth—that we can account for them only by supposing
that a blackleg, who was liar enough to be scouted by his own associates,
was at the elbow of the Editor prompting him when he wrote his accounts,
or the editor was very gullible, and gave ear to a great many idle tales."[35]

William Mills's vexation with stories that suggested the tendentious-
ness of the one he told is somewhat understandable, as a few supposed
eyewitness accounts that circulated in the national press may well have
been falsehoods. One man who said he had been in Vicksburg claimed
that an unnamed gambler had been lynched on the night of July 5, before
the evacuation deadline established at the courthouse meeting had expired.
Another reported that after hanging North and the men in his house, the
crowd in Vicksburg whipped and then mutilated for their own amusement
a sixth man by "sticking pins through his nose and ears." Perhaps Mills was
even right that the "gentlemen" eyewitnesses who appeared in the offices
of the *Louisiana Advertiser* were gamblers fortunate enough to escape the
wrath of the mob. If they told "idle tales," though, they were not alone.
Several accounts of the riot that were never intended for publication also
indicate that Mills's story was a decidedly partial one.[36]

George Featherstonhaugh, a British geologist who traveled extensively
in the Southwest, read Mills's account of the Vicksburg riot in the *Register*
but also spoke to someone who had seen the hangings and who recounted
for him a gallows procession that "baffled all description." Featherston-

haugh's witness saw not Mills's silent crowd but rather the *Advertiser*'s "tumultuous mob, showing a savage impatience to hurry on the execution." Led "by a drunken black fiddler," North and the other men were "reluctantly dragged to the fatal tree" as those watching screamed curses at them. Some of the doomed, the man told Featherstonhaugh, were "dogged and malignant to the last," but at least one "was thoroughly terror-stricken." Until the moment he hanged, "he wept, he implored, he cried aloud for mercy, and evinced the most abject despair."[37]

The Reverend Richard Wynkoop, meanwhile, sent a letter from Vicksburg to a clerical colleague in Maryland in which he wrote that the men pulled from the site of Hugh Bodley's shooting were not even gamblers but rather "poor drunken creatures that happened to be in the house, the real culprits having escaped." The mob, more interested in revenge than accuracy, rushed them all to the gallows anyway. Wynkoop wrote that the assembled hesitated briefly before the platform dropped from the feet of the accused as a dark cloud crossed the sky, and an awkward silence fell over the crowd while they listened to the condemned pray for mercy. The moment was a fleeting one. Someone, in a "deep horrible tone of suppressed rage," roared curses at the noosed men, and in the next instant there were "five human beings in the last agonies of death."[38]

Unlike Featherstonhaugh's witness or those who provided information to the *Advertiser*, Wynkoop described a Vicksburg population that felt at least a modicum of shame. Once the men on the gallows had stopped pleading for a jury trial, begging for their lives, and praying, some in the crowd understood the magnitude of what they had done. "All the mad, blind fury that a moment before agitated their breasts had now subsided and conscience seemed to strike them as it were dumb at the horrible act they had just now perpetrated," Wynkoop wrote. "They turned from the scene guilty in the sight of God, in the sight of men, and their own consciences."[39]

IV.

William Mills could peevishly brush aside descriptions of the riot in Vicksburg that made its residents look impulsive, vindictive, and irrationally violent as lies told by gamblers who continued to cause problems even after they had been chased from the city's borders. Richard Wynkoop's letter, however, might simply have baffled him. Mills knew what had happened in Vicksburg was "startling" and he had expected reproach, but the idea that professional gamblers deserved any sort of quarter or compassion was bewildering, and the vehemence with which the nation's newspapers castigated Vicksburg mystified him. Mills scoured the national press for editorials supporting what had happened in Vicksburg. Yet he found just a smattering that backed his assertions that gamblers were a menace beyond the reach of ordinary legal proceedings who could be disposed of only through extralegal force that communities could rightfully exercise in extenuating circumstances.[40]

There was a Kentucky newspaper that cheered the hangings, describing professional gamblers as men for whom "the law had lost all its terrors" and who "were already steeped in infamy so deep that human execrations could not move them." By this editor's reckoning, "death, instant and terrible, was inflicted, *and should have been inflicted*, upon the assassins," and the residents of Vicksburg had merely shown "prompt and salutary energy" that ensured "the safety of the whole community." That so few other editors shared those sentiments, however, genuinely surprised Mills.[41]

For one thing, mob actions were not unusual in the United States. If anything, they were on the upswing in the 1830s, as economic strains, racial and ethnic tensions, and political divisions yielded increasingly frequent outbursts of violence throughout the nation as the decade wore on. Newspaper editors rarely approved of such things, and Hezekiah Niles spoke for many when he wrote that the "spirit of riot or a disposition to 'take the law in their own hands,' prevail[ing] in every quarter" indicated that "many of the people of the United States are 'out of joint.'" But the notion that events in Vicksburg singularly brought disrepute on the entire country seemed hyperbolic and unwarranted. This was especially so considering that instigators of mob violence in many parts of the country were often led, as in Vicksburg, by people presenting themselves as moral guardians of their communities.[42]

Equally confusing about the emphatic reproof of Vicksburg was that, particularly among the emerging American middle class of which many editors considered themselves members, gambling was widely condemned as an exceptionally dangerous vice. Strewn through periodicals, published sermons, tracts, advice books, and other prescriptive literature in the United States were cautionary tales of promising young men persuaded against their better instincts to gamble with friends or play the lottery. What followed was seemingly inevitable—dissipation, loss of reputation, financial ruin, familial destruction, physical decline, crime, imprisonment, and death, not infrequently by suicide. As one author concluded, "in the whole catalogue of unfortunate and criminal habits, there is no one which results so soon and so completely in loss of character, squandering of property and depravement of principle, as indulgence in gambling."[43]

Part of the problem with gambling lay in its impiety. To evangelical Christians, gambling was sinful, immoral, and condemned its practitioners to damnation. It encouraged avarice, covetousness, and the unearned enrichment of self at the expense of one's neighbors, and it often occurred in environments where drunkenness reigned, blasphemy was a source of amusement, and ruthless disregard for others was a virtue. There was a reason Americans commonly referred to gambling houses as "hells."[44]

Yet gambling was hardly problematic just as a matter of irreligion. Above all else, gambling promoted economic activity and morality out of keeping with how middle-class Americans believed success ought to be pursued. Those fashioning themselves "respectable" placed premiums on mores and behavior that reflected frugality, temperance, probity, industriousness, and self-discipline. They argued there were no shortcuts to wealth and success, and that the only reliable path up the ladder of economic mobility was slow and steady gain from honest and productive labor. But gambling, one commentator lamented, "produce[d] a contempt for the moderate, but certain profits of sober industry." It yielded financial rashness, encouraged a craving for money so insatiable that fraud could be sanctioned in its pursuit, and undermined a decent work ethic. It fostered the notion that something could be had for nothing, that riches could be gained instantly through sheer luck, and that fortunes could be augmented merely by willingness to take a chance. The consequences of gambling for individuals and the nation alike could only be devastating, because its "direct tendency is to undermine the foundations of the public prosperity and happiness."[45]

Given how profound the damage Americans saw potentially inflicted by gambling, it followed that men who gambled for a living were almost universally regarded to be among the most detestable creatures to walk the earth. Few characters were more widely feared and loathed than the professional gambler, who, in the words of one critic, would play cards "upon his brother's coffin" or "his father's sepulchre." Stock villains for editors, ministers, and advice writers, professional gamblers were confidence men who schemed to tempt the virtuous and left them corrupted and destitute. Stereotypically disguising themselves as refined gentlemen and targeting naive and inexperienced young people, professional gamblers befriended their victims, gained their trust, and assured them they could make easy money, their deceptions working all too well as the callow dupes were plundered by gamblers' cheating confederates and eventually became drunken wretches unfit for decent society.[46]

Selfish, indifferent to the fates of others, and socially poisonous, gamblers were deceitful men who would destroy America's future by destroying its youth, and mothers and fathers had to be vigilant. "Every parent who has the good of his offspring at heart," wrote a columnist for a ladies' magazine, "should not hesitate to expose the vipers, nor let the consideration that 'he is a gentleman,' have any weight in restraining him from withdrawing his children from the society and influence of such men." William Mills and other residents of Vicksburg, however, were not alone in thinking that leaving matters in the hands of parents might be insufficient for dealing with such revolting characters. As a Massachusetts author argued nearly a year before the Vicksburg riot, professional gamblers were "enemies to the state," and "if they will not submit to the laws, if they will do nothing for the common good—let them have no benefit from the laws, nor from the institutions of society."[47]

Critiques of gambling and gamblers could be found most readily in the Northeast, where urbanization was taking place at an especially accelerated pace, and where young people alone in cities for the first time seemed particularly vulnerable and in need of protection from duplicitous strangers. But antigambling diatribes could be found even in parts of the country rarely thought congenial to the causes of reformers or to their periodicals. One fulmination that was disseminated widely in the Southwest in the months before the riot in Vicksburg and that helps point toward an explanation for its outbreak was Charles Caldwell's "Address on the Vice of Gambling." Born in North Carolina in 1772, Caldwell trained as a physician in Philadelphia under Benjamin Rush before accepting a faculty position in 1819 at the medical college of Transylvania University in Lexington, Kentucky. Speaking to students there in November 1834, he warned that gambling was "a practice, which is, in fact, a revolting incorporation of almost every description of vice and profligacy."[48]

Caldwell was a notoriously cantankerous man who managed to alienate colleagues everywhere he went, and if the scathing tone and uncompromising content of his address on gambling give any sense of his personality, it is not hard to fathom why. Caldwell blasted gambling of every conceivable kind as an unparalleled evil. Whether it was a family playing card games at home or a man wagering his last penny in the most abandoned gambling den, "any game of hazard, *on which things of value are staked*" amounted to "an attempt made by one person, to deprive another of his property or possessions, against his consent, and *without the return of an equivalent*," and was thus essentially criminal. Caldwell had no patience for those who maintained that gambling could serve as an innocent source of entertainment or that those who gambled mutually agreed to venture money they knew they might lose. These were merely pitiful excuses for "a pursuit congenial only to the degraded and the vulgar" that "steeps the soul in the dregs of corruption and panders to its worst habits of turpitude and profligacy."[49]

Caldwell concurred with most critics that gambling wasted time, encouraged bad habits, led inexorably to despair and bankruptcy, and produced a range of other unwanted consequences both for individuals who gambled and for society as a whole. He condemned parents who exposed their offspring to supposedly harmless friendly betting as practically abusing their children and setting them on the road to ruin, and elites who gambled as debasing themselves and providing "terrible examples of vice and mischief" for "thousands of inferior beings" who looked to them as models of how to behave. But even these criticisms, to Caldwell's way of thinking, missed the "real viciousness and crime" of gambling, which was that it depended on trying to take someone else's property without exchanging anything of value and thus intrinsically entailed fraud. "Each gambler," he insisted, "is endeavouring to rifle the pockets of his companions" no less than if he were attempting larceny at gunpoint. Gambling, in Caldwell's framework, was therefore not only "closely allied to theft, pocket-picking, and robbery." It was "as indefensible, as murder." Indeed, given the prevalence of gambling, "it surpasses murder greatly, in the extent of the misery it produces, and the amount of moral corruption it diffuses through society."[50]

Caldwell thought it disgusting that some who gambled retained an estimable reputation and could be "welcomed into fashionable society" because they "assume the *mask* of some other calling, *by day*, and consort with the *Black-leg* and the ruffian, *by night*." But he reserved special vitriol for those blacklegs, the professional gamblers, warning his student audience that some were probably among them right now, "waiting 'in grim repose,' ready to pounce on you, and make you their prey" like "the tiger crouching in the jungle, eager to glut himself with the blood of the unwary." Caldwell urged his listeners never to trust anyone who proposed a mere "*social* game of cards." Such a man might be "an artful profligate" and a "traitor" who would betray "with the *insidious smile* and prostitute courtesy of *proffered hospitality*." He should be shunned as one would "the breath of pestilence," for "his eye is on your purse, and he will beggar it if he can."[51]

Charles Caldwell's only immediate goal was to encourage the medical students of Transylvania University to form an antigambling society and commit to joining it, which more than 120 of them did immediately following his address. He issued no call for the kind of violence that would erupt in Vicksburg eight months later and did not even demand as a matter of public policy that gambling houses be shut down. It was rather Caldwell's drawing of an absolute and unambiguous line between iniquitous gambling, on the one hand, and morally salutary economic activities, on the other, that exposed why gambling was so unsettling that a community might sanction the public murder of those believed to be making their living doing it.[52]

V.

There was nothing new in the 1830s about the fact that Americans liked to gamble, nor that opportunities to place bets, play cards, and roll dice could be found nearly everywhere from Boston and New York down to Natchez and New Orleans. If anything, critics of gambling argued that one sign of its malignancy was people's apparent inability to stop doing it. Over and over again, moralists noted that gambling tapped into something dark and uncontrollable in the human soul that, once accessed, could not be curbed by reason.

To one, gambling was "a fatal whirlpool, and those who are once drawn within its vortex, but seldom escape." Another argued that "gaming corrupts the best principles in the world: like a quicksand, it swallows up a man in a moment." A third encouraged anyone who saw a loved one "approaching this vortex [of gambling], to rush to him—and plead with him—and if necessary, throw their bodies across his path; for if not arrested, his body and his goods may escape—but his soul will die." Even

Charles Caldwell, who professed that those given a good education and raised with sound morals would never indulge in gambling, conceded that regardless of background no one ought to try betting, for it created a compulsion that could not be contained and led to "a form of positive and permanent *monomania.*"[53]

Concerns about what in modern parlance would be classified as gambling's addictive quality reached new heights as the nineteenth century progressed because gambling's popularity and its appeal to the passions indicated that Americans could not control themselves or their desire for gain at the very moment when the developing forces of capitalism made such control increasingly imperative. As Americans undermined traditional social structures and cultural norms while they jostled to accumulate wealth in a competitive market economy, distinguishing morally between socially constructive moneymaking and socially destructive gambling was a vital means of defining the boundary between legitimate and illegitimate kinds of economic striving. Yet making that distinction often seemed hopeless. The line so clear to Charles Caldwell was in fact blurred at best and nonexistent at worst.[54]

Never was that ambiguity plainer than in the flush times, whose economic contours facilitated becoming rich through speculation that looked as if it demanded no productive labor at all. It was alarming that millions of Americans thrilled to games of chance that distilled the calculations of risk and reward, luck and skill, and profit and loss central to many economic pursuits in a speculative age. Worse still was that they rushed to participate in supposedly legitimate economic activities that appeared little different from gambling. As the *Philadelphia National Gazette* noted in the spring of 1835, thousands of Americans who never would have considered themselves gamblers or approved of gambling nonetheless willingly engaged in behavior just as dangerous and reckless as playing poker with a professional gambler. "Speculation in stocks and real property," the editor of the *Gazette* observed, "is more general and extravagant than it has been before for many years, in all our principal cities. . . . Multitudes are now prominent and desperate dealers in the stock and other speculation markets, of all classes and ages, callings and positions in life, that formerly were never seen nor expected and themselves never thought of action, in such scenes. Small tradesmen, shopkeepers, clerks of all degrees, operatives of town and country, members of the learned professions, students in the offices, beginners in the world without capital or with a little, all frequent the exchanges and the auction grounds to try their fortunes as with the lotteries."[55]

The editor of the *Gazette* worried deeply about this trend, arguing that "this diffusive excitement . . . is unfavorable to productive industry, to steady habits and sure aims, and to morals which are always more or less in danger when hazard whets cupidity, governs actions, and determines fate in a general whirl of spirits and thoughts." But if Americans in northeastern industrializing cities such as Philadelphia wondered whether individual quests for fortune unloosed in the flush times would lead to untrammeled greed, foolhardiness, and financial devastation, those anxieties were even more fraught in the Southwest. And they came to a head in Vicksburg.[56]

The presence of slavery obviously set Vicksburg socially and economically apart from a place like Philadelphia, and it was true that residents of the city believed that professional gamblers forged alliances with one another, committed a variety of crimes, and frequented tippling houses where slaves could buy alcohol and trade in stolen goods, all of which made them seem not unlike members of the mystic clan of John Murrell and thus subjects of special scrutiny in the summer of 1835. With Vicksburg having a substantial slave population in its own right and its prosperity depending on cotton, Francis Cabler's disruption of Independence Day festivities while rumors floated about an impending insurrection nearby revealed him to be both impressively obnoxious and in possession of exquisitely bad timing.[57]

But when William Mills tried to explain what had happened to Cabler and his colleagues, he never made the case that professional gamblers were dangerous because of the threat they posed to slavery. By the time he published his account of the gambling riot in the *Register*, in fact, he had known about the insurrection scare blowing up just fifty miles from his office for nearly a week yet he said nothing about it. Such was the case because what happened in the city in the summer of 1835 was bigger than even the prospect of that fearsome and economically cataclysmic event.

Taking another, closer look at exactly what Vicksburg was and what it was not reveals that it exhibited the culture of American capitalism in the flush times in its most concentrated form, and that the convergence of the city's local social and economic circumstances served to magnify and sharpen much broader concerns in the United States about order and morality. In July 1835, Vicksburg's rioters were not just hanging professional gamblers, and William Mills was not just telling a story when he reported about it. They were all enforcing a version of Charles Caldwell's imaginary line and, in the process, inventing a respectable place for themselves in Jacksonian America.

~ ~

CHAPTER SIX

Defining a Citizen

Even as it grew commercially successful and became integrated into the national and international economies, Vicksburg remained a rootless and unformed place. Plenty of people were drawn to Vicksburg, but few were inclined to remain for very long. In the 1830s nobody was actually "from" Vicksburg. Rather, visitors and more permanent residents alike noted that it was a city filled with "strangers," itinerants from a wide variety of places who lacked strong ties to each other or to any given community. As a new arrival to Vicksburg put it in 1836, the city attracted "men from every corner of the world" but there was "hardly one native of the place." Until the Civil War, in fact, Vicksburg's population was relatively impermanent, with a minority in any given year still present ten years later. From boatmen and businessmen to doctors and lawyers to vagabonds and ne'er-do-wells, Vicksburg was a place people tended to pass through rather than stay.[1]

The city's physical and institutional development reflected the transience of its population. British social reformer and author Harriet Martineau, who made a brief stop in Vicksburg during a steamboat voyage in 1835, described it as a "raw-looking, straggling place," which it was. Vicksburg's streets were unpaved, and many were "full of dirt and rubbish." Because the city was built on a series of steep hills, deep gullies and ravines formed during hard rains and were filled in only "very badly." Vicksburg had a much-admired brick courthouse, but practically all of the town's hastily constructed commercial buildings were wooden and unpainted, and accommodations for travelers were filthy. Residents had formed a temperance association and a colonization society in the early 1830s, but the city had no regular school and just two churches, though the building housing the Presbyterian church was in disrepair and neither it nor its Methodist counterpart had a permanent minister. Instead, men who practiced law during the week often served as lay preachers on Sundays.[2]

If any one thing bound together people living in Vicksburg in 1835, it was their insatiable desire to become wealthy. Commerce never stopped in Vicksburg. "The Sabbath," Virginia lawyer and land agent William Gray noted, was "but little observed." Rev. Richard Wynkoop agreed. Sundays, Wynkoop wrote, were rather "more like a holliday than a day of prayer. The stores are open, and business is carried on the same as if there was no sabbath." Such sacrilege was inevitable, as steamboats traveled on Sundays and arrived at the wharves ready to be loaded and unloaded regardless of whether that seemed the Christian thing to do. Not that many Vicksburgers were overly concerned about the impact of their business practices on the state of their souls. Nearly everyone agreed that trying to talk to most people in Vicksburg about salvation or anything else was a waste of time unless it was "connected with making DOLLARS and CENTS." Gray summed up the state of affairs neatly. "This is a busy place," he wrote in his diary. "All appear to be intent on making money."[3]

Money was why people came to Vicksburg in the flush times, and with good reason. Whether a person was buying and selling land, growing or brokering cotton, dealing in slaves, tending the sick, working at a mercantile firm, or facilitating the endless number of legal transactions and lawsuits, opportunities to become wealthy seemed boundless in Vicksburg, as they did throughout the Southwest. Different people had different plans for getting rich, but the road was less important than the destination. The place was packed with men whom lawyer James Davidson described as "gentlemen adventurers who have dreamed golden dreams."[4]

Among those "gentlemen adventurers" were professional gamblers. They were drawn to the Southwest by the same sorts of profiteering impulses as other migrants, and the decision made in July 1835 by the residents of Vicksburg not to countenance their presence had little to do with hostility to gambling in and of itself. On the contrary, not only were Vicksburgers particularly, and southwestern migrants generally, enthusiastic gamblers, but in a very real sense gambling for a living was precisely how people in Vicksburg survived in the flush times. Having flocked to a town that had not even existed twenty years earlier in pursuit of quick profits that booms in land, cotton, and slaves made unimaginable almost anywhere else in the country, William Mills and his fellow "citizens" sought their fortunes in ways any professional gambler would have recognized. They searched for the optimal chance, sized up their prospects, wagered on the future, and occasionally lied, cheated, or stole if it improved the odds.

But Mills, those who rioted against gamblers, and those who supported them preferred not to think of themselves that way. Though they lived in a city that was nearly bereft of well-established institutions and communal networks that composed "society" as the term was conventionally defined, they seized upon the fracas with Francis Cabler at the Independence Day barbecue as an opportunity to imagine community, impose order, and affirm what they maintained were widely shared standards and mores. Not everyone was pleased that matters turned deadly, but there was no looking back. Contrary to all appearances and even their own doubts, the people of Vicksburg maintained they were not unscrupulous speculators and grasping adventurers jockeying on a wild frontier but worthy Americans living upstanding lives in a wholesome and substantive place.

I.

By all accounts, professional gamblers were ubiquitous in the Southwest. Working sometimes alone but often in small teams, they tended to be as itinerant as other whites in the region, moving from place to place along the rivers and in the interior, running faro banks, playing card games like brag and poker, and spinning roulette wheels. A few larger cities such as New Orleans housed permanent and elaborately outfitted and furnished gambling establishments, but professional gamblers plied their trade just about anywhere they could find people with money. They played on steamboats and at hotels, in taverns and at vacation resorts, alongside racetracks, and at public land sales and revival meetings. In every river city and town the interested could find alcohol and gambling tables at businesses clustered along the waterfront, where vice districts such as the Swamp in New Orleans, the Pinchgut in Memphis, and Under-the-Hill in Natchez became so famous that tourists made them standard parts of their itineraries. Even in the smallest villages, though, everyone knew they could gamble at nondescript and innocuously named "coffee houses" or "groceries." Advertised outside with signs offering baked goods and produce for sale, inside proprietors served the liquor and designated the upstairs rooms and back tables for gambling that earned their establishments the colloquial nicknames of "doggeries," "tippling shops," and "devil's churches."[5]

No matter where they worked, professional gamblers seem never to have starved for lack of customers. A preponderance of southwestern migrants came from older parts of seaboard southern states, and southern men were notably willing to bet on almost anything. The risk taking, boasting, winning, and losing inherent in wagering allowed men to express sociability while also subtly maneuvering for rank, thus confirming cama- raderie and hierarchy in ways that resonated with a masculinist code of southern honor. Yet even by southern standards, southwestern men were renowned for gambling, their appetites legendary across the class spec- trum and among all professions and occupations. In his chronicle of the flush times, Joseph Baldwin was likely being facetious when he claimed to have seen a little boy give an adult ten dollars just to lift him high enough to place a bet at a faro table. But Baldwin was probably serious when he claimed to know a judge who repeatedly canceled court so he could offici- ate at horse races, and he was certainly both serious and right that every southwestern hamlet had at least half a dozen "groceries" that were "all busy all the time."[6]

Gambling's popularity and prevalence in the Southwest were owed only partly to the pedigree of its residents. The region's entire economic envi- ronment required a gambler's sensibility. It offered the prospect of making a fast fortune out of nothing but entailed a disposition to borrow money, take the risk that one could make large profits on paper, and then cash out into something tangible and valuable before the bubble burst or the loans got called in. More than a vehicle for substantiating and reaffirming honor's class-bound pecking order, gambling in the Southwest enabled presump- tively equal men to distinguish themselves individually for daring, wealth, and social prowess among unfamiliar male rivals. What people preferred to gamble at was as instructive as the mere fact of their gambling, and while the elite sport of thoroughbred racing supremely popular among white southerners in the East had more than its share of southwestern adherents, it was faro that really captured the attention and the spirit of southwestern- ers in the flush times.[7]

Probably originating in France and owing its name to the image of an Egyptian ruler that frequently appeared on the backs of French playing cards, faro was the most widely played game of chance in the United States for much of the nineteenth century. It was relatively straightforward in its fundamentals. Players placed money or tokens on a table spread with a cloth known as a "layout" that was illustrated with images of thirteen cards denominated from ace through king, betting on which card the dealer would draw from a shuffled deck. In each round, or "turn," of a faro game, the dealer drew two cards off the top of the deck, which was usually kept in a specially designed spring-loaded box. The first card was the banker's card, and the person or establishment furnishing money for the game won all bets placed on it that turn. The second card, the player's card, paid to anyone who had bet that card the amount he had wagered on it. Turns continued until the deck was spent, at which point the cards were reshuffled and play began again.[8]

Although faro's appeal both predated and outlasted the flush times, the value of the game as a metaphor for that particular economic moment helps explain the fervor with which southwestern migrants played it. Faro was fast paced and easy to play. Any number of people could play it simultaneously, and a player could venture stakes that were relatively small, stunningly large, or anywhere in between. It was a distinctly commercial game designed solely for winning and losing money, and while faro did offer plentiful opportunities for deceptions that helped give professional gamblers who ran it their reputation as "sharpers," the odds in a fair game were nearly as good for players as they were for the bank. To be sure, the contents of one's pocket could disappear quickly. But players were drawn to the table because they believed that figuring the percentages could enable them just as quickly to break the bank. Democratic, exciting, nakedly materialistic, and doling out in an instant the highs of victory to some and the lows of defeat to others, faro condensed the siren call of the flush times in each turn of the cards.[9]

If the Southwest was thus both literally and figuratively filled with gamblers, Vicksburg exemplified the tendency. Its residents were not just profit oriented. In the words of one diarist, they were "run mad with speculation" and did business in "a kind of phrenzy." And Vicksburgers absolutely loved to gamble. Writing in his memoir, former professional gambler John O'Connor remembered that sales of cotton lands in Vicksburg's vicinity made the city "the central point of speculation in the Southwest" in the 1830s. Flooded with money and filled with "adventurous spirits of every description," Vicksburg was also a prime location for professional gamblers. O'Connor claimed that they ran at least fifty faro banks there, "nearly all of which did a thriving business, in spite of the abuse heaped upon their owners by the press of the city." Similarly, Jonathan H. Green, the "reformed gambler" who became famous in the 1840s and 1850s as an antigambling crusader, wrote in one of his many books that in the early 1830s Vicksburg "was distinguished above most places, even at the south, for bad morals. It might be called an emporium of vice." By Green's reckoning, during the flush times "as many as three-fourths of all the citizens of Vicksburg, were more or less addicted to gambling."[10]

Both O'Connor and Green penned their recollections years after the gambling riot had given Vicksburg a reputation for having been a hotbed of gamblers, but contemporary sources confirm the flavor of their observations. H. S. Fulkerson, who migrated from Kentucky to Mississippi in the 1830s, claimed that the "better class" of people in Vicksburg "loathed and condemned" gambling. But he conceded that gambling dens could be found "on every business thoroughfare of the city, conducted openly by day and night, and all day of Sundays," and that gambling was "encouraged by some of the most prominent people" in Vicksburg. Richard Wynkoop, meanwhile, wrote about a man accused of a crime who claimed as an alibi not only that he had been playing cards at the time the crime was committed, but that he had been doing so with the judge presiding in his case. More specifically, Wynkoop wrote that the accused gamblers hanged in the summer of 1835 "were encouraged by a great many of the citizens, and they actually associated with them in their vile practices."[11]

Several newspaper editors who commented on the riot suspected as much. One noted that gamblers "did not trouble virtuous, moral citizens. They obtained no money from men who did not gamble with them; and probably their murderers were, in that very particular, the greatest criminals." Another took Vicksburgers to task for the "laxity of morals" that must have pervaded their city and "permitted an accumulation of vice to such a dangerous mass." Still others reported that the rioters formed a committee whose job it was to divide money they found inside North's house among members of the mob who had lost it while gambling there themselves. The rumor was so widespread that William Mills felt compelled to refute it in the *Register*.[12]

One of the more comical accounts of how gambling in Vicksburg obliterated expected moral and class boundaries comes from traveling Briton George Featherstonhaugh. Boarding a steamboat in Arkansas en route to New Orleans in December 1834, Featherstonhaugh was repulsed by the company with whom he shared passage. On his first night aboard the vessel, a wealthy, drunk, and belligerent young man threatened him with a knife before staggering away, vomiting all over his own clothing, and collapsing in someone else's berth. The next morning a party of ten "notorious swindlers and gamblers" embarked. Armed to a man with pistols and long knives, they drank, swore, spit, smoked, fought, and gambled all day and all night long, stopping only periodically to eat and sleep. Irritated and disgusted, Featherstonhaugh looked for relief to those he believed might share his sentiment, to no avail. Two military officers whom Featherston-haugh hoped would be "on the side of decency at least, if not of correct manners" proved instead to be "familiar intimates" of the men, drinking and gambling with them, and the ship's captain refused to enforce the posted rules calling for the ejection of anyone annoying other passengers. He told Featherstonhaugh that the men's behavior was "the customs and manners of the country, and that if he pretended to enforce the rules he should never get another passenger."[13]

When the steamboat reached Vicksburg several days later, Featherston-haugh was tempted to get off and try his luck, so to speak, on a differ-ent vessel. He decided to stay, however, when "informed that eight or ten *gentlemen*, some of whom were planters of great respectability," would be joining them, including a member of the Vick family for whom the city was named. Certain that there would now be a sufficiency of moral and mannered men to counterbalance "the ruffians in the cabin" and that the captain "would now interfere to keep some order" lest he lose their fu-ture business, Featherstonhaugh thought his troubles were over. He was wrong. After the last meal of the day was served, the gamblers set up their faro bank, and to Featherstonhaugh's "horror and astonishment," the men who boarded at Vicksburg sat down to play, "gambling, drinking, smok-ing, and blaspheming, just as desperately as the worst of them." When the steamboat stopped in Natchez, it emptied enough for Featherstonhaugh and a companion to take refuge in the ladies' cabin, which they never left except for brief meals until they arrived in New Orleans. But the shocked and bewildered Featherstonhaugh never forgot the "specimens of *gentle-men* belonging to the State of Mississippi."[14]

II.

It is perhaps counterintuitive that Vicksburgers lived in a city prospering on a collective gamble and filled with men who relished their time at the card tables and yet also loathed professional gamblers enough to kill them.

Someone, after all, had to provide the faro banks, which few Americans ran for personal recreation. But whatever Vicksburg was, it fell far short of what at least some of its residents liked to believe it was or insisted it would become. The gambling riot became part of an ongoing process by which rioters and their supporters tried wrenching into being a sense of place where there was none and an economically virtuous community where individual self-interest was ascendant if not triumphant. They wanted to see Vicksburg as a city of stability, industry, and sobriety, and it was good for business and their sense of their own moral standing to attest their dedication to honest economic progress and strong communal ties. Where many looked at Vicksburg and saw only speculative fantasies, they declared there was something real.

The violence of the gambling riot did not come out of nowhere, despite William Mills's assertion that it was "startling." What happened in the summer of 1835 grew in part from tensions that had been escalating for some time in Vicksburg. Gambling prosecutions had been on the rise in Warren County for several years, increasing from just one between 1817 and 1822 to nearly thirty during the 1830s, and numerous individuals had been charged in the early 1830s with crimes of faro dealing and keeping a "disorderly house." Ten men were charged with faro dealing and almost twenty others with "keeping a tippling house" just during the November 1834 term of the Warren County Circuit Court, suggesting that county authorities had been making a concerted effort to crack down on gambling and gamblers for months before the riot broke out.[15]

Yet some of those charges had already been dismissed by July 1835, and nearly all the rest remained outstanding. When Mills complained that gamblers habitually thwarted attempts to prosecute them using regular legal proceedings, he may have had a point. Among the charges dropped since November was one against Francis Cabler for faro dealing, and for him of all people to act so brazenly during the Fourth of July celebration a few months later must have seemed especially galling. The decision to lynch him likely reflected the unique provocation his behavior presented to individuals who knew him just well enough to neither like nor trust him. The subsequent decision to warn professional gamblers out of Vicksburg altogether bore out the broader anger and frustration that had been brewing in the city, and the hangings represented a spontaneous explosion of that anger and frustration into murderous rage in response to Hugh Bodley's death.[16]

But if those who supported evicting gamblers from Vicksburg did not premeditate hanging them, they nonetheless saw immense value in defending what they had done. In the weeks and months after the executions, they folded the specifics of local events into an evolving narrative with expansive cultural meaning and implications, using what had happened to Vicksburg's gamblers to project a description of themselves as hardworking people trying to make a decent place for their families rather than a bunch of transient opportunists out for a quick buck. It seems clear that William Mills disguised the uglier aspects of the gambling riot and covered up any opposition to it. But he was not wrong about the kinds of people involved in the riot or the wider backing their actions had.

The names of everyone in the mob that carried out the riot and the executions cannot be known. But ten men can be identified with reasonable certainty, having been named in newspaper articles as active participants or as members of the Vicksburg Volunteers. The eight of those ten to whom it is possible to attach significant information shared similar profiles. All had lived in Vicksburg less than ten years, and most had lived there less than five. None was especially wealthy and only a few owned slaves, but seven were on career paths that often led to wealth and status. There were three merchants, including the militia captain, Pennsylvania native George Brungard; two physicians; one lawyer; and one hotelkeeper. Befitting their commercial and professional orientations, and in keeping with the political leanings of many other whites in western and southwestern Mississippi whose counties most benefited from and depended on the market production of cotton, five were active in the Whig Party. In short, they were aspirants to the emerging southern middle class whose members, like their northern counterparts, sought mantles of moral and cultural authority in their cities and towns.[17]

Examining the public response in Vicksburg in the aftermath of the riot and the hangings reveals that members of the nascent professional and commercial classes also played a central role in explaining and justifying what had happened there, contrasting professional gamblers with the kinds of people they imagined themselves to be and touting the executions as a sign that they were dedicated to protecting the peace and morals of their city. As the editor of Vicksburg's only newspaper, William Mills saw his role to be telling the rioters' story to the nation and offering an account of the violence that made it seem rational, just, and something to which all estimable people rallied. But more than anyone else, Hugh Bodley made possible a transformation of the hangings into a source of respectability.

In death Bodley became a martyr, and his body was barely cold before Vicksburgers began appropriating him to forge a public memory of the riot. On the night of July 6, with five dead men still suspended from the nearby gallows, a group of "citizens" gathered at a hotel. William Benton, who was not only a lawyer chosen to speak at the Fourth of July barbecue days earlier but also Vicksburg's postmaster and its former mayor, chaired the meeting. Richard Lyons, a merchant, served as secretary. Attendees passed a resolution expressing sympathy to Bodley's family and proposed building a monument "in commemoration of the virtues of the deceased, and particularly of the enthusiastic public spirit in the exercise of which he met his mournful and untimely fate." They resolved that Vicksburgers should wear a badge of mourning for thirty days and that all businesses should be closed the following day so that the entire city could attend Bodley's funeral, which would depart from the home of his friend, Planters' Bank cashier Robert Riddle.[18]

The Bodley memorial, erected several years later, took the form of a marble obelisk atop a trapezoidal base. On one side of the base a woman grieves next to an oak tree with a fractured branch, while another side bears an inscription reading that the monument was "erected by a grateful community to the memory of Dr. Hugh Bodley, murdered by the gamblers, July 5, 1835, while defending the morals of Vicksburg." By the time the monument was built, however, Vicksburgers had long since crafted the story they told themselves about who Hugh Bodley was and why he had died.[19]

The crux of it appeared in his obituary, which described Bodley as a "beloved citizen" and a "universally" admired man of "sterling virtues and amiable deportment" who participated in expelling gamblers from Vicksburg because of an "enthusiastic public spirit which marked all his conduct." Bodley had a "susceptible and generous heart" in which "the claims of duty, friendship and benevolence ever found a ready advocate." That "miscreants" such as professional gamblers had killed him was tragic, but Bodley's death, the obituary writer concluded, would "ever remain a damning testimony against that infamous class of individuals to whose desperate vengeance he fell a sacrifice." His name would "be a watchword to rally the friends of virtue against any one of them who may hereafter dare to obtrude his person within the limits of our city or county."[20]

Hugh Bodley was in many ways the perfect counterpoint to the men at whose hands he met his demise. Professional gamblers supposedly profited from fraud and preyed on human weakness to the detriment of society, but as a physician Bodley had dedicated his life to healing, and he earned a living by helping communities stay whole. Originally from Lexington, Kentucky, the twenty-eight-year-old Bodley was part of a prominent family, and his father, Thomas Bodley, had served as an officer during the War of 1812, a general in the Kentucky militia, and a member of the Kentucky legislature, and was a presidential elector several times over. Hugh Bodley belonged to an American elite that, to those fashioning themselves respectable in Vicksburg, deserved to benefit from America's progress. Gamblers, by contrast, were the dregs of society, ruthless killers who had cut down a young man on the cusp of a brilliant future.[21]

We need not doubt that many people in Vicksburg held Hugh Bodley in high esteem to see that memories of him constructed almost instantaneously on his death served to make the riot and the hangings seem virtuous, and Vicksburg a place where communal roots ran deep. The Hugh Bodley Vicksburgers chose to remember may well have resembled the person he really was. A writer for the *Frankfort Commonwealth* in Bodley's native Kentucky who claimed to have known him since his infancy described him much as his obituary in the *Register* did—as "a young man, in the flower of his days, the idol of the society in which he moved, adorned with all the charms which amiable manners, a cultivated mind, a high and lofty sense of honor and indomitable courage can give." Born to a father known "for his hospitality, for his public spirit, [and] for his pure and ardent patriotism," Hugh Bodley was mourned in Kentucky as having "just entered upon his professional career, with every promise of honor and profit to himself, and usefulness to his community." The death of such an individual surely was exceptionally devastating.[22]

But there is a critical difference between how Hugh Bodley was remembered in Mississippi and how he was remembered in Kentucky. Those who commemorated Bodley's life and death in Vicksburg wrote and spoke of him as if he was a venerable and long-standing friend to all who knew him, when in fact Bodley had been in the city only slightly more than two years. He was unmarried, owned neither land nor slaves, and before settling in Vicksburg had been something of a wanderer, rambling about the Southwest for so long while deciding where to live that his father started worrying about him. His estate comprised just under two hundred dollars in cash, a grocer's tab, and a few outstanding bills for subscriptions to some newspapers and medical journals, all published in Kentucky. Bodley's only real attachment to Vicksburg was that two of his siblings lived there, and his sister had moved there even more recently than he had.[23]

Bodley may have made many friends in Vicksburg in a brief time, but those friends grounded their assessments of his character on a relatively shallow base of experience. Mourned and memorialized by people who had known him for two years as if they had known him since the day he was born, however special Hugh Bodley was in reality, he was also the person those lamenting his loss wished him to be. If he represented a segment of Vicksburg's population at its finest, then by extension his virtues were their virtues, his righteous deeds their righteous deeds, his imagined depth of feeling for the good people of Vicksburg the depth of feeling all good people in Vicksburg had for each other and their city. If a man like Hugh Bodley led a mob in breaking down the door of a gambling house, then any worthy person had to stand behind that mob.

And if professional gamblers were so base as to kill a man like Bodley, then surely they deserved to die with as little mercy as they had shown him. Such, at least, was the opinion of the "large and respectable meeting of the citizens of Warren county" that convened at the courthouse three weeks after the hangings. Its attendees unanimously resolved "that the late expulsion of the Gamblers from Vicksburg, by the citizens, was a measure highly necessary for the well-being of the citizens of the place, and to the welfare of the county, and to communities at large." Moreover, they concluded "that the summary justice inflicted upon the murderers of our late estimable citizen, Doct. Hugh S. Bodley, was justifiable; and that the citizens of the county do, and will sustain the citizens of the town, in that execution of speedy and retributive justice."[24]

However large this meeting was, the status of the thirty-six men whose names appeared in the public report of the gathering is beyond doubt. As the meeting represented Warren County and not just the city of Vicksburg, some of those who attended were inhabitants of the countryside, including more than a dozen men whose wealth and slaveholdings placed them firmly in the planter class and several of whom were residents of about as long standing as any white person could be. Russell Smith, for example, owned more than eighteen hundred acres of land and more than forty slaves, and he had lived in the county since at least the 1810s.[25]

That men like Smith turned out to show support for the rioters in Vicksburg indicates the interdependencies of rural and urban elites on the southwestern frontier. Those in Vicksburg aspired somewhat more to the bourgeois values of city dwellers elsewhere in the United States and those in the countryside somewhat more to the achievement of patriarchal dominance and mastery characteristic of southern planters. But the two groups had overlapping and intertwined economic interests in the development of the cotton kingdom, and both benefited from the elimination of any elements perceived capable of disrupting the smooth production and marketing of cotton, whether they were rebellious slaves, gangs of white bandits, or professional gamblers. Indeed, along with a resolution backing the gambling riot, those gathered at the meeting decided to create a "Committee of Safety and Vigilance" for the county like the one that had been created in Livingston, the job of its members being to arrest and bring to trial "all idle vagrant persons whom they may have good reason to suspect of entertaining or promoting any designs against the peace and safety of the community." Whether purging professional gamblers or hunting for John Murrell's "band of vagrant and unprincipled men," those with the most at stake in Mississippi saw the need to work together and "exercise the utmost vigilance and energy for the preservation of our lives and property."[26]

Most of those at the courthouse meeting were not planters, however. They were men much like the rioters themselves. They were, on average, somewhat better established financially and of somewhat longer residence in Vicksburg or Warren County than the rioters. But few had lived there longer than a decade, and they were occupationally typical of a small antebellum city's prominent classes. Seven were merchants, nine were lawyers (including Warren County sheriff Stephen Howard and Vicksburg mayor Robert McGinty), two were physicians, and one was a minister. Seven were running for office and had recently served as county or state officials, and of the twelve with identifiable political affiliations, ten were Whigs. "Citizens" all, they offered their "hearty approbation" for the measures rioters had taken against gamblers and their "aid hereafter in similar measures, should it be required."[27]

III.

The effort to prove that violence could create respectability in Vicksburg culminated six months after the riot with a ceremony that served as an appropriate if less contested bracket to the Independence Day celebration of the previous summer. On New Year's Day 1836, in front of the Planters' Bank, a group of women known only as "the ladies of Vicksburg" publicly presented the Vicksburg Volunteers with a flag bearing the unit's insignia. Speaking before what the *Register* described as a "very large concourse of ladies and gentlemen," a young woman named Mary Ann Fretwell praised the Volunteers for their "gallantry and courage," singling out their actions of July 1835. With the militiamen still touchy about criticism they had received in the national press, Fretwell noted that the "uncandid and censorious" could have their say but that the ladies of Vicksburg knew the Volunteers' actions were grounded in "noble and virtuous motives" and had inspired "improvement in the moral and social condition of the community."[28]

George Brungard received the flag on behalf of the Volunteers he commanded. Expressing his gratitude, he assured the donors that their gift would motivate the unit's members to fulfill their duties as "citizens and soldiers," particularly since it came from women, whose "approbation ... we find more than a recompense for all the probable toils and perils incident to our station." Like Fretwell, Brungard reflected on the gambling riot. He insisted that the Volunteers had acted as they believed necessary, that the passage of time had only further convinced them of the justice of their actions, and that those actions would be repeated should the "moral pestilence" of gamblers reappear in Vicksburg.[29]

Brungard acknowledged that even "a few of our own citizens" had condemned the riot, a rare concession that opponents of the mob violence could rightly be called "citizens" or that there were opponents in Vicksburg at all. But Brungard maintained that such people were not really part of what he considered the community. Instead of rallying around the rioters, local critics were liars who undid the project of respectability by "adding fuel to the flame, and by misrepresentations exciting citizen against citizen and friend against friend." For Brungard, July 4, 1835, had been a moment when people living in Vicksburg had to decide on which side of a moral line they stood. The rioters and their supporters had chosen virtue and could consequently claim a place among the decent in the city. Critics might still reside in Vicksburg, but they were entitled only to "the contempt of the friends of morality, and the good wishes of those excrescences of all communities, the professional gamblers."[30]

Brungard's rhetorical division of the moral from the immoral in Vicksburg reflected the rioters' demarcation of the boundaries of respectability. Their line was not predicated on a categorical divide quite so rigid as the one Charles Caldwell laid down between gambling and legitimate economic activity, but they saw a related division between different types of gambling and different types of gamblers. Vicksburgers do not seem to have been especially troubled that the prospects of speculative money-making had initially attracted so many of them to the city. But *professional* gamblers were men whose devotion to making money knew no bounds, who cared only for themselves, and who neither produced nor contributed anything useful to the society in which they lived. They came, they fleeced whom they could, and when they stopped making money or went bust, they vanished. Anyone trying to stop them might not live to tell the tale. Professional gamblers were speculators too. But in speculating on the lust for easy winnings, they represented and exploited what many Vicksburgers feared were their worst inclinations to greed without the constraints of social obligation, gain without the imperatives of productive labor, and riches without any substantive economic or moral foundation.

Moreover, they did it with so little sense of propriety. Part of what incited Vicksburgers to riot was that professionals either did not understand or did not care that even as many "citizens" gambled they also viewed gambling as a vice, and that indulgence of that vice was supposed to be contained within a particular space and time. That men gambled was no secret, but where professional and amateur gamblers might mingle promiscuously on steamboats, at racetracks, and in "coffee houses," men who considered gambling a pastime rather than an occupation preferred to leave sordid things behind them when play ended. A witness to events in Vicksburg told the *Richmond Enquirer*, for example, that it was professional gamblers' failure to recognize limits that had driven Vicksburgers from exasperation to rage. "Not content with carrying on their 'dreadful trade,' in the silence of night and apart from public observation," they had begun dealing openly and everywhere around the clock and were thus guilty of "break[ing] down the barriers of society."[31]

So long as gamblers did their business after dark, stayed near the waterfront, and let customers come to them, they were merely a "nuisance" and could "receive the benefit of the laws." Confronting amateur gamblers and their families by daylight, however, brought supposedly worthy community members face-to-face with their own abandon in an especially disconcerting way. People already wondering whether they could be both scrupulous and speculators could tolerate confrontation of this kind for only so long.[32]

Such an understanding of the relationship among time, space, and vice makes Francis Cabler's offense on the Fourth of July all the more clear. Even before he arrived on the scene, the planners of the day's events had intended them implicitly to confirm the uprightness of Vicksburg's "citizens" in particular contradistinction to professional gamblers. As the *Lexington Intelligencer* reported hearing from one witness, Vicksburgers "had determined to discountenance a gang of *black-legs*, that infested their society, and ... made arrangements for peaceably excluding them, by a use of tickets, from the public festivities for the occasion." But Cabler showed up anyway, stood his ground when confronted, and later intruded again into a celebration designed to demonstrate that he and his sort specifically were unwelcome. By the time he fully grasped that Independence Day in Vicksburg was for citizens and not for gamblers, he had become an unanticipated part of the day's revelry.[33]

Attempts at establishing these sorts of divisions did not convince everyone. At his plantation home near Centreville in Amite County southeast of Natchez, William Winans read about what had transpired in Vicksburg and failed to see on what basis the rioters could effectively declare that the city belonged exclusively to them. A Methodist minister, Winans had lived in Mississippi for more than twenty years when he wrote to the Reverend Benjamin Houghton, a colleague then living in Vicksburg, with profound concerns about the supposed moral character of the people among whom Houghton lived. "The gamblers," Winans wrote, "had just as much *right* to order the citizens to leave Vicksburgh, and murder them in case [of] refusal, as the citizens had to give them such orders, and murder them in case of refusal." The riot and executions, as Winans saw them, were "clearly a case of wanton usurpation and tyranny—of lawless power against right."[34]

In his response Houghton tried clarifying for Winans the way those in Vicksburg saw the matter, explaining in the process exactly how the rioters set their collective enterprise on the cotton frontier apart from that of their victims. "Many of them," Houghton conceded, "doubtless do all in the way of gaming, that gamblers themselves do; but at other times, they pursue an honest avocation; and if they are fleeced, it is amongst one another; but they will not again soon suffer those to live and game it here who are dependent wholly on *that business* for support, and have no other visible means of subsistence." The problem with professional gamblers, then, was not that they gambled, or even that they cheated. At least as Houghton understood it, the problem was that professional gamblers did not do anything *but* gamble and cheat. To those considering themselves "honest," speculation so shameless, so unrestrained, and so single-minded was unacceptable. Vicksburg may not have ended up being their home for very long either. They too may have understood the city as a way station where gambling helped pass the time and perhaps make some fast cash while they assessed economic opportunities elsewhere in the Southwest. But as they proved at the gallows, at least they pretended to be "citizens" while they stayed.[35]

Ultimately, it is debatable whether those who purged the men they claimed transgressed the limits of acceptable economic behavior differed fundamentally from the purged, even discounting the rumor that the rioters turned to violence as much to retrieve betting losses as to uphold morality or administer justice. Little information can be gleaned about the four men dragged out of the house by the mob on July 6. William Mills identified them only as "Hullams, Dutch Bill, Smith, and McCall." But it is likely that the house's owner and the fifth hanging victim, a man named Truman North, was a professional gambler. The same can be said of Francis Cabler and of another man named James Hoard, whom Mills described in his reports on the gambling riot as a perpetrator of "shameless profligacy" and as having escaped Vicksburg ahead of the mob's wrath. Both North and Hoard were charged in 1834 with "keeping a tippling house," and Hoard, like Cabler, was charged with faro dealing as well as with "indecency and fornication." Hoard, Cabler, and North were certainly associates, as Hoard both repeatedly posted bond for men, including Cabler, accused of these sorts of crimes, and he owned a building adjacent to North's house at the corner of Washington and Grove Streets, one block from the city landing.[36]

But Truman North, Francis Cabler, and James Hoard were not itinerants who came and went as the financial winds blew. On the contrary, all had lived in Vicksburg longer than Hugh Bodley, and all owned property in the city, investments that provided them—despite William Mills's claim that gamblers were "unconnected with society by any ordinary ties"—with the most ordinary tie of all to an American place. Arguably, property ownership made their stake in Vicksburg and its future more concrete than Bodley's was. Truman North even owned a slave, a twenty-eight-year-old woman named Cherry, and North's eight-year-old son Alfred, who became an orphan on July 6, 1835, had depended on his father more than anyone in Vicksburg had depended on Hugh Bodley. To the rioters, however, what separated Truman North from Hugh Bodley was unambiguous. Through riot, rhetoric, and public ritual, the mob and its supporters made clear that whether or not professional gamblers had families, and no matter how much property they acquired, the way they made their living meant they would never be legitimate members of "society."[37]

IV.

People in Vicksburg were not the only Americans in 1835 who felt that professional gamblers embodied a disreputable speculative impulse that had to be checked lest it produce social decay and economic disorder. In the immediate wake of events in Vicksburg, Americans across the country became terrified that they were about to be inundated with members of the "blackleg gentry." Through the summer and into the fall they turned to legal and extralegal means to evict gamblers from dozens of cities and towns and to ensure that any others considering locating there would think twice and keep moving.

The effect of the Vicksburg riot was especially pronounced in Mississippi. William Mills had called for "all our sister towns throughout the State" to help in "exterminating" gamblers, and many were happy to oblige. East of Vicksburg in Clinton, notices were posted warning that all gamblers found in the town "after 12 o'clock, will be used according to Lynch's Law," adding particularly that "the importations from Vicksburg will look out." Townspeople in Pontotoc and Columbus, northeast of Vicksburg, held meetings, passed resolutions, and formed vigilance committees to expel gamblers by force if necessary. To Vicksburg's southwest, in Washington and Woodville, crowds raided gambling houses and engaged in fistfights as they chased supposed gamblers out of town. In Grand Gulf, nine men accused of being gamblers were beaten and tarred and feathered.[38]

In Natchez, where Vicksburgers had sent a special delegation to ask for assistance "in the expulsion of professional gamblers from the country," people gathered at a public meeting in the courthouse, expressed condolences for the death of Hugh Bodley, and promised their cooperation. Residents soon gave gamblers twenty-four hours to evacuate the city. When the deadline passed, a mob went to the Under-the-Hill district, drove out all those who had refused to leave, and destroyed faro tables and roulette wheels in the streets. In short order the *Columbus Argus* could brag that the example set in Vicksburg was "being carried out by almost every town and hamlet in the State." The *Jackson Banner*, published in the state capital, concurred, asserting that "ever since the memorable movement in Vicksburg against this class of men, the Gamblers have been routed and expelled from almost every city" in the vicinity. By September, anyone suspected of being a professional gambler had nowhere safe to go in Mississippi.[39]

But they had to go somewhere. In the Mississippi and Ohio river valleys particularly and the western United States generally, people became convinced that hordes of exiled professional gamblers were heading their way, and they were determined not to sit by and watch the anticipated influx. In New Orleans and Mobile, in Little Rock and St. Louis, in Memphis and Nashville, in Lexington and Louisville, in Cincinnati and Wheeling, and in innumerable smaller places throughout the region, residents sometimes warned gamblers out with deadlines and promises of lynching, sometimes physically assaulted them and destroyed their equipment, sometimes arrested and jailed them, and sometimes convened public meetings where attendees formed antigambling societies and vowed to help enforce local antigambling and vagrancy laws.[40]

Hezekiah Niles concluded in his *Weekly Register* that "all the river towns are alarmed at the fearful introduction of a 'legion of devils' amongst them," but he missed the larger reality by limiting his observations to those spots only. In truth, it seemed no place was big enough to absorb the swarms of gamblers imagined to be floating western rivers and traipsing western roads, and no place was too small to fear being the next target of gamblers' supposed depredations. If the reaction against gambling did not produce the fatalities elsewhere that it did in Vicksburg, surely that was in part because it began in Vicksburg, giving authorities in other places a chance to act ahead of lynch mobs and giving gamblers fair warning that taking a stand as the men in Truman North's house had done would be ill advised.[41]

The mayor of Cincinnati, for example, made aware that city residents were contemplating "strong and violent measures" against gamblers they believed were headed their way, co-opted the gathering anger before it became uncontrollable. He issued a proclamation assuring the public that he had one hundred citizens ready to aid police in evicting gamblers and knew five hundred more he might call on in an emergency, thus making "a resort to violence, by well intended assemblages of the inhabitants . . . entirely unnecessary." In Natchez, meanwhile, the mob that determined to clear the Under-the-Hill district had to resign itself primarily to demolishing gambling equipment after finding that most of the area's occupants had already "fled upon the reception of the news from Vicksburg."[42]

That the West saw the most marked reaction against gamblers is unsurprising. It is impossible to determine how many Americans made their living as gamblers in the 1830s, but an exceptionally large number of them seem to have been in the Ohio and Mississippi valleys. Drawn by abundant cash among a fluid population of risk takers, by river and steamboat systems facilitating movement, and by the inability and unwillingness of legal authorities to take concerted action against them, gamblers found the region fertile ground for their enterprises. Not without justice has one scholar referred to the antebellum Southwest as "the headquarters for the emergence of the professional gambler."[43]

The Vicksburg riot in particular reflected cultural characteristics that were not only western but southern as well. William Mills sprinkled his reporting on the riot with allusions to how gamblers threatened the honor of other white men in the city, and the use of music and ritual humiliation in chasing gamblers from Vicksburg suggests the charivari that some historians have argued was peculiarly southern. Violence in general seems to have been more prevalent in the Southwest than elsewhere in the United States too, even excluding the violence of slavery that undergirded settlement of the region, the prevailing consequences of which remained all too clear in the Mississippi interior as events in Vicksburg were unfolding.[44]

Travelers reported large numbers of short-tempered young men carrying weapons in every southwestern town they visited, and most concluded that given the ferocity of economic competition, the impotence of criminal law enforcement, and the consumption of voluminous amounts of alcohol, interpersonal violence broke out with less provocation in frontier areas than elsewhere in the country. Henry Foote recalled about the Southwest in the 1830s that between widespread drunkenness and "the deplorable fact that nearly all classes of the population went habitually armed, the number of scenes marked with personal violence . . . [was] really astounding to contemplate." One need only read William Gray's accounts of two very prominent and very drunk lawyers fighting in Vicksburg's muddy streets and of the corpse of a man shot dead on Christmas Day that still lay in one of its thoroughfares the next morning to sense that the city was an extraordinarily and even casually violent place.[45]

Whatever the regional tendencies manifest in the antigambling movement of 1835, however, the movement was national. Efforts and calls to evict or arrest gamblers appeared not just in cities such as New Orleans and Natchez but in urban areas along the Eastern Seaboard as well. In Norfolk, police raided a gambling house and piled and burned the equipment they found there in the public market on orders from the city's mayor. In Richmond, the *Enquirer* reported that "every considerate man hears with indignation the whispers of threats to lynch the Gamblers," and the offices of the *Richmond Whig* were threatened with destruction after its editor refused to publish what he considered "inflammatory papers, inviting the *young men* of the City to assemble to extirpate the *gamblers.*" The chief justice of the City Court of Baltimore received an anonymous communication that hundreds of gamblers were flooding into the city, that the police had been bribed not to arrest them, and that he ought to encourage "any energetic means that may be devised to get rid of the population that is odious to all but the profligate and abandoned." Philadelphians feared that southern gamblers were invading the city, as did New Yorkers, while on Long Island a judge, a sheriff, "a large corps of constables, and a posse of the most respectable of the citizens" attacked more than half a dozen men who belonged to a gang of gamblers that had been drawing off attendees at a revival meeting.[46]

One can empathize with Americans' fear of professional gamblers. Men who made their living that way could be dishonest and dangerous. Even granting the sensationalism, bias, selectivity, exaggeration, and embellishment that compromised the accuracy and objectivity of newspaper accounts, travelers' diaries, and narratives penned by former gamblers, the evidence is overwhelming that professional gamblers marked cards, colluded in confidence games to gull the unsuspecting, resorted to violence and sometimes to murder, and associated with thieves, counterfeiters, and other criminals of varying stripes. By and large, professional gamblers were not the sort most people would ever want to cross.

But worries about professional gamblers in 1835 were well out of proportion to any conceivable reality, betraying an apprehension that crossed the boundaries of reason into absurdity. Americans who lived hundreds of miles from the Southwest dreaded not merely that gamblers were about to swarm into their cities but that gamblers chased specifically from Vicksburg would do so. However credible that concern might have been in New Orleans, where steamboats that had passed through Vicksburg routinely docked, the emergence of seemingly earnest news stories out of Pittsburgh and Philadelphia that exiled Vicksburg gamblers could be spotted by the kind of hat they wore or the watch they carried indicated that the targets of the Vicksburg riot struck an especially sensitive nerve in American culture.[47]

That nerve was fully exposed for anyone to see in the very same newspaper reports that excoriated the residents of Vicksburg for having hanged Truman North and the men in his house. The horror most editors expressed about the hangings in Vicksburg was not disingenuous. But if few of them supported the extralegal violence of the Vicksburg mob, even fewer defended professional gamblers, and the language they used to describe them spoke to concerns and fears similar to those articulated by William Mills and his fellow Vicksburgers. All across America, professional gamblers were not just dangerous criminals. They were "vampyres," "blood-suckers," "vultures," "harpies," "living ulcers," "plague spots," and "blood-gouts": seductive men who alternately fed off and introduced toxic impurities to the healthy energy and vitality of others. They left their victims dead or desperate shells of their former selves, inestimably damaging the larger society. As the *New York Sun* put it, somewhat mixing the corporeal metaphor through which Americans made their revulsion known, gamblers were "bullying blackguards . . . who have long been draining the life blood from the moral walk of the community."[48]

Most specifically, editors everywhere lamented that gamblers ruined enterprising and industrious young men—men like Hugh Bodley. Aspiring to join the ranks of professionals, clerks, and other white-collar occupations, young men drawn to cities by economic opportunity were hungry to make their fortunes, optimistic about their futures, in possession of some cash, and hopelessly naive, making them easy marks for gamblers who would undermine their morals as they took their money. The *Philadelphia Inquirer*, for example, noting that "the recent scenes in Vicksburg have induced hundreds to contemplate" gambling and gamblers, argued that the "merchants and wholesale dealers" in every city on the Atlantic seaboard ought to consider remedies for the problem. Merchants in particular had "young men in their service as clerks, book-keepers, and so forth," and "in nine cases out of ten" it was young men in such occupations who were most "tempted to the gaming table." They were "ardent, unsuspecting, and inexperienced," susceptible to the wiles of professional gamblers who disguised themselves as "gentlemen" and who would in short order unburden the credulous "of every thing worth taking." By forming antigambling societies, breaking up gambling halls, and publishing the names of known gamblers in the newspapers, the *Inquirer* argued, "citizens" could collectively prove that "the public mind was never more alive to the horrors of gambling."[49]

Tellingly, while the editor of the *Inquirer* mustered outrage enough to call for a crackdown on professional gamblers and their havens, he neglected to link that call to the larger economic temptations that many young American men found impossible to resist in the 1830s. The editor of the *Inquirer*, William Mills, and the ministers, advice writers, and others who devoted their energies to condemning gamblers and the gambling that took place in the demoniac "hells" of Jacksonian America found it easy to see a class of malevolent villains and deceivers who connived against the upstanding and virtuous and left them morally and financially bankrupt. It was harder and required more abstract vision to see that gamblers' seductions worked because they offered sudden fortunes for nothing more than a readiness to take a risk on a hand of cards or a spin of the wheel. Professional gamblers may indeed have presented false fronts, plied customers with alcohol, and cheated, but it was the prospect of easy money that pervaded American economic life in the flush times that got young men to sidle up to the faro table.

The anxieties present in Vicksburg in 1835 were thus like those in many parts of the United States. Residents of the city were not unusual in finding the consequences of an expanding market economy confusing and sometimes maddening. Americans everywhere struggled with uncertainty and ambivalence as they confronted life amid transient and anonymous populations. Americans everywhere tried forging new forms of community and respectable morality in unfamiliar environments. And though optimistic, Americans everywhere wondered whether the desire for individual gain unleashed in a world of speculative capitalism inevitably produced what Thomas Dew, professor of political economy at the College of William and Mary, saw as a "reckless profligate gambling spirit . . . spread through the country." If some in Vicksburg found deadly violence against professional gamblers who crystallized their misgivings as appropriate a way for negotiating with the new realities and moving forward as sermons and advice manuals, that decision was brutal, but it was a deeply American impulse understood throughout the nation.[50]

V.

One person who did not understand what was happening in Mississippi was the Reverend Duke W. Hullum, who followed events in Vicksburg as closely as he could from his home in Hardeman County, Tennessee. His son John was one of the four men trapped in Truman North's Vicksburg Coffee House on July 6. Shot several times as the mob launched its final assault, and insensible to his ultimate fate, he had been noosed and thrown unconscious from the gallows. The elderly Rev. Hullum grieved and waited for some indication that members of the mob would be tried for their roles in his son's death. Surely they could not get away with murder. But late in September 1835, having neither seen nor heard any sign that officials in Mississippi intended to take action, Hullum wrote a letter to Mississippi governor Hiram Runnels and released the text of it to the press, where it appeared first in the *Liberty Hall and Cincinnati Gazette* before being reprinted in papers all across the country.[51]

Hullum wanted Runnels to do his job. Virtually every newspaper in America had published reports of what had transpired in Vicksburg. Surely Runnels had heard and read enough to be convinced that known killers were walking the streets of the city with impunity. Yet he had done nothing about it and seemed content to continue to do nothing about it, putting Hullum in the flabbergasting situation of having "to ask that justice as a favor which the laws of my country entitle me to demand as a matter of right."[52]

Hullum saw nothing complicated or unclear in the circumstances surrounding his son's death. John Hullum had been inside a house. He had been charged with no crime, and no warrant had been issued for any legal authority to enter the premises. A mob had surrounded the house, and those inside had warned that they would shoot at anyone who approached the building. The mob attacked the house anyway, John Hullum opened fire in self-defense, and he had consequently been hanged without ever seeing a jury or a courtroom. Duke Hullum told the governor that he would have come to Mississippi himself to help prosecute his son's executioners but had been cautioned that he would be killed if he tried to do so. "This," Hullum wrote to Runnels, "is an alarming state of society, and which, if not shortly corrected by an energetic and efficient administration of the laws, we may bid adieu to liberty and justice, the wisdom and purity of our boasted institutions, and all those constitutional rights and privileges which are the pride and glory of every virtuous American citizen."[53]

Duke Hullum recognized that the question of whether his son had been a "virtuous" American citizen was at least partially at issue because it was "alleged he was a gambler." As a minister, the elder Hullum offered no extenuation for what may or may not have been the vices of the younger. To Duke Hullum, gambling was "a great and growing evil, and should receive the pointed reprobation of the civilized world." But if John Hullum *had* been a gambler, "it was susceptible of proof, and he was amenable to the laws." And if the citizens of Mississippi had not figured out how to criminalize gambling effectively, then they had a responsibility to address such a systemic flaw.[54]

Hullum, though, suspected that the problem in Mississippi was less a matter of administration than morality. To Hullum, a "greater distinction is drawn between the professional and the occasional gamester, than comports with my ideas of moral philosophy. . . . [O]ne act of gambling is as much an evidence of an evil propensity, as that one theft distinctly marks the rogue." For Vicksburgers to be so outraged and disgusted by the presence of professional gamblers in their city was hypocritical and disingenuous, because "notwithstanding the apparent shock of the moral sensibility of the citizens of Mississippi, there is no part of the United States where the despicable vice is so generally practiced, among the officers of the law, from the supreme judge down to the constable."[55]

In fact, Hullum had heard that "one of the principal actors" in the mob

"was in the constant habit of visiting gaming houses" and had "by his seductive arts, contributed perhaps more than any other man, to lead the
unfortunate victims of his personal vengeance into those sinks of iniquity."
Duke Hullum did not believe that his son had been killed because he was a
gambler, or that he had been killed because he had murdered Hugh Bodley.
Rather, given the habits and temperaments of Mississippians, Rev. Hullum could only conclude that "the recent crusade at Vicksburgh was not
so much the result of a deep and abiding sense of justice and virtue, as it
was of wicked hearts, bad passions, personal revenge and a reckless spirit of
insubordination to the laws."[56]

If John Hullum had been a gambler, his father failed to see how the
men who had killed him were any different than he was. Perhaps they were
worse. And if Runnels needed evidence before he took action, Hullum enclosed the names of sixteen men who had participated in the mob and nine
witnesses to the riot, all of which he hoped Runnels would "forward without delay to the attorney general or other officer at Vicksburgh charged
with the prosecution of the defendants." Hiram Runnels did not reply to
Duke Hullum's letter. Instead, Hullum waited for prosecutions that never
came. No one was ever criminally charged with his son's murder.[57]

But he was not alone in wondering what was going on in Mississippi.
By the end of the first week of July 1835, months before Duke Hullum's
letter became public, the whole country started hearing about dead gamblers, dead bandits, and dead slaves in the state, and no one could offer a
thoroughly convincing explanation as to why, venture a guess as to when
it would cease, or account for authorities who seemed to be doing nothing
to end it. White Mississippians could not have understood with clarity
how the social, cultural, and economic currents of their times produced the
violence they perpetrated, any more than we can glean real wisdom or gain
perspective on our own historical moment while also living inside it. But
as the violence in Mississippi continued past July 6 and spread ever further
beyond Warren and Madison counties, some of them finally realized that
it had to stop.

PART FOUR

~~~~~~

Slave Holders
and Slave Stealers

~ ~

CHAPTER SEVEN

Suborning Chaos

On the afternoon of July 7, 1835, after witnessing what he considered the farce of Angus Donovan's trial, Henry Foote mounted his horse and started back toward his home in Clinton. He had gotten only about a mile south of Livingston when he came across a large crowd alongside the road. Pausing to see what was going on, Foote observed that the crowd's attention centered on a "good-looking white man" who had been "tied to a tree, and stripped to the waist, whilst he was receiving a terrible castigation with rods." The man had been tried by the Livingston Committee of Safety and released. But he was a steam doctor, and on those grounds some who had gathered by the room where the committee was meeting decided regardless of the committee's verdict "that he ought at least to be decently scourged."[1]

What Henry Foote witnessed was the flogging of Lee Smith. Banished from Mississippi by the Livingston Committee of Safety, Smith did not even make it out of Madison County before a party of men grabbed him, took him into the woods, and gave him three hundred lashes—a beating so severe that he carried the scars for the rest of his life. Only then was he finally allowed to leave the state. Who exactly perpetrated this brutalization is unknown. But every witness account noted that they were people who lived near Smith's home in Hinds County who decided to make clear that Smith was not a pariah to the residents of Madison alone. Knowing what had happened to William Saunders and Joshua Cotton, it seems unlikely that Lee Smith seriously wondered whether he really needed to start his life over somewhere very far from frontier Mississippi. If he did, his neighbors left no doubts.[2]

Numerous public reports in Mississippi tried to suggest that a very different atmosphere prevailed in and around Madison County during the insurrection scare that continued on past the hangings of the gamblers in Vicksburg, and that the Livingston Committee of Safety had successfully introduced order to a situation that might otherwise have escalated into an uncontrolled orgy of violence. *Natchez Courier* editor William Mellen concluded from what he had heard that the proceedings of the committee were "conducted with the utmost coolness—not a harsh expression is suffered to be used to those on trial; they are permitted to introduce all the evidence they can in their behalf, and to tell their own story." A man who had been in Livingston on the day of Lee Smith's trial concurred, telling the editor of the *Clinton Gazette* that the committee's proceedings were marked by "the utmost calmness and dignity" and "conducted in a manner that would not do discredit to the most dignified judicial tribunal of the country." Marveling that defendants could cross-examine witnesses, introduce exculpatory information, and generally participate in hearings that, though extralegal, were well designed to elicit findings "entirely in accordance with truth and justice," the man claimed that the same spirit ramified throughout Livingston. "The utmost order seems to pervade the community there," he reported. "An intense excitement certainly exists among the whole white population; but the excitement is of that awful and profound character which discloses not itself in noise and uproar."[3]

Lee Smith's battered and bleeding form gave the lie to such accounts. So did the letter Angus Donovan wrote to his wife right before he died, in which he noted that "the excitement is so great that we are not tried by a regular jury, but by a committee of planters appointed for the purpose, who have not time to wait on any person for evidence." Indeed, if at the end of the first week of July Livingston even resembled the calm and composed place described by William Mellen and the correspondent for the *Clinton Gazette*, it was just about the only spot for miles that did. Apparently the warning notices first dispatched at the end of June from Livingston to neighboring villages, towns, and counties were extremely effective, because in short order whites throughout central and western Mississippi began manifesting the sense that they too believed themselves under siege.[4]

I.

Although several people asserted that committees like the one in Livingston had formed in every part of Mississippi by the middle of July 1835, no definitive accounts exist of them in the northeastern or southeastern parts of the state, which were still sparsely settled by whites, had relatively small slave populations, or both. The bulk of the evidence points instead to a more focused geography, something along the lines of Henry Foote's recollection of "vigilance committees" in roughly a dozen counties with the largest slave populations in the state. A territorial belt along the Mississippi River stretching northward from Mississippi's boundary with Louisiana nearly 250 miles toward Tennessee and inland roughly 75 miles toward the center of the state, this area clearly felt the tremors radiating outward from Madison County.[5]

Israel Campbell told of the fury unleashed on the slave population near the plantation where he lived in Warren County, and another account from there described an improvised court that had been created to try a number of white men accused of being "concerned with the negroes." A New Orleans newspaper reported that "great alarm" existed "in consequence of a discovered plot for an insurrection among the slaves" in Warren as well as in Claiborne County, also situated to Madison's southwest along the Mississippi River, and the story at least one man told bore that out. Writing from Claiborne to a friend, he indicated that whites there had found several slaves whom they believed had tried to poison their owner and his family, and got them to confess that two white men of "a suspicious character" had prompted them to make the attempt and "promised to take them to a Spanish country."[6]

From near Natchez, about forty miles south of Claiborne, a plantation governess wrote in her diary about "insurrections, hangings, patrolling, and all sorts of frights" in the area, and one man wrote from Natchez itself that everyone in the city was "under arms all the time" and "hourly expect[ed] an insurrection, as the celebrated negro stealers Murrel and his band, are at the head of all the negroes." All the towns upriver from Natchez, the man reported, were similarly guarded, and people in those places were "catching from 5 to 20 every day . . . and they hang them without judge or jury." The editor of the *Woodville Republican* reported that in Washington County, north of Claiborne, a number of white men had been taken into custody for involvement in an insurrection plan. Moreover, he described how residents of his own Wilkinson County in Mississippi's southwestern corner had formed patrols and urged extreme caution "against any improper movements or disorder among the slaves" because they believed an insurrection plot had been "instigated and headed by a considerable number of white men." Some of those men had "been apprehended and executed," but the danger remained, as several of the uprising's "ringleaders" had "furnished a list of white persons as concerned in said insurrection throughout this State, and elsewhere, in the Southern Country."[7]

The grisliness attending to this expanding dread could be seen in Yazoo County, northwest of Madison. A white man from Tennessee named Hunter arrived there in early July and began asking people in the county seat of Benton about prospects for landing a position somewhere as a teacher. After he was seen speaking with a slave, he was taken into custody by a band of regulators and "accused of endeavoring to excite insurrection," which he denied. He was then "slicked." Stripped naked and tied facedown with his arms and legs extended and bound to four posts in the ground, Hunter was whipped while the men surrounding him demanded a confession and the names of his accomplices. Hunter continued to assert his innocence and demanded a trial so that "he could *prove* his character." Instead he was told that if he confessed his guilt he would be released on the condition that he leave the state. After receiving nearly five hundred lashes, Hunter's body had "become sadly mangled" and he confessed, only to find that his tormentors intended to execute him anyway. He immediately recanted, saying that the names he provided were fictitious and "that his only reason for confessing was to escape torture," to no avail. He was hanged and then decapitated. His head was taken to a local physician for dissection after which it was tossed into the street where it was eaten by hogs.[8]

The horror of this particular episode notwithstanding, and no matter how far the insurrection scare spread, the panic was always most intense nearest to where it began. Even putting aside events in Livingston itself, Madison County, Mississippi, was a frightening place to be in early July. Night after night, all across the county, patrols of armed men arrested people at will and burst into the homes of the enslaved, and whites in the county remained convinced they were in grave danger regardless. People at Beattie's Bluff were still so unnerved on July 7 that sixteen men signed a letter to the Livingston Committee of Safety urging its members to have all the roads in the county "strictly guarded" because they were sure that "spies" lurked everywhere monitoring their actions. In the village of Canton, about twelve miles northeast of Livingston, patrollers filled the jail to overflowing by July 3 yet continued to bring in more prisoners every day. Residents formed a militia company "prepared with guns and ammunition," created a committee that sentenced several whites and blacks to lashings, and may have hanged several people. None of it stopped them from writing to the secretary of war in Washington to ask him "to send a company of soldiers to protect the citizens of the county."[9]

If anyplace rivaled Madison for hysteria during the insurrection scare, it was its immediate southern neighbor, Hinds County. Jackson, Mississippi's capital, was about twenty miles south of Livingston, and news of what was happening in Madison got there fast. On July 2, Jackson residents formed what one of the capital's newspaper editors called a "most rigid and vigilant patrol," which monitored the area for at least a week straight. That same editor insisted that patrollers failed even to find a "rumour" of insurrection among slaves in the area, but that failure did not keep them from commandeering every last gun in the capital's arsenal. Neither, apparently, did it persuade many people living in and around Jackson that they had nothing to worry about, as one man wrote from there on July 8 that "the whole country is in arms and assembled at different points to protect their families." Even the justices of the state supreme court were unsure what to make of the situation and went into indefinite recess.[10]

The caution taken in Jackson was mild compared with what prevailed elsewhere in Hinds. From a spot southwest of the capital known as Mississippi Springs, a man wrote to his brother on July 7 that there was "great distress among the women in the villages" nearby. Every night, he claimed, "the women and children are stowed away in the largest house the place affords . . . [and] the men, with arms, guard the town." Then, every morning, those men went to reclaim their families, a ritual sorting the letter writer thought "amusing." He may have found the whole affair a little silly, but he rode with a patrol all night every night anyway and told his brother that he had not slept "a wink."[11]

Burrell Fox, who lived about ten miles north of Jackson in Meridian Springs, was not amused in the least. On the contrary, he was shaken by what he observed during the insurrection scare, writing to his brother-in-law in North Carolina that he "never saw such unhuman feeling in my life befour as they inflicted upon som of the people som of the people would go and take up white man out of his bed dead hours of the night whip them." William Thomson evoked a similarly troubling scene. From his home near the village of Raymond, about twenty miles southwest of Jackson, Thomson wrote on July 12 to his wife in Tennessee that everyone in the area seemed afraid "of a design on the part of the negroes to rise against the whites." The "many different rumors and contradictory accounts of it" made it "impossible at present to arrive at the truth," so confusion reigned. "The little towns around here are guarded every night," Thomson reported, and the guards were quick on the trigger. Just a few nights earlier, Thomson wrote by way of example, a patrol had shot at an elderly black midwife who was hurrying through Raymond to deliver a baby and had not stopped when hailed.[12]

More generally, Thomson continued, the regular workings of the law had been set aside almost entirely in west-central Mississippi. The enslaved had special reason to worry, as "the citizens are scouring every part of the country and every negro they meet who does not give a good account of himself they take up or shoot down." But considering that steam doctors and other white men had also fallen victim to "regulators who have a summary mode of administering justice," Thomson wondered "how far this phrenzy will drive the people. . . . It has already been carried to an alarming length involving the innocent with the guilty, and promises to become a greater evil than that it was intended to correct. The regulators," Thomson concluded, "need regulating."[13]

Hinds County did not descend entirely into uncoordinated mayhem. In Clinton, residents formed a committee of safety like the one in Livingston. It met daily, tried both white and black prisoners, sentenced a number of men to beatings and banishment, and may have condemned at least one slave and several white men to be hanged. Still, as was the case in Livingston, the fact that respected and wealthy men considered the supposed insurrection plot a serious concern served less to ease tensions than it did to further the belief that the threat was real. Henry Foote recalled that "after the first organization of the vigilance committee" in Clinton "the excitement . . . increased perceptibly every hour," and he remembered that every night in town a scene unfolded like the one in Mississippi Springs, with the women and children of Clinton "assembled at a central position, where they remained till daylight, while all the male citizens moved in armed squads over the settlement." Everywhere they looked those squads found "suspected persons, both white and black," and some they brought to the committee for trial. But, Foote recalled, those "whose guilt seemed to be fully established" they simply "hung without ceremony along the roadsides or in front of their own dwellings."[14]

A man who had business in Clinton during the summer of 1835 confirmed Foote's recollection that turmoil prevailed despite the efforts of the town's committee of safety. Arriving in Clinton on July 4, the day the insurrection was purportedly going to take place, the man found everyone he met on the road and in town armed. For his part, the man thought the threat so vastly inflated that he laid his guns on a table before going to bed and asked the slave working at the tavern where he stayed to wake him and bring him his weapons should an insurrection break out. Nonetheless, after staying in Clinton for the better part of five days and helping guard a plantation for a night during which he and his fellows nearly opened fire on a patrol whose members failed to identify themselves, he acknowledged that a sort of delirium had overtaken the area. "I never saw people so blind with excitement in all my life," he wrote to a friend in Kentucky. "The populace, breathing fury and vengeance, are up for blood—they have tasted some, and God alone knows where they will stop."[15]

II.

The geographical shape of the insurrection scare of 1835 had a fairly clear logic. Most of the counties in the western and central portions of Mississippi had or nearly had slave majorities, and they tended also to have the greatest concentrations of plantations, banks, railroads, businesses, and other capital repositories that John Murrell and his men supposedly intended to plunder. White people living in those places had the most to fear and the most to lose in the event of a slave rebellion. As Henry Foote noted, the counties with the largest slave populations were those where "the slaveholding class was more sensitive to the cries of alarm which at this time literally rang through the whole community."[16]

The route that whites came to believe insurgents would follow in the event of an uprising marked a projection of their fears onto the map. While the confessions whites extracted and the rumors they shared about how the insurrection was supposed to unfold varied slightly in details, all agreed that the rebellion would begin in Madison County and that insurgents would move steadily south and west, ravaging villages and towns as they made their way through areas with the densest enslaved populations. At Beattie's Bluff, Jesse Mabry got the enslaved man Joe to say that the rebels would head from there to Livingston and then on to Vernon, Clinton, and Natchez. William Saunders told the "gentleman" he supposedly met while trying to escape from Madison County essentially the same thing, adding that the conspirators would stop in Jackson to retrieve a cache of weapons they had stashed nearby. The editor of the *Clinton Gazette* had heard that "the insurgent army" would head toward the river and lay waste to Warren and Claiborne counties after burning Clinton to the ground, while a man writing from near that town was sure that the insurrectionists were going to pass from Jackson through Raymond and then Port Gibson, the county seat of Claiborne, before moving on to Natchez. In short, panic manifested itself where it did in Mississippi because whites in those places believed their slaves provided the most fuel for the insurgents' fire. Certainty that the revolt would pass their way followed from that.[17]

Nor is it surprising that outside of Madison County, trepidation was most pronounced in Hinds. For starters, it made a certain topographical sense. The Big Black and Pearl rivers defined Madison's northwestern and southeastern boundaries, and while neither was impossible to cross, information flowed more easily and readily along and between those rivers than across them. One needed to ford no rivers to leave Madison to the northeast, but Attala and Leake counties were just two years old and had relatively scattered and mostly white populations. Hinds County, however, was contiguous with Madison, connected to it by two reasonably well-traveled roads that went directly through Livingston, and its northern edge was close to where the insurrection fear was most extreme. Indeed, the roughly four miles from Livingston to the border between Madison and Hinds counties was less than half the distance than that between Livingston and Beattie's Bluff.

Whites from Hinds County were both involved and implicated in the insurrection scare practically from the very beginning. Arguably, the scare did not spread from Madison into Hinds so much as it mushroomed from rumor to panic in the area where the counties came together. Men from Madison and Hinds alike voted to create the Livingston Committee of Safety, and Thomas Shackelford's report of the committee's proceedings makes clear that people in Livingston considered northern parts of Hinds to be "adjoining neighborhoods" to the village. Moreover, both suspected insurrectionists and the patrols looking for them routinely ventured back and forth across county lines. Joshua Cotton and Lee Smith were taken into custody in Hinds County, and Cotton, William Saunders, and Albe Dean had worked, traveled, and lived in both Hinds and Madison. The residents of Hinds County who took it upon themselves to give Smith a thrashing on top of the banishment ordered by the Livingston Committee of Safety obviously had no compunctions about acting in someone else's jurisdiction. It probably never occurred to them that they were doing so.[18]

Even had Hinds not shared its artificial and porous border with Madison, and even had the white populations of the two counties been wholly unfamiliar to each other, Hinds, like Madison, was the kind of place where the anxieties Virgil Stewart's pamphlet preyed on were particularly acute. In some ways Hinds was more established and substantial than Madison. It was older, for one thing. First created in 1821, Hinds County initially encompassed a sizable chunk of the land that had been taken from the Choctaw a year earlier at the Treaty of Doak's Stand, and it was named for one of the federal commissioners who had negotiated the transfer. By the 1830s Hinds had become physically much smaller, as six other counties, including Madison, had been hewn from its original limits. But American colonization of Hinds County had advanced significantly. It had four settlements larger than Livingston, including Jackson, which had been chosen in November 1821 to replace Natchez as the state capital and which was slated to be linked by railroad to the Mississippi River at Vicksburg. Hinds had three newspapers, numerous churches, a courthouse, a college, a female seminary, a number of hotels, several banks, and more than a score of stores and lawyers' offices. The county's institutional development was matched by considerable population growth. Where almost no white or black Americans had lived in Hinds when it belonged to the Choctaw, by 1830 more than eight thousand did, including three thousand who were enslaved.[19]

But if Hinds was somewhat more refined than Madison in 1835, it was still quite rugged. The largest town in the county, Clinton, had only about seven hundred residents. The smallest, a place called Amsterdam, was just a few years old, had a population of about two hundred, and was less a town or even a village than a commercial entrepôt perched on a bluff over the Big Black River. Raymond, the county seat, was not much older, having been founded in 1828. It had a brick courthouse, a school, a few stores, and the offices of some doctors and lawyers, but only three or four hundred people lived there. A traveler passing through in 1835 noted that the road from Raymond to Port Gibson, nearly fifty miles away, was mostly "enveloped in the gloom of the primeval forests," and that Raymond itself had essentially been cut out of the woods "in an open space among the lofty forest trees which enclose it on all sides."[20]

Hinds did house Mississippi's seat of government, but saying that Jackson lacked the grandeur suggested by its status is putting it kindly. The sole reason the capital had been moved to Hinds County at all was because it sat roughly in the middle of the state and thus met demands from a white population shifting toward northern and eastern parts of Mississippi for a governmental hub more centrally located than Natchez. Even so, when the state legislature selected Jackson to be the capital in 1821, it had done so provisionally. Only in 1832 did it decide to make the designation permanent, which meant that by 1835 Jackson had been serving as the capital for almost fifteen years, but there was still not much to it.[21]

One problem was that Jackson had limited natural advantages as an economic center. It was situated on a slightly elevated spot about a quarter of a mile from the Pearl River, but it sat at a point where the river, in the words of one observer, was "narrow, shallow and crooked." Flatboats and keelboats could navigate past Jackson well enough, but steamboats could do so only when the water was high, and even then it was possible only for very small crafts. Times of high water had their significant downside, though, as the river overflowed to within just a couple of hundred yards of the town and made the environs swampy and sickly.[22]

Occasional noxiousness and commercial impracticality hampered Jackson's economic development, and its interim status as the capital before 1832 meant that no one wanted to waste resources on its physical development. The state's legislature and supreme court met in a plain two-story brick building that a correspondent for one of Jackson's newspapers conceded in 1834 could be mistaken for a barn or a stable, and access to the river was achieved via a steep and winding path through the woods. By 1835, funds had been appropriated to build a proper statehouse, but as of November of that year work had been temporarily halted with only the basement completed, and Jackson remained little more than a half-mile square of ground cleared from the forest. It had about six hundred residents but neither a church nor a school, and Joseph Ingraham showed a gift for understatement when he wrote that unless the legislature or the court was in session Jackson was "a very uninteresting village." Despite progress having been made in the years since 1832, it is hard to blame William Gray for thinking Jackson's condition so dismal that the capital probably would have to be moved somewhere else.[23]

None of which is to say that Hinds County lacked promise. The same rivers that bracketed Madison County bracketed Hinds, and while improvements would have to be made to realize the commercial prospects of the Pearl River, on the Big Black farmers from several counties converged to load their products onto steamboats at Amsterdam. To be sure, Amsterdam was not a full-fledged port, and in the 1830s most agricultural goods from the countryside were brought to Clinton and then hauled by wagon thirty-five miles over hilly terrain to Vicksburg. But the chartered railroad promised to make transport easier and more efficient, and in any case, paramount for the prosperity of Hinds County was that its soil and climate were perfectly suited for producing the commodity most in need of delivery to market. With the cotton farmers and planters of Hinds nicely situated to take advantage of the flush times, it was boosterish but not unreasonable for the same writer who disparaged the "statehouse" in Jackson to assert as well that "it cannot but be obvious to the most superficial observer, that Hinds possesses local advantages superior to any other county in the State."[24]

Yet headiness was accompanied by unease in Hinds County, as it was in many parts of the cotton frontier in the flush times. Real estate prices in Hinds skyrocketed in the early 1830s as speculators and settlers scrambled to acquire the best parcels of cotton land. Residents of Hinds County may have been even more attuned than most to the frenzy surrounding the quest for property in Mississippi, as the town of Clinton owed its prominence in part to the fact that the Mount Salus federal land office was located there. One did not need to have witnessed firsthand the swarms of prospective buyers who flooded Mount Salus for more than six months when Choctaw Cession lands went on sale in the fall of 1833, however, to feel the urgency of the moment. Even the boosterish Jackson newspaper correspondent was stunned by the avidity with which people sought Hinds County property in the middle of the 1830s, noting that land purchased for $1.25 an acre in 1832 sold eighteen months later for five or ten times that, and that the mania showed no signs of slowing down.[25]

Hinds County thus had larger and more concentrated areas of settlement than Madison County, but in 1835 it was still heavily forested, devoted more to burgeoning cotton farms and plantations than to villages and towns, and fully engaged in the speculative and debt-fueled real estate madness of the flush times. Its demographic growth similarly reflected both the rush to the region and the ultimate reason why it was so susceptible to the insurrection panic first rumored at Beattie's Bluff. Though not quite as explosive and racially unbalanced as they were in Madison, the trends were equally striking. Between 1830 and 1840 the population of Hinds County jumped more than 130 percent from a little over 8,000 people to more than 19,000. Where the white population grew by about 25 percent from around 5,500 to nearly 7,000, however, the black population grew more than ten times that fast, from a little more than 3,000 in 1830 to more than 12,000 a decade later. In 1830 nearly two of every three people in Hinds County had been white. By 1840 that proportion had been reversed almost exactly.[26]

Hinds County and Madison County shared many of the characteristics that explain the vulnerability of whites in Mississippi to rumors of a slave insurrection—a dramatic and rapid shift in racial demography from majority white to majority enslaved, a massive influx of unfamiliar white people whose economic futures depended on those slaves, dizzying profits from land speculation and cotton growing that seemed limited only by how much a man's credit allowed him to accumulate, and the contingency that inhered to it all. Yet Hinds County was also where the reaction against the insurrection scare of 1835 really began and where the whole affair started slowly grinding to a halt, thanks in no small measure to a man named Patrick Sharkey.

III.

Born near Knoxville in 1789, Patrick Sharkey served as an officer in the First Tennessee Regiment during the War of 1812, was present at the Battle of New Orleans, and moved to Mississippi soon after it became a state. Sharkey began farming near the Walnut Hills close to what would eventually become the city of Vicksburg, and family legend has it that he first scouted the spot as he traveled up the Mississippi River back toward Tennessee after the war. The reality was more prosaic than pioneering, as he was almost certainly just following in the footsteps of an uncle who had moved in 1803 to that part of the Mississippi Territory. However Sharkey decided to move to Mississippi, by the late 1820s he had acquired his own land, married, and been widowed. He soon remarried to Matilda Puckett, a Kentucky native who had been raised in Hinds County by an elder sister, and that family tie prompted Patrick Sharkey to move to Fleetwood, a small Hinds County settlement ten miles northwest of Clinton, fifteen miles southwest of Livingston, and about two miles south of the Madison County line.[27]

In the summer of 1835 Patrick Sharkey was forty-six years old, owned 320 acres of land, and paid taxes on twenty-four slaves. He was a slight man, his son remembering that he never weighed much more than about 130 pounds, and his holdings did not make him extravagantly wealthy by frontier Mississippi standards. He was nonetheless unambiguously prosperous, solidly in the planter class, a local justice of the peace, and considered by his neighbors to be a man of substance and repute. When the residents of the area around Fleetwood decided to form a committee to investigate whether they ought to worry about the insurrection rumors from Madison County, Patrick Sharkey was an obvious choice for membership.[28]

Meeting for the first time on July 5, the members of the Fleetwood committee, unlike most white people living in their vicinity, do not seem to have seen much reason for concern. The committee examined five or six slaves suspected of having knowledge of the insurrection plot, found no evidence that they had any, and decided they ought to be released and sent back to their owners. Had the committee in Fleetwood been left to its own devices, its members might have proceeded as whites were proceeding in other nearby communities—meeting daily, questioning suspects, and periodically beating or banishing or hanging someone. But given the equanimity and speed with which they discharged supposed slave insurrectionists at their first meeting, they might just as well have resolved simply to disband. Patrick Sharkey, at least, appears to have been so inclined, as he and fellow planter and committee member James Kilborn asserted in a letter to Governor Hiram Runnels that it was "acknowledged on all hands that the danger of an insurrection is over. No person that we can learn stands in any farther fear of negroes."[29]

But if Sharkey, Kilborn, and the other members of the Fleetwood committee were finished with the insurrection scare, the insurrection scare was not finished with them. They were right that fear of the enslaved had waned by the time their committee held its first meeting. But white plotters remained a popular bugaboo, and among the white people who lived in the Fleetwood neighborhood were several members of the Rawson family, who Joshua Cotton had claimed were clansmen of John Murrell's so important that they had a list of scores of fellow conspirators.[30]

The Rawsons were unlikely sorts to be entrusted with such powerful information, as they had so little real power themselves. Not even their full names can be known for sure. Contemporary accounts of the insurrection scare describe them only as "the Rawsons." An Abner Rawson appears in the tax records for Hinds County, but only in 1834, at which point he owned no land and one slave. Patrick Sharkey's son remembered that the men of the family were farmers so poor that some of them worked as manual laborers picking cotton on another man's plantation alongside his slaves, and that their last name was actually Ransom. The 1830 census for Hinds County does list a William Ransom as the head of a nonslaveholding family containing three young children, a teenaged boy, two men and a woman in their twenties, and a man in his thirties. But no other personal details about William Ransom or any of his family members exist in county tax or property records.[31]

Rawsons or Ransoms, these were not people of means, but the Livingston Committee of Safety wanted to talk to them. Accordingly, on July 6 the committee dispatched a posse to Hinds County to find them, take them into custody, and bring them back to Livingston for interrogation. Leading the party was Hiram Perkins, owner of nine slaves and 160 acres of land northeast of Livingston. Perkins had been riding patrol for at least several days already and was among those who abortively chased Andrew Boyd through the woods with a pack of dogs on July 4. He had greater success tracking down the Rawsons, three of whom he and his men arrested in Hinds County within a few hours of leaving Livingston.[32]

Only two things are clear about what happened next. Patrick Sharkey was not letting the Rawsons go back to Madison County, and that made Hiram Perkins furious. Several accounts indicate merely that Sharkey "rescued" the Rawsons from Perkins and his company, while another describes Sharkey as having "caused the discharge of some suspected men in the custody of a guard from Madison." Henry Foote recalled that Sharkey, knowing that Perkins and his men would be escorting the Rawsons to certain death in Livingston, "had ventured to protest against their action, and . . . turned the alleged culprit[s] loose." Sharkey's son Clay recounted being told that Perkins and his men had already pronounced a death sentence for the Rawsons, whereupon Patrick Sharkey ordered their release and backed up his demand with a pistol when Perkins refused. In describing to the governor what had transpired, Sharkey made himself less central to the story, reporting only that Fleetwood committee members "were called upon to examine three white men taken up in this neighborhood by a company of armed men from Madd[ison] County. On examination we believed that two of them ought to be discharged & one taken before a justice of the peace for further examination."[33]

Whatever Patrick Sharkey did or said, it was obvious that no one in Fleetwood intended either to do anything to the Rawsons or to allow Perkins and his men to take them to Livingston. At that point Sharkey, Perkins, his posse, the members of the Fleetwood committee, and everyone else at the scene began yelling at each other; or as Sharkey more delicately put it, "a confusion ensued and all talked none reasoned." The Rawsons saw an opportunity that might not come again and slipped away amid the pandemonium. Eventually, Perkins and his men mounted their horses and rode off too. But they did not go far. They spent the night of July 6 skulking in the woods that surrounded Patrick Sharkey's plantation and plotting their revenge.[34]

However many men Hiram Perkins commanded, it was not enough for what he had in mind. The next morning, July 7, he and his posse returned to Livingston and reported what had happened in Fleetwood. The mood of the crowd that was gathering, as it did every day during the proceedings of the Livingston Committee of Safety, turned hostile as Perkins told his story, which "excited the greatest indignation" toward Sharkey. Then the mood turned darker still. Whether Perkins led the members of the crowd toward the conclusion or whether they arrived there on their own, "the suspicion of many" was aroused that Patrick Sharkey himself had to be "an accomplice" in the plot. Virgil Stewart had warned them that John Murrell had men of "high standing" in his mystic clan. How else could one explain why Sharkey had so resolutely defended the Rawsons?[35]

Yet even as many concluded that Sharkey's behavior proved the conspiracy involved members of the planter class as well, a screaming match ensued in Livingston too, with others "loudly" insisting upon "a scrutiny of the motives which influenced" Sharkey in his actions toward the Rawsons. The members of the Livingston Committee of Safety, nearly all planters themselves, were unwilling to assume the worst about Patrick Sharkey just based on a story told by Hiram Perkins. But they did not like what they heard, and they were willing to give Perkins the resources he needed to fulfill his original mission. Reinforcing him with more men, they "ordered the recapture of the Rawsons at all hazards."[36]

Perkins had no intention of using his newfound muscle to go after the Rawsons again. He had been frustrated days earlier in his efforts to capture Andrew Boyd. Now the Rawsons, embarrassingly, had been snatched right out from under him and allowed simply to walk away. Conspirator or not, Patrick Sharkey was going to pay for his meddling. Perkins led his newly enhanced company back to Sharkey's plantation, and the lot of them spent the afternoon and early evening of July 7 casing the premises and devising a plan. If Sharkey could be taken into custody, they would bring him back to Livingston. If he refused to surrender, Perkins was prepared to do whatever he thought necessary. He was going to take Sharkey, dead or alive.[37]

Which he might have done, except Sharkey knew that Perkins and his men were coming. Someone had told Sharkey that his house was being staked out for a second consecutive night and that this time he and his family were in serious danger. If Sharkey had a chance to run, he made no effort to do so. That his wife and his eighteen-month-old son William were by his side as the sun went down suggests that escape was not a viable option, but courage was not something Sharkey lacked in any case. Arming himself with a shotgun, a rifle, and several pistols, Sharkey moved with his family to an outbuilding on his plantation and waited. As it started getting dark, he lit several fires around the building and extinguished every interior light so that he might see the riders approaching and prevent them from drawing a bead on those inside. When night fell, they came for him.[38]

Hiram Perkins led the charge. As he rode past an open window, Sharkey rose from a crouch and opened fire, blasting Perkins right off his horse. Five or six of Perkins's men responded with a fusillade of shots, and they kept on firing. Sharkey's wife fled the room in such stark terror that she left William behind with her husband, who threw a pile of pillows and bedclothes over the child and continued shooting. A bullet discharged in the first barrage had caught Sharkey in the right hand and almost completely shattered it, so he used his left hand instead, unloading on the raiders every weapon he had. After several minutes of exchanged gunfire, Perkins and his men retreated back into the darkness. Once all was quiet, Sharkey and his family crawled into an adjacent garden and concealed themselves in the growth.[39]

The full scope of the damage could be assessed only when the sun rose on the morning of July 8. It was considerable, and frightful. Bullets and buckshot pellets riddled the window frame, walls, and furniture of the room where Patrick Sharkey had been hiding, including the pillows and clothing that Sharkey had tossed hastily on his infant son. Miraculously, neither William nor Matilda Sharkey was injured. Patrick Sharkey was less fortunate; he would never regain effective use of his right hand. Still, those in the patrol from Madison who had tried to kill him could not have looked back on their attempt and thought it had been a good idea. Sharkey had put a bullet in the thigh of a man named Stanford Hodge. He had shot and killed two horses, including one ridden by a man named Hiram Reynolds, who himself barely missed being killed when gunfire grazed his neck and sliced open the collar of his shirt. The wound Sharkey dealt Hiram Perkins, meanwhile, proved mortal. Perkins died before he ever got back to Madison County.[40]

Even had Patrick Sharkey been able to foresee that refusing to allow Hiram Perkins and his company to take the Rawsons to Livingston would escalate from a heated argument to a deadly shoot-out, he might not have backed down. Sharkey knew the Rawsons, and while they may have been poor they had lived in his neighborhood long enough for him to have "formed a favorable opinion of their honesty and integrity." He was not about to turn them over to a gang of ruffians just because they said the Rawsons were guilty of inciting a slave rebellion that he no longer thought a serious concern. Sharkey especially was not going to turn them over to a gang led by Hiram Perkins. Sharkey knew Perkins too. He had lived in Hinds County before moving to Madison in the early 1830s, and theirs had not been a friendly relationship. Indeed, given how it ended, one observer's reflection that Sharkey "entertained an adverse opinion" of Perkins both euphemized the antagonism and failed to acknowledge that the feeling surely was mutual.[41]

Sharkey may or may not have heard that Joshua Cotton named the Rawsons in his confession. Presumably Perkins told him as much in an effort to convince him that the Rawsons' culpability was not based on Perkins's word alone. If Sharkey was so informed, he did not care. Cotton also had lived in Hinds County. Perhaps Sharkey knew him as well and did not believe him a likely insurrectionist. Or perhaps he did. What Sharkey did know was that white men were being hanged nearly every day in Livingston, and he doubted that information acquired or justice dispensed in such an environment could result from a process that accorded with the law. Conservative in temperament and a justice of the peace himself, Sharkey fundamentally distrusted such extralegal expedients as improvised committees and regulator bands. Explaining to the governor why Perkins and his men were angry with the Fleetwood committee, Sharkey concluded it was less because of how the Rawsons' hearing had turned out than because they were "exasperated at us for not consenting to trample upon the laws of the country." That was their prerogative, Sharkey continued, but "the emergency did not seem to us to warrant rash or illegal proceedings." Similarly, Burrell Fox had heard that Perkins and his men tried to take Sharkey not because he failed to consign the Rawsons into their custody but rather because Sharkey had insisted "that 99 men that was gilty better go unpunish then one inosense one to be punish."[42]

Sharkey accepted that emergency circumstances sometimes called for emergency measures. He had agreed, after all, to sit on the committee in Fleetwood, despite its lack of legitimate legal standing. But if such a crisis did present itself, he felt that, at the very least, regular jurisdictional boundaries ought to continue to apply. One observer, for example, noted that Sharkey intervened on behalf of the Rawsons in his capacity "as a magistrate." Henry Foote similarly recalled that Sharkey acted "in his official character" by "claiming jurisdiction of the case," and a third man suggested that Sharkey rejected the proposition that Hiram Perkins, "a citizen of another county," was within his rights to arrest the Rawsons. Individuals from Hinds County had been acting in Madison County and vice versa for nearly a week by the time Perkins captured the Rawsons, so clearly not everyone in Hinds agreed with Sharkey. Nonetheless, Sharkey did not care for men who did not live in his county riding into his community and abducting his neighbors. There was nothing he could do anymore to protect Joshua Cotton or Lee Smith. But he could save the Rawsons, and he was going to do it.[43]

This interplay of the personal and the principled explains what Patrick Sharkey did the morning after his firefight with Hiram Perkins and his men. Now accused in Madison of being a conspirator in the insurrection plot and responsible for the death of one man and the wounding of another from that county, Sharkey needed protection. And he needed his side of the story heard by people he knew well enough to trust would be reasonable and fair. He understood that the prevailing climate in west-central Mississippi would not allow for regular legal proceedings to run their course, and he suspected that he might well be hanged if he was dragged off to Livingston. Considering his alternatives, Sharkey chose to surrender himself to the committee of safety in Clinton and allow its members to decide what ought to be done with him.[44]

Clinton was the largest settlement in the county and legal district where Sharkey lived. It was the cultural capital of Hinds County, with several schools and churches, a temperance society one hundred members strong, a Masonic lodge, and a lyceum for public lectures. It was the commercial center of the county too, with two banks, numerous merchants, and many people who wanted to advance the economic modernization promised by the railroad, which was to pass through Clinton on its way from Jackson to Vicksburg. Clinton had more resident lawyers than the state capital, had itself nearly been chosen in 1829 as the site of the capital, and was the sort of place inhabited by individuals, like Sharkey, of Whig political sensibilities who at least proclaimed their devotion to upholding the rule of law. Sharkey's wife had grown up nearby, so he likely had friends and relatives living in or near the town. Finally, Clinton was not far from Jackson, home to the person Sharkey thought could to do more on his behalf than anyone else. Early on the morning of July 8, just before turning himself in, Patrick Sharkey dispatched a letter to his first cousin explaining the situation and beseeching him to come from Jackson "as soon as possible to intercede for his life." His cousin was William Sharkey, chief justice of the Supreme Court of Mississippi.[45]

It was a given that William Sharkey would respond to his cousin's plea for help. Patrick Sharkey, the elder of the cousins by eight years, was named for William's father, and the two men had remained close throughout William's meteoric rise over the course of a decade from freshly minted lawyer to state legislator to circuit judge to chief justice. Whether there was much William Sharkey could do was an entirely different story. After receiving and reading Patrick Sharkey's letter, he was unsure that he could help, but he thought he knew someone who might. At a nearby hotel, Sharkey knocked on the door of Henry Foote, who had stayed in Jackson the previous night on his way home from Livingston. Sharkey showed Foote the letter and asked if he would accompany him to Clinton, thinking that as one of the town's most prominent residents Foote "might be able to exercise some influence in favor of his imperiled kinsman." Foote agreed, and with no time to waste the two rode off in Sharkey's carriage.[46]

Foote and Sharkey arrived in Clinton in the middle of the afternoon, just as Patrick Sharkey's trial was about to begin. Outside the hearing room they found a sizable number of men from Madison County demanding that Patrick Sharkey be turned over to them for trial in Livingston. Inside they found Patrick Sharkey, exhausted and in so much pain from the injury to his right hand that he could barely sit upright. Foote addressed the Clinton committee of safety first and briefly urged them not to surrender the man before them to the mob waiting outside, as it was his belief "that our fellow-citizen, Mr. Sharkey, had a right to claim an investigation at the hands of a committee of his own county."[47]

Foote then introduced William Sharkey. Well trained in sizing up an audience and choosing just the right words to persuade it, Sharkey understood that throwing his weight around would be of little use in this situation and that questioning the legitimacy of the Clinton committee or its authority to conduct legal proceedings could only make matters worse for his cousin. Instead, Sharkey conceded that regular courts were helpless to act in light of the exigency facing the white people of Mississippi. All he could ask on his cousin's behalf, he said, was that the members of the committee demonstrate the discernment he was sure they possessed, reject the ludicrous claim of Patrick Sharkey's complicity in the insurrection plot, and take seriously their duty to protect the citizens of their county from all dangers, including being tried by those "already too much prejudiced" against them to provide "a fair and dispassionate hearing."[48]

William Sharkey's speech was clever. It tactfully fed the self-regard of committee members in Clinton and avoided making any special plea on his cousin's behalf while simultaneously making clear what he wanted. Neither sophistic nor entirely transparent, it was devastatingly effective. Few committee members could have been unmoved as they heard the preeminent judicial authority in the state humbly defer to their wisdom. There is no record of the actual testimony the committee heard after William Sharkey finished speaking and left the room. Whatever its content, the committee spent little time deciding to acquit Patrick Sharkey "of all dishonorable motives or intentions."[49]

Acquittal, however, did not guarantee Patrick Sharkey's safety. Tensions in Clinton may have been lower than in Livingston, but the man who observed that the residents of the town were "breathing fury and vengeance" was not exaggerating. Just one day earlier people from Hinds County had demonstrated on the back of Lee Smith that they took matters into their own hands when they did not like a committee's decision, and Smith's was not an isolated affair. Hours before the committee of safety in Clinton heard Patrick Sharkey's case, they heard that of an enslaved man named Vincent. Long the property of a Virginia native and prominent Clinton landholder named Robert Bell, Vincent remained part of Bell's estate after his owner's death in 1834 and continued to live with Bell's family. When gunpowder and ammunition were discovered in Vincent's possession after the insurrection scare broke, he was brought to the committee for a trial, at which he was sentenced to three hundred lashes and sale outside the United States. The ubiquitous Henry Foote had not arrived from Jackson in time for Vincent's trial, but afterward members of the committee told him that they would have preferred to release Vincent altogether and had decided to give him some sort of punishment only because they "dreaded the indignant rage of the population of the town."[50]

Yet the population was not appeased. Vincent was brought out from jail the evening following his trial "to receive his stripes," but many in the crowd that had gathered to watch felt the committee's sentence was "insufficient for the punishment of so enormous a crime." They preferred hanging instead. So they decided to take a vote. Whether recognizing that the sentiment for severity was not unanimous or making a concession to the fact that the committee had rendered a different judgment, this was a mob that liked its vigilantism democratic. When the votes were counted, "the hanging party had it by an overwhelming majority," and Vincent was returned to prison so preparations might be made for his execution.[51]

On the morning of July 9 an even larger throng assembled before a store on one of Clinton's busiest streets to see Vincent hanged. Robert Bell's widow, Susan, had been allowed to visit Vincent in jail, and when she emerged she implored the crowd not to carry out its plans. Weeping, she asked them to remember their respect for her husband and to trust that she knew Vincent well enough to be certain of his innocence. Sensing indifference to her plea, she asked if anyone would stand up on her behalf. Henry Foote stepped forward. He had been too frightened to say anything on behalf of either Angus Donovan or Patrick Sharkey except behind the closed door of a committee room, and he knew that even here on the streets of his own town this was a dangerous moment. Right in front of him he saw "a man notorious for his violent and blood-thirsty character" carefully fingering a newly purchased rope to be sure it was strong enough to snap a human neck. But Robert Bell had been Foote's friend, and he found it hard to watch his friend's widow reduced publicly to tearful begging. Asking the crowd to consider that the "excitement" in Clinton would eventually subside and that someone might try to prosecute Vincent's murderers after things returned to normal, Foote suggested they take another vote to be sure that "whatever is done in this affair shall be the act, as it were, of the whole community."[52]

It is hard to imagine that Henry Foote really believed he would persuade the crowd to think carefully about the consequences of their actions, or that they would be cowed by the theoretical prospect of prosecution for murdering a slave. Vengeance is a shortsighted impulse, and fear clouds moral calculations. No one objected to taking a second vote, but these were people who wanted blood. Of the hundred or so people assembled, only eight or ten had the courage or the consciences to vote against ending Vincent's life. Fifteen minutes later Vincent was led to a blackjack oak and hanged by a rope from one of its branches.[53]

Given the willingness of whites in Clinton to enact this sort of reprisal on people they believed to be conspirators regardless of what any committee said, Patrick Sharkey could not have failed to wonder whether an acquittal would matter in his case. If the men from Madison did not take him, those from Hinds might. But Sharkey was spared Vincent's fate. After finding him innocent, the members of the committee in Clinton "declared their determination to protect him against all further molestation," and it stuck. Had the men from Madison County been able to get hold of Sharkey and bring him to Livingston, his status as a wealthy planter rather than a slave might have been irrelevant. But in Sharkey's own county it made all the difference in the world. He would still have to watch his back. The men from Madison were seething as Sharkey emerged from the committee room a vindicated man. They still wanted him, and one witness reported that they continued to "swear they will have him." But that same witness noted too that "the people of Hinds" were "arming and rallying in his defence."[54]

IV.

Only with hindsight is it evident that the conflict between Patrick Sharkey and Hiram Perkins marked the moment when the insurrection scare of 1835 peaked and then began to ebb. At the time, the progression from a clash over bailiwick and procedure to an accusation of collaboration and a gunfight on Sharkey's plantation suggested instead that a new and exceptionally perilous dynamic threatened to take hold in Mississippi. Guilt by association had always played some role in determining who got incriminated as an insurrectionist. But when the owner of nearly twenty-five slaves had to defend himself against charges of helping plan a slave rebellion because he thought suspected insurgents deserved more than a perfunctory hearing before being executed, it augured the onset of an all-too-familiar human drama.

Henry Foote, who claimed that during the insurrection scare the Southwest became "so full of danger to those who relied on the laws of the land for protection and security" that he considered leaving the region altogether, was reminded of the French Revolution's Reign of Terror. Reflecting that large slaveholders were hauled before vigilance committees because they had been able "to preserve their mental equipoise as to disapprove most strongly [of] the[ir] confused and bloody proceedings," Foote concluded that "nothing was wanting but the kindly offices of the *guillotine*, to usher in all the imagined glories of Jacobinical violence." Foote might have chosen from countless historical episodes in which accusations of being subversives in disguise attached to dissenters, but the comparison was not inapt. The allegation against Patrick Sharkey was a classic sign that Mississippi sat perched on the brink of a full-blown witch hunt.[55]

The vow of the people of Hinds County to sustain Patrick Sharkey against pressures to send him to Livingston may have been a boon to Sharkey, but it was not necessarily a sign that things were turning around in the state of Mississippi. Prior to the skirmish on Sharkey's plantation, whites in Madison and Hinds counties had been working largely in tandem. Believing that their lives and their profits were endangered by white saboteurs working to undermine their control over their slaves and bring the rickety edifice of the cotton frontier crumbling down, white people in Madison and Hinds alike had spent more than a week identifying supposed insurrectionists, squeezing them for information, and destroying them. Their actions were neither tidy nor wholly rational, but they shared the same goals.

Now they were working at cross-purposes. It is telling that in his account of the proceedings of the Livingston Committee of Safety, Thomas Shackelford wrote not a word about Hiram Perkins, Patrick Sharkey, their clash, or its aftermath. Shackelford made no secret of the fact that patrols worked across county lines or that residents of Hinds County helped create the committee in Livingston. But there was no way to discuss what happened on Sharkey's plantation and still make it seem that white Mississippians were united against a common foe. Rather, with men from Madison County intent on bringing Patrick Sharkey to Livingston and men from Hinds County equally resolved to stand in Sharkey's defense, the unavoidable conclusion was one drawn by a traveler who happened to be in Clinton at the time of the scare. Should anyone from Madison attempt to take Patrick Sharkey by force, he wrote to a friend in Kentucky, "a civil war must ensue. . . . It is no longer the negroes, but white man against white man. The Mississippians are ruining their own state. By their own high-handed and violent measures, they are giving a magnitude and terror to the contemplated insurrection which it otherwise never could have gained."[56]

The traveler, moreover, thought he knew whose duty it was to keep white Mississippians from destroying everything they were trying to establish in the Southwest. "As yet," he wrote, "the Executive has not interposed to arrest this violent infringement of the civil power. No minister of the law has attempted to stay a course of procedure which threatens the property—the lives and respectability of citizens." Others also wondered why Governor Runnels had failed to take any action. Rumors about the insurrection scare had reached Jackson by July 2. Runnels may have been away from the capital then and for several days afterward, as he was absent on July 6 when the Livingston Committee of Safety sent a rider requesting weapons from the state arsenal. But in his office or not, a wave of terror and disorganization had been rolling across Mississippi for a week by that point. Surely somebody knew how to locate Runnels and tell him there was a problem. If somehow that was not the case, Runnels could not have been ignorant of the situation by the afternoon of July 7 when he was back at his desk reading the letter Patrick Sharkey and James Kilborn had sent him earlier that day.[57]

Sharkey and Kilborn had not written simply to inform the governor what had been happening in the Fleetwood neighborhood. They wanted him to do something about it. With a company of men plotting an attack on Sharkey's plantation and extralegal committees carrying out executions, it seemed obvious to them that "the lawless pashions of man . . . have broke loos, and unless there is a stop put to the shedding of blood confusion & desolation must shortly reign over the land. . . . We respectfully beg leave to suggest to your Excellency that energettic measures be immediately taken to put a stop to this terable State of things."[58]

Essentially, having tried on their own and to no avail to restore reason, Sharkey and Kilborn wanted Runnels to fulfill his job description and execute the law. Specifically, they called on him to dispatch messengers to every county with a proclamation ordering "all illegal tribunals to desolve," demanding that they "deliver up all their prisoners to the civil authoritys," and insisting on the dispersal of "all unlawful bands under the name of Regulaters." Sharkey and Kilborn believed that "all tried & faithful citizens" would willingly help carry out such instructions, but in case Runnels had forgotten, they reminded him that he also had legitimate armed forces at his disposal. Most localities had a sheriff or a board of police, and there was always the state militia. Command "all officers civil and Millitary to be diligent in carrying this Proclamation into execution," Sharkey and Kilborn concluded. "We fully believe it would be efficient."[59]

Over the next few days, more calls came into the governor's office imploring Runnels to act. On July 8, George Wyche, a planter who also lived in the Fleetwood neighborhood, sent a note informing Runnels that "an excitement to an unparalleled extent prevails in Madison [and] in our neighborhood & will soon spread over the State. All law is put down & the government of the country is in the hands of the Mob, whose minds are in a State of feverish excitement." Like Sharkey and Kilborn, Wyche wanted the governor to issue a proclamation calling for "peace & moderation, & submission to the Civil Power."[60]

Four days later the governor received a letter from the committee of safety in Clinton indicating that conditions there had worsened. The letter contained a resolution asking Runnels to organize a unit of sixty armed men in Clinton "for the protection of that town and its vicinity" and to call out the state militia "for the protection of the citizens generally & for searching the woods swamps & other places in order that all persons supposed to be concerned in the insurrectionary movements now in agitation in this state may be apprehended." Accompanying the resolution was an explanatory note from two members of the committee, Anderson Hutchinson and William S. Jones. They thought the governor needed to know that the community had created the Clinton committee of safety in part "for its self defence in the midst of actual insurrection" but also "for the suppression of irregular and precipitate movements resulting from extreme excitement

& the protection of suspected persons until the just & sure ascertainment of their guilt." That allusion to the trial of Patrick Sharkey, the hanging of Vincent, and the standoff between the men from Madison and Hinds counties, made in the context of asking for state military reinforcements, conveyed an unmistakable message: our command of this situation is shaky at best.[61]

When the Clinton committee of safety wrote to Governor Runnels, he had known about the insurrection scare for at least six days. Untold numbers of white and black men had been beaten, banished, or executed, and white people from two different counties were ready to kill each other for reasons that had become only tangentially related to the scare at all. Yet Runnels did nothing. After the scare had finally passed, a number of supporters tried to explain away the governor's inaction. A man from Clinton, who identified himself only as "A Voter" in a letter to the *Jackson Mississippian*, wrote that during the scare he had gone to Jackson to visit the governor himself, having thought it "a little strange" that Runnels remained silent while his constituents were frantically tracking down and trying purported white insurgents and slave rebels just miles from the capital. The man wrote that he had found Runnels in his office, fully apprized of what was happening and reading a letter asking him to call out the militia. Whose letter it was is unknown, but Runnels told "A Voter" he was not inclined to fulfill the request. Runnels said that the residents of Jackson had been patrolling the capital and its surroundings and saw no cause for worry. Moreover, he claimed that he had gone personally to a plantation near Jackson whose owner had expressed apprehension about his slaves and discovered the whole matter to be "a false alarm."[62]

"A Voter" came away from his meeting with Runnels impressed by the governor's steadiness and in agreement with his decision not to get involved. While conceding that there had been more "just cause of alarm in Madison [County]" than near Jackson, the man concluded that using the militia to stamp out the threat of an uprising and using the law to prosecute the white men responsible for it would have been ineffectual. Even if militiamen had caught the insurrectionists, the only evidence against them would have come from their enslaved recruits and would thus have been inadmissible in a regular court. Noting that none of the calls for the governor to take military action came from Madison County itself, the man asserted that the people there, like him, knew full well that "no law is so well adapted to such villains as *Lynch's*."[63]

The editor of the *Mississippian* himself, George Fall, took a somewhat different tack, arguing that using the militia would have been either a strategic debacle or utterly futile. Even were state forces organized enough to carry out a serious military operation—and Fall thought they were not—this was not a situation that called for conventional warfare. The enemy here was not so much an army as it was "unembodied" guerrillas with "no particular plantation or neighborhood [that] could have been made the theatre of [the militia's] operations." Insurrectionists could be anywhere and everywhere, and had Governor Runnels ordered the white men of Mississippi to form militia units and prepare for battle, "many families would have been unprotected while their dwellings were surrounded." That was assuming, of course, that any white men would have answered the governor's call. Fall imagined that no one "would have been willing to have left his home in the performance of a public duty, while his family was exposed to massacre." Whether tactically foolish or practically pointless, turning to the militia was not the most effective course of action. "A strict Patrol," Fall concluded, "is all that is necessary to the successful overthrow of the raw and untutored schemes of negroes, although led on by white men."[64]

Neither of these rationalizations was completely coherent. On the one hand, George Fall thought the threat of insurrection so insignificant that regular patrols could stifle it, but on the other, he worried that taking the wrong step in response to the threat would result in the mass slaughter of white families. As for "A Voter," he felt sure that the dearth of admissible evidence would have allowed any insurrectionists who ended up in a Mississippi courtroom to walk away scot-free, and at the same time he claimed that Joshua Cotton, William Saunders, and the other white men executed in Madison County were hanged more because of "other testimony obtained and finally full confessions made" than because of information acquired from the enslaved.[65]

Hiram Runnels himself did not bother crafting a public explanation for his failure to intervene during the scare, and it is hard to fathom what he was thinking. To say he was inept would suggest he tried to do something substantive. To say he dithered would suggest he indicated that he was seriously concerned. It is tempting to say Runnels was simply so clueless that he actually thought the "false alarm" he saw on one plantation represented what was going on elsewhere in the state. But the conclusion seems inescapable that he knew better. Runnels knew from Patrick Sharkey and James Kilborn that at least one planter was under siege on his own property less than a day's ride from where he sat reading their letter. He knew that members of the Livingston Committee of Safety, among them his own brother, believed the situation so perilous that they wanted the state to buttress their weapons supply. And when he wrote back to them, he had to tell them that he had no weapons to spare because the people in and around Jackson had already seized them all. They were scared, and Runnels knew that too. "Like yourselves," he wrote to the Livingston committee, the residents of Jackson "were much alarmed from the apprehension of a general insurrection among the slaves."[66]

To a certain extent, Runnels genuinely did not grasp the nature or scope of the events unfolding around him. Communications were slow and conducted almost entirely by messengers on horseback, yet rumors flew so quickly that it was impossible to know which to believe and which to dismiss. Rhetorical formalities of notes and letters, meanwhile, could disguise feelings of real urgency and impart a tone so measured as to be misleading. In his letter to the Livingston Committee of Safety, Runnels left open the possibility that things were more grievous than he imagined, writing that he could not provide them immediately with guns but that he would try to retrieve some and send them along "if in your opinion the insurrectionary movements are not sufficiently quelled to secure the safety of the people of your county."[67]

Still, in some measure Runnels's folly was willful. He plainly thought the "apprehension" of the capital's residents overblown, and one gets the sense that it would have taken a lot to persuade him the situation was so bad that he had to use the militia. Thirty-eight years old, Runnels had been born in Georgia but had moved to Mississippi as a child. The son of a man known as someone who "would fire up and fight anybody and at any time," Runnels became accustomed to violence at a very young age and grew up on a frontier so rough that his family were the very first white people to build a house in what eventually became the village of Monticello, on the Pearl River about sixty miles south of Jackson. As a young man he worked as a schoolteacher, and he had no formal legal training, but he served nonetheless as state auditor, state treasurer, and in the state legislature before becoming governor. Runnels was a devoted Jacksonian Democrat politically, and he indicated in his letter to the Livingston Committee of Safety that he believed "nothing but the vigilance of the people" could protect Mississippians from a slave revolt. Given his modest background, he may have taken to heart the populist bombast that helped bring his party to power in the United States. Perhaps he sincerely believed "the people" knew best how to handle their own affairs and ought to be left to their own devices in all but the most desperate cases. Or perhaps his behavior owed itself less to psychology and political leanings than to the fact that the committee on which his brother served sat at the epicenter of the scare but had given no indication that it thought state military intervention necessary.[68]

Whatever factors Runnels took into account as he pondered his options, the result was clear. The letter from Patrick Sharkey and James Kilborn received no reply. The Clinton committee of safety heard nothing from Runnels right away either, prompting William Jones to send another messenger to Jackson the next day just to be sure the governor had received his initial letter. But Runnels was content to let white Mississippians exhaust themselves purging the enemy within, and he effectively encouraged the vigilantes who had grabbed the reins of law and order in his state to do whatever they thought proper. Closing his letter to his brother and the rest of the Livingston Committee of Safety, Runnels offered his "sincere hope that by your vigilance you may be enabled to protect yourselves against all danger from a deep laid conspiracy, for the destruction of yourselves and families."[69]

V.

By the time Hiram Runnels did respond publicly to the insurrection scare, it was far too late for Ruel Blake. Blake had not been seen anywhere near Livingston since July 1, when he borrowed a horse and some cash from Thomas Hudnall and fled the village after trying to shield his slave, Peter, from a beating. Though not suspected as a conspirator at the time, Blake had never been liked much by most white people in Livingston. And over the ensuing days, as his name became part of the confessions elicited from the slaves at Beattie's Bluff and the admissions pried out of Joshua Cotton and William Saunders, the residents of Livingston reached the conclusion after all that "something *more* than sympathy for his negro had influenced him to act as he had done."[70]

But Blake had not heard about any of that. Nor had he heard that a five-hundred-dollar reward had been offered for his arrest. If he had, he would have known that he needed to get as far from Madison County as humanly possible. Instead, he stayed far enough away so as not to be found easily but close enough that he might get a sense of when "the excitement" had subsided. Then, he figured, it would be safe to go home and keep the departing promise he had made to Hudnall to make amends. Once he realized that it would never be safe for him to go home, the window for his escape had closed. Blake was fifty miles from Livingston in, of all places, the city of Vicksburg, where he was passing himself off as a boatman from Indiana. On July 6 someone in a posse that had come from Livingston looking for Blake saw him, and one man from Madison County even heard that Blake had been spotted in the crowd gathered to watch the execution of the gamblers. Blake was taken into custody and word was sent back to Livingston that their man was on his way.[71]

Given all that had transpired between when rumors of insurrection first began making their way around Madison County and when Ruel Blake was captured, it is hard to envision things turning out for Blake differently than they did. Nevertheless, the report of his arrest could not have reached Livingston at a more inopportune moment for him than eleven o'clock on the morning of July 8, which was almost precisely when news arrived in the village that Hiram Perkins had been killed in Hinds County. From the time when the summary executions of Peter and of William Johnson's slave on July 2 had prompted the initial formation of the Livingston Committee of Safety, there may have been no moment when the atmosphere in the village crackled with more paranoia, rage, and fear than when the people there learned that one of their own actually had died in pursuit of men believed to be conspiring with the slaves against their lives.[72]

Whether residents of the village would get to exact revenge on Patrick Sharkey remained an open question, but they would not be denied the chance to give Ruel Blake what they thought he deserved. He had already escaped once, and they were sure that John Murrell's clansmen would try to rescue him now, so as soon as they heard he was coming they sent thirty to forty armed men on horseback to intercept the guard escorting him from Vicksburg. Led by Albert Bennett, a planter, the company took charge of

Blake on the road, turned around, and headed right back to Livingston. Worried they might be ambushed, the riders stopped only when absolutely necessary and not at all to sleep. When they arrived in Livingston around three o'clock in the afternoon on July 9, they had been riding for more than twenty-four hours straight. Their instincts toward violence may have simmered down as the time Blake spent in their custody slowly passed, but those of the people in Livingston had not. Blake's appearance "created a most alarming excitement," and Thomas Shackelford was sure that had the committee of safety not been in session, "in all probability he would have been forcibly taken from the guard, and immediately executed." Pausing to prepare for Blake's trial was not an option. His captors took him directly to the committee room. This had to happen now.[73]

Blake's own slaves testified that he had told them there would be an insurrection on July 4, that he had recruited them to participate, and that he had promised to help them. The committee introduced into evidence the confessions of the slaves executed at Beattie's Bluff that Blake was one of the white men "actively engaged" in the conspiracy, and they managed to have a few slaves from near the Bluff who were still alive corroborate the claim. Joshua Cotton had been dead for days, but the committee had not forgotten his assertions that Blake was "deeply concerned" in the plot and one of its "chief men," and that Blake had said he would assist his own slaves in rebelling. "After hearing all the testimony," Shackelford reported, Blake was given "every opportunity . . . to produce counteracting testimony, which he failed to do." Not that it would have mattered. Everyone knew what was going to happen, including Blake himself. Before he was even led out of the room so the committee might consider his fate, he asked its members at least "to give him time to settle his affairs." Once he was gone, they voted, unanimously, that he was guilty. All together, roughly one hour elapsed from when Albert Bennett's guard brought Blake into Livingston to when the committee of safety sentenced him to hang.[74]

Given how badly the residents of Livingston wanted to see Blake dead, it was remarkable that the committee agreed to give him a day to get his affairs in order. More remarkable still were the arrangements Blake chose to make. Sitting in the Livingston jail on the morning of July 10, Blake wrote his will. It was a brief document, for he had relatively little property in need of disposal. There were Prince, Edmund, Dick, Sylvy, and Lottey—the five slaves he owned who were still alive after Peter's execution. There was a small lot in Livingston on which sat Blake's house, and there were tools, furniture, and other household items. Blake also had some outstanding accounts—a few debts he had yet to pay and a few customers from whom he had yet to collect. Keeping things simple, Blake left all his property to one man and asked that same man to collect on his bills and pay his creditors. The man was Thomas Hudnall.[75]

At first glance, Ruel Blake's decision to leave all his worldly possessions to someone who had voted to sentence him to death just hours earlier for participating in a nonexistent conspiracy is astonishing. But it suggests the depths of Blake's isolation and probably his loneliness on the cotton frontier. He had lived in Madison County for six years, yet he obviously had few friends and maybe even fewer people in whom he genuinely thought he could place his confidence. Thomas Hudnall had been fair in their business dealings over the course of several years. He had been interested enough in Blake's well-being to intervene on his behalf at a critical juncture and gave him a chance to make himself scarce. Whether or not that made Hudnall Blake's friend, he was someone Blake thought he could at least trust to execute his wishes. Under the circumstances, that would have to do.

It is fair to ask why Hudnall failed to take a stand on Ruel Blake's behalf at his trial. By their own rules, committee members had to vote unanimously to hang someone, so Hudnall required only the courage to vote not guilty to save Blake's life. It is possible that Hudnall actually believed Blake was a conspirator. But it is unlikely. He had never shared the opinion prevalent among his neighbors regarding Blake's "rascality." He had helped Blake escape from Livingston even as other white men were falling under suspicion, and despite having voted for Blake's execution Hudnall was willing to have it known publicly that he would pay and collect Blake's debts. Even if Hudnall had wanted to rescue Blake from an ignominious fate, however, he must have seen that doing so probably was impossible. He had had confidence enough in his own wealth and standing to protect Blake once, and Blake had almost gotten away for good. But this time, nothing and no one could save Blake whether he was guilty or not. Hiram Perkins and his men had nearly killed Patrick Sharkey for trying to insulate suspected conspirators from their wrath, and there were people in Livingston who were certain Sharkey was an insurgent and who would kill him notwithstanding his status as a planter if they could just manage to get him out of Clinton. Hudnall had to know that had he voted to acquit Ruel Blake at his trial, there was a chance he would have ended up alongside him on the gallows.

It is debatable how much the planters of Madison County who sat on the Livingston Committee of Safety ever restrained—or wanted to restrain—the anxieties of the white populace, and how much the committee was merely a vehicle for enacting those anxieties. When it came to Ruel Blake's trial, though, the mob clearly ruled. Whatever the opinions or desires of the committee members, in this instance they did its bidding. Blake himself seems to have recognized this and to have understood that Thomas Hudnall was in a hopeless position. At two o'clock on the afternoon of July 10, 1835, guards led Blake from jail to a blacksmith who hammered the irons off his wrists and ankles. Blake washed his hands and his face, donned a white suit, and walked to the same crude gibbet in the center of the village on which Albe Dean and Angus Donovan had died days earlier. Standing at its base, he paused for a moment and looked up, and his eyes filled momentarily with tears. He asked for a few people, Thomas Hudnall almost certainly among them, and "requested them to attend to some worldly concerns." Then he shook their hands and said good-bye.[76]

A committee member asked Blake if he had anything to say to the "immense concourse" of people who had gathered. According to a witness, Blake told the crowd that although he was about to meet God possessed of many "sins and imperfections," he would not have been afraid to die if he "was as innocent of all other sins, as I am of the charge for which I am now about to suffer." While flatly denying his guilt and invoking "the wrath and imprecations of heaven if I am not utterly and absolutely innocent," however, he did not blame the members of the Livingston Committee of Safety for their verdict. Believing "they have been influenced by the best motives for the benefit of the community," he conceded that the evidence they heard "was amply sufficient to warrant my condemnation. But," he concluded, "I am not less innocent on that account."[77]

How much of this speech Blake actually delivered is hard to say. A second witness agreed that Blake denied his guilt to the end. Thomas Shackelford similarly noted that Blake insisted "that his life was sworn away," though Shackelford also wrote that Blake said publicly and privately that the committee "could not have done otherwise than condemn him, from the evidence before them." On the surface, of course, Shackelford's assertion that Blake absolved committee members for their actions at his trial seems hopelessly self-serving. But if we consider the possibility that Blake spoke less to the committee as a whole than specifically to Thomas Hudnall, such a declaration appears more a gesture of sympathy and understanding for a man who did his best than a general exoneration of the committee for the cowardly injustice they perpetrated. Moreover, it utterly belies the notion supposedly shared among Livingston's white population that Ruel Blake was coldhearted, cruel, and hateful. On the contrary, if Blake really said the things he said about his executioners, he was far bigger, more generous, and more compassionate than every one of them.[78]

After speaking to the crowd, Blake asked a minister to pray on his behalf, and he ascended to the scaffold. A rope was placed around his neck and he asked that his face be left uncovered. Asked a last time if he had anything to say, Blake replied once more that he was innocent, adding, "I bear malice towards no one. May God have mercy on my soul! I am ready." The man appointed to release the trapdoor tried to trip it, but it jammed. Ruel Blake, turning and seeing that the mechanism had failed, stepped forward and jumped from the platform, "launching his soul into that terrible abyss from whence no traveller returns." It is not recorded whether the crowd cheered or observed the scene in silence.[79]

CHAPTER EIGHT

Imposing Order

On July 13, after receiving the second letter in as many days from William Jones on behalf of the Clinton committee of safety imploring him to call out the state militia, Hiram Runnels replied. Refusing their entreaty, he told the committee he did not think he had "the necessary information to authorize such an extreme measure" and that he believed there was "ample power invested in the members of police" to contain the crisis, "if properly exerted." Runnels wrote that he would "be happy to be placed in poss[ess]ion of such facts" as "would show the necessity of calling on the militia," though he gave no indication of what sorts of facts could demonstrate such a necessity. In the meantime, he had decided "the best rule for my action is to exhort the proper authorities to the necessity of keeping up strong and efficient patroll service in every county and neighborhood."[1]

The executive proclamation Runnels issued later in the day reflected that decision. Published widely in newspapers throughout and beyond Mississippi, the proclamation stated flatly that there was "a band of lawless base villainous whitemen traversing the country endeavoring to get up an insurrection among our slaves" and that "disclosures" had been made creating "the most serious apprehensions that a widely extended conspiracy is on foot." Because the situation appeared "calculated to produce alarm and to call forth the vigilance and energy of the people," Runnels urged "all good citizens" and every civil and military officer in the state "to suppress all such insurrectionary movements and to apprehend all suspicious persons and deliver them over to the proper authorities that they may be brought to condign punishment." He particularly called on local boards of police to organize "active and efficient patrols" and ordered that the "arms of the State" be delivered "into the hands of the people for their defence" should it become necessary.[2]

Runnels's proclamation is a peculiar document, to say the least. To begin with, it is not evident what prompted him to issue it, as nothing especially desperate or even especially notable had taken place in the days immediately prior to its issuance. No one from Madison County ever did launch an attack to try and take hold of Patrick Sharkey after the Clinton committee of safety acquitted him, and after hanging Ruel Blake on July 10 the Livingston Committee of Safety spent the next few days examining and in most cases releasing people who had been taken into custody while spotted "exploring the country." With the intensity of the crisis fading, no good reason suggests itself to explain the proclamation except perhaps Runnels's desire to make it appear that he was taking some kind of public action.[3]

Adding to the proclamation's peculiarity—and strengthening the notion that Runnels crafted it mostly for the sake of appearances—is that it proclaimed nothing in particular. Runnels called for the organization of "active and effectual patrols" even though patrols were already riding all across the state. He authorized the state's cache of weapons to be distributed among its citizens even though the citizens, in Jackson at least, had already taken every gun in the arsenal. He called for "all suspicious persons" to be turned over to the "proper authorities" yet left the meaning of the latter term deliberately vague, effectively sanctioning any extralegal committees—about which the proclamation said nothing—to keep acting as they chose. Mostly, the proclamation amounted to Runnels encouraging the "vigilance" of white Mississippians even as he acknowledged that fear of an uprising had already made them quite vigilant.

The hollowness of Runnels's proclamation elicited open ridicule from *Natchez Courier* editor William Mellen, who wrote in an editorial that he had published the "silly document, simply because it is the Governor's," but then proceeded to lambaste it and its author alike. Mellen called the proclamation "*injudicious*, because it is calculated now to create an altogether unnecessary alarm"; "*ill-timed*, because, to have been of benefit, it should have been issued a fortnight ago"; and "*useless*, because all the measures which the Proclamation recommends, had been already taken." In fact, Mellen considered the proclamation "*injurious* to every interest in the State—because the danger which might have existed, is, without reason, presumed to exist still."[4]

Mellen could understand how events had taken the course they did in Madison County and thought the actions of its residents "perfectly justifiable." They were afraid, they saw no signs that "the officers of the law" were going to do anything to alleviate their fear, and the duly constituted justices of the peace proved unable to exercise control "during a moment of an excitement." But Mellen considered the governor's behavior unfathomable. "What has the Chief Magistrate of Mississippi," he asked, "been about for the last three or four weeks, that he has just given evidence of being awake? Why was he not upon the scene of action?" Ultimately, Mellen argued that if Runnels had issued a proclamation as soon as he heard what was happening in Madison County and had helped local magistrates execute the law, he could have both "prevented unnecessary alarm in other counties" and "quieted the troubled waters in Madison." The only thing Mellen could say on the governor's behalf was that at least he would always have "a shield against a charge of *rashness!*"[5]

Not everyone appreciated Mellen's sarcasm. The *Courier* was a Whig paper, and editors of several Democratic papers saw Mellen's criticism as an exercise in opportunism that dismissed the plight of whites in west-central Mississippi. From Gallatin, a town in Copiah County due south of Hinds, the editor of the *Democrat* thought Mellen's piece "most insulting" evidence of a "persecuting spirit" rooted in the facts that the residents of Natchez had not felt the "great anxiety and probable peril" induced by the insurrection scare and that the proclamation had come "from a Democratic Governor." The *Democrat*'s editor, sure that Mellen's attack would backfire and redound to Runnels's benefit, concluded that the *Courier* was a paper "whose columns have long been prostituted to the most degrading, selfish, and unprincipled purposes."[6]

In Jackson, George Fall responded to Mellen in the *Mississippian* with similar invective and even harsher slurs. Like the editor of the *Democrat*, Fall asserted that Natchez was far enough from the counties that felt the fear of insurrection most acutely so as not to sense the "state of anxiety, hitherto unparalleled" that "pervaded the public mind." But he claimed that in those counties the governor's proclamation "has been warmly approved; it has quieted the alarm of many individuals, encouraged the county committees of vigilance and safety, and no doubt had a most salutary effect." Writing that "the smiling buffoon of the Courier" would have pilloried the governor no matter what he did, Fall asked whether there was "ever a grosser or more disgusting and shameful evidence of party spirit" than Mellen's criticisms. Brushing aside the attack of the New Hampshire–born Mellen, Fall concluded that the state executive would not be undone "by the simpering, snuffling Yankee, who is hired to assume the editorial black-guardism of the Natchez Courier."[7]

Politically active men in Mississippi viewed nearly every event through a sectarian prism, and both George Fall and the editor of the *Democrat* were probably right that politics partially motivated Mellen's savaging of Governor Runnels and his proclamation. But they were wrong that the white residents of Natchez had not considered their lives in jeopardy during the insurrection scare. And they were wrong that Runnels would survive and even thrive politically. Voters in Mississippi were not pleased with Runnels's torpor during the crisis. Four months after it ended they turned him out of office and replaced him with a Whig chief executive named, of all things, Charles Lynch. Politics in Mississippi could be volatile and unpredictable—Lynch had identified himself as a Democrat just a few years earlier—but at least one Democratic operative thought he understood this particular turn. "The recent insurrectionary movements in this state," he reported to party leaders in Washington, "lost us Madison and Hinds Counties, and injured us in several others." There was just no getting around the fact that William Mellen properly called attention to the emptiness and especially the belatedness of Governor Runnels's proclamation. By the time Runnels got around to taking a public position on the matter, the fear that there were white men prowling his state to provoke the enslaved to rebellion was moving toward its denouement.[8]

I.

In Madison County, residents had hanged Joshua Cotton, William Saunders, Albe Dean, Angus Donovan, and Ruel Blake, nearly all of whom they believed were "ringleaders" of the conspiracy. Supposed confederates like Andrew Boyd and the Rawsons had managed to escape but had been so terrorized that they were unlikely to show their faces in the area again. About a dozen of the enslaved purported to be involved had been executed too, and surely the rest of the slave population was sufficiently cowed not to consider carrying off the plot without whites to instigate and organize it. Additionally, to the extent that a consensus ever had existed in Mississippi that the emergency demanded unquestioning acceptance of the methods used to contain it, the Patrick Sharkey affair and the Clinton committee of safety's vow to defend him demonstrated that such consensus had fractured. Perhaps most important, while the belief that an insurrection was at hand persisted and even strengthened for several days after it was supposed to have begun on the Fourth of July, time passed with no sign that there was going to be one. If the conspiracy had been broken, if the slaves seemed disinclined to rebel, and if white men of standing in Mississippi were beginning to turn their suspicions on each other, perhaps it was no longer worthwhile running to ground every lead and every grievance.

When Governor Runnels tardily revealed that he was monitoring the situation, the members of the Livingston Committee of Safety had already decided the worst of the crisis had passed and the occasion had about arrived for the committee to adjourn permanently. Committee members, however, did want to express gratitude to those who had stood by them. So on the same day that Runnels issued his proclamation they passed a resolution thanking the residents of Vicksburg and Warren County in particular "for their active, energetic, prompt and efficient conduct, respecting the recent alarms and difficulties that have threatened and disturbed the peace and quiet of the people of this county, and this State generally." Vicksburgers had helped take Ruel Blake into custody and make sure that he came back to Madison for trial, and they had provided extra weapons when Governor Runnels had failed to supply them. But it was not just people in Warren County who deserved the committee's recognition. Its members wanted to be sure to acknowledge the white citizens of Mississippi more broadly and to "fully and properly appreciate such acts of conduct among our people throughout the state generally."[9]

The resolution the members of the Livingston Committee of Safety passed was cleverly calculated. It marked an effort to put the scare behind them, invest it with larger meaning as an event during which white Mississippians faced down a threat with courage and resolution, and paper over the divisions among them that had cost Hiram Perkins his life and nearly led to anarchy. It even tied together the insurrection scare and the gambling riot, which no one had seen before as anything other than discreet if coincidentally timed events, by praising Vicksburgers for "arresting and speedily bringing to condign punishment, those inhuman monsters who have been engaged in plotting and maturing such diabolical measures for the destruction of the lives of the innocent and virtuous." Taken as a whole, the resolution enabled the Livingston committee to present itself as one group of actors in a much larger play in which Mississippians were "co-operators in a humane cause impelled by that imperious sense of duty in protecting the lives and virtues of our wives and daughters against the disgraceful and diabolical attempts of mercenary wretches."[10]

But nothing could disguise how deeply troubled a place the insurrection scare had revealed frontier Mississippi to be. To a certain extent, that whites in Madison, Hinds, and other counties in central and western Mississippi would respond as they did to the prospect of a slave uprising is to be expected. Slaves composed a restless and discontented population whose efforts to undermine the regime that held them in bondage were systematic, surreptitious, and widespread. Constantly resisting their captivity and conceiving how they might end their subjugation, periodically the enslaved did actually conspire to overturn slavery altogether.

The revolt foremost in the minds of white Mississippians was the Southampton Insurrection, commonly known as Nat Turner's Rebellion, which had broken out in Virginia in 1831. But scattered across the history of the Western Hemisphere stretching back more than two centuries were hundreds of instances of slave insurgency, and the most successful had occurred in West Indian colonies where the enslaved outnumbered their white captors. The Haitian Revolution that began in 1791 particularly haunted slaveholders in the United States, leading as it did to the overthrow of slavery in the French colony of Saint Domingue, the execution or exile of thousands of whites, and the establishment of a black republic. Slaves outnumbered whites in Haiti on the eve of that revolution even more dramatically than in most parts of frontier Mississippi, but in their desire to maximize the profits to be made from cotton, white settlers in Madison County and other places like it had imported slaves faster than they crafted interpersonal connections and organizational structures that could mitigate the enmity of the enslaved or at least tamp down its virulence. It was a truism of life under slavery in the United States that white southerners feared their slaves might rise against them. But in the Southwest, Americans had created ideal circumstances for the situation they dreaded most. The repercussions for the enslaved were bound to be fierce when any convincing evidence at all indicated that whites, in the words of one correspondent of Governor Runnels, were "sleeping over a volcano."[11]

Nor is it especially startling that white settlers in Mississippi believed other white men were encouraging the enslaved to rebel. Slaveholders often saw economically marginal whites as shifty individuals with suspect racial loyalties whose status made them just as likely to subvert the planta-tion order as sustain it, and American history is replete with examples of white fears of slave rebellion accompanied by the belief that unreliable white people were complicit in the planning. In reality, relationships between lower-class whites and the enslaved were fraught with ambivalence, and while poorer whites commonly socialized and dealt economically with the enslaved, they rarely manifested a desire to overturn slavery itself. Moreover, those white people singled out as insurrectionists during the summer of 1835 were not universally or even mostly poor, and frontier Mississippi had little in the way of a plantation "order" to be subverted. Nevertheless, the wealth of the planters who sat on the various committees of safety depended on making such an order viable. Doing so entailed clearing the region of whites whose racial or economic solidarity seemed tenuous or ambiguous no less in places where order was already established. Arguably, doing so was part and parcel of making the plantation economy possible at all.[12]

But the paroxysm of violence that convulsed Mississippi in the sum-mer of 1835 was the deadliest outbreak of extralegal violence in the slave states between the Southampton Insurrection and the Civil War. This was no ordinary insurrection scare, and we might ask why whites in Madison County and elsewhere in Mississippi believed at all in the particular plot Virgil Stewart warned of in his pamphlet. John Murrell, the scheme's mas-termind, was languishing in the Tennessee State Penitentiary. The notion that his incarceration had led his clan to advance the date of the uprising he supposedly conceived to July 4, as opposed to the December 25 date Stew-art named, came entirely from the imagination of white Mississippians. Most dumbfounding, the story Stewart told in his pamphlet was incredible at best, preposterous at worst, and downright weird either way. The nag-ging questions about Stewart's background, motives, and basic veracity had yet to become widespread public knowledge, but one would think a person did not need to know anything at all about Stewart to wonder whether he ought to swallow a tale as outlandish as *The Western Land Pirate*.

Historians have long observed that Americans are particularly prone to believing in conspiracies, and social, cultural, and political life in the Jacksonian era was shot through with what Richard Hofstadter famously referred to as the "paranoid style." Some Americans worried that the Ma-sons were a secretive and aristocratic group that threatened constitutional government. Others feared the sinister influence of Catholics or Mormons, slaveholders or abolitionists, bankers or workers. Believing that treacherous forces machinating in secret explain the workings of the world or endanger its future is one way to make sense of baffling change, and Americans in the 1820s and 1830s lived in a turbulent time. Their society was becoming increasingly democratic and individualistic, their economic lives increasingly abstruse, and the traditional frameworks that structured society increasingly disaggregated. It was contradictory, perhaps, to maintain that mysterious cabals were plotting against the cherished liberties of the individual while also fretting that Americans had become too atomized to defend themselves against those whose power and influence derived in part from their organization. But the sources of American anxiety were contradictory too, and such presumptions and suspicions helped impart a measure of elemental coherence and clarity to the disorientations of the age.[13]

Not all conspiracy theories appeal to all people in all places, though. The ability of any given theory to gain popularity and acceptance depends on the cultural and social ground of the time and location where it takes root. Moreover, not every conspiracy theory merely or wholly reflects the irrational and paranoid delusions of those who believe in it. Sometimes there really are conspiracies. At the very least, beliefs in conspiracy are not infrequently based in some sort of reality, albeit usually a distorted version of it. And on closer examination the conspiracy posited by Virgil Stewart, while ridiculous on the whole, contained just enough verisimilitude to make it seem credible and astonishingly dangerous to white settlers on Mississippi's cotton frontier.

II.

Banditry in the Southwest had a lengthy history before John Murrell ever began his career of petty crime in western Tennessee and before Virgil Stewart ever published his pamphlet. Going back to the late eighteenth century the region had a reputation as an unsafe and morally degraded section of the North American continent lousy with highwaymen, pirates, and brigands. Capitalizing on dark and lonely stretches of water and road that provided perfect conditions for robbing traders and ambushing travelers, and acting without compunction thanks to the administrative and practical challenges of establishing reliable law enforcement on the frontier, criminals appeared as if from nowhere and then vanished back into the forest before their victims quite understood what had happened to them.[14]

Some of the most famously perilous routes for travelers, such as the Natchez Trace, had fallen into disuse by the 1830s, and the notoriety of the Southwest had begun to metastasize from its origins in reality into the Twainish mythology for which the American frontier is still renowned. The region had not seen a genuine confederacy of killers and thieves since the days of Samuel Mason, who spent several decades leading a band of about a dozen desperadoes in southeastern Illinois, Kentucky, Missouri, and the Mississippi Territory until 1803, when two of his own men turned on him, chopped off his head, and tried to claim a reward offered for his arrest. But legends die hard. The Southwest continued to be staggeringly violent. And especially along the Mississippi River and anywhere state boundaries came together, outlaws remained a considerable problem. Samuel Mason may have been long gone, but it was not necessarily far-fetched to believe an enterprising, charismatic, and ruthless villain like him could exist again.[15]

White settlers of frontier Mississippi did not even have to reach into the distant past to know that men with a frightful combination of charm, intelligence, and sheer criminal ferocity were real and lived among them. Alonzo Phelps was one of those men. His story is worth telling in some detail here because more than any other individual person, Phelps prepared Mississippians in 1835 to believe that John Murrell could be as nefarious as Virgil Stewart said he was. Born in New England in 1804, Phelps was already a murderer twice over when he appeared in the Southwest in the mid-1820s, and he proceeded to spend the late 1820s and early 1830s menacing the countryside from Vicksburg to New Orleans. By the time he was captured, tried, and sentenced to hang in Warren County for the 1833 murder of Owen Rhodes, Phelps had killed more than half a dozen men, assaulted or fought with dozens more, and committed an untold number of highway robberies.[16]

The infamy Alonzo Phelps achieved in Mississippi was attributable only partially to his extensive criminal catalog. Phelps seemed to be a creature encountered in fairy tales. Just under six feet tall and weighing around 165 pounds, Phelps was heavily muscled and extraordinarily strong. His long pointed chin, large mouth, small gray eyes, bushy yellow brows, deeply tanned skin, and the unkempt knots of curly dark red hair that stuck out in all directions from his head made him appear a sort of demon. The fact that he spent the bulk of eight years living outdoors in the forest, subsisting on stolen crops or on squirrels and other small game that he ate raw if too famished or rushed to take the time to cook them, only added to his reputation. It was not for nothing that among the nicknames Phelps acquired, one was simply "the wild man."[17]

Enhancing Phelps's stature as a nearly supernatural villain was his spectacular death. Phelps had no intention of expiring on the gallows, telling anyone who would listen that he planned instead to die "like a soldier." The exact meaning of that became clear the day before his scheduled execution in March 1834, when Phelps requested that a minister be sent to his cell in the Vicksburg jail to provide spiritual solace. The jailor, Martin Anding, noticed while escorting the clergyman into the cell that Phelps had somehow managed to get hold of a small knife or a file and had sawed most of the way through the manacles around his wrists. Understanding that Phelps was trying to escape, Anding immediately backed out of the cell. He armed himself with a large butcher knife, asked a burly man named William Everett to accompany him, and returned with the intention of chaining Phelps more securely.[18]

But Anding and Everett were no match for Phelps. When they came back, Phelps was standing behind the cell door. His hands still fettered, he bashed Everett in the head with a lead inkstand wrapped in a stocking, then scuffled with Anding and snatched the knife from his belt. Anding, Everett, and the minister fled and locked themselves in an adjoining room as Phelps headed for the exterior door of the building. But it too was locked, giving Sheriff Stephen Howard, several deputies, and a small crowd time to assemble in the yard outside the jailhouse. On Howard's signal the exterior door was broken down, and the first man through it found himself face to face with a knife-wielding Phelps. The man fell back wounded, the crowd parted, and Phelps stepped into the prison yard and began making his way toward the main gate. Howard clubbed him over the head with a rifle stock and the crowd began bombarding Phelps with brickbats, rocks, sticks, axes, and anything else they could find to throw at him, but still Phelps moved forward, slowly losing strength with each step. He had made it through the gate and started stumbling down the hill beyond it that led to the Mississippi River when someone hit him square with a brick in the small of his back. Realizing he could go no farther and in tremendous pain, Phelps began screaming for someone to shoot him. Stephen Howard obliged. He stepped out of the crowd and shot Phelps once in the back, sending him sprawling face-forward to the ground, where he died.[19]

The tale of Alonzo Phelps, however, did not end on a hillside by the Vicksburg jail. Ten days before his scheduled execution, Phelps had written to Governor Runnels asking for a postponement so that he might finish writing a document he described as "the history of the last nine years of my life." Runnels refused the request, but Phelps completed the short book anyway, determined to shape not only the circumstances of his demise but also the way Mississippians would remember him. If Phelps's crimes, appearance, and manner of death were not enough to distinguish him in Mississippi as a practically folkloric figure, the *Confession of Alonzo Phelps*, published in Jackson in the spring of 1834, surely was.[20]

Read as autobiography, Phelps's *Confession* is a breathtakingly bleak chronicle of life among the southwestern white underclass. By his own account Phelps had few friends, no family, no steady employment, and no home. He developed fleeting attachments to several women, forged tenuous personal connections with numerous men, worked sporadically at a variety of jobs, and briefly enlisted in the army. But he rarely stayed in one place longer than a few months and had neither the wherewithal nor the inclination to make real plans for a future. He got involved in so many brawls and altercations and could be turned in for reward money in so many jurisdictions that he could trust no one, and he committed so many robberies in part because for every one that brought a windfall there were many that netted him only enough money to survive for a couple of days or weeks. Once, Phelps became so fond of a woman that he considered settling down with her and opening a roadside grocery and timber stop, but his efforts to help her leave her abusive husband ultimately led to the murder for which Phelps was sentenced to hang. By and large, Phelps led an aimless, cruel, destitute, and sad existence consisting of a series of bloody confrontations punctuated by rare and ephemeral stretches of peace and contentment.[21]

But to read the *Confession* solely as a saga of wretchedness is to miss its point and its significance. Phelps framed his exploits throughout as matters of honor, acts of self-defense, or actions undertaken on behalf of the poor and downtrodden. Casting himself as a sort of "social bandit" who stole from the prosperous, aided the penniless, protected the vulnerable, and championed the weak against the strong, Phelps clearly hoped people would be telling stories about him long after his demise, writing that dying at age twenty-nine meant his fame had not "become as fully established, and as widely diffused, as I have heretofore desired it to be." Had he lived to be forty, he assured readers, he would have successfully established himself as "the most celebrated Robber that modern times have produced."[22]

Befitting someone who bragged about being a prolific criminal while claiming his crimes were planted in noble soil, Phelps emerges from the *Confession* as an ambiguous and contradictory figure. On the one hand, he reveled in his own lewdness. Phelps frequented prostitutes whenever he had the opportunity and the means, claimed that at one brothel the madam worried that his behavior and language were so foul that he would corrupt the morals of its residents, alluded to having acquired a venereal disease, and wrote poetry so vulgar the printers of the *Confession* excised it from the published text. On the other hand, Phelps professed an abiding affection for women, asserting that like most "personages who have been considered worthy to figure upon the pages of history" he had "ever been a devoted worshipper at the shrine of Venus," and he became indignant or lashed out with chivalrous rage whenever he encountered or even heard about someone mistreating a woman.[23]

Phelps took delight in boasting about his capacity for violence and relished the gory details of his crimes. Of the men he killed, he described cutting out the heart of one, clubbing another with such force that the man's "brains spouted from his brain-pan, and bespattered my clothing," and slowly "ringing and twisting" the head of a third until he detached it from the man's body. At the same time, Phelps cultivated refinement and erudition, insisting that while a blackguard he was no ignoramus. Though lacking much formal education, Phelps claimed to have read on his own "more extensively than most men." He considered himself especially knowledgeable in "history and moral science" but also believed he was "somewhat better versed in scriptural lore than most of the ministers of the gospel whom I have encountered in my travels" and that he had "attentively examined every work that has fallen in my way in opposition to the Christian system." Never eschewing the chance to scandalize readers, Phelps added that he had "as little respect [for Christianity] as either Voltaire or Tom Paine."[24]

The most notable tension running through the *Confession* was that Phelps gleefully touted his assaulting and stealing from people but also insisted that he adhered to a certain ethical code. He rifled the pockets of those he killed and considered robbing nearly anyone he met on the road. But he maintained that he "never was willing to kill any man, merely for money," and he often spoke with or at least tried visually to size up potential targets in an effort to determine their station in life. Guided by the precept of "robbing the rich to feed the poor, and stripping the miser of his useless hoards to succor the helpless," Phelps unhesitatingly took what he wanted from those he thought could spare it, let pass those who appeared to need the cash they had, and claimed he gave away the bulk of his spoils "to distressed persons whom I casually met."[25]

To no class of people did Phelps extend more compassion than the enslaved, however, and for no class of people did he bear greater enmity than slave traders. Phelps gave money or food to runaway slaves he encountered in the forests, and on one occasion he sawed shackles off of two runaways chained together and told them which roads led north toward freedom. By contrast, when Phelps discovered that a man he was robbing traded professionally in slaves, he stole everything the man had and berated him, saying that not even he would stoop to profit by driving "human cattle to market" and denying his "fellow men of all chance of ever seeing their wives and children again." When the man replied that if he "did not buy and sell negroes, others would," Phelps sneered: "and if I did not rob you of your cash, some other person might." If his *Confession* is to be believed, Alonzo Phelps saw race as meaningless. No one was more friendless than a runaway slave, no one deserved what was in his pockets less than someone who bought and sold others for a living, and nothing was more hypocritical than a moral order in which the same people who felt "furious indignation" toward Phelps when he stole "a pitiful sum of money" would have gladly accepted a reward for returning "poor slaves to the custody of an unfeeling master."[26]

Whether or not we *can* believe Phelps's *Confession* is another matter. Phelps engaged in much self-aggrandizement and probably told some outright lies, but few of the specific incidents he described are implausible, and several Mississippi newspaper editors thought his account largely accurate. The main prosecuting attorney in Phelps's murder trial, Sargent S. Prentiss, had no patience for the notion of Phelps as a magnanimous and charitable outlaw and scoffed in court at his efforts to be thought of as "the Rob Roy of the Mississippi." Phelps, however, liked that moniker so much that he adopted it as the subtitle of the *Confession*. Ultimately, Phelps's truthfulness is less important than his talent for self-promotion. Crafting a narrative laced with social criticism and abounding with violence, sex, and other elements likely to horrify and thrill readers, Phelps forged a personal mythology so successful that poems about him were still appearing in Mississippi newspapers six years after his death.[27]

While it is impossible to say just how many copies of the *Confession of Alonzo Phelps* actually sold, Phelps's influence on the insurrection scare that broke out a little more than a year after his death was substantial. In the most general sense, Phelps exemplified the kind of itinerant, poor, malevolent, and bloodthirsty white man whose disrespect for property rights and especially for slavery presented the kind of obstacles to the establishment of a plantation economy that someone like Joshua Cotton supposedly did. No matter how many Mississippi planters may have read and remembered Phelps's *Confession*, though, one reader mattered more than any other, because Alonzo Phelps was unmistakably among the leading inspirations for John Murrell as Virgil Stewart depicted him in *The Western Land Pirate*.

That Stewart was in central and western Mississippi in the fall of 1834 as he was writing his pamphlet tells us only that he would have heard about Alonzo Phelps and had the opportunity to read the *Confession*. Several details, however, indicate that Stewart both read and directly lifted specific elements of it to make John Murrell a more credible villain. Like the Murrell of *The Western Land Pirate*, Alonzo Phelps considered affecting the disguise of a Methodist minister to gull people into giving him money. John Murrell spoke of visiting a house of prostitution in New Orleans run by a woman known as "old mother Surgick," an obvious reference to the brothel proprietress named "Mother Sedgwick" in Phelps's account. Most tellingly, Phelps described numerous instances when he disposed of murder victims by gutting them, removing their entrails, and sinking their bodies to the bottom of rivers, a signature technique of Stewart's Murrell.[28]

None of these particulars was necessarily unique to Alonzo Phelps or his *Confession*. Southwestern settlers were often skeptical of men purporting to be Methodist preachers; Phelps wrote that Mother Sedgwick was a woman "of extensive notoriety"; and he did not originate disembowelment as a method of body disposal. Clinching the notion that Virgil Stewart had Alonzo Phelps on his mind when he developed the character of John Murrell is that Stewart made Phelps himself a minor but vital character in *The Western Land Pirate*.[29]

According to Stewart, Murrell said that he and Phelps first met when Phelps and a man named Haines robbed him in New Orleans but returned Murrell's money and joined him for a night of revelry on discovering that Murrell was a fellow thief. That night proved seminal for Murrell, and he remembered it as "the commencement of my greatness, in what the world calls villany," because amid the drinking and fornicating Phelps and Haines also gave Murrell the names of every significant participant in the criminal underworld of New Orleans and the entire lower Mississippi Valley. Using that list of names as a guide, Murrell soon began recruiting members for his "mystic clan" and developing his plan to instigate a slave rebellion.[30]

In truth, there is no evidence that Phelps and Murrell ever met or knew each other, though Stewart both included Phelps on the inventory of clan members he provided in *The Western Land Pirate* and cleverly denoted Phelps's first name as "Soril"—a nickname referring to Phelps's sorrel red hair that he noted in the *Confession* was "frequently applied by my associates." Phelps's presence in *The Western Land Pirate* was more than just a touchstone that lent credence to Stewart's narrative, however. Stewart also used Phelps as a benchmark to make Murrell seem more vicious than Phelps at his worst. According to Stewart, when Murrell spoke about Phelps he acknowledged that he was "a noble fellow among the negroes; he wants them all free, and he knows how to excite them as well as any person." But Phelps was too humane for Murrell. "He has been in the habit of stopping men on the highway and robbing them, and letting them go on," Murrell told Stewart, "but that will never do for a robber: after I rob a man he will never give evidence against me; and there is but one safe plan in the business, and that is to kill."[31]

The differences between Alonzo Phelps and John Murrell help explain the dread Stewart's pamphlet instilled among white Mississippians as much as their similarities do. Virgil Stewart's John Murrell was Alonzo Phelps stripped of his pretenses to being a latter-day Robin Hood. Murrell was thoroughly selfish, merciless, and misanthropic, his sympathies for the enslaved nothing more than an affectation used to advance his own ends. Moreover, where Phelps was a loner who lacked the drive to make long-term plans, Murrell was organized and ambitious and had spent years carefully building a criminal syndicate. It might be inconceivable that anyone could effectively command and coordinate the activities of more than one thousand men arrayed over nearly one million square miles of territory as

Stewart alleged Murrell said he did. But Stewart's presentation of a south-western landscape whose criminal elements sometimes worked together to maximize their effectiveness was nonetheless another credible component of his pamphlet.

Alonzo Phelps, for example, noted that he had declined to join "a band of pirates" who worked the rivers around New Orleans and described how he and a man named Charles Bill briefly joined forces "in the business of robbing on the highway." In addition, as the case of Samuel Mason and his men suggests, organized gangs of criminals could be more durable than the roving bands of highwaymen and aimless freebooters whose attacks unnerved travelers and made hair-raising copy in the newspapers. Indeed, there was a tantalizing if enigmatic coda to the insurrection scare of 1835 suggesting that if the criminal organization depicted in Virgil Stewart's pamphlet had just enough plausibility to terrify slaveholders, it also had just enough to give slave stealers the idea to animate it.[32]

III.

Maybe all that Joshua Cotton, William Saunders, and Albe Dean did to-gether was sell Thomsonian medicines. Maybe the stories told to the Liv-ingston Committee of Safety about Cotton and Andrew Boyd collaborat-ing to steal slaves, about Cotton and Dean using the pretense of hunting for horses to speak with plantation slaves, and about Saunders never seeming able to account convincingly for his whereabouts could all be explained away or were lies procured from witnesses under duress. Then again, maybe not. If steam doctoring was a perfectly legitimate way to make a living, it was not an especially lucrative one, and it enabled a nomadic lifestyle that could be a fine front for shady activities and criminal associations. Nothing conclusively indicates that Cotton, Saunders, and Dean had anything other than an aboveboard business relationship, that they stole slaves, or that they even knew who John Murrell was. But it is not unreasonable to wonder whether their steam doctoring disguised more illicit pursuits.

The story of the brothers John and William Earl elevates such questions at least a step beyond the realm of conjecture. The Earls lived in War-ren County, having moved there in 1834 from the Kingston area of Adams County about fifteen miles southeast of Natchez. Joshua Cotton named the Earls in his confession as being among his co-conspirators, but they had remained peripheral figures in whom patrollers and vigilance committees showed little interest and whose connection to the alleged plot was indeterminate. Until the evening of July 15, when half a dozen men from Warren County rode into Livingston with the Earls in tow, intending to turn them over to the village committee of safety for examination. With the committee no longer meeting regularly and most people who lived in and around the village having gone back to their homes, Livingston was relatively deserted, so the Earls were placed in the jail for safekeeping.[33]

It would not be a peaceful night. Unwilling to wait until the committee could reassemble in the morning, a small party of men gathered at the jail and began questioning the Earls, demanding information about the insurrection plot. The brothers were tight-lipped, conceding that they had heard of the conspiracy, that they were acquainted with Andrew Boyd, and not much else. But their interrogators remained convinced they knew more. So they took William Earl, the older of the two, out of his cell and tried scaring him into confessing his involvement and providing the names of his associates. When threats and harassment failed to elicit information, they began whipping him, but Earl gave them nothing. Finally, they stripped him naked, laid him facedown on the ground, dragged a feral cat by the tail across his already bruised and lacerated back, and poured hot sealing wax directly into his wounds.[34]

Whether this sadistic treatment gave its perpetrators the results they wanted is unclear. A resident of Madison County wrote to the *Natchez Courier* that William Earl told his tormentors only "a few *lies*" while they abused him before begging them to stop with a promise that "he would next morning, when he would be more composed, make a full confession of his connexion with the conspirators and of the conspiracy, and of all other villany, in which he was concerned." Thomas Shackelford, however, claimed that Earl made a series of valuable disclosures on the spot. Among other things, Earl supposedly admitted that he, his brother, Andrew Boyd, Joshua Cotton, William Saunders, George Rawson, William Donley, and two other individuals known only as Samuels and Lofton were all complicit in a slave uprising that was to have taken place on the Fourth of July, and that John Earl and Andrew Boyd in particular had spent three weeks riding plantation districts recruiting "as many negroes as they could."[35]

That William Earl lied and that he provided information are not mutually exclusive propositions. The insurrection plan Earl purportedly described, which was to have begun in Madison County and moved southwest with the goal of reaching Natchez, was suspiciously similar to the one whites had beaten slaves into divulging at Beattie's Bluff. Earl could have heard about the plan, the details of which had been circulating through west and central Mississippi by this point for more than two weeks, and then admitted his own involvement under pressure, or perhaps his interrogators fed him the information. Alternatively, Shackelford may have simply fabricated Earl's "confession" after the fact. At the very least, Shackelford's assertion that Earl started talking without having been subjected to "any fear or compulsion" was nonsense. The text of Earl's admission as Shackelford recorded it, in fact, consists mostly of a series of rambling and repetitive declarations that read like they came from a man so far out of his mind with pain as to be unable to maintain his train of thought or form coherent sentences, and willing to say or agree to anything a questioner wanted him to say.[36]

Still, for all that Earl's supposed confession trod what had become familiar ground, there were names in it that had never surfaced before in anyone's testimony to the Livingston Committee of Safety. It was hard to know what to make of that, but the full complement of committee members would never get to hear William Earl talk about it. When Earl's inquisitors were through with him, they returned him to jail, and sometime during the night, he stood as high as the chains fixing him to the floor of his cell would allow, tied one end of a handkerchief to a rung of a ladder, and fastened the other end around his neck. Then he sat back down. When guards came to retrieve him on the morning of July 16 he was dead.[37]

John Earl, however, was still very much alive, and he wanted to stay that way. He appeared nearly jubilant on hearing of his brother's death, claiming that even the limited information he had provided the previous evening was damaging enough that William would have killed him had both of them been released. Now that his older brother was gone, he was ready to talk. The Livingston Committee of Safety reconvened, and John Earl told its members that he had first met Andrew Boyd in the fall of 1834 and that Boyd stole slaves. Moreover, he said that Boyd recently had gone on trial for slave stealing in Warren County and that he, Earl, had been strong-armed by his brother into providing Boyd with a bogus alibi that got Boyd acquitted. Earl asserted further that the man identified by his brother as Lofton had told him a slave insurrection was going to begin on the Fourth of July and asked him to join an organization known as the "Domestic Lodge," whose members included Lofton, Boyd, Saunders, Cotton, Albe Dean, Ruel Blake, William Donley, William Earl, John McKnight, and someone John Earl knew only as Scrugs. Contrary to his brother's statements, John Earl claimed that he had refused to join the group and that he was afraid of it, saying that his brother "told me he would shoot me or any one else who would divulge any thing."[38]

Among the oddities attending to the Earl brothers and their experience in Livingston is how and why they ended up in the village in the first place. The Madison County correspondent of the *Natchez Courier* reported that a committee in Vicksburg had sent the Earls to Livingston on the presumption "that more proof of their guilt could be obtained here, than at Vicksburg." A few weeks after the Earls arrived in Livingston, however, a Warren County man who signed his name "HUMANITY" wrote to the *Vicksburg Register* stating that the residents of Vicksburg would never have hauled "their own criminals from county to county" for trial and that there was no committee in Vicksburg that might have ordered such a thing. Rather, "HUMANITY" claimed, "a few unauthorised individuals" effectively kidnapped the Earls and brought them to Livingston on their own accord, hoping the brothers might never return to Warren County.[39]

That was about right. The *Natchez Courier* correspondent replied to "HUMANITY" with his own letter to the *Vicksburg Register* and admitted that there was no formal committee in Vicksburg. Rather, the Earls had been conveyed to Madison by "five or six highly respectable men of Warren County, who had organized themselves into a committee for their own safety," believing "they were surrounded by such a set of scoundrels, had they attempted to have tried [the Earls], some personal or pecuniary injury would have been offered them." One wonders why those "scoundrels" would have been any more forgiving of abduction and rendition than a local trial. A less generous way of putting things was that a few people from Warren County thought the Earls a squirrelly pair, could see no way to get rid of them through legal means, were uncomfortable personally dispatching them through extralegal means, and concluded that the folks in Livingston might do the dirty work for them instead. Thomas Shackelford said as much in a rare moment of candor, claiming that "several respectable citizens" of Warren County heard that Joshua Cotton had named the brothers in his confession, "and believing the Earles to be rascals, from the course in relation to Boyd . . . determined on bringing them to Livingston and have them tried."[40]

When it came to the Earls, though, the Livingston Committee of Safety failed to administer the kind of justice it had been doling out since the beginning of July. William Earl committed suicide before he ever got a hearing, and after listening to John Earl's testimony, committee members found him guilty of "aiding and abetting the negroes in the late contemplated insurrection" but decided neither to sentence nor punish him. Instead, they sent a transcript of his trial back to Warren and waited for a reply. This too was curious. Committee members in Livingston had never been squeamish or hesitant about whipping or hanging people they decided were involved in the insurrection plot, no matter where they came from or where they lived, and the committee had never bothered soliciting anyone else's opinion as to what to do.[41]

If anything, considering how the residents of Vicksburg had dealt with Truman North and the men in his house, they would seem among the least likely people from whom the Livingston Committee of Safety might need approval before taking action. Still, bringing the Earls to Madison County was irregular even by the standards of extralegal justice, and the members of the Livingston committee did not want to see a reprise of what had happened at Patrick Sharkey's plantation or outside the committee room in Clinton during and after his trial. After those debacles, they would think twice about executing a resident of another county before they were sure it was what those claiming authority in that county wanted.

That hesitation proved wise, as people in Warren were not unanimous in their opinions about the Earls. On July 20, word reached Vicksburg that William Earl had been tortured and that John Earl had been found guilty of involvement with the insurrection plot, whereupon city residents met and appointed a six-person guard to retrieve the brothers. The guard carried a series of resolutions passed at the meeting, including one absolving "the good people of Madison" of any responsibility for how the Earls had been treated and reaffirming their approbation of "the zeal and devotion" residents of Madison County "displayed in the cause of public safety" during "these troublesome times." Nonetheless, when the retrieval party discovered that William Earl was in fact already dead, at least one of its members was disturbed enough to speculate publicly that Earl had been murdered and to assert that what had happened to the Earls was too cruel even "for savages."[42]

After his guards returned John Earl to Warren County, they apparently let him go home and continue on with his life. Perhaps they thought he had already been through enough of an ordeal, or they may have believed his claims that his brother had goaded him into his misdeeds. Whatever its motivation, the leniency shown to John Earl prevented those who provided it from carefully examining the admissions he made to the Livingston Committee of Safety. There is some irony in this, because those admissions pointed toward a more believable explanation of the actual connections among at least some of the men suspected of involvement in the insurrection plot than outlandish theories about John Murrell and his plans.[43]

Throughout Virgil Stewart's pamphlet and the insurrection scare of 1835, the criminal syndicate masterminded by Murrell was always called the "mystic clan" or simply "the clan." What, then, was the "Domestic Lodge" to which John Earl referred? Moreover, who were those other men he mentioned whose names had never before been connected to the conspiracy? Any number of fraternal organizations and secret societies called their basic organizational units lodges. The term carried with it more sinister connotations in the first half of the nineteenth century than it does today, and Earl could have stumbled on it in a frantic mental scramble to identify the league of criminals to which Livingston committee members already believed he belonged. The names Earl and his brother provided, meanwhile, need not have originated with them at all. Given the events of the preceding weeks, names like Cotton, Saunders, Dean, and Blake would have come up during any interrogation. The others could have been their Warren County analogs—people whose behavior or attitudes made them locally disreputable, and whose names the men who initially brought the Earls to Madison offered the residents of Livingston as likely confederates of the brothers. Some prompting backed by torture and fright took care of the rest.

Yet John Earl's story does have elements that lend themselves to an alternative reading. The court papers of Andrew Boyd's slave-stealing trial have not survived, but John and William Earl probably did lie to exculpate him. That the two admitted having done so does not necessarily indicate it was true, but it was something that would have happened publicly and predated the brothers' arrival and mistreatment in Livingston. Moreover,

Boyd and Joshua Cotton did have a personal connection, and maybe even a criminal one. All the way back on June 30, before the Livingston Committee of Safety even existed, when William Saunders was asked to account for himself and his associations he asserted that Cotton and Boyd had colluded to steal the slaves for which Boyd had been tried, and other than those of his ostensible business partners Cotton and Albe Dean, Boyd's was the only name Saunders offered. It was widely rumored that Boyd and Cotton frequently pretended to be siblings, and after being acquitted on the slave-stealing charge in Warren, Boyd had supposedly been headed for Livingston to reconnoiter with Cotton when he learned that Cotton was already in custody and made his own escape through the swamp. Tying Cotton, Boyd, and the Earls together more firmly still was Cotton's naming John and William Earl in his confession. By the time the Earls showed up in Livingston it had become accepted fact that Cotton was an insurrectionist, and we might dismiss the Earls giving his name as the result of coercion. But the best explanation for Cotton having offered the names of the Earls is that he already knew who they were.[44]

If we accept that Cotton, Saunders, Boyd, the Earls, and perhaps some of the other men whose names emerged during the Livingston investigations knew one another and may at times have worked in criminal concert, it is not unthinkable that they might have tried to create an organization like the "Domestic Lodge" mentioned by John Earl. Like other southwestern migrants, criminals sought opportunities for economic gain, and when they located one they took it. John Earl claimed Lofton first approached him about joining the Domestic Lodge in March 1835, which was precisely when Virgil Stewart began distributing *The Western Land Pirate*. The timing may be coincidental, but Stewart's was a work that could speak to people's fantasies as well as their fears. Surely it is not hard to imagine some balefully disposed individuals coming across Stewart's pamphlet, reading about John Murrell's mystic clan and its designs on the wealth of the Southwest, and thinking it ingenious to build an outlaw gang on that model.[45]

In Livingston, both Earl brothers demonstrated a flick of the wrist and a secret handshake they said was the "sign" of the Lodge, and John Earl echoed an assertion William Saunders had made before his death that some members of the group intended to rob James Ewing, a commission house agent they knew to be on his way from New Orleans to Madison

County. No incipient and miniaturized version of Murrell's mystic clan, however, could be complete without using the pretense of orchestrating a slave uprising to create unease among whites and encourage unrest among blacks. That a genuine plot existed in 1835 for a gang of white robbers to collaborate with the enslaved in a massive region-wide rebellion on the Fourth of July is highly improbable. That some slaves in Madison County heard rumors of such a thing not only by eavesdropping on their masters but also from white men creeping about plantations and representing themselves as the plot's operatives may have been a case of life imitating art.[46]

In the end, we cannot know whether John Earl's Domestic Lodge was a total fiction, a pipe dream, or a fledgling copy of the mystic clan. The story of the insurrection scare of 1835, like all histories and perhaps more than most, is open to different readings of the available sources and different trajectories of plot. Given the fragmentary evidence and the biases of those who produced the bulk of it, crafting any narrative in which everything that seems like a revealing clue fits together to yield a neat and tidy account is beyond our ken. If anything like the Domestic Lodge ever existed, though, it did so only briefly. Invented in March 1835, just four months later several of its originators were dead or dispersed, and no one bothered pursuing those who remained behind. By the third week of July, the murderous energy of the white settlers of frontier Mississippi was spent, at least for the moment. As the Madison County correspondent of the *Natchez Courier* observed, whether or not anyone else got arrested barely mattered anymore. "I think the internal danger has passed," he wrote, "and we need apprehend none from the disbanded and scattered villains, who have infested this part of the country. . . . The excitement has entirely subsided, and the countenances of our careworn citizens, have again assumed their wanted cheerfullness."[47]

IV.

Ultimately, for whatever credible conclusions we might draw about how Virgil Stewart's pamphlet reminded white Mississippians of the wildest bandits on the old frontier or inspired the formation of an inchoate criminal confederacy that came unraveled before it was knit, Thomas Shackelford showed anyone who read the proceedings of the Livingston Committee of Safety that he compiled exactly what about Stewart's pamphlet so spooked him and his fellow settlers. To the proceedings Shackelford appended the section of *The Western Land Pirate* in which John Murrell described his insurrection scheme, ostensibly to illustrate what Joshua Cotton had meant when he confessed to "trying to carry into effect the plan of Murrel as laid down in Stewart's pamphlet." But the plan as Murrell supposedly explained it to Stewart took up just one paragraph, while the excerpt Shackelford reprinted went on for nearly three pages, most of which said little about what was supposed to happen during the uprising. Instead, the core of the extracted material consisted of Murrell detailing how he and the members of his clan managed to persuade the enslaved to participate in the plot in the first place.[48]

According to Stewart, Murrell claimed that the success of his plan did not depend on enlisting every slave in the United States. Rather, he had clan members approach only "the most vicious and wicked disposed ones, on large farms, and poison their minds, by telling them how they are mistreated." Clan members were to tell potential rebels that they deserved their freedom as much as any white man and that their bondage was the consequence of "power and tyranny" rather than racial inferiority. Likely recruits were to be reminded that their hard work and degradation made possible the luxurious lives of their masters and that it was wrong for "all the wealth of the country" to be "the proceeds of the black people's labor" even as they received none of it.[49]

To encourage hesitant slaves to be resolute, clan members were to tell them that Europe had abolished slavery; that West Indian slaves had achieved their freedom through violent rebellion; that slaves everywhere were already in on the plot; that thousands of southern whites were ready to die to help the enslaved revolt; that northern whites would not interfere if southern slaves "were to butcher every white man, in the slave holding states"; and that if they were bold enough to fight for their freedom they would "become as much respected, as if they were white." Promised a share of whatever spoils the clan acquired while plundering the countryside and of being ushered to freedom in Texas should the plan fail, the "blood thirsty devil[s]" who agreed to join the conspiracy were to start subtly sowing rebelliousness among the rest of the enslaved population, getting "the feelings of the negroes harrowed up against the whites, and their minds alive to the idea of being free."[50]

Of course, even as Murrell promised the enslaved the liberty, wealth, status, and vengeance their masters denied them, he did not care sincerely about their suffering or their freedom. Stewart wrote that Murrell admitted that the pledges made to recruits were lies and that he recognized that most slaves would have to be tricked or pressured into rebelling. Most were not even supposed to be told about the insurrection until the night it began, at which point the clan's "black emissaries" would invite fellow slaves to secret gatherings, ply them with alcohol, reveal the plan, and announce that revolts were taking place across the country. Murrell foresaw that the enslaved would thus "be forced to engage, under the belief, that the negroes have rebelled every where else, as in their own neighborhood, and by those means every gathering or assemblage of negroes will be pushed forward even contrary to their inclination." But Murrell took no chances. Slaves were also to be told that anyone "refus[ing] to fight would be put to death."[51]

Though ventriloquized through John Murrell's explication of how the insurrection he envisioned was supposed to work, Virgil Stewart's anger and sense of grievance are no better disguised here than anywhere else in *The Western Land Pirate*. By way of Murrell, Stewart projected his own craving for respect onto the enslaved and expressed his resentment toward wealthy people who he felt did not deserve their riches. Stewart's fear of humiliation and of being exposed as a liar and a fraud transmuted easily into wrath and a persecution complex that were barely sublimated by his having Murrell trumpet his own indifference toward the consequences of what was to be his greatest scheme. "I am confident that I will be victorious in this matter," Stewart claimed Murrell told him, "and I will have the pleasure and honor of seeing and knowing, that my management has glutted the earth with more human gore, and destroyed more property, than any other robber who has ever lived in America, or the known world." In Virgil Stewart's mind, America had betrayed its promise to give him the life he wanted, and those who managed to acquire the country's benefits were to blame. Part of him wanted to see it all burn.[52]

But we ought to look past Stewart's psychological intertwining with the character of John Murrell he created and pay attention, as Thomas Shackelford did, to the substance of Murrell's recruitment message and strategic vision. When we do, we can see that planters in Madison County and elsewhere in Mississippi responded so viscerally to Stewart's pamphlet because through Murrell, Stewart pinpointed a fundamental insecurity attendant to the state's economic order that was simultaneously more abstract and more concrete than the generic threat of a slave insurrection. It hardly required great insight to recognize that the social conditions of the cotton frontier allowed for the possibility of slave resistance on a large and coordinated scale, or even that white criminals could help organize that resistance. The demographic imbalance, the antagonism between masters and slaves, the harsh labor regime, the unformed institutions, and the nascent state of most farms and plantations combined to create circumstances in which formal surveillance and more subtle mechanisms of control alike were flimsy. Anyone could see how a rebellion might smolder in the breach.

But Virgil Stewart's John Murrell saw an especially artful and insidious way of stepping into that breach. Thanks to his extensive experience in stealing them, Murrell grasped that the enslaved were both the most valuable and the most uncertain form of property present on the cotton frontier, that the humanity that made them so prized was also what made them so hard to control, and that he could profit handsomely by appealing to slaves' very human desires for freedom. For years, on a small scale, he had used that incisive understanding of how slavery forged the connection between the social and economic contingencies of the developing plantation order and capitalized on the fact that southwestern settlers were not always scrupulous about having clear title to everyone in their workforce. Now he intended to use that understanding as the linchpin of a plan to steal everything those settlers had and undo slavery altogether.

Ironically, in some important ways Murrell was not so different from the planters he saw as his sworn enemies. Both sought to manipulate the enslaved for their own selfish and avaricious ends, and both understood they needed the cooperation of the enslaved to get their enterprises to work. Murrell, in fact, characterized the varying criminal projects he detailed for Virgil Stewart, including his planned uprising, as opportunities for "speculation," and prospective cotton planters were nothing if not speculators when it came to their slaves. But John Murrell and southwestern planters were less the same than they were mirror images of one another, and in that lay the most tangible connection of all between the slave insurrection scare and the gambling riot that made Mississippi so harrowing a place to be in the summer of 1835. Professional gamblers exploited what residents of Vicksburg feared were their basest impulses toward greed and embodied their deepest anxieties about the prospects for a correspondence of speculative capitalism and moral respectability. John Murrell and his mystic clan of slave stealers created analogous yet more specific and cataclysmic challenges. By exploiting the multivalence embedded in human capital, they called into question whether speculative capitalism on the cotton frontier could be sustainable at all.[53]

Southwestern planters often worried that slave traders sold them damaged or delinquent goods whose value they could not accurately assess, and they understood that any slave who saw a way to satisfy his hunger for liberty was an unsteady asset and an enemy of their profits. But John Murrell was preternaturally talented at locating the most rebellious of slaves and then using their rebelliousness to serve his own ends. He was a slave stealer one step ahead of the slaveholder, a master more in tune with the enslaved than their putative actual masters, and a better speculator than even the shrewdest planters. These were not wholly dissimilar men whose coexistence was completely impossible. Damaging enough when he persuaded one slave to run away only to be resold to some other white person, if John Murrell had hundreds of associates everywhere in the slave states methodically and systematically using the same techniques to get the enslaved to do their bidding at will, then property rights in slaves could never be safe or trustworthy. And if that was true, the economic promise of the cotton frontier could never be fulfilled. It could rebound from the trauma of even an extensive slave rebellion. But unrestrained slave stealing would leave slaveholders with nothing but their debts and would doom them all to financial oblivion.

George Fall, the editor of the *Jackson Mississippian*, saw precisely how disastrous a threat like that posed by Murrell could be for the future of the Southwest, whether or not it was as real as planters in Madison County seemed to think. In an editorial published as the insurrection scare subsided, Fall wrote that other newspapers had vastly exaggerated the danger of an uprising. "We live in an adjoining county to that where the plot was first discovered," Fall asserted, "and are convinced from all we can learn, that not one negro in every five hundred ever dreamed of, or was in the slightest degree connected with it." He assured readers that the conspiracy grew mostly out of a small cluster of plantations and owed itself to the machinations of "a few degraded and lawless white men," all of whom had since been hanged as a lesson to those "who are disposed to tamper with our slaves."[54]

Tellingly, though, even as Fall downplayed the scare he stressed that slavery in the Southwest was absolutely secure. Professing to be worried less about Murrell's plot than that "a stranger would suppose . . . that the whole white population of the State had narrowly escaped massacre and death, by the rising of savage and infuriated blacks," Fall had his priorities straight as he sought especially to put at ease anyone considering moving to or spending money in Mississippi. "We can assure those who are disposed to emigrate hither," Fall concluded, "that they have nothing more to fear in Mississippi from insurrectionary movements among the blacks. . . . Property and life are as safe here as in any of the States where slavery exists, and recent occurrences should not prevent emigration to our State, or deter capitalists from investing their funds in our Stocks; for we repeat the assurance, that they can do so with as much security and profit as ever; and that our negroes, uninfluenced by base and designing white men, are as orderly and obedient as the negroes of any State in the Union."[55]

~ ~

Memory and Meaning

Though panic had waned substantially by the end of July 1835, fears reverberated for months that John Murrell's mystic clan still lurked in the slave states. In August, Alabamians in and around Huntsville created committees to watch for signs of clansmen instigating the enslaved to rebel. In Tennessee, two men arrested for horse theft in Charlotte were supposed "to be of Murel's gang," and a number of "suspicious transactions" convinced Nashville residents that there had "been some connection between the agents of the intended Mississippi insurrection and certain persons of our colored population." South of the Tennessee capital, in Bedford County, ten or fifteen slaves were whipped until they confessed that a white man "who refused to tell them his name" and who had since left "to aid in doing something for the rescue of Murrel" had recruited their involvement in a planned uprising.[1]

A greater sense of siege was evident in southeastern Louisiana. In New Orleans, the City Council appointed three men to draft a circular detailing Murrell's plot so residents throughout the state might be prompted "to the adoption of such energetic precautionary measures, as may secure the safety of their lives and the preservation of their property." And adopt those measures they did. East Feliciana Parish residents hanged a man they believed was "one of Murel's gang" after they caught him holding five hundred dollars in counterfeit money, and whites in St. Helena Parish considered some "preachers who had been found busy amongst the negroes" to be members of "the Murel gang" and sentenced them to death. One of those men managed to escape and make his way to Baton Rouge, but people there expressed confidence that "Judge Lynch" would take care of him and the "great many" other "villains prowling about" nearby slave quarters trying to spark a rebellion.[2]

In the towns of Donaldsonville and St. Francisville, whites crafted a more formal response to the threat, holding public meetings at which they re-

solved to enforce stricter discipline of the enslaved population and maintain armed vigilance against the Mississippi "banditti" who sought to "excite mischief" and subvert "good order." If the experience of St. Francisville
resident Rachel O'Connor indicated the state of things, however, formalities restrained the impulses of a terrified population in Louisiana little
better than they had in Mississippi. Late in August, more than a month
after townspeople held their first meeting to address the crisis, O'Connor
informed her brother-in-law that "the people are afraid of all strangers . . .
fearing they might belong to the party that has caused so much trouble in
many parts. They are taken up on all occasions and whipd like dogs and
confined until they stand their trial. It is thought there is a great number
of Murell company yet." Matters had not improved by September, when
O'Connor told her niece that unfamiliar white men were still being taken
into custody. One was about to be hanged, and O'Connor thought that a
sort of mercy, "for they generally whip them nearly to death. They call it
Lintch's Law, giving from two to three hundred lashes, and then let them
go with orders to be out of the state in eight hours."[3]

The flood of stories about skulking clansmen eased as the summer of
1835 wound down but continued in a steady stream through the end of the
year. Georgians arrested an individual purported to be one of "Murrell's
Men" riding a stolen horse and imprisoned several others accused of slave
stealing. Arkansans shot and killed an alleged member of the "Murrel Banditti." Virginians jailed a man "believed to be one of the desperate Murel
clan." Floridians banished, under threat of lynching, a number of men they
concluded were part of Murrell's "confederacy."[4]

Concern spiked again, especially in Mississippi, as Christmas approached. Jackson residents were urged to keep up "vigilant patrols" amid
warnings that "the Murel plan . . . may yet be attempted." Vicksburgers,
remembering "that Murrel himself, in his confession, stated, that the 25th
of December was the day fixed upon" for the uprising, created extra patrols
and coordinated their activities with those of militia units to guard the city.
The chairman of a "Committee of Vigilance" established in the wake of the
gambling riot even encouraged city officials to compel tavern keepers and
boardinghouse owners to collect the names, addresses, and occupations of
those patronizing their establishments. H. L. Green, writing in late November from the Madison County village of Mount Olympus, admitted
to a relative that he was "almost frightened to death at the ap[p]roach of

Christmas" because he thought there would "be an attempt made by the negroes and the Murel gang." Townspeople in Vernon resolved not to let slaves leave plantations during the holidays, and they determined to watch out for "vagabond white men" given that "the danger of the insurrection instigated by that arch villain John A. Murrel . . . is still pending." An Alabama woman writing to her brother in Yazoo County in January 1836 put it neatly when she observed from her reading of the previous month's newspapers that "with regard to the insurrection of the negroes, and Murrell's plans . . . there are some scared people in Miss[issippi]." Truth be told, though, the people where she lived had been scared too. "Before about Christmas," she confessed, "there was the greatest excitement up here I ever saw."[5]

I.

No one benefited from all this more than Virgil Stewart. When Stewart first published *The Western Land Pirate*, responses from newspaper editors had ranged from doubt to derision, and Matthew Clanton had disparaged him publicly and in as humiliating a fashion as he could muster. For many observers, however, the panic that swept Mississippi demonstrated that Stewart must have been telling the truth all along. Newspapers across the United States began publishing lengthy summaries of *The Western Land Pirate*, and several serialized it in its entirety.[6]

Editors who had jeered at or ignored Stewart suddenly fell over themselves to applaud him. From his desk at the *Jackson Mississippian*, George Fall argued that Stewart's pamphlet had "been fully corroborated by circumstances" and that "the people of the Western and Southern States" owed Stewart "a debt of gratitude, for his exertions in the exposure of an extensive and well organized band of robbers and counterfeiters." Fall's colleague at the *Jackson Banner* thought it likely that Stewart would "gain for himself in the South a name that will live till time itself shall be no more." The *Bolivar Free Press* in southwestern Tennessee considered Stewart "fearless and intrepid," and in Stewart's native state of Georgia the *Augusta Chronicle* concluded that "if patriotism ever deserved a monument, assuredly that of Virgil A. Stewart does." Stewart attracted commendations outside the South too. The *New York Journal of Commerce* suggested he had earned "the lasting gratitude of whole Counties and States," and the *Philadelphia Enquirer* wrote that "the population of the south and west will never be able to repay the obligations they are under to Mr. Stewart" for discovering a plan that "would inevitably have led to scenes of carnage and murder without parallel in the history of this country."[7]

Tributes to Stewart were not limited to the journalistic realm. Israel Campbell remembered farmers and planters gathering near Vicksburg around "a long table set in the woods" for a dinner in Stewart's honor. Celebrating with copious amounts of wine and champagne, guests drank to Stewart's health and toasted him as "the protector of our families and firesides." Henry Foote similarly recalled Stewart being feted "in the most enthusiastic manner" in Jackson and throughout Mississippi, recollecting that nearly everywhere Stewart went he was accorded "public honors ... such as the most illustrious benefactors of the human race have seldom enjoyed" and showered with "presents of much value ... by those who lent credence to his alarming revelations." Residents of Clinton bought Stewart a two-hundred-dollar horse "as a token of their respect," and the legislatures of Mississippi and South Carolina considered bills to reward Stewart financially for arresting Murrell's plot.[8]

As the accolades piled up, Stewart doggedly pursued additional evidence for his response to the charges leveled by Matthew Clanton. Accompanied by a small guard of young white men on horseback, Stewart spent the summer and fall of 1835 riding across northern Mississippi and western Tennessee collecting affidavits from anyone he thought able and willing to confirm elements of his story about John Murrell or to call into question Clanton's integrity. He sent a few of these to newspapers for publication, usually with an indignant letter attached, and in November he showed the entirety of what had become a sizable sheaf of documents to the editor of the *Clinton Gazette*, who looked them over and pronounced that he "regard[ed] them as conclusive." When they appeared in print, the editor continued, Matthew Clanton, "the vile calumniator of Stewart," would "be exhibited in colors dark as midnight."[9]

At a minimum, Clanton was exhibited extensively, because by means that remain unclear Stewart stumbled into a publishing coup. In the early summer of 1836 the New York firm of Harper and Brothers published *The History of Virgil A. Stewart, and His Adventure in Capturing and Exposing the Great "Western Land Pirate" and His Gang, in Connexion with the Evidence*. Compiled by one H. R. Howard, the book essentially comprised an expanded and aptly retitled version of *The Western Land Pirate* written in a somewhat more formal style and interspersed with the supporting materials Stewart had collected since the publication of Clanton's pamphlet. Thomas Shackelford's account of the insurrection scare and William Mills's initial *Vicksburg Register* article describing the gambling riot were included as appendices.[10]

The appearance of *The History of Virgil A. Stewart* culminated a remarkable streak of luck for its author that in some ways belied his legion of complaints about his life in the Southwest. Stewart's arrogance and sense of entitlement had led him to make a series of extravagantly myopic decisions during the first half of the 1830s, most of which backfired in the short term and any one of which might have ruined him permanently. Yet circumstances turned in his favor such that by 1836 he had become a widely celebrated man with a book published by one of the leading houses in the United States. Attracting notice in major literary journals, *The History of Virgil A. Stewart* went through at least three printings by the early 1840s.[11]

Yet Stewart's newfound renown brought with it no real sense of triumph. Famous or not, Stewart was never entirely able to dispel the skepticism that followed him and his story. Sometimes he could still see it in the newspapers. An editor in Nashville was among those who considered themselves agnostic in the pamphlet war between Stewart and Clanton even after the insurrection scare in Mississippi had come and gone. He conceded that if Stewart were telling the truth, then his "living without a splendid reward would be . . . a disgrace to the Southern part of the United States," but he also allowed that Stewart might well be "a villain fit only to be an associate with Murel." The editor of the *Liberty Hall and Cincinnati Gazette* cast all circumspection aside. No matter how many people thought otherwise, he believed the insurrection scare a phantom menace and *The Western Land Pirate* a hoax. All a person had to do was read it. "Its details," he wrote, "violate all probability, insomuch that its circulation is an offence against the common sense of the country." Stewart could gather as many affidavits testifying to his character as he wished, the editor continued. They would make him no less "a swindler, and a thief."[12]

Stewart could shrug off such comments, given that acclaim far outweighed criticism. He found it harder to ignore the rebukes that kept coming his way from Madison County, Tennessee. In 1834 he had done property holders there what he considered a favor by bringing down John Murrell, yet they showed neither sincere gratitude nor a disposition to trust him.

Now he was a bona fide hero and still they sniped at him. In August 1835, for example, as some people in Estanaula passed the time talking about what had become of Stewart and his Murrell story, a man named Joab Wilson chimed in that Stewart "was not allowed to visit any respectable family or house in Madison county" and that when he managed to make his way into decent company "he was watched, lest he should steal something." When word of this reached Stewart, he responded with a public letter darkly hinting about Wilson's "motives for so unwarrantable and uncalled for slanders at a time when I have the influence and operation of every villain in America to oppose."[13]

A few weeks later, Wilson and half a dozen other men signed a certificate in support of Matthew Clanton and several of their neighbors "whose character we believe to have been foully aspersed in the publication of Virgil A. Stewart," averring that they could acquire signatures from hundreds more. Stewart answered with another letter, this one filled with his distinctive blend of pomposity, anger, and self-pity. Accusing Wilson and his fellow signatories of being "a big-headed aristocratic hierarchy, an asperser of character, [and] a fit subject for the operations of Clantonism," Stewart wondered that anyone in Madison County or any part of Tennessee "can be my enemy." He consoled himself with the knowledge that he was "guilty of the enormous crime of feeling more for a people than they are capable of feeling for themselves; of having more public spirit than is laudable; of doing more than I am thanked for; of inviting dangers, turmoils and destruction, without the pleasing prospect of making one friend; of standing up in the defence of a country, single-handed, without its approbation; of enlisting and incurring the never-dying vengeance of all the villains in America, to no end but the displeasure of the country I thought I was serving." Melodramatically concluding that it had all been a waste of time, Stewart discouraged other young men from taking the risks he had taken and wished for "a home on the lonely cliffs of mountain heights where the proud eagle delights to soar alone."[14]

Lest he leave standing any bridge that might be totally incinerated, Stewart made one last trip back to Madison County in October 1835. He collected affidavits there from John and Richard Henning and from some of the other men who had formed the guard that initially took John Murrell into custody. But Stewart could not resist riding into the town of Jackson, where he harangued bystanders about the nefariousness of Joab Wilson and announced that "there were not half a dozen honest men in Madison County." After a while people had heard enough. One report had it that Stewart was "called to account . . . and ordered to leave the town." At the very least, according to another, "the general feeling of indignation against him" was such "that common parlance would have suggested a departure."[15]

In light of this tirade, several editors in western Tennessee decided it was time to stop pussyfooting around Virgil Stewart and to call him out for what he was. The editor of the *Randolph Recorder* thought it a "pity" that Stewart "did not pocket silently the silver penny he made out of his Murrel book and mind his business like a prudent man." The editor claimed no personal acquaintance with Stewart, but he did know that Stewart was "rash and imprudent," that in western Tennessee he had acquired "many enemies and evil-thinkers, that before thought well enough of him," and that "a malignant asperity" characterized "all his writings." The editor recognized that Stewart's pamphlet had done "some good," but he suggested that instead of "stalking about the country, defended by bullies, hunting certificates defending his own character, and destroying that of others," Stewart ought to "go to work and thereby establish his character, if it be now repudiated." The editor of the *Jackson Truth Teller* concurred, as did the editor of the *Nashville Banner* and that of the *West-Tennessean*, published in Henry County, who thought "that the attention which has been paid [Stewart] has filled his mind with vain and foolish notions, and induced him to pursue a very imprudent course."[16]

Really, even as the appearance of *The History of Virgil A. Stewart* made its protagonist a celebrity nationally, his fame within the Southwest had already crested. It was not just a few Tennessee newspaper editors who thought by the end of 1835 that Stewart ought to move out of the public eye and go about whatever his business might be. No state government ever did approve any reward money for Stewart. Even in the Mississippi legislature, the effort to grant him "a donation . . . for his honesty, integrity, and philanthropy" failed by a more than 2-to-1 margin. And given the ubiquity of stories about Stewart and Murrell in the southern press in the immediate aftermath of the insurrection scare, it was striking that a year later hardly a single paper in the region mentioned *The History of Virgil A. Stewart* at all.[17]

In the end, being ignored was about the worst thing that could have happened to Virgil Stewart. He never cared much about money and seems to have made very little from sales of either *The Western Land Pirate* or *The History of Virgil A. Stewart*. But he could not simply "go to work and thereby establish his character," because he had no business to attend and no inclination to find one. Obstinate and oblivious to the last, he still had no sense, despite everything he had learned about the link between wealth and standing, that grit, force of will, a good lie, and a little luck were not enough to garner importance or respect. For a brief moment his experience had deceived him in this regard, because when the Mississippi insurrection scare broke out, being the "capturer of Murrell" had provided him with the eminence that he wanted more than anything else in the world. But fame was fleeting, "aristocrats" still disparaged him, and soon enough Stewart was once again a forgotten man in the disregarded masses.

By the latter half of 1836, newspapers had stopped mentioning Stewart's name almost entirely, and while the public record reveals only glimpses of his life from that point forward, its trajectory is plain. In December 1836 Stewart was living in Mississippi and sold the last forty acres he owned in Yalobusha County to Matthew Clanton in what must have been among the more awkward real estate transactions of the era. Six months later a man named Elisha Battle came across Stewart on the road to Natchez, still riding the horse that the residents of Clinton had given him. The animal was probably the most valuable thing Stewart owned, for although Battle asserted in a letter to a Mississippi newspaper that Stewart must have had "a good stock of funds of his own," he could not help but notice that Stewart had clearly "suffered many privations." Battle wrote mostly "with a hope of something being done for" Stewart at the next session of the state legislature.[18]

Some respite from Stewart's deteriorating circumstances came in the spring of 1838 when a jury acquitted him of Matthew Clanton's larceny charge, but the reprieve was small and temporary. One rumor had Stewart becoming a wealthy farmer in Pennsylvania. Another maintained that he embarked on a failed run for Congress in Mississippi. More likely was a newspaper report in 1840 that Stewart had "exiled himself to Texas," claiming that he had no choice "in consequence of the malignity with which he had been pursued by the friends of Murrell, the land pirate." The author of the story was having none of it, concluding that Stewart's excuse was "most extensive fudge and humbug." Perhaps, but the Republic of Texas in the 1840s remained a place many disgraced Americans thought a fine one to expatriate themselves, and reports circulated in 1841 that Stewart got himself elected there as a circuit judge. But another author writing years later maintained that Stewart lived out the rest of his days as a recluse. Thinking himself "in constant danger" and letting his hair and beard grow long and scraggly, Stewart would neither leave his home after sundown nor light a lamp to keep the darkness at bay. Withdrawn into the nightmares of his own imagination, Virgil Stewart had made his own destiny after all. He probably died in 1846. Some said he expired of natural causes, others that he was assassinated. No one much cared either way.[19]

As for John Murrell, for a few months after the insurrection scare he was about as illustrious a criminal as could be found in the United States. A well-known playwright wrote a dramatic composition about him to be performed onstage. A racehorse was named for him. A famous phrenologist visited him in the Tennessee penitentiary and declared that had Murrell "had the advantage of a proper education in youth, and of respectable connexions or society," he might have led a reasonably upstanding life and "bask[ed] in the sunshine of plenty and popular favor." The editor of the *Nashville Republican* fretted that Americans were making too much of the "Western Land Pirate" and that "the *éclat* which Murel has acquired, and the great anxiety there is to visit him, and hear him talk" would preclude Murrell's reformation and lead "weak-minded persons" to think crime a likely path to glory.[20]

The editor of the *Republican* would not have worried had he known what the future held in store for Murrell. He was spared the psychological implosion that was perhaps Virgil Stewart's just and inevitable fate, but Murrell's years in prison took an enormous toll nonetheless. He passed his time at manual labor, sometimes working as a blacksmith, and rarely received visitors of any kind. His mother, Zilpah, died in 1838, leaving an estate that amounted to just under $140 after debts. Murrell's wife, Elizabeth, whose poverty led her to spend six months in jail for larceny shortly after her husband's incarceration, divorced him in 1841 and married another man just a week later. In April 1844 John Murrell was paroled from prison four months early, his body wracked by a decade of toil and by the consumption he contracted shortly before being released. He died, alone, seven months later in Pikeville, Tennessee. He was thirty-eight years old.[21]

II.

By the time Virgil Stewart and John Murrell died, their stories and the events in which they had been involved had long since moved past them both. The process had begun even before the summer of 1835 ended. For several weeks after the insurrection scare in Mississippi subsided, practically no one imbued the events with broad significance. George Fall's efforts at the *Mississippian* to minimize the scare may have been motivated by concerns that it would halt the flow of migrants and capital to his state, but others too thought the upheaval overblown, albeit disturbing. The editor of the *Nashville Banner* thought a plot on the scale feared to have existed impossible to pull off and wrote that he would "not be at all surprised if the late alarm about an insurrection in Mississippi, should turn out to have been a mere chimera, without ever having had any actual foundation." At least some people there agreed, like a man from Clinton who in early August informed a correspondent, "after all, I believe it was much ado about nothing."[22]

Especially notable was the absence of any serious effort to connect the scare to the political controversy surrounding the abolitionist movement, whose rapid growth in the early 1830s discomfited many white Americans north and south. White southerners especially might be expected to have made that connection, as it was not uncommon for slave unrest to be attributed to destabilizing abolitionist influence. Nothing about the Mississippi scare, however, appeared to bear the marks of their "interference." Attentive readers of *The Western Land Pirate* noticed Virgil Stewart's John Murrell employing a critique of the peculiar institution. But Stewart never hinted that Murrell, his men, or his plot had ties to any larger antislavery efforts in the United States, or that the "mystic clan" was anything but an agglomeration of bandits and looters. After hearing the details of events in Mississippi, even individuals who had initially leapt to the conclusion that antislavery forces were to blame, such as the editor of the *Mobile Daily Commercial Register and Patriot*, felt compelled to admit that "it does not appear, that these disturbances were connected, as was supposed at first, with abolition emissaries. The object of the incendiaries appears rather to have been, the kidnapping of negroes."[23]

Such judiciousness soon vanished. As July came to a close, unsolicited antislavery periodicals began appearing by the tens of thousands at southern post offices. The first wave of a campaign during which abolitionists would send more than one million pieces of literature through the mails, the sudden and unanticipated influx of newspapers and tracts touched off a regional reaction unprecedented in scope and ferocity. In Charleston, three thousand people gathered to watch the burning of abolitionist propaganda stolen from the city's main post office. Mass meetings all across the South condemned abolitionists as "reckless fanatics" and "vile incendiaries" and called for boycotts of abolitionist-owned businesses, for stricter enforcement of state bans on printing and importing antislavery publications, and for northern states to pass similar legislation cracking down on abolitionism within their borders. Bounties were put on the heads of prominent abolitionists, rewards were extended for the arrest of anyone caught with abolitionist writings, and just about any unfamiliar white man in the South became a target for legal authorities and extralegal mobs whether in possession of antislavery materials or not. "Almost every mail," one northern editor observed in early September, "brings intelligence of outrages committed upon persons suspected of tampering with slaves."[24]

By the middle of August, as public awareness of the abolitionists' postal campaign spread, the link that few white southerners had fashioned at first between the Mississippi insurrection scare and the designs of antislavery activists became practically axiomatic. Some argued that abolitionist teachings promoted slave rebelliousness and slaveholder insecurity that led inevitably to the ruthlessness displayed in the face of the Murrell scheme. From Washington, D.C., the editor of the *National Intelligencer* referred to the executions in Livingston as "the fruits of fanaticism" and the logical result of abolitionists' "extravagance and folly," "recklessness," and "criminal plots against the lives" of their "fellow men." From Nashville, the editor of the *Republican* now claimed that "the late dreadful occurrences in Mississippi were probably the result of the 'seed which [the abolitionists] have sown.'" A Natchez correspondent of the *New York Journal of Commerce* wrote that he still had no idea whether an insurrection plot had even existed in his state, but he felt certain "that what has been done, has been the consequence of apprehensions of the agency of emissaries of abolition, following up the incendiary publications with which we have been assailed."[25]

Participants at a large public meeting in Richmond, seeking an example of how abolitionism was "essentially wicked and mischievous as well towards the black man, as towards the white," looked to Mississippi. There, they asserted, "the machinations of a few, very few *banditti*, have thrown that whole community into commotion, and brought on the heads of the white and black offenders the summary vengeance of a wronged and enraged people." What transpired had been "deplorable," perhaps, but such was antislavery agitation's "tendency and result." George Fall, pivoting from soft-pedaling the scare to asserting that the doctrines of "deluded abolitionists" were surely "the chief cause of . . . the recent attempted insurrection in Mississippi," made a similar case about the harm done by antislavery activists. "Instead of ameliorating the condition of the African," he wrote, "they are throwing fire brands among them, which if they were to take effect, would utterly destroy the whole race." Opponents of slavery, Fall continued, needed to understand that white southerners would always "rise in their strength with the law in their own hands for the punishment of all those wretches whose infamous designs are to scatter fire brands and death among them."[26]

Some white southerners went even further and began arguing that John Murrell and the members of his clan were effectively indistinguishable from or literally were abolitionists. In Alabama, the editor of the *Tuscaloosa Flag of the Union* observed that Murrell and Arthur Tappan, the silk import magnate who funded much of the abolitionists' postal campaign, "seem to be 'the lions' of the day." So far as the editor was concerned, that was about right, because Tappan and Murrell "are a *nice* pair, and worthy coadjutors in a kindred cause." Almost needless to say, he also hoped the two would "meet with kindred punishment." In Mississippi, a correspondent of the *Woodville Republican* wrote of his certainty that Murrell's men were "nothing more than weak headed Abolitionists, who through a false religious zeal would think they were doing God service to murder all the white inhabitants of the United States, who do not believe just as they do." More than three dozen men from Clinton addressed a letter to American Anti-Slavery Society publishing agent R. G. Williams accusing him of spreading "slanderous *filth* against the South" and of actively conducting the "operations in attempting an insurrection of our slaves" that had been "lately exposed." At the statehouse in Jackson, the legislature's Committee on Domestic Slavery expressed its "deepest concern and indignation" at ongoing abolitionist agitation and pointed to the Murrell scare as "a practical illustration that we are determined not to become the dupes of their vile treachery." By September, when a North Carolina editor referred offhand-edly to the arrest of "three abolition incendiaries of the Murel gang," few readers would have blinked at the casual association.[27]

Even Virgil Stewart remembered a connection between John Murrell and abolitionism that he had somehow neglected to mention before. In *The History of Virgil A. Stewart* he claimed that after Murrell explained how he pitched his insurrection plan to the enslaved, he talked about "the advantage he expected to derive from an English lecturer on slavery" and then quoted that lecturer explaining how a slave uprising would both ruin white southerners financially so that they would become disgusted with slavery and turn northern capitalists against the institution by making the South appear an insecure place to invest their money. English antislavery activist George Thompson did embark on a controversial lecture tour of the United States in 1834, but not until more than six months after Stewart and Murrell traveled together. Moreover, there is no evidence that Thompson (or any other abolitionist) ever said or wrote the things Stewart's Murrell attributed to him. The understanding of slavery rooted almost entirely in terms of economic interests and power, however, was classic Stewart, as was a willingness to be flexible with the facts. If enfolding his story within the day's most heated political controversy might keep him in the news and sell some books, then he could make that happen.[28]

Given what they believed about the desires and tactics of antislavery forces in the United States, that white southerners blurred the distinction between abolitionists and John Murrell's mystic clan is no more surprising than Virgil Stewart's mendacity. Indeed, much of the language people used to describe the former might also have been applied to the latter, practically without alteration. Possessed of "Assassin like Character[s]," abolitionists were "stealthy marauder[s] of the night" who prowled the South "under the cloak of Religion" encouraging "a rebellious or insurrectionary character among the black population" and "distilling the most deadly poison into the ear of the ignorant, but . . . happy and contented negro." Driven by "false notions of philanthropy" and organized into societies that were "treason-able in design and effect," abolitionists would "drench the southern states in blood, ravage them with fire, and scourge them with discord and commo-tion." As any number of antislavery activists arrested in the decades before the Civil War on charges of "slave stealing" could attest, white southerners considered them no different from the men affiliated with John Murrell. Villains of the darkest dye, they all sought "to rob, murder, plunder and devastate" the South.[29]

No less than "Murrell men" or abolitionists, professional gamblers were part of the constellation of miscreants troubling the Southwest in the summer of 1835, and while the hangings in Vicksburg at first seemed connected to the insurrection scare mostly by their proximity, timing, and gruesome violence, white southerners soon tied gamblers in with the other reprobates in their midst. In late July a "committee" from Vicksburg searched several steamboats for "a party of gamblers, who had absconded from Mississippi with kidnapped negroes," and William Mills soon began cautioning readers of the *Vicksburg Register* that expelled gamblers, "with the aid of the Murrel gang," were planning a military assault on the state. The *New Orleans Bee* reported that a gang of "gambling abolitionists" had been routed from the Louisiana town of Greensburg, and another paper expressed concern that "refugee gamblers and abolitionists" were beginning to cluster in the Arkansas Territory. A Nashville editor informed abolitionists that white southerners had "nothing in common with that philanthropy which finds associates among horse-thieves, gamblers, black-legs, and cut-throats," and white men in one Tennessee county issued a public admonition "to all Gamblers, Blacklegs, Negro Stealers, and Negro Insurrectionists—All the clan of John A. Murrell, and all Mississippi Refuse of every character" to stay out of the state. Proclaimed from "the palace of the Guillotine," the warning itself contained the consequences of failing to heed it.[30]

There was a certain sense to these connections as well. Forging abolitionists, members of the mystic clan, and gamblers into a triumvirate of malevolence tidily accounted for a series of profoundly disconcerting events, fitting them all into a story in which evil men worked in concert to undermine the economic prosperity produced by slavery on a burgeoning frontier. As constructed by Virgil Stewart, in fact, John Murrell and his clan sat perfectly at the intersection of where white southerners imagined these disparate scoundrels operated. Like professional gamblers, members of the mystic clan were itinerant and often vagrant, would do anything for money, and associated with the enslaved against their masters' interest in maintaining discipline and authority. And like abolitionists, they sometimes disguised themselves as men with respectable professions even while absconding with slaves and hoping to spark a wholesale rebellion. Put together, they loomed as monsters of nearly unparalleled wickedness.

Such fiends deserved no quarter, an argument delineated most vividly by Charles Caldwell. In November 1835, reprising his 1834 address to the students of Transylvania University, Caldwell reminded his audience that every form of gambling, no matter how benign it might seem, spread corruption and crime throughout American society. He delighted in what he saw as the progress made against gambling since his initial speech, expressed hope and confidence that it would soon be eradicated altogether, and urged Americans to take whatever measures they deemed necessary to "expel black-legs, and expunge gambling" from their midst. Lest anyone doubt "that assassination, and all forms of individual violence and dissoluteness enter into the aggregate of evils that cluster around the vice of gambling," Caldwell asserted that one need only look to the summer's events in Mississippi.[31]

As Caldwell saw matters, "the conspiracy between black-legs and horse-thieves, robbers and rebellious slaves, to spread conflagration and havock through the south" demonstrated that "a new and more inhuman element" had entered the catalog of savagery gamblers were willing to perpetrate. Exposing themselves as a "gang of desperadoes" who held "the assassin's knife . . . at the throat" of Mississippians, gamblers and their associates were "a curse to society, and a scandal to their race." Threatening the lives of "thousands of the orderly and virtuous," they sought to bring about "a promiscuous and wide-spread scene of burning and butchery" that would leave the waters of the Mississippi River so "reddened and reeking with blood" that it would "reflect the glare of the midnight conflagration." Mississippians in Vicksburg and throughout the state were right in undertaking the "vigorous re-action" they did. Allowing the "existence and freedom" of men like these was "to invite ruin." With "their reformation . . . hopeless," nothing short of "exterminat[ion]" would suffice.[32]

Caldwell did not explicitly reference abolitionism or abolitionist involvement in the supposed plan for insurrection in Mississippi, but they were clearly on his mind as he blasted "certain eastern writers, and other noisy meddlers, at a distance" who had criticized "the prompt and stern proceedings of our brethren of the south." Advancing an argument white southerners would make ever more frequently to defend themselves from what they considered unwarranted assaults on slavery, Caldwell asked rhetorically why "captious and obtrusive railers" interfered "with a matter that in no way concerns them," and he inveighed against "shallow and censorious news-mongers" who knew nothing about the dangers posed by the prospect of a "*servile war.*" Carping about the rule of law, Caldwell concluded, was merely "*cautious, time-serving* nonsense" and "the counsel of cowardice, ignorance and indecision."[33]

Many white northerners shared Charles Caldwell's outrage. Mob violence directed against abolitionists skyrocketed in the North during the summer and fall of 1835, and meetings convened in dozens of northern cities mirrored those held in the South as attendees expressed solidarity with their fellow Americans in the slaveholding states and assured them that they too found abolitionists to be repugnant extremists. And like their southern counterparts, white northerners explicitly drew on the summer's events in Mississippi to attack the antislavery cause, often fusing abolitionists with gamblers and John Murrell as they did so. In Bangor, Maine, participants in an antiabolition meeting agreed that "recent disastrous events in the South" revealed "the actual tendencies of [abolitionists'] measures, to produce dissension and bloodshed." In New York City, five thousand people gathered in City Hall Park listened as a lawyer named Willis Hall blamed the insurrection scare in Mississippi on "a few persons from the North who co-operate with the horse thieves and black-legs of the South."[34]

Editors from New York City, in fact, were especially vociferous. One had "no doubt" that "the slave insurrection in Mississippi is traceable to [abolitionist] influence," and another asserted that "the late extensive plans developed in Mississippi . . . clearly demonstrate a preconcerted and most atrocious conspiracy set on foot by the incendiaries of the Tappan and Garrison School, to light up the torch of civil war over every part of the Southern States." A third, comparing abolitionists to gamblers because they "swindle society out of its money and its good sense at the same time," concluded that "the card and dice-box gentry have been co-partners and fellow laborers with the sanctimonious emissaries of Tappanism, in projecting the plan of a negro insurrection in the South-western States." A fourth got right to the point, calling abolitionists "robbers and pirates," claiming that John Murrell was an abolitionist "agent in the south," and lambasting the "Murrell and Tappan gang" as men who "invoke the aid of the North in support of their designs, and threaten the vengeance of all *Christendom* upon the Southern States, if they dare to resist."[35]

Yet Caldwell was not wrong that there were Americans horrified by the lawlessness Mississippians displayed during the summer of 1835 or that abolitionists were the most stridently "censorious." Although many northerners criticized the executions in Vicksburg even as they sympathized with southerners who felt themselves on the brink of insurrection, northerners opposed to slavery understood everything that had happened in Mississippi as the natural outgrowth of a society that condoned inequality and the abuse and exploitation of human beings. In his *Liberator*, William Lloyd Garrison denied that abolitionists had anything to do with what transpired in Mississippi, and instead considered what took place a case of "masters reap[ing] the fruits of their ungodly scheme of keeping their bondmen in Egyptian darkness." Noting that criminals had supposedly enlisted the enslaved to the plot by promising freedom, Garrison argued that slaves who desired liberty but lacked sophistication were "easily ensnared by the first imposter who comes along." In that regard slaveholders had put themselves in a bind. If the enslaved "were taught to examine and reflect, they would reject the plans of wretches," Garrison observed, but they would recognize all the more that those wretches were "moved by as much avarice as their own *kidnappers*, or the robbers of their wages, or the 'associated negro-thieves.'"[36]

Others too thought the insurrection scare a consequence of slavery's warping influence and blamed slaveholders for a situation of their own making. The editor of the *Amherst Cabinet*, for instance, argued that "the accounts from Mississippi of the meditated insurrection among the blacks, afford a melancholy picture of the evils of slavery." It was no wonder, he continued, that slaveholders were "ever in fear of detection and just retribution." They led sinful lives, "trampling on the rights of others and appropriating to themselves their property unjustly gotten and holden." Eventually they would all "be visited with the fruits of their evil doings. If slave holders persist against entreaty, light, reason, and known natural consequences, they must endure them, with none to pity them but for their obduracy."[37]

Elizur Wright, editor of the *Quarterly Anti-Slavery Magazine*, similarly saw the insurrection scare as a natural by-product of slavery, though he focused less on tensions between slaves and their owners than on the economic logic slavery dictated among the southern white population. In a lengthy review of *The History of Virgil A. Stewart*, Wright maintained that because slavery devalued free labor, southern whites with no direct financial interest in slavery "must live by preying, in some form or other, upon the profits of the slaveholders." They might begin by joining "the horse-racers, cockfighters, gamblers and speculators in general, who swarm through the South and contrive to relieve the great slaveholding planters of any inconvenient plethora." But as wealth increasingly concentrated in the hands of slaveholders, the class of nonslaveholding whites would become larger and more desperate, and concomitantly "less scrupulous about the morality of its mode of preying upon the great 'domestic institution' of its country. It is by no means difficult to conceive," Wright continued, "that it may ere long become sufficiently hungry and audacious to give serious trouble to the security of slave property itself." For his part, Wright doubted Virgil Stewart's story. But the fact that so many white southerners did not exposed the rottenness at slavery's core and amply demonstrated "that causes are at work in southern society, which if they have not produced this, must of necessity produce similar conspiracies."[38]

White southerners sowing the seeds of their own destruction was one thing, but other opponents of slavery used the convulsions in Mississippi to make the case that slavery's pernicious effect could not be contained within the states that condoned it and that the institution had begun to poison the rights of free people everywhere in the country. In 1836 the Executive Committee of the Ohio Anti-Slavery Society deplored mob attacks on antislavery newspapers in Cincinnati and argued that they showed how the previous summer's extralegal executions of gamblers and suspected insurrectionists had initiated a "REIGN OF TERROR" that was extending into the free states. Along the same lines, the American Anti-Slavery Society remarked that the Mississippi insurrection plot had been blamed on abolitionists despite a lack of evidence that any plot had existed and concluded that it had become impossible almost anywhere in the United States for Americans to express opinions about slavery. "This state of feeling in regard to all moral interference with slavery," the society declared in its 1836 annual report, "has not been created by the abolitionists, but [merely] brought to light. . . . The unbounded wrath and railing and murdering at the South, show how far, if not fatally, the disease has triumphed there; and the proslavery meetings and mobs at the North, will show how far the same disease has worked its way here."[39]

Even as stories about the riots and scares and executions in Mississippi faded from the newspapers, slavery's opponents continued harkening back to them. In 1838, when Abraham Lincoln was explaining to an audience of young northern men how mob violence imperiled American political institutions, he noted that such "outrages" took place all over the country, but he selected what happened in Mississippi as "the most dangerous in example, and revolting to humanity." Describing a "process of hanging, from gamblers to negroes, from negroes to white citizens, and from these to strangers," Lincoln depicted a scene where "dead men were seen literally dangling from the boughs of trees upon every road side; and in numbers almost sufficient, to rival the native Spanish moss of the country, as a drapery of the forest." In 1839, when Theodore Dwight Weld sought to refute claims made by slavery's defenders that the law protected the lives of the enslaved, he observed that the law had failed to prevent the residents of Vicksburg from executing professional gamblers without trial and that no one in Mississippi seemed inclined to punish those who "laughed the law to scorn" in carrying out the hangings.[40]

Abolitionists' efforts to use events in Mississippi to bolster their cause reached their apogee in 1840 with the publication of a cartoon titled "*Our* Peculiar *Domestic Institutions*" in the *American Anti-Slavery Almanac*. A large tree with a sign reading "Vicksburg" fills the center of the image, and a small gang of white men gathered around it watches as the last of five noosed men is hoisted to dangle from one of its limbs. In the background to the right, a score of white southerners crowd together at a cockfight, and horses race around a track to the left. In the foreground, two more cocks fight, two men tussle on the ground, and a man whips an enslaved child. Occupying the middle ground are two men dueling with pistols, two others engaging in a bare-chested knife fight, and another man dragging a cat across the naked back of a prostrate slave. Amid them all, four men sit at a card table filled with liquor bottles. At the side of one man kneels an enslaved child, his body and labor the stakes for which the men play. One of the foursome will never see whether his hand would have landed the big prize, however, as the fellow across the table has just shot him through the head. All told, the collage of images delivered a powerful message. Debased by greed and accustomed to the violence on which slavery rested, white southern men had become little better than animals, as indifferent to suffering and conditioned to mutilate and murder one another as the fighting cocks they cheered.[41]

What happened in Mississippi in 1835 did not cause the Civil War. But it was not unrelated to the war's outbreak. By fitting into the developing narratives of abolitionists and their opponents and propelling those narratives forward, Mississippi's dreadful summer was like dozens of other small irritants, largely forgotten amid the familiar narrative of sectional conflict, that produced moments of friction and mutual recrimination that slowly but surely drove the wedge deeper between the sections. And it continued to echo through the years leading up to the outbreak of hostilities, sometimes in ironic fashion. In January 1861, Virginian Sherrard Clemens implored his fellow members of the House of Representatives to do whatever they could to avoid the impending breakup of the Union. With extremists in both the North and the South having led the nation down a dangerous road, Clemens looked back to 1835 to explain his certainty that the road led to disaster. Reminding his colleagues that John Murrell had once imagined economic catastrophe and physical devastation for nearly every white person touched by the institution of slavery, he wondered whether Murrell's fantasy was to become America's nightmare. "Was this prophecy," Clemens asked, "and is it about to become part of the history of this country?" The most proximate reasons for the Civil War may have been the breakdown of the political system and the failure of American politicians to compromise on the issue of slavery expansion. But the violence in Mississippi in 1835 was one of many events that left a sedimentary layer of grievance and provocation behind as it rushed through the riverbed of American life. When the sediment rose high enough, it nearly choked the nation to death.[42]

III.

The transformations of John Murrell, Virgil Stewart, and what transpired in Mississippi in 1835 have never stopped in the more than 175 years that have unfolded since. Murrell, Stewart, their lives, and the events that made them famous contained violence, crime, conspiracy, mystery, and frontier adventure that provided rich and malleable raw material for storytellers of varying stripes, and they all became fodder for popular culture from the instant they entered the American imagination. Their presence waned over the course of the nineteenth century as the generation of Americans who remembered them departed the scene and as the Civil War and its aftermath moved to the center of nearly every facet of American life. But Murrell and Stewart returned to prominence again by the second quarter of the twentieth century, and they remain remarkably persistent figures on the landscape of American myth to this day.[43]

Repurposed again and again, stories involving Stewart and Murrell have served as the foundation of countless pieces of short fiction and more than a dozen novels. To be sure, Stewart and Murrell have animated more than their share of pulpy material. No work in the nineteenth century did more to popularize the life of Murrell, for example, than a lurid biography serialized in 1846 by the *National Police Gazette*, a pioneering tabloid that reveled in tales of the sordid and seedy. Published as a single volume in 1847, the currency and general familiarity of that biography prompted Herman Melville to mention it as one of the cheap and sensationalistic pamphlets sold by hucksters aboard the steamboat that served as the setting of his 1857 novel, *The Confidence-Man*.[44]

In the twentieth century, schlocky variations on the Murrell and Stewart story frequently were shoehorned into the increasingly fashionable western genre. Onscreen, the story appeared in the 1940 film *Virginia City*, with Humphrey Bogart in the Murrell role; in a 1959 episode of the television series *Riverboat*, with boat pilot Burt Reynolds wary of an assault by Murrell and his gang; and in the 1960 movie *Natchez Trace*, which promised that no matter if it was "a fortune or a female . . . John Murrell took what he wanted." In print too, twentieth-century authors like their nineteenth-century counterparts, inclined toward hackneyed prose and plotlines, with most extrapolating on Stewart's work and depicting Murrell as a devilish genius with flash, charm, and diabolical charisma. Whether it was C. William Harrison's 1960 novel *Outlaw of the Natchez Trace*, which described Murrell as "well-dressed and soft-spoken, but with eyes of steel and a heart as cold as a swamp snake," or Paul Wellman's 1964 *Spawn of Evil*, which depicted Murrell as "Satan's satrap," the "arch-criminal" of his day who had "a lust for women, the more depraved the better," and likely had "the smell of sulphur on his breath," heat rather than light carried the day stylistically.[45]

But Murrell and Stewart have provided inspiration as well for authors as canonical as William Faulkner, Jorge Luis Borges, Eudora Welty, William Gilmore Simms, and Mark Twain. They too used Murrell's supposed banditry and the insurrection he purportedly tried organizing to portray the southwestern frontier as a place of legend. But theirs is a legend rooted by and large in profound darkness, evocative of a place defined less by melodrama and derring-do than by silences and secrets. One scholar has suggested that Murrell served in part as the model for Thomas Sutpen, the protagonist of the novel that is arguably Faulkner's masterpiece, *Absalom! Absalom!* It would only be fitting if that was the case. In the minds of white southwestern settlers, criminals such as John Murrell undermined the successful building of a glorious and profitable plantation world. But the ruthless ambition, indomitable will, and total lack of conscience that allowed Thomas Sutpen to escape dire poverty, appear seemingly out of nowhere in Mississippi in the 1830s, and install himself as the wealthiest cotton planter in Faulkner's fictional Yoknapatawpha County sat on a foundation of slavery, racial hierarchy, lies, and deceit that was depraved, criminal, and thoroughly rotten in its own right. If Sutpen's mystifying rise pointed toward what someone with Murrell's reputed brilliance might otherwise have become, Sutpen's baroque and spectacular fall demonstrated that ruin was the cotton kingdom's destiny no less than it was Murrell's. Consequences could be avoided for only so long.[46]

For Faulkner, the Civil War itself served as judgment on the ways men like Thomas Sutpen made their fortunes and led their lives. In reality, though, the meaning of Mississippi's experience during the flush times was to be found neither in fiction nor in the political controversies surrounding abolitionism. In reality, the meaning transcended the matter of whether John Murrell was a criminal mastermind, whether Virgil Stewart was a hero, or whether slave stealers and gamblers genuinely conspired against the prosperity of the Southwest. In reality, the meaning came when the reckoning came, and it came much sooner than the Civil War.

IV.

Some people saw its approach. James Davidson, traveling through Mississippi in 1836, found the overheated economic atmosphere to be dispiriting because he was sure the entire state would "be a fine field for Lawyers in two or three years." Others, like a correspondent of the *Jackson Mississippian* calling himself "Curtius," could not make sense of what was happening. Within a matter of weeks as winter became spring in 1837, the abundant

flow of cash that had fueled the flush times dried up, property values plummeted, and farmers and planters throughout the state faced bankruptcy and
destitution. Convinced that Mississippi remained "in the highest state of
prosperity" and that "the intrinsic value of property" had "in nowise dimin-
ished," Curtius insisted that "the present pressure" was "purely artificial."
In most circumstances a believer in "letting trade regulate itself," Curtius
now called on the state government to take remedial action for those who,
"when all the productive industry of the country was in the full tide of success," failed to "anticipate that an unseen hand would hurl back the flood,
and leave the stranded on the naked shore." Without relief, he argued,
"Mississippi will stand a MONUMENT OF DEVASTATION."[47]

Curtius was not entirely wrong to blame an "unseen hand" for the crisis
he saw unfolding in Mississippi in 1837, at least to the extent that people
and forces outside the state played important roles in precipitating it. He
certainly could not have chosen a more apt metaphor than the shifting
tides for what transpired, as the dynamics that inundated Mississippi with
the appearance of boundless wealth early in the 1830s reversed themselves
almost completely in the second half of the decade. Where land sales had
once filled Mississippi bank vaults with federal monies, congressional legislation passed in June 1836 provided for redistributing federal surpluses
among the states based on their representation in Congress, presaging a
currency drain from the Southwest and leading bankers to begin calling
in loans and restricting credit terms. President Jackson's executive order
requiring federal land purchases to be made in gold or silver, issued just
weeks later, might have helped stem the prospective outflow of money
from Mississippi. But it also threatened an abrupt curtailment of speculation in the state and raised the specter of undercapitalized banks unable to
pay hard money to note holders demanding redemption. These conflicting
congressional and presidential policies only enhanced doubts foreign investors and creditors had already begun to have about the overall strength
of the American economy. Late in the summer of 1836 the Bank of England raised interest rates, and that fall it tightened credit available to British firms engaged in business and trade with the United States. Monetary
pressure on the American side of the Atlantic intensified accordingly, and
when cotton prices then fell by 25 percent between November 1836 and
April 1837, collapse was inevitable.[48]

The suffering experienced in the United States during the depression that followed the Panic of 1837 was severe, widespread, and long lasting, and signs of its impact were seen and felt first in Mississippi. On May 4 both the Planters' Bank and the Agricultural Bank in Natchez suspended specie payments, touching off a cascade of suspensions by nearly every bank in the country before the month ended. Cotton's indispensability to the American economy made Mississippi a logical bellwether of a broader downturn when market prospects for the crop declined. Nonetheless, Curtius's position that Mississippians themselves bore no responsibility for their predicament was hard to square, as the enticements offered by the Southwest were matched only by the giddy carelessness the region's residents displayed as they gave in to them. Behaving as if the flush times would last forever and as if they could extend themselves indefinitely without repercussions, Mississippians were left hopelessly exposed and vulnerable to changing conditions.[49]

The underlying weaknesses of Mississippi's economy were reflected in the extent of its desolation in the years after 1837. Speculators and other purchasers of public land who had yet to make payment defaulted and forfeited title to tens of thousands of acres when they could not muster the necessary specie, and new federal land sales in the state plummeted from more than three million acres in 1836 to fewer than half a million in 1837. Farmers and planters who had borrowed against future cotton crops scrambled desperately to keep their enterprises afloat as prices fell, but court dockets still became crammed with so many debt lawsuits "that some of the lawyers had their declarations in *assumpsit* printed by the quire, leaving blanks only for the names of the debtor, creditor and the amounts." Announcements of sheriff's sales would fill the columns of Mississippi newspapers for years.[50]

William Wills, a merchant, cotton planter, and minister from North Carolina, was shocked by what he observed in Mississippi when he traveled there in 1840. "The actual condition of affairs," he wrote in his diary, "is much worse than the report." Real estate that had recently been some of the most coveted in the nation was practically worthless, and Wills estimated that in the counties he passed through "it may probably be said that *not one man in fifty*, are solvent and probably less a number than this." Wills tried to withhold judgment, but he could not help thinking that Mississippians had failed to note when "limits have been passed, lost sight of & forgotten as things having no existence." As a result, Mississippi was "ruined, her rich men are poor and her poor men beggars. Millions on millions have been speculated on and gambled away by banking, by luxury, and too much prosperity until of all the States in the Union she has become much the worst. We have hard times in No. Ca.; hard times in the east, hard times everywhere, but Miss: exceeds them all." Mississippi plantation owner Martin Philips would not have argued the point. He recorded in his own 1840 diary that the state was "now paying penance for her past extravagance." To him it seemed that all of Mississippi was "*bankrupt*; never was there a time when insolvency was more general."[51]

The depression hit especially hard in the central and western portions of the state that had seen some of the most unrestrained speculation of the flush times. By the spring of 1837 the collective debts of Madison County and two of its neighbors alone had already come due in the amount of nearly three million dollars, and one observer wondered whether "a sacrifice of property, unheard of in the annals of calamity," would be enough to pay them. It seemed unlikely, as William Wills noted that "some of the finest lands in Madison & Hinds Counties may now be bought for comparatively nothing." Real estate once valued at fifty dollars an acre could be purchased for five, and land formerly valued at ten or twenty dollars an acre was available for as little as fifty cents. Small and promising villages such as Livingston never recovered from the Panic of 1837, and larger and more established towns such as Vicksburg would not see prosperity return for years. The Reverend J. R. Hutchison recalled that by 1838, economic misery "spread like a funeral pall over the young city. The hum of business began to die away. The wheels of industry moved sluggishly. The sinews of trade were cut; and ere long every citizen experienced the effects of a wide-spread embarrassment." Vicksburg, he wrote, "became but the shadow of its former self. Its wealth had taken to itself wings like an eagle, and had fled."[52]

Slaves and slavery sat alongside real estate at the core of Mississippi's economy before the crash, and many white Mississippians consequently turned to their enslaved property as they tried staving off financial disaster. Bearing the brunt of their owners' failures, thousands of slaves who had already lost families and communities through forced migration to the Southwest disappeared back into the cash nexus as planters stanched losses by selling off their most valuable remaining assets along with their land and their livestock. In other cases, whites had put themselves so deep in a hole that they forsook any expectation of getting out of it and abandoned their land altogether, sometimes in the middle of the night and one step ahead of their creditors. But even as they left fires burning, cows in their pens, and wagons in their places, they never left behind their slaves. If they could just make it out of the United States and into Texas, land and food could be replaced, but no property could help a farmer start over faster than enslaved laborers. Martin Philips was not the only planter who noticed his formerly rich neighbors "running off with their negroes."[53]

Creditors sometimes chased down debtors attempting to abscond to Texas, but arguably flight remained the most effective salvaging strategy, as the dramatic drop in slave prices during the depression significantly limited the utility of most other approaches that relied on the enslaved to bail white men out of debt. Prices driven unreasonably high during the flush times bottomed out in the early 1840s at less than half what they had been at their peak a few years earlier, but stories emerged from Mississippi in the earliest stages of the panic about farmers whose needs for cash were so pressing that they sold slaves for a quarter of what they might have been worth months before. Most problematic, of course, was that many white Mississippians had purchased the slaves in their possession with borrowed money that they had yet to pay back. Selling those slaves at depreciated prices might mean some small return for banks, slave traders, and other creditors, but it could not forestall overgrown plantations and humiliating auctions, every one of which reminded the white farmers and planters of Mississippi how foolish their decision to gamble their livelihoods on someone else's misery had been.[54]

As Mississippi's governing officials confronted the dire situation of the state and flailed about for solutions, they too looked to slavery. In part, like their constituents, they tried extracting whatever value remained from enslaved property in an attempt to regain fiscal soundness and avoid a complete fiasco. Desperately endeavoring to revive capital flows, for instance, the state legislature created more banks, the largest and most important of which was the Union Bank of Mississippi. Chartered early in 1837 as the grievously distressed condition of the banking sector became clear, the Union Bank was authorized to raise the substantial sum of $15.5 million, mostly through the sale of bonds backed by the credit of the state and secured by mortgages on the property of bank stockholders, who were required by law to be Mississippi residents. Slaves buttressed those bonds, as along with cotton and land they constituted a substantial portion of the estates stockholders mortgaged to secure them.[55]

A few months later, as bank suspensions rolled across the state and the nation, legislators sought to address the longer-term problem of capital that left Mississippi to pay nonresident creditors and turned to slavery yet again, this time enacting a law that actually implemented the 1832 constitutional ban on the importation of slaves for sale in Mississippi. Imposing a fine of up to five hundred dollars and as much as six months in jail for each slave a violator brought into the state, the law also voided all contracts signed and debts incurred for illegal slave purchases after its passage. If chartering the Union Bank potentially rescued some Mississippi planters through loans exchanged for mortgages on their property, putting the force of law behind the prohibition on the interstate slave trade potentially protected those planters from their own folly, removing the temptation to buy more slaves on credit in the deluded belief that their labor and possible future appreciation could push accounts back into the black. Neither legislative action fixed the enormous problems white Mississippians had created for themselves, but at least the policies nudged them away from assuming additional bad debts and toward paying down those they had already incurred.[56]

Some Mississippi slaveholders, in fact, tried using the new law banning the slave trade to evade paying some of those debts altogether—by simply denying they owed them. If the law annulled sales made in violation of a ban that had been in place for years, then perhaps every sale made after the ban was enacted had been illegal all along and slaveholders had no liability to fulfill their terms. This was a fairly radical reading of the legal situation, but an interpretation of the law retroactively nullifying slave sales could collectively save Mississippi property owners millions of dollars and might go a long way toward easing the debt burden of the state as a whole. Such considerations surely entered into the minds of Mississippi judges, including those on the state supreme court, who began ruling that deals made for imported slaves anytime after May 1, 1833, were not legally binding. That taking possession of someone else's enslaved property without paying for it was the very definition of a slave stealer seems to have occurred to no one.[57]

Ultimately, none of these gambits worked. The Union Bank scheme proved a failure, and cotton prices, which rebounded briefly in 1838, nosedived in 1839. They would not return to what they had been in the mid-1830s for decades. In 1841, the U.S. Supreme Court ruled in the case of *Groves* v. *Slaughter* that Mississippi's constitutional ban on interstate slave sales had required enabling legislation in order to be made operational and that all sales made prior to 1837 were thus legitimate and enforceable. It is doubtful that a different outcome could have saved Mississippi, but by the time the decision came down it was too late anyway. The state had defaulted on interest payments for Union Bank bonds several months earlier, and in 1842 the state legislature repudiated the bonds altogether. By the end of the 1840s only two banks operated in Mississippi. The state would neither charter another one nor receive foreign credit again until after the Civil War.[58]

V.

Americans engaged in a great deal of soul-searching in the wake of the Panic of 1837. As their faith in self-reliance collided with the realities of epidemic economic misfortune, many wondered whether those who fell into the financial and psychological abyss had only themselves to blame and had thus not merely failed but were actually failures. Others, such as minister and reformer Henry Ward Beecher, used the panic as an opportunity to blast speculators especially, asserting that they lured their fellow citizens to their downfall no less than the "vulture-flock" of professional gamblers. "Indeed," Beecher argued in 1843, "a Speculator on the exchange, and a gambler at his table, follow one vocation, only with different instruments. One employs cards or dice, the other property. . . . Both burn with unhealthy excitement; both are avaricious of gains . . . both depend more upon fortune than skill; they have a common distaste for labor; with each, right and wrong are only the accidents of a game; neither would scruple in any hour to set his whole being on the edge of ruin, and going over, to pull down, if possible, a hundred others."[59]

Antislavery activists, however, located a more immediately material and systemic cause for the crisis of the age. Joining critiques that focused on individual culpability with those that condemned a spirit of speculation, they maintained that blame for the unraveling economy and the scope of its impact could be placed directly on the extent to which slavery was woven into the fabric of the nation's economic life. The Executive Committee of the American Anti-Slavery Society articulated such an argument from the very outset of the panic, observing in the spring of 1837 that "the commercial world is now passing into one of those collapses which never fail to succeed an overblown system of credit" and asserting that substantial responsibility for this particular collapse lay with slaveholders and their financial enablers around the country. No people in the United States had more avidly or extensively sought credit during the flush times than slaveholders, and their inability to cover their debts was now bringing "the whole system to its ruin." Northern merchants were no less reproachable. "Anxious to partake the rich plunder," they had "furnished their capital for the extension of slave labor" and "reap[ed] great profit from the carrying trade" even as "the enormous extravagance and mad speculation that have grown out of the slave system" made "a re-action upon the system itself" inevitable. That northern capitalists were paying a steep price for their greed, the committee concluded, was their own doing. "Madly hastening to be richer, they have outbid each other in long credits, to secure Southern custom, till the South, like all well-trusted and prodigal customers, has squandered her own means and theirs, and they are left in the lurch."[60]

Abolitionists continued into the early 1840s to harp on the notion that America's economic misery owed itself to the intertwining of northern capital and southern slavery. One of the most widely circulated and influential tracts of the era, for example, was Joshua Leavitt's *The Financial Power of Slavery*, first published in 1840. Contending that slavery was "the chief source of the commercial and financial evils under which the country is now groaning," Leavitt called on readers to recognize how slavery systematically sucked capital out of the economy and how every American suffered for the lost millions northern investors had sunk into the South. "Ask any man of business in our cities," Leavitt suggested, "where his capital is gone, and where his *hopelessly irrecoverable* debts are, and he will point to the South. . . . And behind every one of these stands another class, who have sold goods, or lent money, or given their endorsement to others that have trusted their all at the South, and now cannot pay. And behind these another class, and another, and another, until there is hardly a remote hamlet in the free States that has not been directly or indirectly drained of its available capital by the Southern Debt."[61]

Leavitt and his fellow abolitionists oversimplified the extent to which slavery and slavery alone could be blamed for the Panic of 1837. Like any economic crisis, it resulted from a complex concatenation of factors. That there was something to their critique was undeniable nonetheless. Whatever profligacy might be attributed to white southerners who gorged themselves on cheap loans for land and slaves, financially facilitating the binge were men outside the region who were no less able to resist the lure of what looked like easy money. Complicity in the flush times was general, and what the Panic of 1837 revealed in especially painful fashion were the imbrications of supposedly free financial markets with the foul violence of slavery that were normally invisible and that many outside the South preferred to pretend did not exist.[62]

When everything foundered, looking away was no longer possible. As the Executive Committee observed, in good economic times, the wealth produced by slavery was "the common plunder of the country. . . . Northern merchants, northern mechanics, and manufacturers, northern editors, publishers, and printers, northern hotels, stages, steamboats, rail-roads, canal boats, northern banks, northern schoolmasters, northern artists, northern colleges, and northern ministers of the Gospel, all get their share of emolument from this general robbery" of the enslaved. At moments when the South suffered the kind of financial failure seen in the late 1830s, however, there was no way to maintain that pecuniary ties to slavery might coexist with moral and political opposition to the institution, because interregional credit networks meant "the natural result of this extraordinary bankruptcy" was "to throw the ownership of large numbers of slaves upon Northern capitalists."[63]

No place better demonstrated such things than Mississippi, as both the Executive Committee and Joshua Leavitt were well aware. More than any other state, the Executive Committee pointed out, Mississippi had resorted to the "necromancy of banking" to keep itself solvent, only to see rampant inflation and the extensive mortgaging of property "to Northern merchants." Nowhere served as a better example of how the slave trade enhanced demands for investments that had vanished in the panic, Leavitt argued, than Mississippi, where the "trade was carried on by the aid of Northern capital ... until the bubble burst, and all that capital is gone, sunk, irrecoverable."[64]

And the Executive Committee's assertion that the credit extended by northerners in the flush times would make them slaveholders in the depression was exactly so. In 1836, a little more than two years after Andrew Jackson began removing federal deposits from its vaults, the charter of the Second Bank of the United States formally expired, and what remained of its liabilities transferred to a new state-chartered institution known as the United States Bank of Pennsylvania. So did its assets, which included millions of dollars of outstanding loans made to Mississippi residents who could not possibly pay their debts in cash. As a consequence, by the middle of the 1840s just one trust created by the United States Bank to recover those debts owned four plantations and was one of the largest slaveholders in the state. A dubious windfall, perhaps, but investors had ventured a risky wager on the Southwest. Such were their winnings.[65]

ACKNOWLEDGMENTS

~ ~

When I first stumbled across the events at the heart of this book, I never imagined I would still be thinking about them nearly ten years later, and although I have tried to be diligent in keeping account of the very many people to whom I owe my gratitude for assistance on this project, I also beg forgiveness from those I neglect to mention. Archivists, librarians, and other staff at the Mississippi Department of Archives and History in Jackson, the Tennessee State Library and Archives in Nashville, the Lower Louisiana and Mississippi Valley Collection at Louisiana State University in Baton Rouge, the Southern Historical Collection at the University of North Carolina at Chapel Hill, the Center for American History at the University of Texas at Austin, and the Beinecke Rare Book and Manuscript Library at Yale University in New Haven all proved tremendously helpful and accommodating. Special thanks go to particular individuals at smaller archives without whose help I would never have found some crucial resources: Debra McIntosh at the J. B. Cain Archives of Mississippi Methodism at Millsaps College in Jackson, Mississippi; Gordon Cotton and George "Bubba" Bolm at the Old Court House Museum in Vicksburg, Mississippi; Hewey Purvis at the Warren County Courthouse, also in Vicksburg; and Louise Lynch at the Williamson County Historical Society Archives in Franklin, Tennessee.

I was very fortunate to receive fellowship support and other financial assistance for work on this project from a number of sources, and it gives me great pleasure to be able to thank them at long last for their confidence in my abilities. The Deep South Regional Humanities Center, the University of North Carolina at Chapel Hill Academic Libraries, and the University of Alabama Research Grants Committee provided funding enabling a series of research trips. The Gilder-Lehrman Center for the Study of Slavery, Resistance, and Abolition awarded a short-term fellowship letting me spend two months in New Haven that ended up being one of the more productive bursts of my scholarly career. My thanks go particularly to David Blight, Dana Schaffer, Tom Thurston, and Melissa McGrath. A fellowship from the National Endowment for the Humanities and the American

Antiquarian Society allowed me to spend six months in Worcester, Massachusetts, that both advanced my research significantly and were far more fun than a New England winter ought to be. I owe much to the AAS staff and to all the other fellows with whom I was in residence, but particularly to Ken Banks, Steven Bullock, Joanne Chaison, Pat Crain, Sara Crosby, Joe Cullen, Ellen Dunlap, Richard Fox, Vince Golden, John Hench, John Keenum, Lucia Knoles, Tom Knoles, Marie Lamoureux, Catherine Manegold, and Caroline Sloat.

Twelve years ago the University of Alabama provided me with the only academic job I have ever had. I feel lucky to have received the university's institutional support as well as to be part of a history department with phenomenal colleagues. My thanks to the university for providing me with a one-semester sabbatical, and especially to Kari Frederickson, who both as director of the Frances S. Summersell Center for the Study of the South and as history department chair has always been willing to provide material assistance for research whenever possible.

Portions of this work were presented at Brown University's Nineteenth-Century U.S. History Workshop and at the University of Georgia's Early American History Workshop. I offer my appreciation to those who participated and offered their feedback, and to Seth Rockman and Claudio Saunt for inviting me to their respective host institutions. The chapters of this book dealing with the city of Vicksburg and its gamblers appeared in somewhat different and significantly condensed form in the *Journal of American History*. My thanks to Ed Linenthal and the editorial and production staff at the journal, and to the readers whose comments sharpened my thinking and prose in important ways.

Over the years, many people have graciously read portions of this manuscript, perused book proposals, advised me on fellowship applications, written letters of recommendation, located and copied primary materials, sent unsolicited tips on sources, commented on conference papers, and provided the general encouragement needed to move a book from conceptualization to completion. Simply to list their names here does not do justice to their support and assistance, but it will have to suffice. My deepest appreciation to Edward Ayers, Elizabeth Blackmar, Jane Dailey, Steven Deyle, Daniel Goldmark, Robert Gudmestad, Kate Haulman, Peter Charles Hoffer, Paul Horwitz, Walter Johnson, Michael Kwas, Andy Lewis, Susan O'Donovan, George Rable, Calvin Schermerhorn, and Brad Wood. Thanks also to Seth

Rockman and Sven Beckert, who kindly thought of my work when they were putting together what ended up being an exhilarating and stimulating conference on slavery and capitalism in the spring of 2011. My paper for that event enabled me to think through many of the ideas that appear in the prologue and epilogue of this book.

I would be especially remiss not to recognize Ed Baptist, John Mayfield, and Scott Nelson for their singular contributions. All three read the manuscript in its entirety and offered very sound counsel for revision. That the changes I made only approximate their suggestions owes itself primarily to my own shortcomings and stubbornness.

Craig Remington and the staff at the University of Alabama's Cartographic Research Laboratory did outstanding work creating the maps for this book, and the staff at the University of Georgia Press has been wonderful and responsive at every stage of the publication process. I am especially beholden to my editor, Derek Krissoff. When I met Derek at a conference years ago almost by happenstance and told him what I was then only about halfway through working on, he not only saw its potential immediately but then also let a contract offer for the book sit on the table for an absurdly long time while I dithered. I am sincerely thankful for his patience and guidance, and I hope the final product is worth the wait.

In a book that turns so much on the assumption of debt and its consequences, it is only appropriate that I save for last an acknowledgment of debts so deep that I can never repay them. I am fortunate indeed that the members of my family are extraordinarily generous creditors. My children, Ben and Abigail, were born as the research and writing of this book unfolded. Both are too young to have any real understanding of what it is I do or what this book is about, and I would have it no other way. They seem genuinely thrilled to see me every time I walk through the door, and that goes above and beyond anything I could ever think to ask of them. They are beautiful and I love them dearly. Finally, I dedicate this book to Rebecca, my kindred spirit and most beloved friend. I have been thoroughly smitten with her since our first date. I have a wondrous life because of her. And I am so, so grateful.

Tuscaloosa, Alabama
January 2012

NOTES

~ ~

ABBREVIATIONS USED IN THE NOTES

ASP *American State Papers, Documents of the Congress of the United States, in Relation to the Public Lands*, 8 vols. (Washington, D.C., 1860)

CAP *Confession of Alonzo Phelps, the Rob Roy of the Mississippi* (Jackson, 1834)

LLMVC Louisiana and Lower Mississippi Valley Collection, Louisiana State University, Baton Rouge, Louisiana

LP Augustus Q. Walton, Esq., *A History of the Detection, Conviction, Life and Designs of John A. Murel, the Great Western Land Pirate* (Cincinnati, 1835)

MC Matthew Clanton, *A Refutation of the Charges Made in the Western Land Pirate, against Matthew Clanton; together with an Exposition of the Character of Virgil A. Stewart, Its Author* (Pittsburg, Miss., 1835)

MDAH Mississippi Department of Archives and History, Jackson, Mississippi

OCHM Old Court House Museum, Vicksburg, Mississippi

PCMC *Proceedings of the Citizens of Madison County, Mississippi, at Livingston, in July, 1835* (Jackson, 1836)

SHC Southern Historical Collection, University of North Carolina at Chapel Hill

TSLA Tennessee State Library and Archives, Nashville, Tennessee

VAS H. R. Howard, comp., *The History of Virgil A. Stewart, and His Adventure in Capturing and Exposing the Great "Western Land Pirate" and His Gang, in Connexion with the Evidence* (New York, 1836)

WCC Warren County Courthouse, Vicksburg, Mississippi

WCHS Williamson County Historical Society, Franklin, Tennessee

PROLOGUE. The Cotton Frontier, United States of America

1. *LP*, 70; *VAS*, 7, 8, 11; William C. Stewart, *Gone to Georgia* (Washington, D.C.: National Genealogical Society, 1965), 163; Yalobusha County Tract Book of Original Entry, vol. 1 (1833–53), 12, 17; *ASP*, vol. 7, 446.

2. John Henning owned twenty-seven slaves in 1830. U.S. Census—Tennessee, Madison County, 1830; *LP*, 20; *VAS*, 12.

3. *LP*, 21, 63; *VAS*, 13–14, 119–23. A number of authors have examined the stories

of Virgil Stewart and John Murrell and the events their interaction set into motion. The most informative and exhaustively researched is James Lal Penick Jr., *The Great Western Land Pirate: John A. Murrell in Legend and History* (Columbia: University of Missouri Press, 1981). Other significant and analytically interesting sources include Clement Eaton, *The Freedom-of-Thought Struggle in the Old South* (New York: Harper and Row, 1964), 95–99; William W. Freehling, *The Road to Disunion: Secessionists at Bay, 1776–1854* (New York: Oxford University Press, 1990), 110–13; Kenneth S. Greenberg, *Honor and Slavery: Lies, Duels, Noses, Masks, Dressing as a Woman, Gifts, Strangers, Humanitarianism, Death, Slave Rebellions, the Proslavery Argument, Baseball, Hunting, and Gambling in the Old South* (Princeton: Princeton University Press, 1997), 135–45; David Grimsted, *American Mobbing, 1828–1861: Toward Civil War* (New York: Oxford University Press, 1998), 11–12, 14–17, 144–56; David J. Libby, *Slavery and Frontier Mississippi, 1720–1835* (Jackson: University Press of Mississippi, 2004), 101–18; Davidson Burns McKibbin, "Negro Slave Insurrections in Mississippi, 1800–1865," *Journal of Negro History* 34, no. 1 (1949): 76–79; Edwin A. Miles, "The Mississippi Slave Insurrection Scare of 1835," *Journal of Negro History* 32, no. 1 (1957): 48–60; Christopher Morris, "An Event in Community Organization: The Mississippi Slave Insurrection Scare of 1835," *Journal of Social History* 22, no. 1 (1988): 93–111; and Laurence Shore, "Making Mississippi Safe for Slavery: The Insurrection Panic of 1835," in *Class, Consensus, and Conflict: Antebellum Southern Community Studies*, ed. Orville Vernon Burton and Robert C. McMath Jr., 96–127 (Westport, Conn.: Greenwood Press, 1982). Among books that straddle the line between scholarship and the sort of bandit folklore that still dominates the popular memory of John Murrell, see Robert M. Coates, *The Outlaw Years: The History of the Land Pirates of the Natchez Trace* (New York, 1930), esp. 169–302; and Paul I. Wellman, *Spawn of Evil: The Invisible Empire of Soulless Men Which for a Generation Held the Nation in a Spell of Terror* (New York: Doubleday, 1964).

4. The boom years of the 1830s were thus a product both of the specific financial circumstances and bank politics of that decade and of longer and more general trends related to accelerated market development that characterized the United States during the first half of the nineteenth century. The most recent synthesis of the historiography of the so-called market revolution is John Lauritz Larson, *The Market Revolution in America: Liberty, Ambition, and the Eclipse of the Common Good* (New York: Cambridge University Press, 2009); the most provocative expression of the market revolution thesis remains Charles Sellers, *The Market Revolution: Jacksonian America, 1815–1846* (New York: Oxford University Press, 1991). Useful essay collections engaging various components and implications of the era's economic developments include Melvyn Stokes and Stephen Conway, eds., *The Market Revolution in America: Social, Political, and Religious Expressions, 1800–1880* (Charlottesville: University Press of Virginia, 1996); and Scott C. Martin, ed., *Cultural Change*

and the Market Revolution in America, 1789–1860 (Lanham, Md.: Rowman and Littlefield, 2005). Valuable as a short introduction to the subject is Sean Wilentz, "Society, Politics, and the Market Revolution, 1815–1848," in *The New American History*, rev. and exp. ed., ed. Eric Foner, 61–84 (Philadelphia: Temple University Press, 1997). A number of historians have criticized the entire notion of the market revolution as an analytical construct; for example, Daniel Feller, "The Market Revolution Ate My Homework," *Reviews in American History* 25, no. 3 (1997): 408–15; and Daniel Walker Howe, *What Hath God Wrought: The Transformation of America, 1815–1848* (New York: Oxford University Press, 2007). Howe concedes that "markets expanded vastly in the years after the end of the War of 1812" even as he argues that "their expansion partook more of the nature of a continuing evolution than a sudden revolution" (5). The literature on Jacksonian-era banking and finance is nearly as daunting as that on the broader market economy. Useful works on the development of the American banking sector, the "war" over the rechartering of the Second National Bank, and the liberalization of credit that ramped up amid its defunding include Howard Bodenhorn, *A History of Banking in Antebellum America: Financial Markets and Economic Development in an Era of Nation-Building* (Cambridge: Cambridge University Press, 2000); Ralph C. H. Catterall, *The Second Bank of the United States* (Chicago, 1902); J. Van Fenstermaker, *The Development of American Commercial Banking, 1782–1837* (Kent, Ohio: Kent State University Bureau of Economic and Business Research, 1965); Bray Hammond, *Banks and Politics in America* (Princeton: Princeton University Press, 1957), esp. chs. 10–15; John M. McFaul, *The Politics of Jacksonian Finance* (Ithaca: Cornell University Press, 1971); Reginald Charles McGrane, *The Panic of 1837: Some Financial Problems of the Jacksonian Era* (New York, 1924); Robert V. Remini, *Andrew Jackson and the Bank War* (New York: W. W. Norton, 1967); Larry Schweikart, *Banking in the American South from the Age of Jackson to Reconstruction* (Baton Rouge: Louisiana State University Press, 1987); William G. Shade, *Banks or No Banks: The Money Issue in Western Politics, 1832–1865* (Detroit: Wayne State University Press, 1972); Walter Buckingham Smith, *Economic Aspects of the Second Bank of the United States* (Cambridge: Harvard University Press, 1953); Peter Temin, *The Jacksonian Economy* (New York: W. W. Norton, 1969); and Jean Alexander Wilburn, *Biddle's Bank: The Crucial Years* (New York: Columbia University Press, 1967).

5. Michael Chevalier, *Society, Manners, and Politics in the United States* (Boston, 1839), 286, 309. Many other travelers had essentially the same observations about Americans' restless movement in pursuit of material gain during that era. See Frederick Marryat, *A Diary in America, with Remarks on Its Institutions* (New York, 1839), 7–9; and Thomas Yoseloff, ed., *Voyage to America: The Journals of Thomas Cather* (New York: Thomas Yoseloff, 1961), 22–23, 79–80, 134–43.

6. Lewis Cecil Gray, *History of Agriculture in the Southern United States to 1860*,

vol. 2 (Washington, D.C., 1933), 898–901, 1027. For one recent exploration of cotton's global significance and the role the United States played, see Sven Beckert, "Cotton: A Global History," in *Interactions: Transregional Perspectives on World History*, ed. Jerry H. Bentley, Renate Bridenthal, and Anand A. Yang, 48–63 (Honolulu: University of Hawai'i Press, 2005). Also see Brian Schoen, *The Fragile Fabric of Union: Cotton, Federal Politics, and the Global Origins of the Civil War* (Baltimore: Johns Hopkins University Press, 2009). Important works on post-Revolutionary settlement and economic development in the Southwest include Carolyn Earle Billingsley, *Communities of Kinship: Antebellum Families and the Settlement of the Cotton Frontier* (Athens: University of Georgia Press, 2004); Joan E. Cashin, *A Family Venture: Men and Women on the Southern Frontier* (Baltimore: Johns Hopkins University Press, 1991); Thomas C. Clark and John D. W. Guice, *Frontiers in Conflict: The Old Southwest, 1795–1830* (Albuquerque: University of New Mexico Press, 1989); William C. Davis, *A Way through the Wilderness: The Natchez Trace and the Civilization of the Southern Frontier* (New York: Harper Collins, 1995); Everett Dick, *The Dixie Frontier: A Social History of the Southern Frontier from the First Transmontaine Beginnings to the Civil War* (New York: Alfred A. Knopf, 1948); Don H. Doyle, *Faulkner's County: The Historical Roots of Yoknapatawpha* (Chapel Hill: University of North Carolina Press, 2001), esp. 23–156; Daniel S. DuPre, *Transforming the Cotton Frontier: Madison County, Alabama, 1800–1840* (Baton Rouge: Louisiana State University Press, 1997); Libby, *Slavery and Frontier Mississippi*; James David Miller, *South by Southwest: Planter Emigration and Identity in the Slave South* (Charlottesville: University Press of Virginia, 2002); John Hebron Moore, *The Emergence of the Cotton Kingdom in the Old Southwest: Mississippi, 1770–1860* (Baton Rouge: Louisiana State University Press, 1988); Christopher Morris, *Becoming Southern: The Evolution of a Way of Life, Warren County and Vicksburg, Mississippi, 1770–1860* (New York: Oxford University Press, 1995); James Oakes, *The Ruling Race: A History of American Slaveholders* (New York: Vintage, 1982); Malcolm J. Rohrbough, *The Trans-Appalachian Frontier: People, Societies, and Institutions, 1775–1850* (New York: Oxford University Press, 1978), esp. chs. 8, 11, 12; and Adam Rothman, *Slave Country: American Expansion and the Origins of the Deep South* (Cambridge: Harvard University Press, 2005).

7. Stuart Bruchey, *Cotton and the Growth of the American Economy: 1790–1860: Sources and Readings* (New York: Harcourt Brace, 1967), 7, 9–10, 16–17, 19, 21, 23.

8. Malcolm Rohrbough, *The Land Office Business: The Settlement and Administration of American Public Lands, 1789–1837* (New York: Oxford University Press, 1968), 226–32; Edwin Arthur Miles, *Jacksonian Democracy in Mississippi* (Chapel Hill: University of North Carolina Press, 1960), 117–20. On Choctaw and Chickasaw removal, also see Mary Elizabeth Young, *Redskins, Ruffleshirts, and Rednecks: Indian Allotments in Alabama and Mississippi, 1830–1860* (Norman: University of

Oklahoma Press, 1961); Clark and Guice, *Frontiers in Conflict*, 233–53; Arthur H. DeRosier Jr., *The Removal of the Choctaw Indians* (Knoxville: University of Tennessee Press, 1970); and Samuel J. Wells, "Federal Indian Policy: From Accommodation to Removal," in *The Choctaw before Removal*, ed. Carolyn Keller Reeves, 181–213 (Oxford: University Press of Mississippi, 1985).

9. More than thirteen banks were actually incorporated in the state between 1829 and 1837, but by 1837 a number of them had already closed. Roughly twenty-eight banks and branches operated in the state by the end of 1836. See Marvin Bentley, "Incorporated Banks and the Economic Development of Mississippi, 1829–1837," *Journal of Mississippi History* 35, no. 4 (1973): 381–401; John Hebron Moore, *Agriculture in Ante-Bellum Mississippi* (New York: Bookman Associates, 1958), 69; Bruchey, *Cotton and the Growth of the American Economy*, 18–19; Miles, *Jacksonian Democracy in Mississippi*, 143–44. On banks and banking in early Mississippi, also see Bentley, "The State Bank of Mississippi: Monopoly Bank on the Frontier (1809–1830)," *Journal of Mississippi History* 40, no. 4 (November 1978): 297–318; Charles Hillman Brough, "The History of Banking in Mississippi," in *Publications of the Mississippi Historical Society*, vol. 3, ed. Franklin L. Riley, 317–40 (Oxford, Miss., 1901); Richard Holcombe Kilbourne Jr., *Slave Agriculture and Financial Markets in Antebellum America: The Bank of the United States in Mississippi, 1831–1852* (London: Pickering and Chatto, 2006); Dunbar Rowland, "Banking," in *Encyclopedia of Mississippi History*, vol. 1, ed. Dunbar Rowland, 181–97 (Madison, 1907); James Roger Sharp, *The Jacksonians versus the Banks: Politics in the States after the Panic of 1837* (New York: Columbia University Press, 1970), 55–88; and Robert C. Weems Jr., "Mississippi's First Banking System," *Journal of Mississippi History* 29, no. 4 (1967): 386–408.

10. Herbert A. Kellar, "A Journey through the South in 1836: Diary of James D. Davidson," *Journal of Southern History* 1, no. 3 (1935): 355. Among its democratic provisions the 1832 constitution eliminated all property requirements for voting and office holding, established term limits for most offices, and made nearly every state and county office an elected rather than an appointed position. This last provision included all judges; Mississippi was the only state in the country where that was the case. See Miles, *Jacksonian Democracy in Mississippi*, 35–43; and Winbourne Magruder Drake, "The Mississippi Constitutional Convention of 1832," *Journal of Southern History* 23, no. 3 (1957): 354–70.

11. William Henry Sparks, *The Memories of Fifty Years* (Philadelphia, 1870), 364; Joseph Holt Ingraham, *The South-West by a Yankee*, vol. 2 (New York, 1835), 86, 95; Burrell Fox to Aaron Neal, November 12, 1835, Neal Family Papers, box 1, folder 8, SHC.

12. *Boston Daily Courier*, July 11 and October 17, 1835; *Chicago American*, July 25, 1835; *Scioto (Ohio) Gazette*, August 19, 1835; *New York Evening Post*, November 10,

1835, and January 15, 1836; *Liberty Hall and Cincinnati Gazette*, May 14, 1835; *Lexington Intelligencer*, October 6, 1835.

13. Joseph G. Baldwin, *The Flush Times of Alabama and Mississippi: A Series of Sketches* (New York, 1853), 50, 82, 83–84, 87, 88.

14. William F. Gray, *From Virginia to Texas, 1835* (Houston, 1909), 26, 28, 41–42, 52–53 (quotations on 28, 52). Gray's cravings lend credence to historian James Roger Sharp's conclusion that in the 1830s Mississippi was "the best example of a state totally absorbed in the boom psychology" (Sharp, *Jacksonians versus the Banks*, 54).

15. Dennis East, "New York and Mississippi Land Company and the Panic of 1837," *Journal of Mississippi History* 33, no. 4 (1971): 305–6; *Lynchburg Virginian* in *Liberty Hall and Cincinnati Gazette*, June 25, 1835.

16. Bentley, "Incorporated Banks and the Development of Mississippi," 387, 389, 390, 399; East, "New York and Mississippi Land Company"; Catterall, *Second Bank of the United States*, esp. 132–63; Edward E. Baptist, "Toxic Debt, Liar Loans, and Securitized Human Beings: The Panic of 1837 and the Fate of Slavery," *Common-Place* 10, no. 3 (2010), www.common-place.org/vol-10/no-03/baptist, accessed January 10, 2012; Kilbourne, *Slave Agriculture and Financial Markets*, 25–55; Miles, *Jacksonian Democracy in Mississippi*, 70–86, 119–22.

17. Kellar, "A Journey through the South in 1836," 355; Baldwin, *Flush Times*, 87, 89, 263; *Jackson Mississippian*, June 24, July 1, July 15, July 22, August 5, August 12, August 19, August 26, and September 2, 1836.

18. A report filed in 1837 by state-appointed bank commissioners, for example, indicated that banks in Mississippi had less than half their authorized capital on hand, and just a tiny percentage of that was in hard money, with the ratio of specie to circulation and deposits just 1 to 15. Even those figures probably underestimated the extent to which banks had bungled their operations, because a number of institutions refused to allow the commissioners to inspect their books. Baldwin, *Flush Times*, 87; Brough, "History of Banking in Mississippi," 324–27; Fenstermaker, *Development of American Commercial Banking*, 152–53; McGrane, *Panic of 1837*, 24–27; and Miles, *Jacksonian Democracy in Mississippi*, 130–31, 143–44.

19. Johnson Jones Hooper, *Simon Suggs' Adventures and Travels* (Philadelphia, 1858), 12. Less aphoristically, William Henry Sparks wrote that in the flush times "there was no common bond but interest.... Society was a chaos, and *sauve qui peut*, or, take care of yourself, the rule" (Sparks, *Memories of Fifty Years*, 365).

20. Important works on the confusion and anxiety wrought more broadly in the United States by antebellum economic change, many of which focus on middle-class formation, religious revivalism, and the creation of bourgeois morality in northeastern cities and towns, include Stuart M. Blumin, *The Emergence of the Middle Class: Social Experience in the American City, 1760–1900* (New York: Cambridge University Press, 1989); Christopher Clark, *The Roots of Rural Capitalism:*

Western Massachusetts, 1780–1860 (Ithaca: Cornell University Press, 1990); Lori D. Ginzberg, *Women and the Work of Benevolence: Morality, Politics, and Class in the Nineteenth-Century United States* (New Haven: Yale University Press, 1992); Karen Halttunen, *Confidence Men and Painted Women: A Study of Middle-Class Culture in America, 1830–1870* (New Haven: Yale University Press, 1982); Rodney Hessinger, *Seduced, Abandoned, and Reborn: Visions of Youth in Middle-Class America, 1780–1850* (Philadelphia: University of Pennsylvania Press, 2005); Paul E. Johnson, *A Shopkeepers' Millennium: Society and Revivals in Rochester, New York, 1815–1837* (New York: Hill and Wang, 1979); John F. Kasson, *Rudeness and Civility: Manners in Nineteenth-Century Urban America* (New York: Hill and Wang, 1990); David J. Rothman, *The Discovery of the Asylum: Social Order and Disorder in the New Republic* (Boston: Little, Brown, 1971); Mary P. Ryan, *Cradle of the Middle Class: The Family in Oneida County, New York, 1790–1865* (New York: Cambridge University Press, 1981); and Ronald G. Walters, *American Reformers, 1815–1860*, rev. ed. (New York: Hill and Wang, 1997).

21. By way of comparison, the enslaved population of Mississippi grew by some thirty-two thousand during the 1820s. The slave population in the state doubled over the course of the decade, but the average number of slaves imported annually during the 1820s was only about a quarter of the average number imported annually during the 1830s. Moore, *Emergence of the Cotton Kingdom*, 118; Moore, *Agriculture in Ante-Bellum Mississippi*, 69.

22. Chevalier, *Society, Manners, and Politics in the United States*, 400; Ingraham, *South-West by a Yankee*, 2:91; and Ulrich B. Phillips, *American Negro Slavery* (New York, 1918), chart opposite 370.

23. As Edward Baptist has recently argued, "enslaved human beings were the ultimate hedge" for anyone looking to profit from the southwestern cotton economy (Baptist, "Toxic Debt, Liar Loans, and Securitized Human Beings"). Also see Ulrich B. Phillips, *American Negro Slavery* (New York, 1918), chart opposite 370; and Robert Evans Jr., "The Economics of American Negro Slavery, 1830–1860," in *Aspects of Labor Economics: A Conference of the Universities–National Bureau Committee for Economic Research* (Princeton: Princeton University Press, 1962), 199.

24. In their studies of the domestic slave trade, Steven Deyle, Walter Johnson, and Michael Tadman all conclude that roughly 60 to 70 percent of slaves moved from the upper South to the lower South over the course of the antebellum era were moved via the interstate trade. David Libby, focusing on Mississippi specifically, concludes that slaves imported by traders "comprised a great part of the African American population in Mississippi before 1835." Charles Sydnor notes that the trade was substantial and that "few, if any, southern States received as many slaves and exported as few" as Mississippi. See Steven Deyle, *Carry Me Back: The Domestic Slave Trade in American Life* (New York: Oxford University Press, 2005), 289;

Walter Johnson, *Soul by Soul: Life inside the Antebellum Slave Market* (Cambridge: Harvard University Press, 1999), 5–6; Michael Tadman, *Speculators and Slaves: Masters, Traders, and Slaves in the Old South* (Madison: University of Wisconsin Press, 1989), 44; Libby, *Slavery and Frontier Mississippi*, 61; and Charles Sackett Sydnor, *Slavery in Mississippi* (New York, 1933), 144–57, quotation on 144. On the financing of the cotton plantation economy, see Harold D. Woodman, *King Cotton and His Retainers: Financing and Marketing of the Cotton Crop of the South, 1800–1925* (Lexington: University of Kentucky Press, 1968), 3–195. For a contemporary source describing the escalating debt assumed by purchasers of slaves in Mississippi, see *United States Gazette* in *New York Observer and Chronicle*, February 22, 1840. On the relationship between local credit systems and mortgages backed by slave property, see Bonnie Martin, "Slavery's Invisible Engine: Mortgaging Human Property," *Journal of Southern History* 76, no. 4 (2010): 817–66.

25. Sydnor, *Slavery in Mississippi*, 157–62. On the speculative nature of the domestic slave trade, see Deyle, *Carry Me Back*, esp. 94–141; Robert H. Gudmestad, *A Troublesome Commerce: The Transformation of the Interstate Slave Trade* (Baton Rouge: Louisiana State University Press, 2003); Johnson, *Soul by Soul*; and Tadman, *Speculators and Slaves*. How much debt white Mississippians engaged to pay for their slaves in the 1830s cannot be reckoned precisely, but the figure was staggering. One man estimated that over the course of the decade Mississippians collectively borrowed ninety million dollars to buy slaves; another asserted in 1841 that Mississippians in 1841 still owed more than three million dollars to slave traders for purchases they made between 1832 and 1837. The *Natchez Courier*, publishing from the site of the largest slave mart in the state, offered a snapshot that may provide a relatively accurate feel for the whole, reporting that white residents of Mississippi bought as many as ten thousand slaves on credit between the fall of 1835 and the fall of 1836 at an average cost of one thousand dollars, thus creating a debt of ten million dollars to be paid out of the 1836 cotton crop. See *United States Gazette* in *New York Observer and Chronicle*, February 22, 1840; *Groves* v. *Slaughter*, 40 U.S. 449 (1841), 481; and *Natchez Courier* in *Christian Secretary*, May 20, 1837.

26. On efforts by southwestern states to ban the interstate slave trade in the years after Nat Turner's Rebellion, see Lacy K. Ford, *Deliver Us from Evil: The Slavery Question in the Old South* (New York: Oxford University Press, 2009), 449–60. The constitutional ban was not Mississippi's first attempt to regulate the slave trade. A law mandating certificates of good character for adult slaves imported for sale to Mississippi was enacted by the territorial legislature in 1808 and reenacted in 1822, and in 1825 the state began taxing the proceeds of slave auctions as well as slave sales conducted by itinerant traders; the tax was revived in 1833. On efforts to control the slave trade in Mississippi, the constitutional ban, and the considerations behind it, see Sydnor, *Slavery in Mississippi*, 162–63; *Groves* v. *Slaughter*, 40 U.S. 449

(1841), 452–54 (quotations at 452); *Green* v. *Robinson*, 6 Miss. 80 (December 1840), 102; and *Glidewell et al.* v. *Hite et al.*, 6 Miss. 110 (December 1840), 111–12.

27. *Groves* v. *Slaughter*, 40 U.S. 449 (1841), 452; Sydnor, *Slavery in Mississippi*, 163–65, 168–69; Ford, *Deliver Us from Evil*, 455–57. The ban's unpopularity was evident almost immediately, and in 1833 the legislature submitted to voters a constitutional amendment that would have repealed it. That November, Mississippians overwhelmingly approved the repeal, but Mississippi law required that constitutional amendments receive at least 50 percent of the total number of votes cast for the legislature in the year they were proposed in order to pass. The amendment to repeal the ban on the interstate trade failed to achieve that standard, and the trade thus remained technically unconstitutional.

CHAPTER ONE. Inventing Virgil Stewart

1. William C. Stewart, *Gone to Georgia* (Washington, D.C.: National Genealogical Society, 1965), 162; W. E. White, ed., *The Early History of Jackson County, Georgia* (Atlanta, 1914), 23.

2. Stewart, *Gone to Georgia*, 162–63.

3. *VAS*, 7; Adam Rothman, *Slave Country: American Expansion and the Origins of the Deep South* (Cambridge: Harvard University Press, 2005), 54; Lewis Cecil Gray, *History of Agriculture in the Southern United States to 1860*, vol. 2 (Washington, D.C., 1933), 682. Virgil Stewart appears to have had at least one brother, named Tapley or Tarpley, who was arrested in Arkansas in 1842 on suspicion of counterfeiting and bank robbery. See *Arkansas Gazette*, October 12, 1842.

4. *VAS*, 7; Joan E. Cashin, *A Family Venture: Men and Women on the Southern Frontier* (Baltimore: Johns Hopkins University Press, 1991), 44–49, 53–61.

5. *VAS*, 7, 8; Gray, *History of Agriculture*, 2:697, 1026–27.

6. *VAS*, 8.

7. Emma Inman Williams, *Historic Madison: The Story of Jackson and Madison County, Tennessee* (Jackson, Tenn., 1946), 1–10, 29–47, 120–35; James Phelan, *History of Tennessee: The Making of a State* (Boston and New York, 1888), 303–4, 309–10; Malcolm J. Rohrbough, *The Trans-Appalachian Frontier: People, Societies, and Institutions, 1775–1850* (New York: Oxford University Press, 1978), 163–66, 168–69.

8. Williams, *Historic Madison*, 29–30, 198–226, 528, 532 (quotations on 29–30 and 198).

9. *VAS*, 8. No public record indicates that Stewart ever purchased or paid taxes on any land in Tennessee. A Madison County man named Hezekiah Askew did sign an affidavit swearing that Stewart "kept a house of his own, until he sold off his property" late in 1832, but Askew described Stewart as having "occupied" the farm he lived on, suggesting that perhaps Stewart rented rather than owned the property. Stewart may have managed to cobble together the funds for a small piece of land,

though, given that he had enough money when he left Tennessee to purchase an extensive stock of goods that he intended to sell in Mississippi. It seems far less likely that Stewart ever owned any of "the negroes" he claimed worked his farm with him. One Tennessean recalled that Stewart worked for a time as an overseer, but no one who knew Stewart in Tennessee ever mentioned his having held any slaves of his own. *VAS*, 169–70; Truman Hudson Alexander Papers, 1817–1975, MF 517, reel 1, TSLA.

10. Malcolm Rohrbough, *The Land Office Business: The Settlement and Administration of American Public Lands, 1789–1837* (New York: Oxford University Press, 1968), 90; Don H. Doyle, *Faulkner's County: The Historical Roots of Yoknapatawpha* (Chapel Hill: University of North Carolina Press, 2001), 54.

11. Rohrbough, *Land Office Business*, 221–34. On the Treaty of Dancing Rabbit Creek, the removal of the Choctaw, and speculation on their land, see Mary Elizabeth Young, *Redskins, Ruffleshirts, and Rednecks: Indian Allotments in Alabama and Mississippi, 1830–1860* (Norman: University of Oklahoma Press, 1961), 22–72; Robert V. Remini, *Andrew Jackson and His Indian Wars* (New York: Penguin, 2001), 180–205, 239–53; Samuel J. Wells, "Federal Indian Policy: From Accommodation to Removal," in *The Choctaw before Removal*, ed. Carolyn Keller Reeves, 181–213 (Oxford: University Press of Mississippi, 1985); David J. Libby, *Slavery and Frontier Mississippi, 1720–1835* (Jackson: University Press of Mississippi, 2004), 101–3; and Thomas C. Clark and John D. W. Guice, *Frontiers in Conflict: The Old Southwest, 1795–1830* (Albuquerque: University of New Mexico Press, 1989), 233–53.

12. Rohrbough, *Land Office Business*, 223–26; Young, *Redskins, Ruffleshirts, and Rednecks*, 159.

13. *VAS*, 8–9, 165–71; *LP*, 79–80 (quotation on 79); *MC* in *Nashville Banner and Whig*, August 21, 1835. Matthew Clanton's work, which no longer exists in its original form, was reprinted over two issues of the *Nashville Banner and Whig* in August 1835. Hereafter, it is cited with the date August 21, 1835, or August 24, 1835, corresponding to the issue of the *Banner and Whig* in which the information cited appeared. On the early histories of Tuscahoma and Chocchuma, see Henry Watterson Heggie, *Indians and Pioneers of Old Eliot* (Grenada, Miss.: Tuscahoma Press, 1989), 226–33, 241–50.

14. *VAS*, 9 (quotation), 166–69; *ASP*, 7:454.

15. U.S. Census—Tennessee, Perry County, 1830; Williams, *Historic Madison*, 335, 336; U.S. Census—Mississippi, Panola County, 1850; *MC*, August 21, 1835; Yalobusha County Tract Book of Original Entry, vol. 1 (1833–53), 1.

16. *LP*, 69; *VAS*, 9–11; *MC*, August 21, 1835 (quotations).

17. *LP*, 70; *VAS*, 11; *MC*, August 21, 1835. Though agreeing broadly on the course of events, Stewart and Clanton recalled somewhat different chronologies. Stewart claimed that Clanton left the Choctaw Cession for Tennessee in November and

did not return until six weeks later in early January; Clanton asserted that he went to Tennessee in October and was gone for just a few weeks. That Clanton was gone somewhat longer than he remembered seems possible, but given that Clanton and Stewart both purchased land in Chocchuma in mid-December, Clanton's memory placing him back in Mississippi by the beginning of that month is probably more accurate.

18. *ASP*, 7:446; Yalobusha County Tract Book of Original Entry, vol. 1 (1833–1853), 12, 15, 17, 19. Stewart would later claim that he never purchased land in the Choctaw Cession because the time he spent after John Murrell's arrest trying to locate John Henning's slaves forced him to abandon any hope of buying property. Stewart's claim in this regard seems odd because it was so demonstrably false. It did, however, allow Stewart to make the case that he was willing to put the interests of his country above his own. It was also in keeping with his tendency toward self-pity. See *VAS*, 126–27. For a somewhat different version of the story, see *LP*, 64.

19. U.S. Census—Tennessee, Tipton County, 1830; U.S. Census—Mississippi, Monroe County, 1850; Yalobusha County Deed Book D, 9, MDAH; *VAS*, 213 (first quotation); *MC*, August 21, 1835 (second and third quotations). Stewart too described these living arrangements as "very intimate," even going so far as to suggest that he and Clanton "lived nearly as one family" (*LP*, 65).

20. Dunbar Rowland, *The Official and Statistic Register of the State of Mississippi* (Madison, Wis., 1917), 442; Dunbar Rowland, *Mississippi*, vol. 2 (Atlanta, 1907), 995. Many works about frontier settlement in the Southwest and elsewhere note that economic failure, disillusionment, and disappointment were relatively common. See, for example, James Oakes, *The Ruling Race: A History of American Slaveholders* (New York: Vintage, 1982), 123–27; Cashin, *A Family Venture*, 64–65, 73–77; Stephen Aron, *How the West Was Lost: The Transformation of Kentucky from Daniel Boone to Henry Clay* (Baltimore: Johns Hopkins University Press, 1996), esp. 124–69; and Malcolm J. Rohrbough, *Days of Gold: The California Gold Rush and the American Nation* (Berkeley: University of California Press, 1997).

21. It is hard to tell how serious Virgil Stewart was about running for office in Yalobusha County. He claimed in 1835 to have "given his name to some of his friends as a candidate" for county clerk, but by 1836 he had stopped making that claim. U.S. Census—Tennessee, Tipton County, 1830; Yalobusha County Combination Tax Rolls, 1834, Auditor of Public Accounts, RG29, MDAH; *LP*, 64 (quotation); *MC*, August 21 and 24, 1835; James Lal Penick Jr., *The Great Western Land Pirate: John A. Murrell in Legend and History* (Columbia: University of Missouri Press, 1981), 56–59; James W. Bragg, "Captain Slick, Arbiter of Early Alabama Morals," *Alabama Review* 11 (April 1958): 125–34; Richard Maxwell Brown, *Strain of Violence: Historical Studies of American Violence and Vigilantism* (New York: Oxford University Press, 1975), 67–133; Richard Maxwell Brown, *The South Carolina Regulators*

(Cambridge: Harvard University Press, 1963); Jennet Kirkpatrick, *Uncivil Disobedience: Studies in Violence and Democratic Politics* (Princeton: Princeton University Press, 2008), 17–61; Rachel N. Klein, *Unification of a Slave State: The Rise of the Planter Class in the South Carolina Backcountry, 1760–1808* (Chapel Hill: University of North Carolina Press, 1990), 36–77.

22. Henry S. Foote, *Casket of Reminiscences* (Washington, D.C., 1874), 251; Joseph G. Baldwin, *The Flush Times of Alabama and Mississippi: A Series of Sketches* (New York, 1853), 228; Diary of Robert Cartmell, vol. 31, February 17, 1913, Robert Cartmell Papers, TSLA.

23. *ASP,* 7:283, 329, 414–47, 734.

24. Several hundred pages of affidavits and testimony collected during a congressional investigation of the Chocchuma land sales detail the workings of the Chocchuma Land Company. See *ASP,* 7:272–73, 283–84, 448–507, 608–22, 732–35, 8:711–88. For historians' accounts of the sales and the company, see Young, *Redskins, Ruffleshirts, and Rednecks,* 155–61; Rohrbough, *Land Office Business,* 226–28; Edwin Arthur Miles, *Jacksonian Democracy in Mississippi* (Chapel Hill: University of North Carolina Press, 1960), 93–96; James P. Shenton, *Robert John Walker: A Politician from Jackson to Lincoln* (New York: Columbia University Press, 1961), 13–17; Thomas D. Cockrell, "The Politics of Land in Jacksonian Mississippi," *Journal of Mississippi History* 47, no. 1 (1985): 11–13; Gordon T. Chappell, "Some Patterns of Land Speculation in the Old Southwest," *Journal of Southern History* 15, no. 4 (1949): 473–76; and H. Donalson Jordan, "A Politician of Expansion: Robert J. Walker," *Mississippi Valley Historical Review* 19, no. 3 (1932): 363–65.

25. Shenton, *Robert John Walker,* 14; Young, *Redskins, Ruffleshirts, and Rednecks,* 158; Cockrell, "Politics of Land in Jacksonian Mississippi," 12.

26. *ASP,* 7:449, 492, 504–5.

27. Ibid., 283–84, 491–505 (quotations on 492).

28. Ibid., 420, 446, 502 (quotation on 502).

29. Shenton, *Robert John Walker,* 11–16, quotation on 12; *ASP,* 7:480.

30. My account of the early life and criminal career of John Murrell owes a great deal to Penick, *Great Western Land Pirate,* esp. 9–31. See also Williamson County Deed Book A-1, 602–3, TSLA; Tennessee Prison Records, 1831–1992, part 2: Oversized Volumes, vol. 42, Convict Record Book 1831–42, 103–4, RG25, TSLA; *State v. John A. Murrell,* 1823, 1826, Miscellaneous Williamson County Original Court Papers, files of the Williamson County Archive, WCHS; Williamson County Will Book 3, 211–12 and 756–57, TSLA. John Murrell's mother's name sometimes appears in the records as Zilpha.

31. Cashin, *A Family Venture,* 100–102; Maury County Circuit Court Minute Book 1821–24, 360–61, 386, TSLA; Dickson County Circuit Court Minute Book 3, March 1825–September 1827, September term 1826 and March term 1827, unpagi-

nated, TSLA; Williamson County Will Book 3, 756–57, TSLA; Penick, *Great Western Land Pirate*, 13, 14; *State v. James Murrell*, 1823, *State v. John A. Murrell*, 1823, 1826, *State v. Jeffrey G. Murrell*, 1828, Miscellaneous Williamson County Original Court Papers, WCHS; Williamson County Circuit Court Minute Book 4, 254, 256, 258, 511, Minute Book 6, 165, 168, and Minute Book 7, 227, TSLA; Tennessee Prison Records, 1831–1992, part 2: Oversized Volumes, vol. 42, Convict Record Book 1831–42, 103–4, RG25, TSLA; *Clinton (Miss.) Gazette*, September 19, 1835.

32. *Franklin (Tenn.) Independent Gazette*, December 26, 1823; Williamson County Circuit Court Minute Book 4, 181–83, 219–20, TSLA; Williamson County Court of Pleas and Quarter Sessions Minute Book 2, 215–22, TSLA; Williamson County Court Minute Book 7, 9, 35, 86, 88–90, 100–101, 125–26, 135, TSLA; *State v. John A. Murrell*, 1823, 1826, Miscellaneous Williamson County Original Court Papers, WCHS; Penick, *Great Western Land Pirate*, 14–15.

33. Williamson County Circuit Court Minute Book 4, 180–81, 184, 216, 252, 346, 349–50, Minute Book 5, 29, 46, 133, TSLA; *State v. John A. Murrell*, 1823, 1826, Miscellaneous Williamson County Original Court Papers, WCHS; *Franklin (Tenn.) Independent Gazette*, December 26, 1823 (quotation); Davidson County Circuit Court Minute Book E, 462–63, TSLA. The branding likely was never inflicted. No one who provided a reliable physical description of Murrell ever indicated that he had a scar reading "HT" or anything else on his thumb. See Penick, *Great Western Land Pirate*, 19–20, for a discussion of the matter.

34. *State v. John A. Murrell*, 1823, 1826 (quotation), *State v. Ira Walton et al.*, *State v. James Cox et al.*, 1824, Miscellaneous Williamson County Original Court Papers, WCHS; Williamson County Court Minute Book 7, 373, 384, 462, TSLA.

35. Williamson County Will Book 3, 756–57, TSLA; Williamson County Circuit Court Minute Book 5, 364, Minute Book 6, 100, 156–57, TSLA; Williamson County Deed Book H, 473, 747–48, and Deed Book K, 567–69, TSLA.

36. U.S. Census, 1830—Wayne County, Tennessee; *River Counties Quarterly* 1, no. 1 (1972): 87; Jill K. Garrett, comp., *Obituaries from Tennessee Newspapers* (Greenville, S.C.: Southern Historical Press, 1980), 251; Tennessee Prison Records, 1831–1992, part 2: Oversized Volumes, vol. 42, Convict Record Book 1831–42, 103, RG25, TSLA.

37. By the time John Murrell entered the Tennessee State Penitentiary in 1834, he was the father of two children. His daughter Arthusy was born in 1832 or 1833, so Elizabeth Murrell was at least pregnant with her sometime in 1831 or 1832. James Penick asserts that Murrell's other child was a son, also named John. The 1840 census listing for Elizabeth Murrell, however, indicates three children living in her household. Two were girls between the ages of five and ten, and one was a boy under age five. It is possible that Elizabeth Murrell became pregnant just before her husband went to prison in August 1834, in which case the boy was likely John and

Elizabeth's infant son. Alternatively, the Murrells had two daughters, both born between 1830 and 1834, which would make them both between five and ten at the time the 1840 census was taken. See Penick, *Great Western Land Pirate*, 25–26, fn. 29, and 29, fn. 34; Tennessee Prison Records, 1831–1992, part 2: Oversized Volumes, vol. 42, Convict Record Book 1831–42, 103–4, RG25, TSLA; U.S. Census, 1840—Madison County, Tennessee; U.S. Census, 1850—McNairy County, Tennessee; Davidson County Circuit Court Minute Book F, 20, TSLA; Madison County Deed Book 3, 325–26, TSLA; Madison County Circuit Court Order Book, 1828–36, 371–72 (quotation on 372), TSLA.

38. *LP*, 19–20.

39. Madison County Circuit Court Order Book, 1828–36, 348, 371–72, TSLA; *LP*, 20.

40. Madison County Circuit Court Order Book, 1828–36, 382–83, TSLA; *LP*, 19. On the social position of poor whites in the antebellum South, see Charles C. Bolton, *Poor Whites of the Antebellum South: Tenants and Laborers in Central North Carolina and Northeast Mississippi* (Durham: Duke University Press, 1994); Charles C. Bolton and Scott Culclasure, eds., *The Confessions of Edward Isham: A Poor White Life of the Old South* (Athens: University of Georgia Press, 1998); Victoria E. Bynum, *Unruly Women: The Politics of Social and Sexual Control in the Old South* (Chapel Hill: University of North Carolina Press, 1992); Jeff Forret, *Race Relations at the Margins: Slaves and Poor Whites in the Antebellum Southern Countryside* (Baton Rouge: Louisiana State University Press, 2006); and Timothy James Lockley, *Lines in the Sand: Race and Class in Lowcountry Georgia, 1750–1860* (Athens: University of Georgia Press, 2001).

41. A few scholars have examined the phenomenon of free blacks being kidnapped and sold into slavery, and there are several published accounts of abolitionists tried in southern states on charges of slave stealing for having endeavored to help people escape their bondage. But essentially no historical work deals with slave theft that involved criminals profiting by exploiting the desire of the enslaved for freedom. This is perhaps to be expected given the challenges of systematically assessing the frequency or patterns of an activity that by its very nature was secretive and shadowy, not to mention the difficulty of ascertaining when a slave was "stolen" and when one simply ran away. Why slaveholders saw slave stealing as serious enough to deserve the death penalty in some states was explained in 1819 by a South Carolina court, which asserted that the law making slave stealing a capital crime there was designed "to give the most ample protection to the most valuable species of personal property, owned in this country; and to effect that object, it became necessary to resort to terms suited to the nature of the property intended to be protected. Negroes, being intelligent creatures, possessing volition, as well as the power of locomotion, are capable of being deluded by art and persuasion, as

well as of being compelled by fear or force to leave the service of their masters."
See Carol Wilson, *Freedom at Risk: The Kidnapping of Free Blacks in America, 1790–
1865* (Lexington: University Press of Kentucky, 1994); and Jenny Bourne Wahl, *The
Bondsman's Burden: An Economic Analysis of the Common Law of Southern Slavery*
(Cambridge: Cambridge University Press, 1998), 132–35 (quotation on 132–33). For
Tennessee specifically, see R. L. Caruthers and A. O. P. Nicholson, *A Compilation
of the Statutes of Tennessee of a Permanent and General Nature, from the Commencement of the Government to the Present Time* (Nashville, 1836), 319. For examples of
southerners referring to those they suspected of being slave stealers as "tampering"
with the enslaved, see *Baltimore Gazette and Daily Advertiser*, August 24, 1835; and
Arkansas Gazette, August 25, 1835.

42. *Randolph (Tenn.) Recorder*, June 20, 1834; *Arkansas Gazette*, March 10, 1835;
Penick, *Great Western Land Pirate*, 55, 60, 62–63, 65; Larry D. Ball, "Murrell in Arkansas: An Outlaw Gang in History and Tradition," *Mid-South Folklore* 6, no. 3
(1978): 65–75. Also see the *Recorder* of June 20, 1835; the *Gazette* of March 31, 1835,
April 7, 1835, and July 7, 1835; and George W. Featherstonhaugh, *Excursion through
the Slave States* (New York, 1844), 87–120.

43. Penick, *Great Western Land Pirate*, 62–63. Also see *Randolph Recorder*, September 16, 1834, and June 20, 1835; *Arkansas Gazette*, March 31, 1835; *Jackson Mississippian*, July 4, 1834; and Tipton County Circuit Court Minutes, 1825–34, 243, 271,
TSLA.

44. *LP*, 21; *Franklin (Tenn.) Independent Gazette*, December 26, 1823; Tennessee
Prison Records, 1831–1992, part 2: Oversized Volumes, vol. 42, Convict Record Book
1831–42, 103–4, RG25, TSLA.

45. *LP*, 20–23; *VAS*, 13–19.

46. *LP*, 23, 26–29, 31–32; *VAS*, 26–30, 34–35.

47. *LP*, 32 (quotation); *VAS*, 36–37.

48. *LP*, 42–45, 48–51; *VAS*, 61–62, 70–91.

49. *LP*, 36, 50 (quotation); *VAS*, 47–49, 83–84.

50. John Henning's belief that John Murrell was heading toward Randolph
likely originated with Murrell himself, as his letter to Richard Henning consisted
mostly of an invitation to join him on a trip there, where supposedly he would see
that Murrell's business was entirely aboveboard. In reality, Murrell intended the
letter as a decoy, anticipating that Henning would shadow him as he headed toward
Randolph, whereupon Murrell would lose him along the road and head instead
into Arkansas. *LP*, 36, 48, 50; *VAS*, 48, 50, 75–76, 80, 99–100.

51. *LP*, 29, 34, 49; *VAS*, 27–28, 42–43.

52. *LP*, 29, 35, 49; *VAS*, 29–30, 42–45, 76–78, 99–102.

53. *LP*, 51–52; *VAS*, 79, 88–95, 152–53.

54. *LP*, 52–53; *VAS*, 96–98.

55. *LP*, 54, 62–63; *VAS*, 102–3, 112, 119–20.

56. *LP*, 63; *VAS*, 120–23. The posse that arrested Murrell included several men with a direct personal interest in seeing him apprehended, including Stewart; two of John Henning's sons; William Long; and Ransom Byrn, a slave trader who believed Murrell had also stolen one of his slaves. Later in the spring of 1834 Byrn sued Murrell for damages and received a judgment of $675, though given Murrell's insolvency Byrn almost certainly never collected. *LP*, 60; *VAS*, 113–14, 123; Madison County Court Minute Book 4, 1833–40, 130, 134, 158, TSLA; Madison County Court Execution Dockets, 1829–44, no. 2391, August term 1834, TSLA.

57. *LP*, 63; *VAS*, 121, 123.

58. Precisely what Virgil Stewart told people in the spring of 1834 about his ride with John Murrell is unknowable, but clearly he began telling a more expansive version of the story he had told John Henning. Stewart said he "acquainted" Henning "with his adventure, and Murel's confessions concerning his negroes." Similarly, Stewart recalled that when he provided information about Murrell in court the day after Murrell's arrest, he "confined himself to such facts as related to the abduction and subsequent disposition of Mr. Henning's negroes." Within weeks, however, he was telling Matthew Clanton all about Murrell and his "accomplices." Clanton recalled that in Mississippi, Stewart "told his Murel story to every man who would listen to it," and Stewart himself acknowledged that by the spring many people in Tennessee knew that he had been boasting about his knowledge of Murrell's supposed criminal organization. Given the story Stewart would tell on the witness stand at Murrell's trial and then again months later in his pamphlet, he could not possibly have talked at any length about Murrell and his associates without at least alluding to some of the many crimes to which he claimed Murrell confessed. *LP*, 63, 64; *VAS*, 123, 128, 129–30; *MC*, August 24, 1834.

59. *LP*, 64; *VAS*, 126–28 (quotation on 128).

60. *VAS*, 128 (quotations); *Vicksburg Register*, March 12, 1834; *Yalobusha Pioneer* 1 no. 1 (1977): 4–5.

61. *LP*, 64; *VAS*, 126, 128. More than a year and a half later, a New Orleans newspaper published a letter purporting that Henning's slaves had been sold in June 1834 in Marksville, Louisiana, where Henning finally recovered them. The letter writer did not conclusively connect Murrell to the theft of Henning's slaves, but his description of what the slaves supposedly said about slave stealers who persuaded them to run away, concealed them for months in a camp in the forest, and sold them as soon as published advertisements for their capture stopped appearing comported well with the way thieves described by Stewart and others operated. *New Orleans Bulletin* in *Vicksburg Register*, September 24, 1835. Also see Penick, *Great Western Land Pirate*, 68–70.

62. *MC*, August 24, 1834.

63. *VAS*, 129; *Vicksburg Register*, March 12, 1834; Rowland, *Mississippi*, 2:995; *Yalobusha Pioneer* 1 no. 2 (1977): 2–3.

64. *LP*, 80 (first quotation); *VAS*, 129–30 (second quotation on 129). Also see *LP*, 64, where Stewart alluded obscurely to "several charges and preferments" launched against him about this time in Tennessee.

65. *LP*, 64; *VAS*, 130–31, 134 (quotations).

66. *LP*, 66; *VAS*, 134–35 (quotations on 134).

67. *MC*, August 21, 1834.

68. Ibid.

69. Ibid. Even before hearing the Vesses' accusation Stewart noticed that the couple appeared to be watching and talking about him. *LP*, 65; *VAS*, 131–36.

70. *MC*, August 21, 1834; *LP*, 69, 70.

71. *MC*, August 21, 1834.

72. Ibid.

73. Ibid.

74. Ibid.

75. *MC*, August 21 (quotations) and August 24, 1834; *VAS*, 145–46; *LP*, 71; *Vicksburg Register*, March 12, 1834.

76. *MC*, August 21, 1834; *VAS*, 209–10.

77. *MC*, August 21, 1834.

78. Murrell escaped on May 7, 1834, from the Brownsville jail in Haywood County, where he had been lodged since February because the Madison County jail was in a state of disrepair. Stewart would later claim that he actually learned about Murrell's disappearance from a letter sent to him in Mississippi by a friend in Tennessee, and that Clanton accused him of theft only after that. Both Saunders and Clanton, however, said they confronted Stewart about the merchandise in his chest around the first of May, and a letter from Tennessee regarding Murrell's disappearance could not have reached Stewart in Yalobusha County until at least a week after that. Clanton and Saunders may have misremembered the timing of their accusations by a few days, but Stewart was almost certainly fudging the facts. In reality, Stewart probably left Yalobusha County about May 4 or 5 and arrived back in Madison County within days of Murrell's escape from jail. Madison County Circuit Court Order Book, 1828–36, 443–44, 498, TSLA; *VAS*, 149–51, 213–14; *LP*, 69, 71.

79. *LP*, 71.

80. *LP*, 71; *VAS*, 151–52; *MC*, August 21, 1834 (quotations).

81. *MC*, August 24, 1834.

82. As described by British geologist George Featherstonhaugh, who traveled from Baltimore to the Mexican frontier and back again, Texas in the early 1830s was

a refuge for outlaws and the bankrupt, "a country which for some time loomed up as an asylum of that portion of oppressed humanity that feels nervous under the restraints of the law" (Featherstonhaugh, *Excursion*, 74).

83. *MC*, August 24, 1834; *VAS*, 152; *LP*, 72; Madison County Circuit Court Order Book, 1828–36, 443, 498, TSLA. Though local legend has it that two slaves played integral roles in capturing Murrell in Alabama, it seems that his mother told Tennessee authorities where he was. Shortly after Murrell escaped from jail, his appeal of his conviction in the William Long case came before the Supreme Court of Tennessee. In his absence the court ruled that Zilpah Murrell would lose the $250 bond she had posted for her son while he appealed unless she could produce him at the next term of the court. A year later Zilpah asked for and was granted a discharge from the forfeiture because she had "delivered over the body of the said John A. Murrell to Mathias DeBerry Sheriff of Madison County." See William L. McDonald, "The Legend of Captain Slick's Company," *Journal of Muscle Shoals History* 5 (1977): 17–18; William L. McDonald, "The Legend of Uncle Tom Brannon and the Capture of John A. Murrell," *Journal of Muscle Shoals History* 5 (1977): 37–38; and Supreme Court of Tennessee, Western Division, Minutes, December 1830–April 1840, 182, 239–40 (quotation on 240), TSLA.

CHAPTER TWO. Inventing John Murrell

1. *Jackson Truth Teller* in *Randolph Recorder*, September 5, 1834. Also see *LP*, 73; *VAS*, 171; *Arkansas Gazette*, September 23, 1834; Madison County Circuit Court Order Book, 1828–36, 442–43, TSLA; Emma Inman Williams, *Historic Madison: The Story of Jackson and Madison County, Tennessee* (Jackson, Tenn., 1946), 38.

2. *Jackson Truth Teller* in *Randolph Recorder*, September 5, 1834.

3. Ibid.; Madison County Circuit Court Order Book, 1828–36, 442–45, 457, 498, TSLA; *LP*, 73; *VAS*, 178–79. Several other newspapers published accounts of the trials, but their reports clearly originated with the story published in the *Truth Teller*. See, for example, *Arkansas Gazette*, August 26 and September 23, 1834. Useful as well in establishing a sense of Stewart's testimony is an article from the *Randolph Recorder* published November 21, 1834. Appearing four months after the trial but before the publication of Stewart's pamphlet, its summary of Stewart's testimony could have come only from someone who witnessed or heard directly about the trial itself.

4. *Jackson Truth Teller* in *Randolph Recorder*, September 5, 1834; *Randolph Recorder*, November 21, 1834.

5. *LP*, 23–24. The editor of the *Truth Teller* wrote that on the witness stand Stewart detailed "many examples of splendid success" that he claimed Murrell gave him to demonstrate how slave stealing was a secure path to riches. In his pamphlet, meanwhile, Stewart recalled that he testified to "all the circumstances and occur-

rences which led to the introduction and acquaintance with Murel and himself,"
but also to many of the "feats of villany" that Murrell boasted about on their travels.
Precisely which "examples" and "feats" Stewart described in court is a matter of
some conjecture. The above account of his likely testimony derives from the conversations Stewart delineated in his pamphlet as having transpired between the
two men up to and including the moment when Murrell supposedly demonstrated
how he coaxed the enslaved to allow themselves to be "stolen." At Murrell's trial
the prosecution would have been most interested in those instances where Stewart
said Murrell talked about John Henning and the slaves Murrell was being tried for
stealing. But Stewart's language in writing about his testimony and the account
from the *Truth Teller* strongly suggest that aside from those moments, the substance
of his evidence lay in stories he asserted Murrell relayed during the early portions
of their journey, most of which went to putting the theft of Henning's slaves in the
broader context of the slave-stealing operation Murrell supposedly bragged about
running. *Jackson Truth Teller* in *Randolph Recorder*, September 5, 1834; *LP*, 73.

6. *LP*, 20, 24–25.

7. Ibid., 25.

8. Ibid., 26, 29–30.

9. Ibid., 26.

10. Ibid., 25.

11. Ibid., 32–34.

12. *Jackson Truth Teller* in *Randolph Recorder*, September 5, 1834; *LP*, 34.

13. *LP*, 23, 35–36.

14. Ibid., 36–39.

15. As Madison County sheriff Mathias Deberry would later attest, Stewart
surely had heard the "circulating reports" about "the infamous character of Murrell"
that were widespread in Murrell's neighborhood (*VAS*, 214).

16. *VAS*, 26, 41–42 (quotation on 41).

17. *VAS*, 100–102 (quotation on 101); R. L. Caruthers and A. O. P. Nicholson, *A
Compilation of the Statutes of Tennessee of a Permanent and General Nature, from the
Commencement of the Government to the Present Time* (Nashville, 1836), 330. In fact,
the cajoling incident may not be so unlikely. In his account of his life as a slave in
Georgia, John Brown recalled having a master so cruel that sometime in the 1840s
he ran off with a white man he barely knew who promised to bring him to a spot
where men affiliated with Murrell supposedly gathered stolen slaves for transport
and resale. The escape attempt had to be aborted when someone informed the
white man that Murrell was in prison. Brown's account not only indicates that
stories about Murrell animated white criminals for years after Murrell was caught,
but also that the enslaved might take any possible avenue for escaping bondage, no
matter how foolhardy it might seem. L. A. Chamerovzow, ed., *Slave Life in Georgia;*

A Narrative of the Life, Sufferings, and Escape of John Brown, a Fugitive Slave, Now in England (London, 1855), 49–51.

18. Russell Fowler, "Milton Brown, 1804–1883: West Tennessee's Man for All Seasons," *West Tennessee Historical Society Papers* 50 (1996): 7–26; Williams, *Historic Madison*, 87–90; Henry S. Foote, *Bench and Bar of the Southwest* (St. Louis, 1876), 258; Mrs. Randall Vann, "Honorable Milton Brown," paper delivered to the Madison County Historical Society, May 9, 1944, in Roy Watterson Black Papers, box 5, TSLA; J. Roderick Heller, *Democracy's Lawyer: Felix Grundy of the Old Southwest* (Baton Rouge: Louisiana State University Press, 2010). Months after Murrell's trial, Stewart, still indignant about Brown's treatment of him on the witness stand, insisted that Brown had taken Murrell's case largely "for the sake of acquiring the character of a great criminal lawyer" (*LP*, 84).

19. *LP*, 82–84. Also see *Western Weekly Review* (Franklin, Tenn.), October 9, 1835; *VAS*, 179; and *Randolph Recorder*, November 21, 1834.

20. *VAS*, 179, 214; *MC*, August 24, 1835; *LP*, 74; Madison County Circuit Court Order Book, 1828–36, 443, 498, TSLA.

21. *MC*, August 24, 1835; *LP*, 74 (quotation), 83.

22. *LP*, 20; *VAS*, 122, 213–14 (quotation on 214).

23. *VAS*, 214. It seems unlikely that Murrell and Stewart had met prior to 1834 because Murrell would almost certainly have said as much, if only to raise doubts that might have helped him avoid conviction. For one historian's inconclusive speculation on the matter, see James Lal Penick Jr., *The Great Western Land Pirate: John A. Murrell in Legend and History* (Columbia: University of Missouri Press, 1981), 89–93.

24. *LP*, 74. In his pamphlet Stewart would repeatedly and vehemently deny the accusation of venality, but McVey's testimony was not the sole evidence at the trial indicating that Stewart pursued Murrell for money. The only material evidence offered against Murrell consisted of some documents discovered on his person when he was recaptured near Florence after escaping from prison, one of which was an uncertified affidavit indicating that Stewart admitted to some of Murrell's Arkansas colleagues that he was after a five-hundred-dollar bounty offered by some wealthy men for Murrell's capture and conviction. Prosecutors introduced the affidavit to show that at the time of his arrest Murrell was planning to smear Stewart's character in the hope of avoiding conviction. Though the affidavit was almost certainly phony, it probably raised questions about Stewart in the minds of jurors, who surely recalled it when Reuben McVey testified. *LP*, 20, 74; *VAS*, 152–55.

25. Madison County Circuit Court Order Book, 1828–36, 444–45, TSLA.

26. Ibid., 442–43, 444–45. Given the stories Stewart told in court, it is possible to conceive of Murrell being charged with a wide range of crimes in addition to slave stealing; horse theft seems a particularly likely candidate. A number of historians

have asserted that Murrell was tried for murder as well, a claim that appears to rely ultimately on one of Milton Brown's daughters, who recollected her father telling some of his fellow lawyers that Murrell was a thief but not a murderer. In fact, there is no definitive evidence regarding the full bill of indictment. See Penick, *Great Western Land Pirate*, 94–95; Harbert Alexander, *Tales of Madison: Historical Sketches of Jackson and Madison County, Tennessee* (Franklin, Tenn.: Hillsboro Press, 2002), 52; and Williams, *Historic Madison*, 87–88. Also see Park Marshall, "John A. Murrell and Daniel Crenshaw," *Tennessee Historical Magazine* 6, no. 1 (1920): 4.

27. *MC*, August 24, 1835; *Jackson Truth Teller* in *Randolph Recorder*, September 5, 1834.

28. *LP*, 80–81 (first quotation on 81, subsequent quotations on 80).

29. *VAS*, 181–83 (quotations on 181 and 181–82). Also see *LP*, 74.

30. *MC*, August 24, 1835.

31. *Randolph Recorder*, June 20, 1834 (first quotation); *Arkansas Gazette*, July 1 (second quotation) and July 22, 1834.

32. *LP*, 20, 74. That Stewart understood the reward money collected on his behalf to be a message that residents of Madison County wanted him to stop talking about his travels with John Murrell is suggested by the second version of his pamphlet. There, Stewart claimed that members of Murrell's gang offered to bribe him if he would refrain from writing and publishing his story, but the location of that claim right at the point in the narrative where he was about to leave Madison suggests he was really talking about the reward money and that he saw it as a bribe from county residents. *VAS*, 183–84.

33. *LP*, 74–78; *VAS*, 184–200; *Randolph Recorder*, November 21, 1834.

34. *LP*, 78; *VAS*, 197, 200–204, 215–16. James Moore owned eighty acres of land along the Pearl River and five or so slaves. Combination Tax Rolls, Auditor of Public Accounts RG29, Madison County, Mississippi, 1834–35, MDAH.

35. *LP*, 78.

36. *Randolph Recorder*, November 21, 1834.

37. *LP*, 77–78; *Randolph Recorder*, November 21, 1834; *Nashville Banner* in *Randolph Recorder*, December 25, 1835. On "John G. Brown," also see Penick, *Great Western Land Pirate*, 102–5. It is perhaps unwise to make too much of the "science" of handwriting analysis, but a graphological reading of the "cramped" style of the letter points toward an "expressive" author who is cautious about money, has a "suspicious temperament," and possesses a "confused character . . . with diffuse thoughts thronging the mind"— traits that characterized Virgil Stewart. See www.igraphology.com/analytical-factors.html, accessed June 2, 2011.

38. *VAS*, 201–2.

39. Stewart would claim that he delivered two thousand dollars to the friend with whom he deposited his papers "for the purpose of defraying the expense of

their publication," and that he saw the threat Murrell posed to the Southwest as so dire that he gave away and surreptitiously distributed rather than sold his pamphlet once it was published. The amount Stewart received just before leaving Tennessee is unknown, but it cannot have been anywhere near two thousand dollars. Moreover, several sources indicate clearly that Stewart's pamphlet was indeed sold. *VAS*, 200 (quotation), 204; *Arkansas Gazette*, June 2, 1835; Henry S. Foote, *Casket of Reminiscences* (Washington, D.C., 1874), 251.

40. On antebellum sensational literature, see especially David S. Reynolds, *Beneath the American Renaissance: The Subversive Imagination in the Age of Emerson and Melville* (New York: Alfred A. Knopf, 1988). Also see Daniel A. Cohen, *Pillars of Salt, Monuments of Grace: New England Crime Literature and the Origins of American Popular Culture, 1674–1860* (Amherst: University of Massachusetts Press, 2006); Patricia Cline Cohen, *The Murder of Helen Jewett: The Life and Death of a Prostitute in Nineteenth-Century New York* (New York: Alfred A. Knopf, 1998); Ann Fabian, *The Unvarnished Truth: Personal Narratives in Nineteenth-Century America* (Berkeley: University of California Press, 2000), 49–78; Karen Halttunen, *Murder Most Foul: The Killer and the American Gothic Imagination* (Cambridge: Harvard University Press, 1998); Shelly Streeby, *American Sensations: Class, Empire, and the Production of Popular Culture* (Berkeley: University of California Press, 2002); and Andie Tucher, *Froth and Scum: Truth, Beauty, Goodness, and the Ax Murder in America's First Mass Medium* (Chapel Hill: University of North Carolina Press, 1994).

41. Of the sizable literature on southern honor, the classic remains Bertram Wyatt-Brown, *Southern Honor: Ethics and Behavior in the Old South* (New York: Oxford University Press, 1982). Also see Edward L. Ayers, *Vengeance and Justice: Crime and Punishment in the Nineteenth-Century South* (New York: Oxford University Press, 1984); Kenneth S. Greenberg, *Honor and Slavery: Lies, Duels, Noses, Masks, Dressing as a Woman, Gifts, Strangers, Humanitarianism, Death, Slave Rebellions, the Proslavery Argument, Baseball, Hunting, and Gambling in the Old South* (Princeton: Princeton University Press, 1997); Stephanie McCurry, *Masters of Small Worlds: Yeoman Households, Gender Relations, and the Political Culture of the Antebellum South Carolina Low Country* (New York: Oxford University Press, 1995); and Steven M. Stowe, *Intimacy and Power in the Old South: Ritual in the Lives of the Planters* (Baltimore: Johns Hopkins University Press, 1987).

42. On the particular significance of violence to honor and on the ways male understandings of honor shifted as a consequence of southwestern migration, see Edward E. Baptist, *Creating an Old South: Middle Florida's Plantation Frontier before the Civil War* (Chapel Hill: University of North Carolina Press, 2002), 120–53; Dickson D. Bruce Jr., *Violence and Culture in the Antebellum South* (Austin: University of Texas Press, 1979); Joan E. Cashin, *A Family Venture: Men and Women on the Southern Frontier* (Baltimore: Johns Hopkins University Press, 1991), 99–118; and

Elliott J. Gorn, "'Gouge and Bite, Pull Hair and Scratch': The Social Significance of Fighting in the Southern Backcountry," *American Historical Review* 90 (February 1985): 18–43.

43. A growing number of works describe how honor intersected, sometimes uneasily, with other value systems and behavioral codes in the pre–Civil War South, and how factors such as race, class, age, location, and occupation helped shape the way antebellum southern men saw themselves. Usefully examining these realities from a variety of perspectives is Craig Thompson Friend and Lorri Glover, eds., *Southern Manhood: Perspectives on Masculinity in the Old South* (Athens: University of Georgia Press, 2004). Similarly, the extent to which honor was a uniquely southern model for masculine behavior has also been called into question. See, for example, Amy S. Greenberg, *Manifest Manhood and the Antebellum American Empire* (Cambridge: Cambridge University Press, 2005).

44. The best recent work grappling with the confused masculinity wrought specifically on the southwestern frontier by the contradictions between honor culture and market culture is John Mayfield, *Counterfeit Gentlemen: Manhood and Humor in the Old South* (Gainesville: University Press of Florida, 2009). On the ways an evolving market culture reshaped masculinity and identity elsewhere in the United States, see Michael Kimmel, *Manhood in America: A Cultural History* (New York: Free Press, 1996), 13–78; Karen Halttunen, *Confidence Men and Painted Women: A Study of Middle-Class Culture in America, 1830–1870* (New Haven: Yale University Press, 1982); David J. Pugh, *Sons of Liberty: The Masculine Mind in Nineteenth-Century America* (Westport, Conn.: Greenwood Press, 1982); and E. Anthony Rotundo, *American Manhood: Transformations in Masculinity from the Revolution to the Modern Era* (New York: Basic Books, 1993). On the fears and realities of failure in antebellum America, see Edward J. Balleisen, *Navigating Failure: Bankruptcy and Commercial Society in Antebellum America* (Chapel Hill: University of North Carolina Press, 2001); and Scott A. Sandage, *Born Losers: A History of Failure in America* (Cambridge: Harvard University Press, 2005), 22–98.

45. Stewart was not alone in undertaking what might be called a strategy of articulation. Personal narratives by common men and women from a variety of backgrounds were increasingly prominent in the United States from the middle of the eighteenth century forward. As Ann Fabian suggests, these Americans wrote in part to turn their experiences into saleable assets and in part because the process of writing was itself a way of taking control of one's life and "a means to assert an imaginative propriety over events by giving them narrative form." At the same time, however, Fabian notes something Virgil Stewart would discover to be all too true, namely that "the authority derived from experience and the bonds built on its articulation are not necessarily either liberating or long-lasting. . . . [I]n paying particular attention to the discursive production of experience we can witness a play

of social forces that grants truth and authority to certain descriptions of experience and not to others" (Fabian, *The Unvarnished Truth*, 7).

46. Stewart would later write that Walton was a friend he encountered in October 1834 on the road somewhere west of Columbus, and that in addition to taking custody of Stewart's papers Walton directed him to the home of James Moore as a place where he might rest. Stewart himself indicated that the name "Augustus Q. Walton" was a false one, but such a person may have existed. Stewart could have had assistance in giving his story some narrative coherence and in introducing him to Moore, and rumors did circulate after the pamphlet appeared that a merchant named William Armour was in fact the author. Still, in the preface to Stewart's pamphlet "Walton" writes that he took much of its language from notes made by Stewart, and months after publication Stewart would write a long letter to a Mississippi newspaper in which he referred to the pamphlet as "my narrative" which "I published." In short, even if Stewart did have help compiling *The Western Land Pirate*, it is fairly clear that he was its primary author. *VAS*, 200; *LP,* 18; *Jackson Mississippian*, February 19, 1836; Penick, *Great Western Land Pirate*, 105.

47. *LP,* 17 (first quotation), 18 (other quotations).

48. Ibid., 17 (first and second quotations), 29 (third and fourth quotations), 63 (fifth quotation), 74 (final quotation).

49. Ibid., 20 (first and second quotations), 71 (third quotation), 74 (fourth quotation), 79 (fifth and sixth quotations), 73 (seventh quotation), 36 (final quotation). In creating this contrast Stewart constructed a crude version of what David Reynolds refers to as the "moral adventure" stories of such authors as James Fenimore Cooper, which "probed the turbulence and linguistic violence of frontier or city life but tried to uphold firm ethical values through the portrayal of a central hero . . . who sustains integrity and moral power" (Reynolds, *Beneath the American Renaissance*, 183).

50. *LP*, 29 (first, seventh, and eighth quotations), 17 (second quotation), 21 (third quotation), 26 (fourth, fifth, and sixth quotations).

51. Ibid., 39 (first quotation), 40, 42 (remaining quotations), 52, 61.

52. Ibid., 36 (first quotation), 51 (second quotation).

53. Ibid., 45–46 (quotations on 45 and 46).

54. Ibid., 47–48, 54 (second quotation), 40 (remaining quotations).

55. Ibid., 41, 58 (quotation), 61–62.

56. Ibid., 64 (quotations), 65.

57. Ibid., 65–66 (quotations on 66).

58. Ibid., 66–69, 71 (first quotation on 66; second, third, and fourth quotations on 68; fifth quotation on 69; final quotation on 71).

59. Ibid., 71 (first, second, and third quotations), 73 (fourth quotation), 83 (fifth quotation), 74 (sixth and seventh quotations).

60. Ibid., 54.

61. Ibid., 17. On advice manuals and etiquette guides, see Halttunnen, *Confidence Men and Painted Women*; Rodney Hessinger, *Seduced, Abandoned, and Reborn: Visions of Youth in Middle-Class America, 1780–1850* (Philadelphia: University of Pennsylvania Press, 2006); and John F. Kasson, *Rudeness and Civility: Manners in Nineteenth-Century Urban America* (New York: Hill and Wang, 1990).

62. *LP*, 33, 45. Stewart's work actually predates the height of the vogue for southwestern humorists, which was just beginning in the 1830s. But stories about the strangeness and casual violence of the southwestern frontier, often told for comic effect, were already becoming familiar to many Americans by then thanks to early newspaper sketches and travel writers. See Hennig Cohen and William B. Dillingham, eds., *Humor of the Old Southwest*, 3rd ed. (Athens: University of Georgia Press, 1994); M. Thomas Inge, ed., *The Frontier Humorists: Critical Views* (Hampden, Conn.: Archon Books, 1975); M. Thomas Inge and Edward J. Piacentino, eds., *The Humor of the Old South* (Lexington: University of Kentucky Press, 2001); James H. Justus, *Fetching the Old Southwest: Humorous Writing from Longstreet to Twain* (Columbia: University of Missouri Press, 2004); Mayfield, *Counterfeit Gentlemen*; and John Francis McDermott, ed., *Before Mark Twain: A Sampler of Old, Old Times on the Mississippi* (Carbondale: Southern Illinois University Press, 1968). On Porter and his *Spirit of the Times*, see Norris W. Yates, *William T. Porter and the Spirit of the Times: A Study of the Big Bear School of Humor* (Baton Rouge: Louisiana State University Press, 1957).

63. *LP*, 45, 58. Even as much of what Stewart unveiled for the first time in *The Western Land Pirate* was the product of his imagination, to the extent there was material that may have come from Murrell himself it was information about Murrell's life and early career. According to Stewart, for example, Murrell mentioned that he sometimes stole slaves in Alabama with the assistance of an overseer named "Nolin" who was his "brother-in-law's brother." Murrell's sister Leanna was married to a man named Nolen, and their residence in Alabama probably explains why Murrell fled there after escaping from jail in 1834. Similarly, Stewart referenced a man named Crenshaw as one of Murrell's first criminal associates. There was a Crenshaw family living in Williamson County at the same time as the Murrell family, and a number of legends point to Daniel Crenshaw as John Murrell's mentor in crime. The Crenshaws and the Murrells were connected by marriage, and Daniel Crenshaw did run afoul of the law for horse theft and forgery. No conclusive evidence other than Stewart's pamphlet, however, actually links Daniel Crenshaw and John Murrell. That does not demonstrate that Murrell really told Stewart the things Stewart said he did, but the fact that Stewart knew Crenshaw's name at all suggests Murrell may have talked about his activities as a young man. See Marshall, "John A. Murrell and Daniel Crenshaw"; Penick, *Great Western Land Pirate*, 21–22, 45; *LP*, 60; and Madison County Deed Book 6, 1838–40, 473, TSLA.

64. *LP*, 71–72. In the expanded edition of his pamphlet, published in 1836, Stewart offered a slightly different explanation of his reticence. He no longer claimed to have been concerned about Murrell receiving a fair trial. Rather, he asserted that he thought no one would believe him and that talking about the clan and the plot might make him look foolish and elicit enough sympathy for Murrell to result in his release from prison. Thus, Stewart claimed, he decided to wait until closer to the time of the supposed insurrection to write about it. In some ways this was a more plausible explanation, and it had the virtue of acknowledging that the entire story was "an imputation upon the good sense of" anyone hearing it. Still, given the scope of the danger supposedly involved, it makes almost no sense that he would wait roughly eight months after Murrell had gone to prison to publish his story. *VAS*, 123–25, 182–83 (quotation on 182).

65. *LP*, 61–62. For a more detailed account of some of the names of "clansmen" provided by Stewart, including many of those listed above, see Penick, *Great West-ern Land Pirate*, 69–81. Also see Larry D. Ball, "Murrell in Arkansas: An Outlaw Gang in History and Tradition," *Mid-South Folklore* 6, no. 3 (1978): 65–75. Ball found that a few of the names of the Arkansans Stewart listed corresponded to real persons with plausible connections to crimes committed in the Morass but that many others were names of people who just happened to live in the area, and some may not have existed at all. On Stephen Foreman, see *Arkansas Gazette*, July 1, July 22, and August 19, 1834, and April 7, 1835. On Alonzo Phelps, see *CAP*; *Jackson Mississippian*, July 4, 1834; and Foote, *Casket of Reminiscences*, 431–35. On Reuben Tims, see *Nashville Republican*, August 22, 1835. On the Lloyds, Bunches, and Bar-neys, see *Randolph Recorder*, June 20, 1835.

66. *Arkansas Gazette*, August 18, 1835; *LP*, 61. The entire list of clansmen can be found in *LP*, 61–62. A Virginia editor who read Stewart's pamphlet and believed Stewart might be telling the truth conceded that he did not recognize a single name of Murrell's clansmen from his own state and asserted about Stewart's list more generally that he "had no doubt that it was vastly exaggerated in number, and indeed that many of the names upon it had no living representatives." Simi-larly, a North Carolina editor praised Stewart for bringing Murrell to justice and preempting the insurrection plot even as he published the list of clansmen Stewart provided so that they might be captured "if the names be not fictitious ones." The editor, moreover, admitted he had never heard of any of Murrell's North Carolina confederates. *Lynchburg Virginian* cited in *Baltimore Gazette and Daily Advertiser*, August 5, 1835; *Raleigh Register*, September 1, 1835.

67. *VAS*, 115; *LP*, 50.

68. *Randolph Recorder*, September 16, 1834.

69. Although few people at the time of Murrell's trial knew about the circum-stances under which Stewart left Mississippi, Stewart had an inkling that the story

would eventually catch up with him. In *The Western Land Pirate* he wrote that soon after he left Yalobusha County "Clanton and his agents" began spreading "over the country that Mr. Stewart had stolen a quantity of goods from Clanton, and run away," and that "[s]uch reports were very mortifying to the feelings of Mr. Stewart" (*LP*, 71).

70. *LP*, 22, 26, 35.

71. Ibid., 32.

72. Ibid., 23. Also see David Grimsted, *American Mobbing, 1828–1861: Toward Civil War* (New York: Oxford University Press, 1998), 150.

73. *LP*, 26 (first and last quotations), 23.

74. Ibid., 31, 32, 35. It requires no great leap into Freudianism to conclude that the early death of Stewart's father shaped his quest for older men on whom he might model his behavior. Numerous historians have noted the contentious relationships between cotton frontier settlers and their fathers and argued that ambivalence between fathers and sons shaped the contours of the frontier itself. See, for example, Cashin, *A Family Venture*, 32–44; and Mayfield, *Counterfeit Gentlemen*, xxiii–xxiv.

75. *LP*, 51 (first quotation), 31 (last quotation), 52 (remaining quotations).

76. Ibid., 41.

77. The question of whether or not class relations among white southerners before the Civil War were harmonious has an extensive historiography. The planter class hardly faced the danger of white revolt from below, but the rhetoric of white male democracy aside, it is beyond dispute that elite southerners condescended to those below them economically. An excellent dissection of class tensions on one southern frontier and the ideological gymnastics necessary to mask them can be found in Baptist, *Creating an Old South*.

78. *Jackson Truth Teller* in *Arkansas Gazette*, June 2, 1835.

79. *Vicksburg Register*, September 24, 1835; *Baton Rouge Gazette* in *Nashville Banner and Whig*, September 21, 1835; *Arkansas Gazette*, August 18, 1835. Also see *Lynchburg Virginian* in *Baltimore Gazette and Daily Advertiser*, August 5, 1835. Stewart recognized how poorly received *The Western Land Pirate* was on its initial publication, writing later that although "it excited great curiosity, and was . . . the subject of much speculation," a fair number of readers considered it a work of fiction (*VAS*, 205).

80. *Jackson Mississippian*, July 17, 1835. Nineteen other men also signed the statement "so far as it relates to Mr. Clanton."

81. *Yalobusha Pioneer* 1, no. 4 (1977–78): 7; *MC*, August 24, 1835. Clanton's response to Stewart first appeared in the *Pittsburg (Miss.) Bulletin* on July 2, 1835, but was soon thereafter available in pamphlet form. *Vicksburg Register*, July 23, 1835; *Nashville Banner and Whig*, August 17, 1835; *Western Weekly Review* (Franklin, Tenn.), September 18, 1835.

82. *MC*, August 21 and 24, 1835.

83. *Yalobusha Pioneer* 1, no. 4 (1977–78): 7; *Vicksburg Register*, July 23, 1835. Stewart's letter appeared in several other newspapers besides the *Register*, including the *Grand Gulf (Miss.) Advertiser*, August 4, 1835; *Jackson Mississippian*, July 31, 1835; *Western Weekly Review* (Franklin, Tenn.), September 4, 1835; and *Nashville Republican*, August 8, 1835. Stewart did try to collect that evidence, his first attempt consisting essentially of finding a group of thugs to manufacture information for him. On July 5, 1835, some three dozen men went to the home of Isham Medford, a resident of Attala County, about two days' ride south of Yalobusha, whose name appeared on the list of clan members Stewart had published in *The Western Land Pirate*. The company whipped Medford until he admitted to being allied with Murrell and brought back a written statement indicating that Medford said he did not personally know Matthew Clanton but that "he had understood from others engaged in the same nefarious practices with himself that said Clanton was a friend of, and belonged to, the clan of counterfeiters and thieves with which he was associated, and which so long had infested the country" (*VAS*, 158–62, 163–64, quotation on 158–59).

CHAPTER THREE. Exposing the Plot

1. *PCMC*, 5.

2. Ibid.

3. Ibid., 6 (quotation); "Transactions in Mississippi," *United States Telegraph*, October 6, 1835 [hereafter cited as "Transactions"]. Thomas Shackelford, a lawyer who compiled the official report of the Livingston Committee of Safety, referred to Mrs. Latham only as "a lady" and as "Madam Latham." The 1830 census lists a 40–50-year-old woman living in the household of Lorenzo Latham with no corresponding man in that age bracket, and the 1840 census lists a 70–80-year-old woman in the Latham household. One of the two census takers probably misestimated Mrs. Latham's age. *PCMC*, 5, 8; Fifth Census of the United States, Population Schedules, Mississippi, Madison County, 95; Sixth Census of the United States, Population Schedules, Mississippi, Madison County, 89; Madison County Deed Book A, 1828–33, 87–88, 272–73, MDAH.

4. *PCMC*, 5–6; "Transactions."

5. *VAS*, 26, 128–29, 201–2, 204. In keeping with his efforts to ingratiate himself with every wealthy or prominent person he met, when Stewart visited Hudnall he not only sought corroboration for Murrell's story but also offered to testify for Hudnall should any of Murrell's associates file a civil suit against him. Murrell had told Stewart that Hudnall realized he had been the victim of a scam after the slave he had just purchased disappeared and had stopped payment on the bank draft he had used for the purchase, which Murrell told Stewart might require a lawsuit to reinstate.

6. "Letters from Mississippi No. 12," *Jackson Mississippian*, March 14, 1834; Carol Lynn Mead, *The Land between Two Rivers: Madison County, Mississippi* (Canton, Miss.: Friends of the Madison County–Canton Public Library, 1987), 11–12, 16; "Beattie's Bluff . . . a Disappearing Part of Yazoo County History," *Yazoo County Herald*, July 28, 1974.

7. "Transactions" (quotation); Madison County Combination Tax Rolls, 1835, Auditor of Public Accounts, RG29, MDAH. Livingston was neither the largest settlement in the county nor the busiest commercially. Those distinctions went to Vernon, population around three hundred, whose location on the Big Black River made it a more promising trade location. Moreover, plans already existed to move the seat of Madison County to the more geographically central settlement of Canton, but Livingston remained the unofficial county seat into the 1850s, by which point the advance of steamboats and railroads had sent the town into significant decline. "Letters from Mississippi No. 12," Jackson *Mississippian*, March 14, 1834; Mead, *Land between Two Rivers*, 13–15, 23–25; "Livingston, Once Madison County Seat, Now a Ghost," *Jackson Clarion-Ledger*, August 16, 1970; "County Seat No Longer Living(ston)," *Jackson Daily News*, January 31, 1984.

8. "Letters from Mississippi No. 12," *Jackson Mississippian*, March 14, 1834; "Transactions" (quotation). Thomas Shackelford too wrote that by the middle of June, "a rumor was afloat through Madison county, that an insurrection of the slaves was meditated" but that no "authentic information" could be obtained and no one knew "where the report originated," so "most of the citizens were disposed to treat it as unfounded." A man writing from Canton similarly indicated that insurrection rumors began circulating in mid-June, but the precise chronology of events immediately preceding the June 27 meeting is impossible to determine. Several witnesses claimed that Mrs. Latham overheard the conversation on June 28 or 29, but one man who lived near Beattie's Bluff reported that he had been out of the county altogether until June 28 and was informed about the conversation on arriving home. Even if Lorenzo Latham and James Lee started telling others what they had heard on the same day they heard it, such timing suggests that Latham's mother overheard the slaves' conversation no later than June 27 and most likely on June 25 or 26. Lorenzo Latham and James Lee probably began telling others what they had found on June 26 or perhaps early on June 27, at which point they or someone else brought the information to Livingston. "Trouble at the South," *United States Gazette*, July 24, 1835; "Transactions"; "The Mississippi Disturbances," *Baltimore American*, August 8, 1835 [hereafter cited as "Disturbances"]; PCMC, 5 (quotation), 6, 8.

9. *PCMC*, 6.

10. Ibid., 6–7.

11. Ibid., 20, 21, 15. According to Thomas Shackelford, Saunders stated flatly on

June 30 that Albe Dean was a conspirator in the insurrection. If he did indeed say that, however, it was surely several days later at Saunders's trial, as Shackelford also indicated that when Saunders was first interrogated he failed to say anything about the supposed conspiracy at all. *PCMC*, 20.

12. "Transactions"; *Woodville Republican*, July 18, 1835 (quotation).

13. *PCMC*, 7. That whites in Livingston initially had no idea when the uprising they were hearing about was supposed to take place "had the effect of creating considerable alarm," as Shackelford put it. Whites in Livingston thus began concocting details about the plot in part to ease their own anxiety, even as doing so served to convince them that the insurrection plan was real. *PCMC*, 7.

14. "Letters from Mississippi No. 12," *Jackson Mississippian*, March 14, 1834 (quotation); John Hebron Moore, *The Emergence of the Cotton Kingdom in the Old Southwest: Mississippi, 1770–1860* (Baton Rouge: Louisiana State University Press, 1988), 7; Madison County Combination Tax Rolls, 1830 and 1835, Auditor of Public Accounts, RG29, MDAH; Fifth Census of the United States, Population Schedules, Mississippi, Madison County; Sixth Census of the United States, Population Schedules, Mississippi, Madison County. On politics in antebellum Mississippi, see Robert E. May, *John A. Quitman: Old South Crusader* (Baton Rouge: Louisiana State University Press, 1985); Edwin Arthur Miles, *Jacksonian Democracy in Mississippi* (Chapel Hill: University of North Carolina Press, 1960); Christopher J. Olsen, *Political Culture and Secession in Mississippi: Masculinity, Honor, and the Antiparty Tradition, 1830–1860* (New York: Oxford University Press, 2000); James Roger Sharp, *The Jacksonians versus the Banks: Politics in the States after the Panic of 1837* (New York: Columbia University Press, 1970), 55–109; and James P. Shenton, *Robert John Walker: A Politician from Jackson to Lincoln* (New York: Columbia University Press, 1961).

15. Joseph Holt Ingraham, *The South-West by a Yankee*, vol. 2 (New York, 1835), 101–3 (quotation on 102–3). Also see William F. Gray, *From Virginia to Texas, 1835* (Houston, 1909), 44–50; and Herbert Kellar, "A Journey through the South in 1836: Diary of James D. Davidson," *Journal of Southern History* 1, no. 3 (1935): 367–69.

16. On the "panic" of 1834, see Ralph C. H. Catterall, *The Second Bank of the United States* (Chicago, 1902), 314–31; Richard Holcombe Kilbourne Jr., *Slave Agriculture and Financial Markets in Antebellum America: The Bank of the United States in Mississippi, 1831–1852* (London: Pickering and Chatto, 2006), 46–52; Miles, *Jacksonian Democracy in Mississippi*, 73–86; and Robert V. Remini, *Andrew Jackson and the Bank War: A Study in the Growth of Presidential Power* (New York: W. W. Norton, 1967), 126–29.

17. On the exploitative and "transitory nature" of agriculture in antebellum Mississippi, see John Hebron Moore, *Agriculture in Ante-bellum Mississippi* (New York: Bookman Associates, 1958), 37–68.

18. Concerns about the impact of the rain on the cotton crop persisted throughout the summer of 1835. See, for example, *New Orleans Observer*, August 1, 1835; *Mobile Daily Commercial Register and Patriot*, August 5, 1835; and *Baltimore Gazette and Daily Advertiser*, September 16, 1835. Not every man had the aggressive and wild temperament for which the region's settlers became known, but the influence of those who did was unmistakable. See, for example, Joseph G. Baldwin, *The Flush Times of Alabama and Mississippi: A Series of Sketches* (New York, 1853), 88–89.

19. Fifth Census of the United States, Population Schedules, Mississippi, Madison County; Sixth Census of the United States, Population Schedules, Mississippi, Madison County, 112.

20. "Letters from Mississippi No. 12," *Jackson Mississippian*, March 14, 1834 (quotation); *PCMC*, 12; "Transactions."

21. On slavery in Mississippi, see David J. Libby, *Slavery and Frontier Mississippi, 1720–1835* (Jackson: University Press of Mississippi, 2004); Charles Sackett Sydnor, *Slavery in Mississippi* (New York, 1933); and Moore, *Emergence of the Cotton Kingdom*, 73–115. On the particularly harsh nature of southwestern frontier slavery, see Joan E. Cashin, *A Family Venture: Men and Women on the Southern Frontier* (Baltimore: Johns Hopkins University Press, 1991), 99–118. Libby suggests that prior to the agricultural expansion of the flush times, white Mississippians had gained enough confidence in their ability to dominate enslaved laborers that they could indulge a relatively moderate approach to racial control. The opening of the northern half of the state for settlement and the rising cotton prices of the 1830s, however, "revived the avarice not seen in Mississippi since the first cotton boom a generation earlier," making slaveholders in the state especially ferocious in their labor demands and especially susceptible to a scare like that born of Stewart's pamphlet. Libby, *Slavery and Frontier Mississippi*, 94–103 (quotation on 103).

22. In 1830 the federal census taker actually found Jesse Mabry in Spartanburg County, South Carolina, where he headed a household of seven white people. They may have been relatives, but their ages do not match those of Mabry's wife or children. In 1830 in Wilkinson County, Mississippi, however, the firm of Ware and Mabry, listed as a household for census purposes, contained a white man in his thirties (suggesting that Mabry himself may have been counted twice), a white woman in her thirties, and several young children of the right ages to be Mabry's. Benjamin Mabry, Jesse and Nancy's oldest child, was born in South Carolina in 1815 or 1816. Their son George was born in Mississippi in 1821 or 1822, and their daughter Mary was born there in 1826 or 1827. It thus seems most likely that the Mabrys began their move to Mississippi sometime around 1820, with Jesse returning to South Carolina periodically over the course of the next decade before removing to the Southwest for good by the early 1830s. Seventh Census of the United States, Population Schedules, Mississippi, Madison County, 312; Third Census of

the United States, Population Schedules, South Carolina, Union County, 133; Fifth Census of the United States, Population Schedules, South Carolina, Spartanburg County, 322; Fifth Census of the United States, Population Schedules, Mississippi, Wilkinson County, 277.

23. Wilkinson County Deed Book G, 1830–32, 317–18, 660–62, MDAH; Wilkinson County Deed Book K, 1836–38, 255–56, MDAH.

24. Wilkinson County Deed Book H, 1833–35, 6–8, 483–86, MDAH; Wilkinson County Deed Book J, 1835–36, 148, MDAH; Wilkinson County Deed Book K, 1836–38, 255–56, MDAH; *Woodville Republican*, November 23, 1833; Wilkinson County Combination Tax Rolls, 1833–35, Auditor of Public Accounts, RG29, MDAH.

25. *Woodville Republican*, January 24, 1835; Madison County Deed Book C, 1835–36, 56–58, 64–65, MDAH.

26. Madison County Combination Tax Rolls, 1835–36, MDAH. Though it would be hard to say what Mark Cockrill's plantation was "really" worth given the boom market distortions, the extravagance of Jesse Mabry's purchase is unquestionable. Young male field hands, the most valuable of all enslaved persons, sold in New Orleans in 1835 for an average price of $1,150. If every one of Cockrill's slaves fit that category, their total market price would thus have been roughly $145,000, making the price Mabry paid for Cockrill's land probably around $30 per acre after accounting for the livestock and farm equipment. In reality, however, the market value of Cockrill's slaves was significantly less than that given that a fair number of them were women and some were certainly children and older men. It seems more likely that Mabry paid at least $40 for each acre of Cockrill's land. Thomas Hudnall, in comparison, purchased more than eighteen hundred acres of Madison County land only a few miles from Cockrill's holdings for roughly $6.50 per acre just two years earlier. Madison County Deed Book A, 1828–33, 703–5, MDAH; Madison County Deed Book C, 1835–36, 64–65, MDAH; Robert Evans Jr., "The Economics of American Negro Slavery, 1830–1860," in *Aspects of Labor Economics: A Conference of the Universities–National Bureau Committee for Economic Research* (Princeton: Princeton University Press, 1962), 199; Ulrich Bonnell Phillips, *American Negro Slavery* (New York, 1918), chart opposite 370.

27. *PCMC*, 9.

28. Ibid.

29. Ibid., 7, 9; Madison County Combination Tax Rolls, 1835, MDAH.

30. *PCMC*, 9.

31. Ibid.

32. Ibid., 9, 10 (quotations).

33. Joe failed to say anything about John Murrell or his men, probably because Mabry, Smith, and Beattie never mentioned them to him. Though the outline of the conspiracy people in Livingston came to believe commingled vague rumors of

rebellion with the particular story told in Virgil Stewart's pamphlet, not everyone in the region had read Stewart's work. People just twenty miles or so from Livingston, for example, found copies of Stewart's pamphlet hard to come by even several weeks after the insurrection scare began in Madison County, and as noted above it probably had not made its way to the intensely rural area around Beattie's Bluff. That Joe seemed to lack knowledge about Murrell reinforces the notion that the "mystic clan" was a product of Virgil Stewart's imagination and indicates that Mabry, Smith, and Beattie proceeded in their interrogations on the basis of an abbreviated version of what those in Livingston thought was happening. *Jackson Mississippian*, August 7, 1835.

34. *PCMC*, 10.

35. Ibid.

36. Ibid.

37. Ibid., 10, 11.

38. The best single work on the intersection of race and rape in the nineteenth-century South and how attitudes toward that intersection changed over time is Diane Miller Sommerville, *Rape and Race in the Nineteenth-Century South* (Chapel Hill: University of North Carolina Press, 2004).

39. *PCMC*, 11.

40. Ibid., 11 (quotations), 37. Elisha Moss appeared in the 1830 census as a white man in his fifties. Four other white men under the age of twenty lived in his household, and another man in his twenties named Ebenezer Moss lived nearby with his wife. Fifth Census of the United States, Population Schedules, Mississippi, Madison County, 95.

41. *PCMC*, 11.

42. Ibid. Curiously, whites at Beattie's Bluff let Joe live. Perhaps they believed him when he said he had nothing to do with the insurrection plot. More likely, as a blacksmith he was too useful to execute.

43. *PCMC*, 7.

44. Ibid., 7, 26.

45. Ibid., 25, 26.

46. Ibid., 25–26; "Transactions" (quotation).

47. "Disturbances" (first quotation); "Transactions" (second quotation); *PCMC*, 23.

48. *PCMC*, 23.

49. Ibid., 26 (quotation), 15.

50. Ibid., 25, 26 (quotations); Madison County Combination Tax Rolls, 1835, 1836, MDAH; "Transactions"; Madison County Deed Book A, 1828–33, 707–8, 775–76, MDAH; *Jackson Mississippian*, December 12, 1834. Respect for Hudnall was almost certainly behind the later claim that Blake left town before any white men

were suspected of involvement in the conspiracy. Given what ultimately became of Blake, it would look bad after the fact for Hudnall to have protected him, while asserting that no one would have ever thought a white man like Blake might be a conspirator absolved Hudnall of any blame for having helped him escape.

51. *PCMC*, 7, 15, 20.

52. Ibid., 7–8, 9, 10 (quotations on 7, 7–8).

53. "Livingston (Madison County)" subject file, MDAH, contains a plat map for the village of Livingston.

54. *PCMC*, 6, 23.

55. "Transactions" (quotation); "Disturbances;" *PCMC*, 13.

56. *PCMC*, 14 (first two quotations); "Transactions" (last quotation).

57. *PCMC*, 12–13, 26.

58. "Transactions."

59. *PCMC*, iv, 12–13.

60. "Transactions"; *PCMC*, 13.

61. "Transactions" (quotation); "Trouble at the South," *United States Gazette*, July 24, 1835; Christopher Morris, "An Event in Community Organization: The Mississippi Slave Insurrection Scare of 1835," *Journal of Social History* 22, no. 1 (1988): 93–111.

62. *PCMC*, iii (quotation); Seventh Census of the United States, Population Schedule, Mississippi, Madison County, 391; *Nashville Republican*, December 12, 1835. Shackelford was only twenty-one or twenty-two years old, owned no land, and was of no particular prominence in the county, and it is unclear why he received responsibility for compiling the report of the Livingston Committee of Safety. Historian James Penick wrote that Shackelford was the committee's secretary, but that was not the case. A man named William Royce acted in that capacity. Shackelford did not transcribe the proceedings of the committee but may have taken notes during the committee's meetings. James Lal Penick Jr., *The Great Western Land Pirate: John A. Murrell in Legend and History* (Columbia: University of Missouri Press, 1981), 118; *PCMC*, 14; "Transactions."

CHAPTER FOUR. Hanging the Conspirators

1. *Nashville Republican*, July 18, 1835; "Transactions in Mississippi," *United States Telegraph*, October 6, 1835 [hereafter cited as "Transactions"]; *PCMC*, 15–16, 21. Although one of the men in the company that rounded up Cotton and Saunders reported the men were arrested on the night of July 3, he also conceded that he was physically exhausted and "not in a condition for writing." He easily could have lost track of dates. Thomas Shackelford's report and other eyewitness accounts make clear that both men were brought back to Livingston on July 2. *Nashville Republican*, July 18, 1835.

2. *PCMC*, 13. One man claimed the committee was actually created on July 2, right after Joseph Pugh called for its formation, and that its members began their work that night by arraigning and charging Cotton and Saunders with inciting an insurrection. Such timing is plausible, especially since Jesse Mabry recalled leaving Beattie's Bluff on July 2 to take his seat on the committee. Given the importance placed on having the committee appear legitimated by the populace and the time necessary to craft resolutions delineating how the committee would operate, however, it seems likely that before the committee really got to work, the crowd on July 3 went through the motions of formally ratifying whatever choices had already been made. "Transactions"; *PCMC*, 11.

3. *PCMC*, 14; Combination Tax Rolls, Madison County, 1835, 1836, MDAH.

4. Henry S. Foote, *Casket of Reminiscences* (Washington, D.C., 1874), 251 (first quotation); "Transactions" (remaining quotations); *PCMC*, 6, 13–14; Fifth Census of the United States, Population Schedules, Mississippi, Madison County and Warren County; Sixth Census of the United States, Population Schedules, Mississippi, Madison County.

5. *PCMC*, 15 (quotations), 17; "Transactions"; *Vicksburg Register*, July 16, 1835.

6. *PCMC*, 13–15.

7. Ibid., 14 (first three quotations), 15 (last two quotations).

8. "Transactions."

9. *PCMC*, 15; Fifth Census of the United States, Population Schedules, Tennessee, Henry County; Hinds County Marriage Record Book 1, 1823–37, 347, MDAH; Madison County Deed Book C, 1835–36, 185, MDAH.

10. The most comprehensive work on Thomsonianism is John S. Haller Jr., *The People's Doctors: Samuel Thomson and the American Botanical Movement, 1790–1860* (Carbondale: Southern Illinois University Press, 2000). Also see James O. Breeden, "Thomsonianism in Virginia," *Virginia Magazine of History and Biography* 82, no. 1 (1974): 150–80; Spencer Klaw, "Belly-My-Grizzle," *American Heritage* 28, no. 4 (1977): 96–105; and William G. Rothstein, *American Physicians in the Nineteenth Century: From Sects to Science* (Baltimore: Johns Hopkins University Press, 1972), 125–51.

11. Haller, *People's Doctors*, ch. 1; Klaw, "Belly-My-Grizzle," 98–99; Rothstein, *American Physicians*, 125–40.

12. Haller, *People's Doctors*, 31–43, 83; Klaw, "Belly-My-Grizzle," 98; Rothstein, *American Physicians*, 140–51.

13. Claudia L. Bushman provides a nice case study of a Virginia planter who relied heavily on Thomsonian methods on his plantation in *In Old Virginia: Slavery, Farming, and Society in the Journal of John Walker* (Baltimore: Johns Hopkins University Press, 2002). On medicine in the antebellum South, also see Sharla M. Fett, *Working Cures: Healing, Health, and Power on Southern Slave Plantations* (Chapel

Hill: University of North Carolina Press, 2002); Ronald L. Numbers and Todd L. Savitt, eds., *Science and Medicine in the Old South* (Baton Rouge: Louisiana State University Press, 1989); Todd L. Savitt, *Medicine and Slavery: The Diseases and Health Care of Blacks in Antebellum Virginia* (Champaign: University of Illinois Press, 1978); Marie Jenkins Schwartz, *Birthing a Slave: Motherhood and Medicine in the Antebellum South* (Cambridge: Harvard University Press, 2006); and Steven M. Stowe, *Doctoring the South: Southern Physicians and Everyday Medicine in the Mid-Nineteenth Century* (Chapel Hill: University of North Carolina Press, 2003).

14. Estate of Joshua Cotton, Probate Packets, Warren County, case 532, file 53, p. 60, September term 1835, MDAH; William H. Thomson to Hannah Lavinia Thomson, July 12, 1835, box 1, folder 1, Ruffin Thomson Papers, SHC; Haller, *People's Doctors*, 83; Klaw, "Belly-My-Grizzle," 98.

15. Haller, *People's Doctors*, 127–31; *Woodville Republican*, May 2, 23, and 30, 1835. See also a similar pair of articles that appeared eight months earlier in the *Randolph Recorder*, whose editor ran a piece referring to Thomson's system as "quackery" only to find himself tempering his remarks and apologizing after some of his readers took offense. *Randolph Recorder*, September 23 and October 3, 1834.

16. *PCMC*, 15.

17. Ibid., 19. The 1830 Tennessee census records no William Saunders living in Sumner County. Three men named William Saunders lived in neighboring Davidson County, however; all were in their twenties or thirties, and none owned slaves. Fifth Census of the United States, Population Schedules, Tennessee, Davidson County, 230, 250, 270.

18. *PCMC*, 19–20 (quotations on 19).

19. Ibid., 20.

20. Ibid., 15. Cotton may have had two children in Tennessee, as the 1830 census indicated a white woman in her twenties, a white girl between the ages of five and ten, and a white boy under age five in his household. Fifth Census of the United States, Population Schedules, Tennessee, Henry County, 13.

21. *PCMC*, 16.

22. Ibid., 16–17 (quotations on 16).

23. Ibid, 17. That hanging white men based entirely on testimony from the enslaved could be problematic is suggested by the fact that the authors of several newspaper articles describing the insurrection scare thought it worth mentioning. A "gentleman" from Hinds County, for example, wrote in early July to a merchant in Nashville that Joshua Cotton, "after being condemned upon negro testimony, made a confession and disclosed the whole plan." Similarly, in mid-August, a letter writer to the *Jackson Mississippian* noted of several executed white men that "though they did not, as I understand, hang on negro evidence, yet from them they

were suspected, and other testimony obtained and finally full confessions made."
United States Gazette, July 28, 1835; *Jackson Mississippian,* August 14, 1835.

24. *PCMC,* 16.

25. Ibid., 12, 16.

26. For a consideration of these issues that reaches roughly similar conclusions, see James Lal Penick Jr., *The Great Western Land Pirate: John A. Murrell in Legend and History* (Columbia: University of Missouri Press, 1981), 118–23.

27. *PCMC,* 17. In reference to the statement entered into evidence that supposedly reflected what Saunders confessed, Shackelford described Saunders as having admitted its contents "to the gentlemen." That the language here indicates Saunders made his confession to several people at once rather than to the single "gentleman" Saunders supposedly met on the road may be merely a typographical error. But it is a suggestive slip that may point directly to the conversations Saunders had with multiple members of the patrol that arrested him, and to Shackelford's inability to keep his own story straight.

28. *PCMC,* 17.

29. Ibid., 20.

30. Ibid.

31. Ibid.

32. Ibid., 21.

33. Ibid., 18.

34. Ibid.

35. Ibid.

36. Shackelford recorded one version of Cotton's confession, but at least three other lengthy witness accounts and several shorter ones appeared in the newspapers during the summer of 1835. Though they differ in their details, all substantially agree on what Cotton admitted and none contradicts the others. The above summary combines information from the several accounts. See *PCMC,* 18–19; "Transactions"; "Disturbances"; *Vicksburg Register,* July 16, 1835; and *United States Gazette,* July 28, 1835.

37. Cotton said that John Rogers lived in Yazoo County, but the John Rogers who witnessed his wedding in Hinds County seems a more likely reference. Until early 1835 Lee Smith had also owned a small piece of land. One account of Cotton's confession indicated that Cotton named Angus Donovan as a fellow conspirator as well, but Shackelford's report does not. *PCMC,* 19, 28; "Transactions"; Hinds County Marriage Record Book 1, 1823–37, 347, MDAH; Combination Tax Rolls, Hinds, Madison, Wilkinson, and Warren counties, 1834–36, MDAH; Hinds County Deed Book 4, 121–22, MDAH; *Woodville Republican,* May 12, 1827, December 2, 1828, and July 24, 1830.

38. "Transactions"; *United States Gazette*, July 28, 1835.

39. "Transactions." Shackelford reported that Cotton's last words were "take care of yourselves to night and to-morrow night," but a man from Tiger Bayou in Madison County claimed Cotton warned Mississippians to "beware of to-night, to-morrow, and the next night." The language above comes from a man who was in Livingston at the time of the insurrection scare and roughly splits the difference between the other two versions. *PCMC*, 19; "Disturbances."

40. "Transactions."

41. *PCMC*, iv, 21, 32–33; *Nashville Republican*, July 18, 1835; "Transactions"; "Disturbances"; *Woodville Republican*, August 15, 1835.

42. One witness reported the second man's name was "Ferry"; another wrote it "Terrel." Neither name appears in Madison County property or tax records in the first half of the 1830s. Combination Tax Rolls, Madison County, Mississippi, 1834–35, MDAH; "Transactions"; "Disturbances" (quotation).

43. *PCMC*, 27–28 (quotation on 28); "Transactions"; "Disturbances"; *Clinton Gazette*, September 19, 1835.

44. *PCMC*, 28–29 (quotation on 29); "Transactions"; "Disturbances."

45. Published accounts indicate one of these two men was named Hiram Hall. The other was mentioned only as "Nicholas." *PCMC*, 28–29 (quotations on 28); "Transactions"; "Disturbances".

46. "Disturbances" (quotation); "Transactions."

47. *PCMC*, 21.

48. Ibid., 21–22 (quotation on 21).

49. Ibid., 21–22 (quotations on 22).

50. *Nashville Republican*, July 16, 1835; *Clinton Gazette* in *Vicksburg Register*, July 16, 1835; and *Columbus Democratic Press* in *Huntsville Southern Advocate*, July 28, 1835. Also see *Jackson Mississippian*, July 24, 1835; and "Transactions."

51. Accounts of just how many slaves died during the insurrection scare of 1835 vary. A man who had been in the patrol that arrested Cotton and Saunders claimed nine slaves were executed. A man who lived about twelve miles from Livingston asserted on July 3 that whites in the village had in custody around fifteen slaves whom they intended to hang in addition to the two already killed on July 2. A third witness wrote on July 8 that ten slaves were to be hanged that day on top of the seven who had already died, and a fourth indicated that ten or so slaves had been hanged by the middle of July. A newspaper editor in Hinds County had heard reports of "some 10 or 15" executed slaves as of July 11; a man writing from Livingston on July 12 claimed that "ten or twelve negroes" had been hanged; another writing from Vicksburg wrote that "12 negroes" had died in Madison County; and William Thomson, in Hinds County, wrote to his wife that "about 20 negros have been executed." Several individuals passing up the Mississippi River by steamboat

during the scare told the editor of an Arkansas newspaper that they heard whites had hanged thirteen slaves as "accomplices" of the white insurrectionists. It seems likely that at least a dozen and perhaps as many as twenty slaves were murdered during the insurrection scare. Whatever the exact number, it is hard to dispute one man's conclusion that "a large number of blacks have been executed in the different counties." *Nashville Republican*, July 18, 1835; *United States Gazette*, July 24, 1835; *New Orleans Bee*, July 14, 1835; *Nashville Republican*, July 16, 1835; *Clinton Gazette* in *Vicksburg Register*, July 16, 1835; *United States Telegraph*, August 1, 1835; *Lexington Intelligencer*, July 28, 1835; William H. Thomson to Hannah Lavinia Thomson, July 12, 1835, Ruffin Thomson Papers, box 1, folder 1, SHC; *Arkansas Gazette*, July 14, 1835; "Disturbances".

52. Israel Campbell, *Bond and Free: or, Yearnings for Freedom* (Philadelphia, 1861), 70–72 (quotations on 71).

53. Ibid., 72–74 (quotations on 72 and 74).

54. *Columbus Argus* in *United States Telegraph*, August 3, 1835; *Columbus Democratic Press* in *Huntsville Southern Advocate*, July 28, 1835.

55. *United States Gazette*, July 28, 1835; PCMC, iv; *United States Telegraph*, August 1, 1835.

56. LP, 61–62. In the aftermath of the insurrection scare some newspapers erroneously claimed that Cotton's and Saunders's names appeared in Stewart's pamphlet.

57. Campbell, *Bond and Free*, 73; *Jackson Mississippian*, August 14, 1835; *Lexington Intelligencer*, July 28, 1835.

58. Combination Tax Rolls, Madison and Hinds counties, Mississippi, 1835, MDAH; Madison County Deed Book C, 1835–36, 185, MDAH; will of Ruel Blake, in "Madison County—1835 Uprising" subject file, MDAH.

59. Foote, *Casket of Reminiscences*, 254. On the suspicion of southerners toward "Yankee peddlers," see Joseph T. Rainer, "The 'Sharper' Imagine: Yankee Peddlers, Southern Consumers, and the Market Revolution," in *Cultural Change and the Market Revolution in America, 1789–1860*, ed. Scott C. Martin, (Lanham, Maryland: Rowman and Littlefield, 2005).

60. Combination Tax Rolls, Hinds County, Mississippi, 1834–35, MDAH; Fifth Census of the United States, Population Schedules, Mississippi, Hinds County, 199; Laurence Shore, "Making Mississippi Safe for Slavery: The Insurrection Panic of 1835," in *Class, Consensus, and Conflict: Antebellum Southern Community Studies*, ed. Orville Vernon Burton and Robert C. McMath Jr., 111 (Westport, Conn.: Greenwood Press, 1982); *Clinton Gazette*, September 19, 1835; PCMC, 27–28; Madison County Deed Book A, 1828–33, 121–22, MDAH; "Transactions." For an account of the insurrection scare that attributes the accusations against white men primarily to their being "strangers who sought money through stealth and trickery," see

Kenneth S. Greenberg, *Honor and Slavery* (Princeton: Princeton University Press, 1997), 144.

61. As Bradley Bond has argued, even as they recognized the dangers of market dependency antebellum white Mississippians believed that engagement with the market economy demonstrated a dedication to productivity and the achievement of personal autonomy that made a white man trustworthy and deserving of citizenship. Bond writes that "suspicion of anyone not at least lightly entangled in the web of the market ran high" and that "when whites without direct ties to the agricultural market associated with blacks" they ran the risk of confronting extreme hostility if not violence. Bond describes the insurrection scare of 1835 largely as an incident that reveals the significance of "controlling the underclass." Such an argument overstates the significance of the economic standing of those targeted during the scare, but the uneasy (and perceived oppositional) relations of certain white men to developing market economies in both cotton and slaves played central roles in their troubles. See Bradley G. Bond, *Political Culture in the Nineteenth-Century South: Mississippi, 1830–1900* (Baton Rouge: Louisiana State University Press, 1995), 81–94 (quotations on 92, 93).

62. *PCMC*, 15.

63. "Transactions"; *PCMC*, 25.

64. *PCMC*, 25.

65. Ibid.; Madison County Deed Book A, 1828–33, 121–22, MDAH.

66. *PCMC*, 22, 24; Foote, *Casket of Reminiscences*, 254–55.

67. *PCMC*, 22.

68. Ibid., 23.

69. Ibid.

70. Ibid., 23–24. Shackelford also reported a white witness against Donovan, a plantation overseer who claimed Donovan told him that "the negroes would soon be all free in this state" and that the enslaved "*could obtain their liberty by force, and that they would do it, not by themselves, but with the aid of thousands of rich, smart white men, who were ready to head them, with money, arms and ammunition for their use.*" The forced and affected tone of these supposed assertions reads like a caricature of the sorts of windy statements Virgil Stewart's John Murrell would have made had he sincerely cared about helping the enslaved escape bondage, and at best it was an exaggerated version of an actual conversation presented to seal Donovan's fate in lieu of any other white witness's testimony against him. Indeed, Shackelford may have entirely invented the overseer witness, just as he did the "gentleman" to whom William Saunders supposedly confessed, to buttress another claim Shackelford made about Donovan. According to Shackelford, Donovan was no ordinary member of Murrell's clan but was actually "an emissary of those deluded fanatics at the north—the ABOLITIONISTS." By Shackelford's reckoning, Donovan had come

to Mississippi as an abolitionist but after stumbling onto the insurrection plot then "joined the conspirators with the hope of receiving part of the spoils." In truth, it is obvious that Shackelford, compiling his report in the fall of 1835 against the backdrop of growing national political controversy over organized antislavery, blamed Donovan's fate on "those who sent him here" as a way of retroactively tying what had happened in Mississippi to that controversy and displacing responsibility for it. In the event, whites in Mississippi were not looking for abolitionists, and even as being an abolitionist in Mississippi was no small thing, not one of the numerous reports about the meetings, hearings, and verdicts of the Livingston Committee of Safety printed in newspapers or recorded privately in diaries during the insurrection scare mention Donovan being tied to the antislavery movement. *PCMC*, 24, 25.

71. *PCMC*, 24–25 (quotations); *Baltimore American*, August 8, 1835; Fifth Census of the United States, Population Schedules, Kentucky, Mason County, 180.

72. *PCMC*, 37.

73. Ibid., 37, 38.

74. Foote, *Casket of Reminiscences*, 255.

75. *PCMC*, 25.

76. Michael Perman, "Henry Stuart Foote," *American National Biography Online*, www.anb.org, accessed June 15, 2011; and John E. Gonzales, "The Public Career of Henry Stuart Foote (1804–1880) (Ph.D. diss., University of North Carolina at Chapel Hill, 1957).

77. Foote, *Casket of Reminiscences*, 251, 254.

78. Cecil L. Sumners, *Governors of Mississippi* (Gretna, La.: Pelican Publishers, 1980), 66; Foote, *Casket of Reminiscences*, 254 (quotations).

79. Foote, *Casket of Reminiscences*, 254.

80. Ibid., 255.

81. Ibid.; *Maysville Eagle* in *Baltimore Gazette*, August 6, 1835 (quotations); *PCMC*, 22, 25, 27.

82. "Transactions"; "Disturbances."

CHAPTER FIVE. Purging a City

1. Letter from L. S. Houghton to Henry Bosworth, July 10, 1835, typescript in "Hanging of Gamblers" vertical file, OCHM [hereafter cited as Houghton letter]; *Vicksburg Register*, July 9, 1835. On Independence Day celebrations in the early Republic, see Len Travers, *Celebrating the Fourth: Independence Day and the Rites of Nationalism in the Early Republic* (Amherst: University of Massachusetts Press, 1997); and David Waldstreicher, *In the Midst of Perpetual Fetes: The Making of American Nationalism, 1776–1820* (Chapel Hill: University of North Carolina Press, 1997).

2. *Vicksburg Register*, July 9, 1835; Seventh Census of the United States, Population Schedules, Mississippi, Warren County.

3. Warren County Circuit Court Papers, Criminal Cases, 1832–49, folder 7, OCHM; Houghton letter; *Vicksburg Register*, July 9, 1835; H. S. Fulkerson, *Random Recollections of Early Days in Mississippi* (Vicksburg, 1885), 96.

4. Houghton letter; *Vicksburg Register*, July 9, 1835.

5. *Vicksburg Register*, July 9, 1835. For a history of the rhetoric and meaning of lynching as a term and a practice, and how the word itself became a political flashpoint in the aftermath of what happened in Vicksburg, see Christopher Waldrep, *The Many Faces of Judge Lynch: Extralegal Violence and Punishment in America* (New York: Palgrave Macmillan, 2002), esp. 13–47.

6. Houghton letter; *Vicksburg Register*, July 9, 1835.

7. Seventh Census of the United States, Population Schedules, Mississippi, Warren County; Combination Tax Rolls, Warren County, 1829, 1834, 1835, MDAH; Warren County Marriage Records, April 23, 1835, book E, p. 48, MDAH; I. M. Patridge, "The Press of Mississippi," *DeBow's Review* 29, no. 4 (1860): 504.

8. Christopher Morris, *Becoming Southern: The Evolution of a Way of Life, Warren County and Vicksburg, Mississippi, 1770–1860* (New York: Oxford University Press, 1995), 105, 108–9. On the perceived beauty of Vicksburg's scenery, see Joseph Holt Ingraham, *The South-West by a Yankee*, vol. 2 (New York, 1835), 170; Rev. Richard Wynkoop to "Reverend Sir," October 1, 1836, published in the *Vicksburg Daily Herald*, December 27, 1912 [hereafter cited as Wynkoop letter]; Charles Augustus Murray, *Travels in North America during the Years 1834, 1835, and 1836*, vol. 2 (London, 1839), 108–9; and William H. Wills, "A Southern Traveler's Diary, 1840," *Southern History Association Publications* 8 (1904): 32.

9. Morris, *Becoming Southern*, 40–41, 109–10; Christopher Waldrep, *Roots of Disorder: Race and Criminal Justice in the American South, 1817–80* (Urbana and Chicago: University of Illinois Press, 1998), 8–10; *Baltimore American*, September 9, 1835; "Letters from Mississippi, No. 9," *Jackson Mississippian*, January 10, 1834.

10. Morris, *Becoming Southern*, 137–38; Timothy Flint, *Recollections of the Last Ten Years* (Boston, 1826; reprint, New York: Alfred A. Knopf, 1932), 282–83; Wynkoop letter; Rev. J. R. Hutchison, *Reminiscences, Sketches and Addresses Selected from My Papers during a Ministry of Forty-five years in Mississippi, Louisiana and Texas* (Houston, 1874), 51–52 (first quotation on 51); "Letters from Mississippi, No. 9," *Jackson Mississippian*, January 10, 1834 (second quotation); Ingraham, *South-West by a Yankee*, 2:169–70 (third quotation on 170).

11. *Vicksburg Register*, July 9, 1835.

12. Ibid.

13. Ibid.

14. Ibid.

15. Ibid.

16. Ibid. Mills reported that Bodley was hit seven times, but H. S. Fulkerson,

who took up residence in Mississippi in 1836, noted in his memoir that Bodley was hit in the chest with a "load of buckshot." Given the number of wounds Bodley incurred, presumably from just four shooters, Fulkerson was likely right, despite having heard the story secondhand. See Fulkerson, *Random Recollections*, 97.

17. *Vicksburg Register*, July 9, 1835.

18. Ibid.

19. Ibid.

20. *Vicksburg Register*, July 9, 1835; *Baltimore Gazette*, August 1, 1835 ("tragedy"); *Louisiana Advertiser* in *Raleigh Register and North Carolina Gazette*, August 4, 1835 ("outrage"); *Niles' Weekly Register*, August 1, 1835 ("outrage"); *Albany Daily Advertiser* in *New York Evening Post*, August 3, 1835 ("outrage"); *Georgetown Metropolitan* in *Baltimore American*, August 7, 1835 ("murders"); and *Richmond Enquirer*, July 28, 1835 ("butchery").

21. *Baltimore American*, August 6, 1835; *Raleigh Register and North Carolina Gazette*, August 11, 1835; *Hartford Times* in *Portland Eastern Argus*, August 26, 1835; *Protestant Vindicator* in *Liberator*, August 15, 1835; *New York Evening Post*, August 4, 1835.

22. *New Orleans True American* in *New York Evening Post*, July 31, 1835. For examples of similar positions taken by editors in other parts of the United States, see *Louisville Advertiser* in *New York Evening Post*, July 31, 1835; *St. Louis Herald* in *Chicago American*, August 8, 1835; *Liberator*, August 22, 1835; *Baltimore American*, August 6, 1835; *Arkansas Advocate* and *Georgetown Metropolitan*, both in *Baltimore American*, August 7, 1835; and *Lexington Intelligencer*, November 24, 1835.

23. *Hartford Times* in *Portland Eastern Argus*, August 26, 1835; *Baltimore Gazette*, August 1, 1835.

24. *Arkansas Advocate* in *Baltimore American*, August 7, 1835; *Fredericksburg (Va.) Arena* in *Baltimore American*, October 26, 1835; *Philadelphia Commercial Herald* in *Baltimore Gazette*, August 1, 1835.

25. *Fredericksburg (Va.) Arena* in *Baltimore American*, October 26, 1835; Peel, quoted in *Chicago American*, October 31, 1835. Similarly, a North Carolina newspaper observed that the "affray at Vicksburg . . . has caused great discussion in the English papers" (*Raleigh North Carolina Standard*, October 22, 1835). Also see the work of Thomas Brothers, who singled out the Vicksburg riot from hundreds of others he noted in the United States in the 1830s to make the argument that "no one in the United States is ever punished by law, whatever his crime, except it be the poorest of the poor, who have no property, nor any power or influence in elections" (Thomas Brothers, *The United States of North America as They Are* [London, 1840], 15).

26. James Burns Wallace Diary, January 12, 1836, LLMVC; *Nashville Republican*, July 25, 1835; *Scioto (Ohio) Gazette*, August 26, 1835; *Randolph Recorder*, September 25, 1835; Herbert A. Kellar, "A Journey through the South in 1836: Diary of James D.

Davidson," *Journal of Southern History* 1, no. 3 (1935): 355. Among foreign travelers mentioning the hangings were George Featherstonhaugh, Alexander Mackay, Frederick Marryat, Harriet Martineau, Charles Murray, and Fredrika Bremer, who noted even as late as 1850 that although she personally found Vicksburg "creditable," the events of 1835 continued to make it a place with a "bad reputation." George W. Featherstonhaugh, *Excursion through the Slave States* (New York, 1844), 138; *America of the Fifties: Letters of Fredrika Bremer*, edited by Adolph B. Benson (New York, 1924), quotations on 266 and 265; Alexander Mackay, *The Western World, or Travels in the United States in 1846–1847*, vol. 2 (Philadelphia, 1849), 117–18; Frederick Marryat, *A Diary in America, with Remarks on Its Institutions* (New York, 1839), 243–47; Harriet Martineau, *Retrospect of Western Travel*, vol. 2 (New York, 1838), 17–18; Murray, *Travels in North America*, 2:108–9. Domestically, one could see the legacy of the gambling riot for Vicksburg's reputation at least into the early 1850s as well. See, for example, Solon Robinson, "Notes of Travel in the Southwest—No. VIII," *Cultivator*, November 1845, 334; and Joseph F. Tuttle, "An Hour with Thomas Hunt," *Christian Parlor Magazine*, May 1, 1851, 22.

27. *Vicksburg Register*, July 9, 1835; *Richmond Enquirer*, July 31, 1835; *Niles' Weekly Register*, August 1, 1835.

28. *Natchez Courier* in *Grand Gulf (Miss.) Advertiser*, July 14, 1835; *Arkansas Gazette*, July 14, 1835.

29. *Louisiana Advertiser* in *United States Gazette*, July 29, 1835.

30. Ibid. The *Advertiser* identified the militia member with whom Cabler quarreled only as a "Mr. Fisher," but a *Vicksburg Register* article identifies by name several members of the Volunteers, including an "Alex. Fisher." *Vicksburg Register*, January 7, 1836.

31. *Louisiana Advertiser* in *United States Gazette*, July 29, 1835. The *Advertiser* asserted that the leader of the Volunteers was named "Baumguard," but he was in fact George Brungard. *Vicksburg Register*, January 7, 1836.

32. *Louisiana Advertiser* in *United States Gazette*, July 29, 1835. Robert Riddle actually confirmed that the *Advertiser* portrayed at least some elements of the Vicksburg riot more accurately than Mills did, at least in spirit. Riddle had once resided in Richmond, was angry that the *Advertiser* suggested he had played a leading role in the riot, and on returning to Richmond disputed that description in a conversation with Thomas Ritchie. According to a report published in Ritchie's *Richmond Enquirer*, Riddle had been at his job in the Planters' Bank during the assault on North's house. Riddle claimed he left the bank and accompanied the crowd to the gallows only after hearing that Bodley, a friend, had been killed so that he could attend to Bodley's body. Riddle denied that the executed men had been mocked or mistreated before being hanged and insisted that the band had not played Yankee Doodle. Nevertheless, he conceded that "the drums were ordered to beat, to prevent

North's addressing the multitude. This order was given by Captain Hurst . . . with the unanimous approbation of the whole crowd, who cried out, 'Don't hear him,' &c." It was left to the reader to determine whether it was more humane to silence desperate men with drums rather than with full musical accompaniment. Richmond *Enquirer* in *Vicksburg Register*, September 10, 1835.

33. *Louisiana Advertiser* in *United States Gazette*, July 29, 1835.

34. Ibid. The *Advertiser* identified Bodley's brother-in-law but mistyped his name as "Hest." See Annie Lee Sanders, "Vicksburger, Descendant of Dr. Hugh Bodley, Has Collection of Old Records," *Vicksburg Sunday Post*, April 29, 1962.

35. *Vicksburg Register*, July 23 and August 6, 1835.

36. *Natchez Courier* in *Grand Gulf (Miss.) Advertiser*, July 14, 1835; *Louisville Journal* in *Lexington Intelligencer*, July 24, 1835 (quotation); and *Baltimore Gazette*, July 30, 1835. Also see *United States Telegraph*, July 25, 1835, containing an article from a New Orleans paper claiming that two gamblers were lynched in addition to the five who were hanged.

37. Featherstonhaugh, *Excursion through the Slave States*, 138.

38. Wynkoop letter. Wynkoop was not the only one to claim that the hanged men were not gamblers. Jonathan H. Green, who made his living as a gambler for years before becoming an antigambling crusader in the 1840s and 1850s, wrote that two of the five men hanged in Vicksburg were gamblers, but the most he could say about the other three was that if they "were not [gamblers], they were found in their company." John O'Connor, also a professed former gambler, claimed in the 1870s that none of the victims were gamblers. Even Francis Cabler, according to O'Connor, was actually a blacksmith who had become a prizefighter. Cabler thus often loitered at gambling houses, but O'Connor asserted he was not a gambler by profession. Jonathan H. Green, *An Exposure of the Arts and Miseries of Gambling* (Cincinnati, 1843), 212; John O'Connor, *Wanderings of a Vagabond* (New York, 1873, edited pseudonymously under the name John Morris), 341–46.

39. Wynkoop letter.

40. *Vicksburg Register*, July 9, 1835.

41. *Frankfort (Ky.) Commonwealth* in *Vicksburg Register*, August 6, 1835. Also see *Huntsville (Ala.) Democrat* in *Vicksburg Register*, August 6, 1835. The small number of papers whose editors were willing to excuse the hangings in Vicksburg were, like the Huntsville paper, almost all located in the Southwest. The anger expressed by the *Commonwealth* can be explained in part by the fact that Hugh Bodley was originally from Kentucky, although most newspapers even in that state were at least ambivalent about the hangings.

42. *Niles' Weekly Register*, August 22, 1835. On mob violence in antebellum America, see esp. David Grimsted, *American Mobbing, 1828–1861: Toward Civil War* (New York: Oxford University Press, 1998). Also see Richard Maxwell Brown, *Strain of*

Violence: Historical Studies of American Violence and Vigilantism (New York: Oxford University Press, 1975); Michael Feldberg, *The Turbulent Era: Riot and Disorder in Jacksonian America* (New York: Oxford University Press, 1980); Paul A. Gilje, *The Road to Mobocracy: Popular Disorder in New York City, 1763–1834* (Chapel Hill: University of North Carolina Press, 1987); Carl E. Prince, "The Great 'Riot Year': Jacksonian Democracy and Patterns of Violence in 1834," *Journal of the Early Republic* 5, no. 1 (1985): 1–19; Leonard L. Richards, *"Gentlemen of Property and Standing": Anti-Abolition Mobs in Jacksonian America* (New York: Oxford University Press, 1970); and Waldrep, *Many Faces of Judge Lynch*, 13–47.

43. "On Lotteries," *Atkinson's Saturday Evening Post*, March 5, 1831. On the history of gambling in antebellum America, see esp. Ann Fabian, *Card Sharps, Dream Books, and Bucket Shops: Gambling in 19th-Century America* (Ithaca: Cornell University Press, 1990). Also see John M. Findlay, *People of Chance: Gambling in American Society from Jamestown to Las Vegas* (New York: Oxford University Press, 1986), 11–109; Jackson Lears, *Something for Nothing: Luck in America* (New York: Viking, 2003), 55–145; and David G. Schwartz, *Roll the Bones: The History of Gambling* (New York: Gotham Books, 2006), 135–57, 247–91. Less scholarly works include Herbert Asbury, *Sucker's Progress: An Informal History of Gambling in America from the Colonies to Canfield* (New York, 1938); and Henry Chafetz, *Play the Devil: A History of Gambling in the United States from 1492 to 1950* (New York: Clarkson N. Potter, 1960). Also see the fine anthology of nineteenth-century gambling tales edited by Thomas Ruys Smith, *Blacklegs, Card Sharps, and Confidence Men: Nineteenth-Century Mississippi River Gambling Stories* (Baton Rouge: Louisiana State University Press, 2010).

44. As the *Religious Intelligencer* concluded wishfully in 1829, "no man who has been attentive to religious duties was ever found to be a gamester." See "Gaming," *Religious Intelligencer*, July 11, 1829. Also see "On Lotteries," *American Baptist Magazine*, October 1830; "Gaming," *Western Messenger*, August 1835; and "The Ruinous Consequences of Gambling" (New York: American Tract Society, 18—).

45. "Gaming," *American Quarterly Observer*, October 1834, 272. On the making of the middle class and bourgeois morality, see Thomas Augst, *The Clerk's Tale: Young Men and Moral Life in Nineteenth-Century America* (Chicago: University of Chicago Press, 2003); Stuart M. Blumin, *The Emergence of the Middle Class: Social Experience in the American City, 1760–1900* (New York: Cambridge University Press, 1989); Nancy F. Cott, *The Bonds of Womanhood: "Woman's Sphere" in New England, 1780–1835* (New Haven: Yale University Press, 1977); Karen Halttunen, *Confidence Men and Painted Women: A Study of Middle-Class Culture in America, 1830–1870* (New Haven: Yale University Press, 1982); Rodney Hessinger, *Seduced, Abandoned, and Reborn: Visions of Youth in Middle-Class America, 1780–1850* (Philadelphia: University of Pennsylvania Press, 2006); Paul E. Johnson, *A Shopkeepers' Millennium: Society and Revivals in Rochester, New York, 1815–1837* (New York: Hill and Wang,

1979); John F. Kasson, *Rudeness and Civility: Manners in Nineteenth-Century Urban America* (New York: Hill and Wang, 1990); and Mary Ryan, *Cradle of the Middle Class: The Family in Oneida County, New York, 1790–1865* (New York: Cambridge University Press, 1981).

46. "The Gambler," *Bouquet*, March 23, 1833. On the presence of professional gamblers as a common type of confidence man in the work of antebellum advice writers, see Haltunnen, *Confidence Men and Painted Women*, 16–20.

47. "But He Is a Gentleman," *Lady's Book*, April 1835; "Gaming," *American Quarterly Observer*, October 1834, 275.

48. Charles Caldwell, "An Address on the Vice of Gambling; Delivered to the Medical Pupils of Transylvania University, November 4, 1834" (Lexington, 1834), 4. Numerous papers in the South and Southwest in 1834 and 1835 excerpted Caldwell's address. See, for example, the *Arkansas Gazette*, December 23, 1834. On Caldwell and his opposition to gambling, also see Fabian, *Card Sharps, Dream Books, and Bucket Shops*, 26–31.

49. Caldwell, "Address on the Vice of Gambling," 6, 7.

50. Ibid., 9–17, quotations on 12, 9, 13, 16, 15.

51. Ibid., 21, 31, 32.

52. Ibid., 33–37.

53. "The Gamester," *Atkinson's Saturday Evening Post*, September 29, 1838; "Gaming," *Religious Intelligencer*, July 11, 1829; "Miscellany," *Episcopal Watchman*, February 9, 1833; Caldwell, "Address on the Vice of Gambling," 23.

54. On the significance of Americans distinguishing between suitable and dangerous forms of moneymaking, the centrality to such distinctions of defining some means of wealth accumulation as "gambling," and the thinness and artificiality of the line between the two, see Fabian, *Card Sharps, Dream Books, and Bucket Shops*, 3–5; and Scott A. Sandage, *Born Losers: A History of Failure in America* (Cambridge: Harvard University Press, 2005), 70–98.

55. *Philadelphia National Gazette* quoted in *Liberty Hall and Cincinnati Gazette*, May 14, 1835. Americans did begin articulating concerns that speculative forms of moneymaking would lead to or were synonymous with gambling as early as the late eighteenth century. Then, the fears reflected a sense that an individualistic financial ethos was replacing the imagined republican virtue of the Revolutionary era, whereas the concerns of the Jacksonian age grew out of the more general changes the expanding market economy wrought in American social and economic life. On concerns about gambling and speculation in the fiction of the early Republic, see Karen A. Weyler, "'A Speculating Spirit': Trade, Speculation, and Gambling in Early American Fiction," *Early American Literature* 31, no. 3 (1996): 207–42.

56. *Philadelphia National Gazette* quoted in *Cincinnati Liberty Hall and Gazette*, May 14, 1835.

57. On the association between professional gamblers and slaves, and fears that gamblers subverted both slavery and white supremacy by their willingness to gamble with anyone who had cash regardless of their race or class, see Kenneth S. Greenberg, *Honor and Slavery* (Princeton: Princeton University Press, 1997), 137–45; Fabian, *Card Sharps, Dream Books, and Bucket Shops*, 36–38; and *Woodville (Miss.) Republican*, August 29, 1835. The percentage of the population that was enslaved in Vicksburg is uncertain because the census taker in 1830 did not separate Vicksburg's total from Warren County as a whole. But in 1840 more than one thousand slaves lived in the city, roughly one-third of the total population. Sixth Census of the United States, Population Schedules, Mississippi, Warren County.

CHAPTER SIX. Defining a Citizen

1. Herbert A. Kellar, "A Journey through the South in 1836: Diary of James D. Davidson," *Journal of Southern History* 1, no. 3 (1935): 356; Richard Wynkoop to "Reverend Sir," October 1, 1836, published in the *Vicksburg Daily Herald*, December 27, 1912 [hereafter cited as Wynkoop letter]; Christopher Morris, *Becoming Southern: The Evolution of a Way of Life, Warren County and Vicksburg, Mississippi, 1770–1860* (New York: Oxford University Press, 1995), 118–19.

2. Harriet Martineau, *Retrospect of Western Travel*, vol. 2 (New York, 1838), 17 (first quotation); William F. Gray, *From Virginia to Texas, 1835* (Houston, 1909), 29 (second and third quotations); George W. Featherstonhaugh, *Excursion through the Slave States* (New York, 1844), 137; "Letters from Mississippi, No. 9," *Jackson Mississippian*, January 10, 1834; Wynkoop letter; William H. Wills, "A Southern Traveler's Diary, 1840," *Southern History Association Publications* 8 (1904): 33; and Morris, *Becoming Southern*, 123.

3. Gray, *From Virginia to Texas*, 27 and 26 (first and last quotations); Wynkoop letter (second quotation); "Letters from Mississippi, No. 9," *Jackson Mississippian*, January 10, 1834 (third quotation).

4. Kellar, "A Journey through the South in 1836," 356.

5. "Letters from Mississippi—No. 19," *Jackson Mississippian*, August 15, 1834; Herbert Asbury, *Sucker's Progress: An Informal History of Gambling in America from the Colonies to Canfield* (New York, 1938), 109–54, 197–262; John M. Findlay, *People of Chance: Gambling in American Society from Jamestown to Las Vegas* (New York: Oxford University Press, 1986), 44–78; Thomas Ruys Smith, ed., *Blacklegs, Card Sharps, and Confidence Men: Nineteenth-Century Mississippi River Gambling Stories* (Baton Rouge: Louisiana State University Press, 2010), 1–24. A lengthy description of a New Orleans gambling hall can be found in Joseph Holt Ingraham, *The South-West by a Yankee*, vol. 1 (New York, 1835), 126–35. Also see the narratives of former professional gamblers such as John O'Connor, *Wanderings of a Vagabond* (New York, 1873; edited pseudonymously under the name John Morris); George Devol, *Forty*

Years a Gambler on the Mississippi (1887; reprint, New York, 1926); and Jonathan H. Green, *The Gambler's Life* (Philadelphia, 1857).

6. Joseph G. Baldwin, *The Flush Times of Alabama and Mississippi: A Series of Sketches* (New York, 1853), 84, 85; Kenneth S. Greenberg, *Honor and Slavery* (Princeton: Princeton University Press, 1997), 135–45; Bertram Wyatt-Brown, *Southern Honor: Ethics and Behavior in the Old South* (New York: Oxford University Press, 1982), 339–50.

7. Findlay, *People of Chance*, 50–51; Jackson Lears, *Something for Nothing: Luck in America* (New York: Viking, 2003), 112.

8. For modern Americans unfamiliar with the game, faro is most analogous to playing roulette with cards; players could place bets on several possible outcomes at once by laying money across two cards, at the corners where four cards came together on the layout, and so on, with payouts adjusted accordingly. If a dealer drew a "split," or two cards of the same denomination, on a turn, the bank took half the money bet on that card. For descriptions of faro and its rules, see Asbury, *Sucker's Progress*, 3–19; Jonathan H. Green, *An Exposure of the Arts and Miseries of Gambling* (Cincinnati, 1843), 110–16; and O'Connor, *Wanderings of a Vagabond*, 56–75.

9. Ann Fabian, *Card Sharps, Dream Books, and Bucket Shops: Gambling in 19th-Century America* (Ithaca: Cornell University Press, 1990), 21; Findlay, *People of Chance*, 60–61. Nearly all sources agree that a fair game of faro provided margins of just a few percentage points for the bank, but most also agree that some measure of cheating was a constant. Herbert Asbury assumed that "cheating soon became as much a part of Faro in America as a pack of cards," and Jonathan Green devoted nearly thirty pages in one of his many books to describing the various ways gamblers tinkered with the box, used sleight-of-hand, and shaved cards to give themselves advantages, concluding that a person "would act more rationally and correctly to burn his money than to bet it on faro." John O'Connor, however, thought gamblers' reputation for cheating overblown and rooted in myth and stereotype as much as in reality. Surely cheating was part of faro as it was played in nineteenth-century America, just as it was of any kind of gambling or other economic pursuit. Asbury, *Sucker's Progress*, 13; Green, *Arts and Miseries of Gambling*, 117–47 (quotation on 117); O'Connor, *Wanderings of a Vagabond*, 65.

10. Kellar, "Journey through the South in 1836," 355; O'Connor, *Wanderings of a Vagabond*, 340, 341; Green, *Gambler's Life*, 137; Green, *Arts and Miseries of Gambling*, 212.

11. H. S. Fulkerson, *Random Recollections of Early Days in Mississippi* (Vicksburg, 1885), 95; Wynkoop letter.

12. *Hartford Times* in *Portland Eastern Argus*, August 26, 1835; *Mobile Daily Commercial Register and Patriot*, July 22, 1835; *Protestant Vindicator* in *Liberator*, August 15, 1835; *Vicksburg Register*, August 6, 1835.

13. Featherstonhaugh, *Excursion through the Slave States*, 134–36 (quotations on 135, 136).

14. Ibid., 137–39 (quotations on 137).

15. Christopher Waldrep, *Roots of Disorder: Race and Criminal Justice in the American South, 1817–80* (Urbana and Chicago: University of Illinois Press, 1998), 43; Warren County Circuit Court Minute Book C, November 1831–November 1834, 36, 46, 158, 353, 545, 546, 548, 552, 553, WCC.

16. Warren County Circuit Court Minute Book C, November 1831–November 1834, 567, 581, 587, WCC; Warren County Circuit Court Minute Book D, May 1835–February 1837, 75, 88, 90, WCC.

17. Information about the Vicksburg rioters is compiled from *Vicksburg Register* articles and advertisements between 1831 and 1836, and from the annual Warren County Combination Tax Rolls between 1829 and 1836, MDAH. On the southern middle class, see Jonathan Daniel Wells, *The Origins of the Southern Middle Class* (Chapel Hill: University of North Carolina Press, 2004). On the correlation among wealth, slaveholding, orientation toward production for national and international markets, and Whig voting in Mississippi, see James Roger Sharp, *The Jacksonians versus the Banks: Politics in the States after the Panic of 1837* (New York: Columbia University Press, 1970), 89–99.

18. *Vicksburg Register*, July 9, 1835 (quotations), October 28, 1831, May 14, 1832, and March 4, 1834.

19. The Bodley memorial originally stood in the yard of the First Presbyterian Church, which donated a small piece of land for the site in 1838. The monument likely was erected soon after that. The inscription on the memorial misstates the date of Hugh Bodley's death as July 5 rather than July 6. Frank E. Everett Jr., *A History of the First Presbyterian Church of Vicksburg, Mississippi, in the Nineteenth Century* (Vicksburg, 1980), 28; Steve Riley, "Vicksburg's Hills Alive with Gambling Legacy," *Jackson Clarion-Ledger*, May 4, 1986, A1.

20. *Vicksburg Register*, July 9, 1835.

21. On Thomas Bodley and the Bodley-Bullock House, which is on the National Register of Historic Places, see "Bodley House," *RootsWeb*, http://www.rootsweb.com/-kyfayett/dunn/bodley_house.htm, accessed July 12, 2011. Also see Lewis Collins, *History of Kentucky*, vol. 1 (Covington, Ky., 1874), 368–69, 524–25.

22. *Frankfort Commonwealth* in *Vicksburg Register*, August 13, 1835.

23. Hugh Bodley first advertised his services as a physician in the *Vicksburg Register* in May 1833, and he paid a poll tax only in 1834 and 1835. His brother William, a lawyer, arrived in Vicksburg in 1830. Their sister Anne moved to the city with her husband, lawyer William Henry Hurst, in November 1834. Warren County Combination Tax Rolls, 1834–35, MDAH; *Vicksburg Register*, January 2 and May 1, 1833; Frank E. Everett Jr., *Vicksburg Lawyers prior to the Civil War* (Vicksburg: F. E. Ev-

erett, 1965, 33, 58; Warren County Deed Book G, 1834–36, 873, 880, MDAH; Thomas Bodley to Hugh Bodley, February 24, 1833, Trigg Family Papers, MDAH; Estate of Hugh S. Bodley, Probate Packets, Warren County, case 518, file 51, 59, December term 1835, MDAH.

24. *Vicksburg Register*, July 30, 1835.

25. Ibid. Information about meeting attendees compiled from *Vicksburg Register* articles and advertisements between 1831 and 1836, and from Warren County Combination Tax Rolls, MDAH. At least two rioters—George Brungard and William Henry Hurst—were also at this meeting.

26. *Vicksburg Register*, July 30, 1835. On the relationship between urban and rural spaces and their inhabitants in Warren County, see Morris, *Becoming Southern*, esp. 114–31.

27. *Vicksburg Register*, July 30, 1835.

28. *Vicksburg Register*, January 7, 1836.

29. Ibid.

30. Ibid.

31. *Richmond Enquirer*, August 11, 1835.

32. Ibid. For similar dynamics at play in other Mississippi towns, see *Woodville (Miss.) Republican*, August 29, 1835; and *Columbus (Miss.) Argus* in *Vicksburg Register*, September 24, 1835.

33. *Lexington Intelligencer*, July 21, 1835. Attaching such exclusionary conditions to Fourth of July celebrations was not wholly out of keeping with the spirit of the holiday in the 1830s, as the day was less an occasion for unity than some liked to pretend. Noting the varied social and political meanings with which Americans invested celebrations of the Fourth (and that for some it was simply an excuse to get drunk), Len Travers argues that "as Americans approached the middle of the nineteenth century, Independence Day increasingly revealed not so much what they held in common as what separated them" (Len Travers, *Celebrating the Fourth: Independence Day and the Rites of Nationalism in the Early Republic* [Amherst: University of Massachusetts Press, 1997], 222).

34. William Winans to Rev. Benjamin A. Houghton, August 29, 1835, box 17, letter book 8, 162–63, William Winans Papers, J. B. Cain Archives, Millsaps College, Jackson, Miss.

35. Rev. Benjamin A. Houghton to William Winans, January 16, 1836, box 20, folder 8, Winans Papers.

36. Although popular memory and legend say that the house in which the accused gamblers barricaded themselves was known as the "Kangaroo," that was not the case. The Kangaroo was especially notorious in Vicksburg, but it burned to the ground early in 1834, nearly a year and a half before the gambling riot. But the entire section of the city along the waterfront and north of the main business district in

which gambling houses, bar-rooms, and other sorts of less "reputable" establishments clustered was known informally as the Kangaroo, which likely explains the persistence of the misattribution of that name to North's house. *Vicksburg Register*, January 29, 1834; Morris, *Becoming Southern*, 121. Regarding the men inside that house, the *Louisiana Advertiser* indicated that "Dutch Bill" was the house "barkeeper." It gave Smith's first name as Samuel, but no Samuel Smith appears in the public records. A Hobson Smith was indicted for faro dealing in 1831, but he disappears from Warren County records after the case was dropped in 1834. Of the four, the only conclusively identifiable man is John Hullum, who was originally from Tennessee. James Hoard had actually been indicted twice for faro dealing, once in 1831 and again in 1834. Interestingly, and perhaps pointing further to the difficulty of separating "citizens" from "gamblers," the men who posted security for Francis Cabler when he was charged with faro dealing in 1835 were Robert McGinty, the mayor of Vicksburg, and E. W. Morris, who would become sheriff of Warren County just months later. *Vicksburg Register*, July, 9, 1835; *Louisiana Advertiser* in *Boston Daily Courier*, August 1, 1835; *Liberty Hall and Cincinnati Gazette*, November 12, 1835; Warren County Circuit Court Minute Book C, 36, 46, 53, 58, 165, 166, 266, 284, 288, 369, 370, 381, 540–41, 545, 546 549, 551, 552, 566, 567, 571, wcc; Warren County Minute Book D, 87, 88, 89, 90, wcc; Warren County Circuit Court Papers, Criminal Cases, 1832–49, folders 7 and 9, ochm; Warren County Deed Book F, 1831–34, 335–36, mdah; Warren County Deed Book G, 581–82, mdah.

37. Truman North had lived in Warren County since at least 1830, and Cabler and Hoard probably arrived in 1831 or 1832. It seems likely that North had a wife named Ellenor, but the records of North's estate make clear that his son Alfred was his only heir and that Samuel McLean of Kentucky was named his guardian. *Vicksburg Register*, July 9, 1835; Warren County Combination Tax Rolls, 1832–35, mdah; Fifth Census of the United States, Population Schedules, Mississippi, Warren County; Warren County Deed Book F, 335–36, mdah; Warren County Deed Book G, 256–57, 286–87, 581–82, mdah; Probate Packets, Warren County, Estate of Truman North, case 589, file 58, 67, July term 1835, mdah; Warren County Minute Book D, 55, wcc.

38. *Vicksburg Register*, July 9 (first two quotations), September 24, and August 13, 1835; *Niles' Weekly Register*, August 8, 1835 (last quotation); *Chicago American*, September 5, 1835; William Winans to Sarah H. McGehee, August 22, 1835, box 17, letter book 8, 151, Winans Papers; *Arkansas Gazette*, July 14, 1835.

39. *Niles' Weekly Register*, August 8, 1835 (first quotation); *Vicksburg Register*, August 13, 1835; *New York Evening Post*, July 30, 1835; *New Orleans Bee*, July 13, 1835; and *Columbus Argus* and *Jackson Banner*, both in *Vicksburg Register*, September 24, 1835 (second and third quotations).

40. In addition to the locales listed above, I have found newspaper reports of

meetings held, warnings issued, antigambling societies formed, and other actions taken against gamblers in Carroll, East Feliciana, West Feliciana, and St. Helena parishes, Louisiana; Tuscaloosa and Huntsville, Alabama; Washington, Helena, and Red River, Arkansas; Maysville and Covington, Kentucky; Jacksonville, Illinois; Dubuques, Missouri; and LaPorte, Indiana. This list is surely not exhaustive. The *Raleigh North Carolina Standard* of October 15, 1835, observed, "it appears that the people of the south-west make common cause against these moral pests. They have been hung, Lynch'd, or driven out of nearly every town in the South and West." Also see *Niles' Weekly Register*, August 8 and 22, and October 31, 1835; *Vicksburg Register*, July 23, August 13 and 27, and September 10, 1835; *Baltimore Gazette*, July 29, August 17 and 25, September 10, and October 26, 1835; *Mobile Commercial Register and Patriot*, July 22, 1835; *New Orleans Bee*, August 19 and August 26, 1835; *Lexington Intelligencer*, July 31 and August 4, 1835; *Portland Eastern Argus*, August 26, September 15, and October 28, 1835; *Arkansas Gazette*, July 14 and 28, August 11 and 25, September 1 and 8, and October 6, 1835; and *Chicago American*, July 11, August 29, and September 5, 1835.

41. *Niles' Weekly Register*, August 8, 1835.

42. Ibid.; *Vicksburg Register*, July 30, 1835.

43. Findlay, *People of Chance*, 46.

44. Wyatt-Brown, *Southern Honor*, 435–61; Joan E. Cashin, *A Family Venture: Men and Women on the Southern Frontier* (Baltimore: Johns Hopkins University Press, 1991), 102–8. Most scholarly accounts of the Vicksburg riot highlight southern sensibilities and cultural systems such as honor, frontier violence intended to import eastern moral standards to the West, or some combination of the two. See Fabian, *Card Sharps, Dream Books, and Bucket Shops*, 29–38; Findlay, *People of Chance*, 64–69; David Grimsted, *American Mobbing, 1828–1861: Toward Civil War* (New York: Oxford University Press, 1998), 14–15; and Greenberg, *Honor and Slavery*, 135–45. Morris (*Becoming Southern*, 120–22) attributes the Vicksburg riot to generalized fear of "outsiders."

45. Henry S. Foote, *Casket of Reminiscences* (Washington, D.C., 1874), 264; Gray, *From Virginia to Texas*, 29 and 57. Also see Ingraham, *Southwest by a Yankee*, 2:45–50, 166–69; Featherstonhaugh, *Excursion through the Slave States*, 94–100; and Baldwin, *Flush Times*, 58–59, 83–85.

46. *Niles' Weekly Register*, August 8, 1835; *Portland Eastern Argus*, August 5 and 12, 1835; *Baltimore Gazette*, August 6 and September 10, 1835; *United States Gazette*, August 5 and 7, 1835; *Liberty Hall and Cincinnati Gazette*, August 20, 1835; *Richmond Enquirer*, August 7 and 14 (first quotation), 1835; *United States Telegraph*, August 15 (fourth quotation), 20, and 24 (second quotation), 1835; *Lexington Intelligencer*, August 7 (third quotation) and 25, 1835, and January 15, 1836; *New York Evening Post*, August 8, 1835; *Chicago American*, August 29, 1835; and *Boston Courier*, October 21, 1835.

47. *United States Gazette*, August 11, 1835; and *Baltimore Gazette*, August 7, 1835. Also see *Boston Courier*, August 5, 1835, which noted that "there are strong reasons for believing that one of the routed Vicksburg gamblers is now, or was a few days since," in Philadelphia. The "strong reasons" consisted of a "gentleman" spotting a loud drunken man in a bar who carried a switchblade knife, asserted that he could win any person's money at cards in half an hour, and claimed that he was "d———d near Vicksburg when *them* fellows *was* hung." The informer said he had seen the supposed gambler previously, in Louisville. Such, apparently, was "evidence" that the braggart was an exiled gambler from Vicksburg. He had not been seen in Philadelphia for several days, prompting the paper to suggest that he was "perhaps at this moment in New-York." The *New York Journal of Commerce* reported a few weeks later that "gentlemen from Vicksburg have recognized in our streets several of the gamblers who were expelled from that place." This was quite a feat amid the half million people in New York in the 1830s. *New York Journal of Commerce* in *Arkansas Gazette*, September 22, 1835.

48. *Frankfort Commonwealth* in *Lexington Intelligencer*, July 28, 1835 ("vampyres"); *Tuscaloosa (Ala.) Flag of the Union* in *Huntsville Southern Advocate*, October 13, 1835 ("vampyres"); *Niles' Weekly Register*, August 1, 1835 ("harpies"); *Louisville Advertiser* in *New York Evening Post*, July 31, 1835 ("plague spots"); *Chicago American*, August 29, 1835 ("blood-gouts"); *Huntsville Democrat* in *Vicksburg Register*, August 29, 1835 ("harpies" and "vultures"); *Manchester (Miss.) Herald* in *Vicksburg Register*, July 20, 1835 ("blood-suckers"); *Philadelphia Inquirer* in *United States Telegraph*, August 15, 1835 ("living ulcers"); *New York Sun* in *United States Telegraph*, August 15, 1835.

49. *Philadelphia Inquirer* in *United States Telegraph*, August 15, 1835.

50. Thomas R. Dew, "On Price," *Farmers' Register* 3 (June 1835): 71.

51. *Liberty Hall and Cincinnati Gazette*, November 12, 1835.

52. Ibid.

53. Ibid.

54. Ibid.

55. Ibid.

56. Ibid.

57. Ibid.

CHAPTER SEVEN. Suborning Chaos

1. Henry S. Foote, *Casket of Reminiscences* (Washington, D.C., 1874), 255–56.

2. *PCMC*, 28; "Transactions in Mississippi," *United States Telegraph*, October 6, 1835 [hereafter cited as "Transactions"]; "The Mississippi Disturbances," *Baltimore American*, August 8, 1835 [hereafter cited as "Disturbances"]; *Baltimore American*, August 7, 1835.

3. *Natchez Courier* in *Lexington Intelligencer*, July 31, 1835; *Clinton Gazette* in *Vicksburg Register*, July 16, 1835. Also see *Columbus Argus* in *United States Telegraph*, August 3, 1835.

4. *Maysville Eagle* in *Baltimore Gazette*, August 6, 1835.

5. *United States Telegraph*, August 1, 1835; *United States Gazette*, July 24, 1835; Foote, *Casket of Reminiscences*, 251; David J. Libby, *Slavery and Frontier Mississippi, 1720–1835* (Jackson: University Press of Mississippi, 2004), 77.

6. Israel Campbell, *Bond and Free: or, Yearnings for Freedom* (Philadelphia, 1861), 70–74; *United States Gazette*, July 24, 1835; *New Orleans Observer*, August 15, 1835; *Woodville Republican*, July 18, 1835.

7. Entry dated July 17, 1835, anonymous diary, 1835–37, LLMVC; *New Orleans Bee*, July 16, 1835; *Woodville Republican*, July 18, 1835.

8. "A Tale of Horror," *Liberator*, December 10, 1836. Also see *Woodville Republican*, July 18, 1835; *Clinton Gazette*, July 11, 1835; "Disturbances"; and *Baltimore American*, August 7, 1835.

9. PCMC, 37; *United States Gazette*, July 24, 1835.

10. *Jackson Banner* in *Grand Gulf Advertiser*, July 14, 1835 (first two quotations); *New Orleans Bee*, July 14, 1835 (third quotation); *Jackson Mississippian*, August 14, 1835; PCMC, 35–36; *United States Telegraph*, August 3, 1835; *Lexington Intelligencer*, July 28, 1835. A number of scholars have pointed to factors such as institutional development and community formation to explain why the scare played out in different ways in Madison and Hinds counties. While these kinds of distinctions were undeniable and the scare proceeded along somewhat different trajectories in Madison and Hinds, the counties were far more alike than they were different and the variance between how whites reacted to the scare in the two places is easily overstated. See Christopher Morris, "An Event in Community Organization: The Mississippi Slave Insurrection Scare of 1835," *Journal of Social History* 22, no. 1 (1988): 93–111; and Laurence Shore, "Making Mississippi Safe for Slavery: The Insurrection Panic of 1835," in *Class, Consensus, and Conflict: Antebellum Southern Community Studies*, ed. Orville Vernon Burton and Robert C. McMath Jr., 96–127 (Westport, Conn.: Greenwood Press, 1982).

11. *Baltimore Gazette*, July 30, 1835.

12. Burrell Fox to Aaron Neal, September 25, 1835, Neal Family Papers, box 1, folder 8, SHC; William H. Thomson to Hannah Lavinia Thomson, July 12, 1835, box 1, folder 1, Ruffin Thomson Papers, SHC.

13. William H. Thomson to Hannah Lavinia Thomson, July 12, 1835, box 1, folder 1, Ruffin Thomson Papers, SHC.

14. Foote, *Casket of Reminiscences*, 252 (quotations), 256; *Jackson Mississippian*, August 14, 1835; *Natchez Courier* in *Lexington Intelligencer*, July 31, 1835; *Baltimore American*, August 7, 1835; *Nashville Republican*, July 18, 1835.

15. *Lexington Intelligencer*, July 28, 1835.

16. Foote, *Casket of Reminiscences*, 251.

17. *PCMC*, 10, 17; *Clinton Gazette* in *Vicksburg Register*, July 16, 1835; *Nashville Republican*, July 18, 1835.

18. *PCMC*, 13; *Nashville Republican*, July 18, 1835; *Natchez Courier* in *Grand Gulf Advertiser*, July 14, 1835.

19. "Letters from Mississippi, No. 9" and "Letters from Mississippi, No. 11," *Jackson Mississippian*, January 24 and February 28, 1834; Joseph Holt Ingraham, *The South-West by a Yankee*, vol. 2 (New York, 1835), 166–75; Mrs. Dunbar Rowland, *History of Hinds County, Mississippi, 1821–1922* (Jackson, Miss., 1922), 5–21; Fifth Census of the United States, Population Schedules, Mississippi, Hinds County.

20. "Letters from Mississippi, No. 11," *Jackson Mississippian*, February 28, 1834; Ingraham, *South-West by a Yankee*, 2:166 (quotations).

21. Rowland, *History of Hinds County*, 12–14; "Letters from Mississippi, No. 11," *Jackson Mississippian*, February 28, 1834.

22. Rowland, *History of Hinds County*, 12–15; "Letters from Mississippi, No. 11," *Jackson Mississippian*, February 28, 1834; William F. Gray, *From Virginia to Texas, 1835* (Houston, 1909), 35 (quotation); Ingraham, *South-West by a Yankee*, 2:173–74.

23. "Letters from Mississippi, No. 11," *Jackson Mississippian*, February 28, 1834; Ingraham, *South-West by a Yankee*, 2:174, 175 (quotation); Gray, *From Virginia to Texas*, 35.

24. "Letters from Mississippi, No. 9," *Jackson Mississippian*, January 24, 1834; Ingraham, *South-West by a Yankee*, 2:169–70; Shirley Faucette, "Clinton–Yesterday," *Journal of Mississippi History* 40, no. 3 (1978): 215–30.

25. "Letters from Mississippi, No. 9," *Jackson Mississippian*, January 24, 1834; Malcolm Rohrbough, *The Land Office Business: The Settlement and Administration of American Public Lands, 1789–1837* (New York: Oxford University Press, 1968), 226.

26. Fifth Census of the United States, Population Schedules, Mississippi, Hinds County; Sixth Census of the United States, Population Schedules, Mississippi, Hinds County.

27. George C. Osborn, "Plantation Life in Central Mississippi as Revealed in the Clay Sharkey Papers," *Journal of Mississippi History* 3, no. 4 (1941): 277–78; Dunbar Rowland, *Courts, Judges, and Lawyers of Mississippi, 1798–1935*, vol. 1 (Jackson, Miss., 1935), 87; James Kilborn and Patrick Sharkey to Governor Hiram Runnels, July 7, 1835, Governor's Papers, RG27, series 714, vol. 21, MDAH; Fifth Census of the United States, Population Schedules, Mississippi, Hinds County, 223.

28. Fifth Census of the United States, Population Schedules, Mississippi, Hinds County, 223; Hinds County Combination Tax Rolls, 1835, MDAH; Osborn, "Plantation Life in Central Mississippi," 278; Henry S. Foote, *The Bench and Bar of the South and Southwest* (St. Louis, 1876), 67; *Lexington Intelligencer*, July 28, 1835;

Kilborn and Sharkey to Governor Runnels, July 7, 1835, MDAH. Several accounts of the insurrection scare suggest Patrick Sharkey was much richer than he actually was. One witness described Sharkey accurately as "a man who has stood high in the estimation of his fellow-citizens" but less so as a man so wealthy that he worked "sixty hands," and Henry Foote erroneously recalled that Sharkey was "one of the wealthiest planters in the county of Hinds." In fact, Sharkey was listed on the 1830 census as the owner of twenty-one slaves. He paid taxes on twenty-four slaves, twenty-four slaves, and nineteen slaves in 1834, 1835, and 1836, respectively, and on the 1840 census he was listed as the owner of twenty-five slaves. Sharkey was not poor, but he owned nowhere near sixty slaves prior to 1840. "Disturbances"; Foote, *Bench and Bar*, 67; Hinds County Combination Tax Rolls, 1834–36, MDAH.

29. Kilborn and Sharkey to Governor Runnels, July 7, 1835, MDAH. In 1835 James Kilborn owned 240 acres of land and twenty-three slaves. Hinds County Combination Tax Rolls, 1836, MDAH.

30. *PCMC*, 18; "Transactions."

31. "Transactions"; "Disturbances"; *Natchez Courier* in *Grand Gulf Advertiser*, July 14, 1835; Hinds County Combination Tax Rolls, 1834, MDAH; Osborn, "Plantation Life in Central Mississippi," 278; Fifth Census of the United States, Population Schedules, Mississippi, Hinds County, 203.

32. Hinds County Combination Tax Rolls, 1835, MDAH; "Transactions"; "Disturbances"; Osborn, "Plantation Life in Central Mississippi," 278. Several sources indicate that Perkins and his company captured a fourth man who may have been named Blackman along with the Rawsons. If so, what became of him is unclear. "Disturbances"; *Natchez Courier* in *Grand Gulf Advertiser*, July 14, 1835.

33. "Transactions"; "Disturbances" (first quotation); *Lexington Intelligencer*, July 28, 1835 (second quotation); Foote, *Bench and Bar*, 67 (third quotation); Osborn, "Plantation Life in Central Mississippi," 278; Kilborn and Sharkey to Governor Runnels, July 7, 1835, MDAH (last quotation).

34. Kilborn and Sharkey to Governor Runnels, July 7, 1835, MDAH.

35. "Transactions."

36. Ibid. Also see "Disturbances."

37. "Transactions"; Foote, *Casket of Reminiscences*, 260; *Lexington Intelligencer*, July 28, 1835.

38. According to Sharkey's son, an enslaved woman belonging to the family had been hired out to work at a hotel where Perkins's company stopped en route to the plantation, overheard them as they plotted, and rushed back to inform her owners that they were in danger. Sharkey himself wrote on the afternoon of July 7 only that it was "reported" that Perkins and his men were ambushing his home "for purposes best known to themselves." Another witness noted simply that Sharkey had been "partially apprized of Perkins' intentions." Osborn, "Plantation Life in

Central Mississippi," 278; Kilborn and Sharkey to Governor Runnels, July 7, 1835, MDAH; "Transactions".

39. *Lexington Intelligencer,* July 28, 1835; "Transactions"; *Nashville Republican,* July 18, 1835; Foote, *Casket of Reminiscences,* 260; Foote, *Bench and Bar,* 67; William H. Thomson to Hannah Lavinia Thomson, July 12, 1835, Ruffin Thomson Papers, SHC; Burrell Fox to Aaron Neal, September 25, 1835, Neal Family Papers, box 1, folder 8, SHC.

40. *Lexington Intelligencer,* July 28, 1835; "Transactions"; "Disturbances"; *Nashville Republican,* July 18, 1835; Foote, *Casket of Reminiscences,* 260; Foote, *Bench and Bar,* 67; Osborn, "Plantation Life in Central Mississippi," 278; William H. Thomson to Hannah Lavinia Thomson, July 12, 1835, Ruffin Thomson Papers, SHC; Burrell Fox to Aaron Neal, September 25, 1835, Neal Family Papers, SHC.

41. "Transactions"; Fifth Census of the United States, Population Schedules, Mississippi, Hinds County, 198.

42. Sharkey and Kilborn to Governor Runnels, July 7, 1835, MDAH; Burrell Fox to Aaron Neal, September 25, 1835, Neal Family Papers, SHC.

43. *Lexington Intelligencer,* July 28, 1835; Foote, *Casket of Reminiscences,* 259; Foote, *Bench and Bar,* 67; "Transactions."

44. Foote, *Bench and Bar,* 67; Foote, *Casket of Reminiscences,* 260.

45. Osborn, "Plantation Life in Central Mississippi," 288; "Letters from Mississippi, No. 11," *Jackson Mississippian,* February 28, 1834; Faucette, "Clinton–Yesterday," 220, 227; Rowland, *History of Hinds County,* 13–14; Rowland, *Mississippi,* vol. 1 (Atlanta, 1907), 455–457; *Clinton Gazette* in *Jackson Mississippian,* July 24, 1835; Foote, *Bench and Bar,* 67 (quotation).

46. Rowland, *Courts, Judges, and Lawyers of Mississippi,* 87–88; Rowland, *Mississippi,* 2:649–53; Foote, *Bench and Bar,* 67 (quotation); Foote, *Casket of Reminiscences,* 259–260. Foote recalled in two different memoirs what he witnessed in the summer of 1835, and given that forty years had elapsed since the events in question occurred, his chronology is sometimes confused. Foote claimed in both works that William Sharkey came to his hotel room in Jackson to ask for help at his cousin's trial, but in one memoir he also claimed to have returned to Clinton the morning after witnessing the whipping of Lee Smith and said that he was not in Jackson until several days later. Newspaper and other accounts from the time, though, make clear that the shootout at Patrick Sharkey's plantation took place on the same day Lee Smith was beaten and that his trial before the Clinton committee occurred the following day. That William Sharkey would have sought someone locally known to introduce him in Clinton is believable, but the only way he could have found Henry Foote in Jackson for that purpose would be if Foote had stopped in the city on his way back to Clinton. Given that Foote often had

legal and political business to attend to in Jackson, that neither of the main roads headed south out of Livingston went directly to Clinton, and that getting to Clinton from Livingston before dark would have required great haste if one left the latter place in the afternoon, Foote most probably chose to head home via Jackson and stayed there on the night of July 7.

47. Foote, *Bench and Bar*, 67–68; Foote, *Casket of Reminiscences*, 260–61 (quotation on 261).

48. Foote, *Bench and Bar*, 68 (quotations); Foote, *Casket of Reminiscences*, 261.

49. "Transactions." Also see Foote, *Bench and Bar*, 68; and Foote, *Casket of Reminiscences*, 261.

50. Figuring the date of Vincent's trial requires a bit of detective work and a bit of guesswork. On July 24 the *Jackson Mississippian* reprinted Vincent's story as it appeared in the *Clinton Gazette*. July 24 was a Friday, and while no copies of the *Gazette* from July 1835 survive, the paper was published on Saturdays, meaning that its article about Vincent appeared in either the July 11 or July 18 edition. The original story indicates that Vincent's execution took place on "Thursday morning last" and suggests that his trial took place the day before that. The language here is ambiguous. If the story originally appeared in the July 11 issue of the *Gazette*, "last" means July 9, the Thursday immediately preceding, as there was no vigilance committee in existence in Clinton on any Thursdays prior to that one. If the story originally appeared in the July 18 issue of the *Gazette*, "last" could mean that Vincent's trial occurred on July 15 or on July 8, but July 8 seems more likely for several reasons. The activities of vigilance committees all over the state, including the one in Livingston, had slowed significantly by the fifteenth. Moreover, Henry Foote claimed to have seen what happened to Vincent when he got back to Clinton the day after seeing the beating of Lee Smith. He may have been mistaken, but an entirely plausible and consistent timeline exists in which Foote saw a mob assault Lee Smith on the afternoon of July 7, arrived in Jackson that evening, accompanied William Sharkey to Clinton on the morning of July 8, and witnessed what became of Vincent in town that afternoon and early the next day. *Clinton Gazette* in *Jackson Mississippian*, July 24, 1835; Foote, *Casket of Reminiscences*, 256.

51. *Clinton Gazette* in *Jackson Mississippian*, July 24, 1835.

52. Foote, *Casket of Reminiscences*, 257–58; Hinds County Combination Tax Rolls, 1834 and 1836, MDAH.

53. Foote, *Casket of Reminiscences*, 258; *Clinton Gazette* in *Jackson Mississippian*, July 24, 1835. We have only Foote's word that he made that speech, but in reporting what happened to Vincent, the *Clinton Gazette* did note that before he was hanged the crowd listened to "every thing favorable to the culprit . . . which could be said" and that it did take a second vote.

54. Foote, *Casket of Reminiscences*, 261; *Lexington Intelligencer*, July 28, 1835.

55. Foote, *Casket of Reminiscences*, 259; Foote, *Bench and Bar*, 66–67.

56. *Lexington Intelligencer*, July 28, 1835.

57. Ibid.; "Transactions"; *PCMC*, 35–36; *Jackson Mississippian*, August 14, 1835.

58. Sharkey and Kilborn to Governor Runnels, July 7, 1835, MDAH.

59. Ibid.

60. George Wyche to Governor Hiram Runnels, July 8, 1835, Governor's Papers, RG27, series 714, vol. 21, MDAH; Hinds County Combination Tax Rolls, 1835 and 1836, MDAH.

61. Clinton Committee of Safety to Governor Hiram Runnels, July 11, 1835, Governor's Papers, RG27, series 714, vol. 21, MDAH. The Clinton committee of safety dated its letter and resolution July 11 but did not send the message to the governor until the next morning.

62. *Jackson Mississippian*, August 14, 1835.

63. Ibid.

64. *Jackson Mississippian*, July 17, 1835.

65. *Jackson Mississippian*, August 14, 1835.

66. *PCMC*, 36.

67. Ibid.

68. Rowland, *Encyclopedia of Mississippi History*, vol. 2 (Madison, Wis., 1907), 60, 580–81 (first quotation on 580); *PCMC*, 36 (second quotation); Cecil L. Sumners, *The Governors of Mississippi* (Gretna, La.: Pelican Publishing, 1980), 52–53.

69. William S. Jones to Governor Hiram Runnels, July 13, 1835, Governor's Papers, RG27, series 714, vol. 21, MDAH; *PCMC*, 36 (quotation).

70. *PCMC*, 26.

71. Ibid., 26–27; *Natchez Courier* in *Grand Gulf Advertiser*, July 14, 1835; "Disturbances."

72. "Transactions"; "Disturbances."

73. Shackelford wrote that Blake arrived in the village and was tried on July 8, but sources written as events were unfolding indicate that he did not leave Vicksburg until that morning and he could not possibly have been brought fifty miles from Vicksburg to Livingston and then tried by the committee all in a single day. The report of one witness that Bennett and his men brought Blake into the village on the afternoon of July 9 is certainly the most accurate. *PCMC*, 27 (quotation); *Natchez Courier* in *Grand Gulf Advertiser*, July 14, 1835; "Disturbances".

74. *PCMC*, 9 (first quotation), 27 (remaining quotations); "Disturbances."

75. "Will of Ruel Blake," in "Madison County—1835 Uprising" subject file, MDAH.

76. "Transactions."

77. *PCMC*, 27 (first quotation); "Transactions" (remaining quotations).

78. *PCMC*, 27 (quotations); "Transactions"; "Disturbances."

79. "Transactions."

CHAPTER EIGHT. Imposing Order

1. Governor Hiram Runnels to the Clinton Committee of Safety, July 13, 1835, Governor's Papers, RG27, ser. 714, vol. 21, MDAH.

2. Proclamation of Governor Hiram G. Runnels, July 13, 1835, Governor's Papers, RG27, ser. 714, vol. 21, MDAH. The proclamation first appeared in the *Jackson Mississippian* on July 17, 1835. Other newspapers across the state and country reprinted it over the course of the next few months.

3. "Transactions." That some paranoia was still evident among white Mississippians is suggested by a letter sent to planter and state official John Quitman a few days after the governor issued his proclamation. The letter, from J. E. Stuart in Vernon, included a seemingly innocuous note confiscated from a man traveling through Vernon who claimed to be from Louisiana. The note reported to friends in Natchez what the man had heard about the number of people killed in Mississippi during the insurrection scare, but Stuart thought the correspondence had a "clandestine character" and that the man might be a "spy travelling through our country to recussitate [*sic*] the disconcerted desperadoes." Stuart asked Quitman to check into the individuals in Natchez the man claimed were his friends. He also told Quitman that the man had been placed under surveillance but had neither been arrested nor charged with anything, indicating that tensions remained high but that the tendency toward speedy trials and executions had waned. J. E. Stuart to John A. Quitman, July 1835, typescript in "Madison County—1835 Uprising" subject file, MDAH.

4. *Natchez Courier* in *Vicksburg Register*, July 30, 1835.

5. Ibid.

6. *Gallatin Democrat* in *Jackson Mississippian*, August 14, 1835.

7. *Jackson Mississippian*, July 31, 1835.

8. *Niles' Weekly Register*, December 5, 1835 (quotation). Mississippi gubernatorial election returns for 1835 can be found in *Jackson Mississippian*, November 20, 1835. Charles Lynch won a majority in twenty-one counties in 1835, thirteen of which comprised almost the entire southwestern quadrant of the state. Most of those counties inclined toward the Whigs and would likely have voted for Lynch under any circumstances, but Lynch won election by only four hundred votes, a margin of victory very plausibly attributed to disappointment with Runnels in just a few counties among individuals who might have otherwise voted for him.

9. *Vicksburg Register*, July 23, 1835 (quotations); "Transactions"; *PCMC*, 36.

10. *Vicksburg Register*, July 23, 1835.

11. Anonymous correspondent to Governor Runnels, undated, Governor's Pa-

pers, RG27, ser. 714, vol. 21, MDAH. It is not impossible that the enslaved in Madison County were actually plotting some sort of rebellion in the summer of 1835. Evidence for such a plot is scant, but Thomas Shackelford's report of the proceedings of the Livingston committee includes scattered details hinting that something more real if less far-reaching than the conspiracy outlined in Virgil Stewart's pamphlet might have been afoot. There was the whispering Lorenzo Latham's mother heard, for example, and there was also the testimony of William Johnson's driver, who reported that he had been told that Ruel Blake's slave Peter had said he intended to steal kegs of gunpowder. These fragments of information are suggestive more than conclusive and point toward the challenge involved in sorting rumors from reality and insurrection fears from real insurrection plots. *PCMC*, 5, 6. David Libby argues that the slaves of Madison County really were planning an insurrection of some kind in *Slavery and Frontier Mississippi, 1720–1835* (Jackson: University Press of Mississippi, 2004), 109–13. On the Haitian Revolution and its repercussions in the United States, see Laurent Dubois, *Avengers of the New World: The Story of the Haitian Revolution* (Cambridge: Harvard University Press, 2004); Alfred Hunt, *Haiti's Influence on Antebellum America: Slumbering Volcano in the Caribbean* (Baton Rouge: Louisiana State University Press, 1988); David Geggus, ed., *The Impact of the Haitian Revolution in the Atlantic World* (Columbia: University of South Carolina Press, 2001); and Ashli White, *Encountering Revolution: Haiti and the Making of the Early Republic* (Baltimore: Johns Hopkins University Press, 2010). The literature on slave revolts and rumors and fears of slave revolts in mainland North America is vast. A reasonable if dated starting point is Herbert Aptheker's pioneering *American Negro Slave Revolts* (New York, 1943). For one controversial debate about distinguishing between an actual insurrection plot and white fears of insurrection, see Michael Johnson, "Denmark Vesey and His Co-conspirators," *William and Mary Quarterly*, 3rd ser., 58, no. 4 (2001): 915–76; and "Forum: The Making of a Slave Conspiracy, Part 2," *William and Mary Quarterly*, 3rd ser., 59, no. 1 (2002): 135–202. A similarly tricky event to sort through in Civil War Mississippi is explored in Justin Behrend, "Rebellious Talk and Conspiratorial Plots: The Making of a Slave Insurrection in Civil War Natchez," *Journal of Southern History* 77, no. 1 (2011): 17–52; and Winthrop D. Jordan, *Tumult and Silence at Second Creek: An Inquiry into a Civil War Slave Conspiracy* (Baton Rouge: Louisiana State University Press, 1993).

12. See Jeff Forret, *Race Relations at the Margins: Slaves and Poor Whites in the Antebellum Southern Countryside* (Baton Rouge: Louisiana State University Press, 2006), esp. 115–56; and Timothy James Lockley, *Lines in the Sand: Race and Class in Lowcountry Georgia, 1750–1860* (Athens: University of Georgia Press, 2001), esp. 98–130.

13. David Libby rightly notes that Virgil Stewart's depiction of the initiation ceremony of John Murrell's mystic clan drew on imagined understandings of Ma-

sonry. See Libby, *Slavery and Frontier Mississippi*, 108. On conspiracy theories in American history, see Richard Hofstader's classic *The Paranoid Style in American Politics and Other Essays* (New York: Alfred A. Knopf, 1965); David Brion Davis, *The Fear of Conspiracy: Images of Un-American Subversion from the Revolution to the Present* (Ithaca: Cornell University Press, 1971); David Brion Davis, *The Slave Power Conspiracy and the Paranoid Style* (Baton Rouge: Louisiana State University Press, 1969); and Peter Knight, ed., *Conspiracy Theories in American History: An Encyclopedia* (Santa Barbara; Calif.: ABC-CLIO, 1993).

14. William C. Davis, *A Way through the Wilderness: The Natchez Trace and the Civilization of the Southern Frontier* (New York: HarperCollins, 1995), esp. 258–79. Also see John D. W. Guice, "A Trace of Violence?," *Southern Quarterly* 29, no. 4 (1991): 123–43; Robert V. Haynes, "Law Enforcement in Frontier Mississippi," *Journal of Mississippi History* 22 (January–October 1960): 27–42; Raymond Friday Locke, "The Natchez Trace: 'Road of Blood,'" *Mankind* 4, no. 12 (1975): 30–37; Virginia Park Matthias, "Natchez-under-the-Hill as It Developed under the Influence of the Mississippi River and the Natchez Trace," *Journal of Mississippi History* 7, no. 4 (1945): 201–21; John Francis McDermott, ed., *Before Mark Twain: A Sampler of Old, Old Times on the Mississippi* (Carbondale: Southern Illinois University Press, 1968); Thomas Ruys Smith, *River of Dreams: Imagining the Mississippi before Mark Twain* (Baton Rouge: Louisiana State University Press, 2007), esp. 141–76; and Jack K. Williams, "Crime and Punishment in Alabama, 1819–1840," *Alabama Review* 6 (January 1953): 14–30.

15. On Samuel Mason and other celebrated regional criminals of his era such as Micajah Harpe, Wiley Harpe, and Joseph Hare, see John Francis Hamtramck Claiborne, *Mississippi, as a Province, Territory, and State*, vol. 1 (Jackson, 1880), 225–28, 530–31; Davis, *Way through the Wilderness*, 272–76; Guice, "A Trace of Violence?"; Joseph Thompson Hare, *The Life and Dying Confession of Joseph T. Hare* (Baltimore, 1818); and Otto A. Rothert, *The Outlaws of Cave-in-Rock* (1924; reprint, Carbondale: Southern Illinois University Press, 1996). The notoriety of the Southwest was always probably somewhat exaggerated, and one can see the conflation of fact, legend, and hyperbole in work on criminality in the region well into the twentieth century. Works that serve as fine (and admittedly rousing) examples of the problem include Robert M. Coates, *The Outlaw Years: The History of the Land Pirates of the Natchez Trace* (New York, 1930); and Jonathan Daniels, *The Devil's Backbone: The Story of the Natchez Trace* (New York: McGraw-Hill, 1962).

16. *CAP*; Henry S. Foote, *The Bench and Bar of the South and Southwest* (St. Louis, 1876), 36; Henry S. Foote, *Casket of Reminiscences* (Washington, D.C., 1874), 432.

17. *CAP*, 29, 33, 46; Foote, *Bench and Bar*, 37; Foote, *Casket of Reminiscences*, 433;

Alonzo Phelps to Governor Runnels, March 11, 1834, Governor's Papers, RG27, ser. 714, vol. 21, MDAH.

18. Phelps to Runnels, March 11, 1834, MDAH (quotation); *CAP*, 44–45; Foote, *Casket of Reminiscences*, 434. The accounts of Phelps's death provided in these sources vary in the details but agree in broad outline. The description above relies most heavily on the version presented in *CAP*.

19. *CAP*, 45–46; Foote, *Casket of Reminiscences*, 434–35.

20. Phelps to Runnels, March 11, 1834, MDAH.

21. *CAP*. The few firsthand accounts we have of the lives of poor whites in the antebellum South comport all too well with Phelps's descriptions. See, for example, Charles C. Bolton and Scott Culclasure, eds., *The Confessions of Edward Isham: A Poor White Life of the Old South* (Athens: University of Georgia Press, 1998), 1–18.

22. *CAP*, 44. The concept of the "social bandit," who achieved heroic status among the masses by flouting authority and casting his actions as being on behalf of the oppressed, was first explored at length by Eric Hobsbawm in two works, *Primitive Rebels: Studies in Archaic Forms of Social Movement in the 19th and 20th Centuries* (Manchester: Manchester University Press, 1959); and *Bandits*, rev. ed. (1969; New York: New Press, 2000).

23. *CAP*, 2–3 (quotation), 10–11, 14, 16, 24–26, 32.

24. Ibid., 19, 22 (first quotation), 34 (second quotation), 2 (remaining quotations). Similarly, in his letter to Governor Runnels, Phelps claimed he devoted much of the time he spent alone in the woods to "readeing books of all kinds." Henry Foote concluded that Phelps was indeed "a ripe and accurate scholar" who had on his person when arrested a "much-worn pocket-copy of Horace" that "he was able to read with much more facility than our ordinary college graduates would be likely to evince." Phelps to Runnels, March 11, 1834, MDAH; Foote, *Bench and Bar*, 36.

25. *CAP*, 42 (first quotation), 22 (remaining quotations).

26. Ibid., 15, 27 (last three quotations), 30 (first two quotations), 31 (third and fourth quotations), 35.

27. *Clinton Gazette* in *Jackson Mississippian*, July 4, 1834; *Jackson Mississippian*, June 6, 1834. Also see *CAP*, 43, 50; Foote, *Bench and Bar*, 36; and Foote, *Casket of Reminiscences*, 433. For one of the poems written about Phelps, see "The Rob Roy of the Mississippi," which appeared in the *Jackson Mississippian*, December 16, 1841, though it was originally published in the *Vicksburg Register* in 1834 under the title "Phelps, the Criminal." *CAP*, 48–49.

28. *CAP*, 16, 14, 22, 34; *LP*, 47.

29. *CAP*, 14.

30. *LP*, 47 (quotation), 54.

31. *CAP*, 33 (first quotation); *LP*, 59 (remaining quotations), 62. It is worth noting that in the *History of Virgil A. Stewart*, Stewart included an affidavit, supposedly authored by Henry Foote in the spring of 1836, purporting that Foote had in his possession the original manuscript of the *Confession of Alonzo Phelps* and that it contained "a statement of a plan for exciting an insurrection among the slaves of the south" and an acknowledgment by Phelps that he had "a large number of associates, whose names he cautiously concealed from the public." Foote further asserted in the affidavit that he withheld that part of the manuscript from publication "on account of my believing it dangerous to publish it," but that any curious party could come examine the text and that its existence inclined him to believe that Stewart told the truth about John Murrell. Henry Foote did act as one of Alonzo Phelps's attorneys at his trial for the murder of Owen Rhodes and claimed in his memoirs to have helped transcribe part of Phelps's *Confession*. Given Phelps's hostility toward slavery and his relationships with other criminals, it is not impossible to imagine him remarking on the prospects for a slave insurrection or saying that he knew the names of other bandits. The notion that Foote would keep secret a plan for a slave rebellion, however, is far-fetched. If anything, the danger posed by that information is precisely why Foote would have shared it. Given that Foote's name is misspelled as "H. S. Foot" on the affidavit Stewart published, it seems not unreasonable to conclude that Stewart fabricated the document. But even if it was genuine, nowhere did Foote claim that Phelps knew John Murrell, that his "plan" for an insurrection resembled the one Stewart described, or that his "large number of associates" was an organization of any kind, much less one like Murrell's mystic clan. *VAS*, 261–262; Foote, *Casket of Reminiscences*, 434.

32. *CAP*, 8, 28.

33. Adams County Combination Tax Rolls, 1834, MDAH; Warren County Combination Tax Rolls, 1835, MDAH; *PCMC*, 19, 29–30; "Transactions."

34. Letter dated July 24, 1835, *Natchez Courier*, August 7, 1835, in *Woodville Republican*, August 15, 1835; *Woodville Republican*, November 14, 1835; "Transactions"; *Vicksburg Register*, August 13, 1835.

35. *Woodville Republican*, August 15, 1835; *PCMC*, 29.

36. *PCMC*, 29 (quotation), 30.

37. Ibid., 30; "Transactions"; *Woodville Republican*, August 15, 1835.

38. *PCMC*, 30 (quotation); *Woodville Republican*, August 15, 1835. These sources provide slightly different but essentially compatible versions of John Earl's testimony to the Livingston Committee of Safety. The version originally published in the *Natchez Courier*, for example, indicates that John Earl claimed both his brother and his mother bullied him into helping Andrew Boyd escape punishment for slave stealing.

39. *Woodville Republican*, August 15, 1835; *Vicksburg Register*, August 13, 1835.

40. *Vicksburg Register*, September 17, 1835; *PCMC*, 29.

41. *Vicksburg Register*, September 17, 1835 (quotation); *Woodville Republican*, August 15, 1835; *PCMC*, 31.

42. *Vicksburg Register*, September 17 (first four quotations) and August 13, 1835 (last quotation).

43. The Madison County correspondent of the *Natchez Courier* reported that he had no idea what happened to John Earl but understood that when Earl got back to Warren he "would not be hanged, [and] that the circumstances under which he acted would be taken into consideration." Earl was still living in Warren County in 1836. *Woodville Republican*, August 15, 1835; Warren County Combination Tax Rolls, 1836, MDAH.

44. *PCMC*, 15, 16; *Woodville Republican*, August 15, 1835.

45. *PCMC*, 30; *VAS*, 204.

46. *Woodville Republican*, August 15, 1835; *PCMC*, 30, 16.

47. *Woodville Republican*, August 15, 1835.

48. *PCMC*, 18 (quotation), 33–35.

49. Ibid., 33.

50. Ibid., 33–34 (quotations on 34).

51. Ibid., 34–35.

52. Ibid., 35.

53. Ibid.

54. *Jackson Mississippian*, July 17, 1835.

55. Ibid. Other newspapers in the aftermath of the scare similarly stressed the danger to property rights in slaves entailed by an insurrection like the one about which Virgil Stewart warned. The *Argus* of Columbus, Mississippi, for example, asserted as calm seemed restored that "this affair should warn our state authorities of the necessity of increased vigilance for the preservation of public safety. We have no fear of the white population—but our planters may lose a great amount of slave property, if this disgraceful nest of thieves and robbers is not entirely broken up." A Georgia newspaper, meanwhile, asserted in writing about organized slave stealing generally and the insurrection scare specifically that "this *crime* and this *crisis* should suggest to the civil authority, and the community at large, the utmost vigilance in hunting down a system of Larceny, which strikes at the very root of our social relations and our rights of property." Looking back on the behavior of Governor Hiram Runnels during the insurrection scare, one wonders whether he hesitated to do anything because even as he knew that pandemonium was taking over ever-larger portions of his state he worried that calling out the militia could signal to potential investors and settlers that Mississippians lacked control over the slave population

and that the state was thus too unstable and dangerous a place to put their capital. *Columbus Argus* in *United States Telegraph*, August 3, 1835; *Milledgeville Standard of Union* in *Jackson Mississippian*, November 27, 1835.

EPILOGUE. Memory and Meaning

1. Daniel S. Dupre, *Transforming the Cotton Frontier: Madison County, Alabama, 1800–1840* (Baton Rouge: Louisiana State University Press, 1997), 225–37; *Nashville Republican*, August 18 (fourth and fifth quotations) and 22 (first quotation), 1835; *Washington Globe*, August 21, 1835 (second and third quotations).

2. New Orleans City Council, "Report of a Conspiracy to Incite a Rebellion throughout the Slave States," August 1, 1835, Cornell University Division of Rare and Manuscript Collections, Carl A. Kroch Library, Ithaca, N.Y., 1 (first quotation); *Nashville Republican*, September 3, 1835 (second, third, sixth, and seventh quotations); *North Carolina Standard* (Raleigh), September 10, 1835 (fourth quotation); *New Orleans Bee*, August 11, 1835 (fifth quotation).

3. *Nashville Republican*, August 20 (first two quotations) and September 3, 1835; *New Orleans Bee*, July 21, August 17 (third quotation), and September 2, 1835; *Baltimore American*, January 21, 1836; Rachel O'Connor to Alfred Conrad, August 24, 1835 (fourth quotation), and O'Connor to Frances S. Weeks, September 7, 1835 (fifth quotation), both in Weeks Family Papers, LLMVC. To some extent, fear remained evident past July within Mississippi as well. In the middle of September, for example, whites in Livingston hanged a slave belonging to Thomas Hudnall who had fled two months earlier on learning that the committee of safety wanted to interrogate him and was later recaptured. See *Niles' Weekly Register*, October 31, 1835.

4. *Baltimore Gazette*, October 6, 1835 (first quotation); *Baltimore American*, October 26, 1835; *Jackson Mississippian*, December 11, 1835 (second quotation); *Baltimore Gazette*, January 21, 1836 (third quotation); Edward E. Baptist, *Creating an Old South: Middle Florida's Plantation Frontier before the Civil War* (Chapel Hill: University of North Carolina Press, 2002), 207 (fourth quotation).

5. *Nashville Republican*, December 12, 1835 (first two quotations); *Vicksburg Register*, December 17 (third quotation) and 31, 1835; H. L. Green to Frances Sprague, November 28, 1835, Winchester Family Papers, Natchez Trace Collection, University of Texas, Austin (fourth and fifth quotations); *Clinton Gazette*, December 26, 1835 (sixth and seventh quotations); Mary Ann Rebecca Wyche to Thomas Wyche, January 15, 1836, Wyche-Otey Papers, folder 2, ser. 1.1, SHC (seventh and eighth quotations). Fears increased again around Christmas Day 1835 in Louisiana as well. See, for example, *New Orleans Observer*, January 2, 1836; *Arkansas Gazette*, February 2, 1836; and *Baltimore Gazette*, January 12, 1836.

6. For one example of Stewart's pamphlet being published serially, see the

Huntsville (Ala.) Southern Advocate, beginning with the August 4, 1835, issue. A summary of Stewart's pamphlet provided by the *Lynchburg Virginian* was republished especially widely. It appeared in part or in whole in the *Baltimore American*, August 6, 1835; *New York Journal of Commerce*, September 8, 1835; *United States Telegraph*, August 6, 1835; *North Carolina Standard* (Raleigh), September 3, 1835; *Arkansas Gazette*, September 1, 1835; *Boston Courier*, August 11, 1835; *Richmond Enquirer*, August 4, 1835; and *Charleston Courier*, August 13, 1835, among others.

7. *Jackson Mississippian*, November 20, 1835; *Jackson Banner* in *Greenville (S.C.) Mountaineer*, September 19, 1835; *Bolivar Free Press* in *Western Weekly Review* (Franklin, Tenn.), October 9, 1835; *Augusta (Ga.) Chronicle* in *Charleston Courier*, August 26, 1835; *New York Journal of Commerce*, September 8, 1835; *Philadelphia Enquirer* in *Baltimore American*, August 10, 1835. Also see *Georgia Constitutionalist* in *Jackson Mississippian*, November 27, 1835.

8. Israel Campbell, *Bond and Free: or, Yearnings for Freedom* (Philadelphia, 1861), 72 (first quotation), 73 (second quotation); Henry S. Foote, *The Bench and Bar of the South and Southwest* (St. Louis, 1876), 66 (third and fourth quotations); Henry S. Foote, *Casket of Reminiscences* (Washington, D.C., 1874), 251 (fifth quotation); *Jackson Mississippian*, June 23, 1837 (sixth quotation), and December 25, 1835; *Journal of the House of Representatives of the State of Mississippi* (Jackson, 1836), 101, 112–13; *Jackson Banner* in *Greenville (S.C.) Mountaineer*, September 19, 1835. Also see J. F. H. Claiborne, *Life and Correspondence of John A. Quitman*, vol. 1 (New York, 1860), 138; and *VAS*, 269–71.

9. *Jackson Mississippian*, November 20, 1835, and February 19, 1836; *Western Weekly Review* (Franklin, Tenn.), October 9, October 16, and November 20, 1835; *Clinton Gazette*, November 21, 1835 (quotations).

10. *VAS*.

11. James Lal Penick Jr., *The Great Western Land Pirate: John A. Murrell in Legend and History* (Columbia: University of Missouri Press, 1981), 164, 170. For reviews and notices about *VAS*, see *Atkinson's Saturday Evening Post*, August 27, 1836; *New-Yorker*, August 27, 1836; *Journal of Belles Lettres*, September 6, 1836; *Western Monthly Magazine and Literary Journal*, November 1836, 689–90; *Family Magazine*, 1837, 160; and *American Monthly Magazine*, November 1836, 502–6.

12. *Nashville Banner and Whig*, August 17, 1835; *Liberty Hall and Cincinnati Gazette*, September 3, 1835.

13. *Western Weekly Review* (Franklin, Tenn.), November 20, 1835.

14. Ibid., October 16, 1835.

15. *VAS*, 13, 50, 122–123; *Randolph Recorder*, December 4 (first and second quotations) and 18 (third quotation), 1835.

16. *Randolph Recorder*, December 4, 18, and 25, 1835.

17. *Journal of the House of Representatives of the State of Mississippi* (Jackson, 1836), 366–67; *Jackson Mississippian*, June 23, 1837.

18. Yalobusha County Deed Book B, 349–50, MDAH; *Jackson Mississippian*, June 23, 1837.

19. *Southern Times and State Gazette* (Columbia, S.C.), February 23, 1838; *New Orleans Daily Picayune*, July 3, 1838; *Pennsylvania Inquirer and Daily Courier*, July 4, 1840; *New England Weekly Review* (Hartford, Conn.), February 1, 1840 (first three quotations); *Daily Atlas* (Boston, Mass.), June 5, 1841; "Uses and Abuses of Lynch Law, No. III," *American Whig Review* 12 (March 1851): 216–17 (fourth quotation on 217); *Fayetteville (N.C.) Observer*, April 28, 1846.

20. N. H. Bannister, "Murrell, the Pirate," Harvard Theater Collection, Cambridge, Mass.; *American Turf Register and Sporting Magazine*, 1836, 587; *Nashville Republican*, September 12, September 19, October 3 (first two quotations), and November 19, 1835 (third and fourth quotations).

21. *Nashville Republican*, November 24, 1835; Diary of Bradley Kimbrough, February 16, 1837, TSLA; Madison County Will Book 2, 1835–39, 409, TSLA; Madison County Will Book 3, 1839–43, 17, 366–68, TSLA; Madison County Circuit Court Order Book, 1828–36, 522, 537, 550, TSLA; Madison County Circuit Court Minute Book 2, 1840–44, 94, TSLA; Madison County Marriages vol. A, 1838–46, 70, TSLA; Tennessee Prison Records, 1831–1992, part 2: Oversized Volumes, vol. 43, Main Prison, 1831–65, RG25, TSLA; *Columbia (Tenn.) Democrat*, April 18, 1844; *Nashville Whig*, November 21, 1844.

22. *Nashville Banner* in *Chicago American*, September 19, 1835; *New York Evening Post*, August 15, 1835.

23. *Mobile Daily Commercial Register and Patriot*, July 22, 1835. There were a small number of exceptions to this generalization. See, for example, *Huntsville Southern Advocate*, July 28, 1835; and *New Orleans True American* in *New York Evening Post*, July 30, 1835.

24. *Niles' Weekly Register*, August 22, 1835; *Boston Courier*, September 3, 1835. On the abolitionists' postal campaign, see Donna Lee Dickerson, *The Course of Tolerance: Freedom of the Press in Nineteenth-Century America* (New York: Greenwood Press, 1990), ch. 4; William W. Freehling, *Prelude to Civil War: The Nullification Controversy in South Carolina, 1816–1836* (New York: Harper and Row, 1965), 340–48; Richard R. John, *Spreading the News: The American Postal System from Franklin to Morse* (Cambridge: Harvard University Press, 1995), 257–80; Leonard L. Richards, *"Gentlemen of Property and Standing": Anti-Abolition Mobs in Jacksonian America* (New York: Oxford University Press, 1970), 51–62, 71–75; Bertram Wyatt-Brown, *Lewis Tappan and the Evangelical War against Slavery* (Cleveland: Case Western Reserve Press, 1969), 149–66; Bertram Wyatt-Brown, "The Abolitionists' Postal

Campaign of 1835," *Journal of Negro History* 50, no. 4 (1965): 227–38; and Susan Wyly-Jones, "The 1835 Anti-Abolition Meetings in the South: A New Look at the Controversy over the Abolition Postal Campaign," *Civil War History* 47, no. 4 (2001): 289–309.

25. *National Intelligencer* in *Niles' Weekly Register*, August 22, 1835; *Nashville Republican*, August 4, 1835; *New York Journal of Commerce*, October 15, 1835.

26. *Niles' Weekly Register*, August 22, 1835; *Jackson Mississippian*, August 14, 1835.

27. *Tuscaloosa (Ala.) Flag of the Union* in *North Carolina Standard* (Raleigh), September 10 and October 8, 1835; *Woodville Republican*, October 24, 1835; *United States Telegraph*, September 24, 1835; *Jackson Mississippian*, February 5, 1835. Also see William Winans to Obadiah Winans, November 14, 1835, box 17, letter book 9, Winans Papers, J. B. Cain Archives, Millsaps College, Jackson, Miss.

28. *VAS*, 58–59. On George Thompson's lecture tour, see C. Duncan Rice, "The Anti-Slavery Mission of George Thompson to the United States, 1834–1835," *Journal of American Studies* 2, no. 1 (1968): 13–31. More than a decade later, the notion that John Murrell had a correspondence with George Thompson was still part of the story people told about Murrell, his clan, and his plot. See, for example, "Uses and Abuses of Lynch Law, Article Second," *American Whig Review* 12 (November 1850): 499.

29. Letter from Macon, Georgia, in *New York Journal of Commerce*, October 12, 1835 (first quotation); *Richmond Whig* in *Nashville Republican*, September 3, 1835 (second quotation); *Nashville Republican*, August 4 (third and fifth quotations) and August 11, 1835 (ninth quotation); *New Orleans Observer*, September 19, 1835 (sixth and seventh quotations); *Clinton Gazette*, September 12, 1835 (fourth and eighth quotations). Also see *Richmond Compiler* in *Baltimore American*, August 7, 1835. On the ease with which southerners made connections between John Murrell and abolitionism in the wake of the postal campaign, also see Penick, *Great Western Land Pirate*, 151–57; Dupre, *Transforming the Cotton Frontier*, 225–26, 231–36; and David Grimsted, *American Mobbing, 1828–1861: Toward Civil War* (New York: Oxford University Press, 1998), 154–56. For instances of abolitionists arrested on charges of slave stealing, see *Narrative of Facts, Respecting Alanson Work, Jas. E. Burr, and Geo. Thompson, Prisoners in the Missouri Penitentiary, for the Alleged Crime of Negro Stealing* (Quincy, Ill., 1842); *A History of the Trial of Miss Delia A. Webster, at Lexington, Kentucky, Dec'r 17–21, 1844* (Vergennes, Vt., 1845); *Substance of an Argument of Samuel F. Vinton, for the Defendants, in the Cause of the Commonwealth of Virginia vs. Peter M. Garner and Others* (Marietta, Ohio, 1846); and *Trial and Imprisonment of Jonathan Walker, at Pensacola, Florida, for Aiding Slaves to Escape from Bondage* (Boston, 1846).

30. *United States Gazette*, August 1, 1835; *Vicksburg Register*, November 19, 1835;

New Orleans Bee, August 19, 1835; *Arkansas Gazette*, August 18 and September 8, 1835; *Nashville Republican*, August 11, 1835; also see *Nashville Banner and Whig*, September 21, 1835.

31. Charles Caldwell, *A Discourse on the Vice of Gambling, Delivered, by Appointment, to the Anti-Gambling Society of Transylvania University, November 2nd and 3rd, 1835* (Lexington, 1835), 16, 11.

32. Ibid., 11, 12–13.

33. Ibid., 11–12, 13, 14. Also see pp. 53–59, an appendix to the address in which Caldwell elaborated on the above themes.

34. *New York Journal of Commerce*, August 28 and September 11, 1835. For examples of mass meetings held in northern cities, see *Niles' Weekly Register*, August 29, September 5, October 3, and October 10, 1835. On anti-abolitionist mob violence, see Richards, *"Gentlemen of Property and Standing"*; and Grimsted, *American Mobbing*, 19–22, 25–27.

35. *New York Journal of Commerce*, July 28, 1835; *New York Evening Star* in *Charleston Courier*, August 14, 1835; *New York Morning Courier and New York Enquirer*, October 9, 1835; *New York Morning News* in *Liberator*, November 7, 1835; *New York Morning News* in *United States Telegraph*, October 22, 1835. Also see *New York Gazette* in *Newport (R.I.) Mercury*, August 8, 1835.

36. *Liberator*, August 1, 1835.

37. *Amherst (Mass.) Cabinet* in *Massachusetts Spy* (Worcester), August 12, 1835.

38. "Land Piracy," *Quarterly Anti-Slavery Magazine* 2, no. 1 (1836): 104–5.

39. *Narrative of the Late Riotous Proceedings against the Liberty of the Press, in Cincinnati* (Cincinnati, 1836), 9; *Third Annual Report of the American Anti-Slavery Society* (New York, 1836), 50–51 (quotation on 51).

40. Abraham Lincoln, "Address before the Young Men's Lyceum of Springfield, Illinois, January 27, 1838," in *The Collected Works of Abraham Lincoln*, vol. 1, ed. Roy P. Basler, 109–10 (New Brunswick, N.J.: Rutgers University Press, 1953); Thodore Dwight Weld, comp., *American Slavery as It Is: Testimony of a Thousand Witnesses* (New York, 1839), 146.

41. "Illustrations of the Anti-Slavery Almanac for 1840" (New York, 1840), Rare Book and Special Collections Division, Library of Congress, Washington, D.C.

42. Speech of Sherrard Clemens, January 22, 1861, *Congressional Globe*, 36th Congress, 2nd session, appendix, 105.

43. James Penick details some of the ways the story of Stewart and Murrell has persisted in popular culture in *Great Western Land Pirate*, 168–74, but his impatience with the more absurd manifestations of the legend is plain. A more thorough and informative exploration of the topic that includes an extensive bibiliography is Thomas Ruys Smith, "Independence Day, 1835: The John A. Murrell Conspiracy

and the Lynching of the Vicksburg Gamblers in Literature," *Mississippi Quarterly* 59, nos. 1–2 (2005–6): 129–60.

44. Herman Melville, *The Confidence-Man: His Masquerade* (New York, 1857), 2. The most recent novel adopting the Murrell and Stewart story is John Wray, *Canaan's Tongue* (New York: Alfred A. Knopf, 2005). The *National Police Gazette* life of Murrell ran from September 12, 1846, through April 24, 1847, and appeared as a single volume in *The Life and Adventures of John A. Murrell, the Great Western Land Pirate* in 1847. Broad interest in Murrell's life during the antebellum era is suggested by some of the more shameless attempts of other nineteenth-century authors to capitalize on it with only tangentially connected stories, such as *The Female Land Pirate; or Awful, Mysterious, and Horrible Disclosures of Amanda Bannorris, Wife and Accomplice of Richard Bannorris, a Leader in that Terrible Band of Robbers and Murderers, Known Far and Wide as the Murrell Men* (Cincinnati, 1847); and *James Wellard, Companion of John A. Murrell, the Great Western Land Pirate* (Cincinnati, 1855).

45. Quotation from original poster for the film *Natchez Trace*, in possession of the author; C. William Harrison, *Outlaw of the Natchez Trace* (New York: Ballantine Books, 1960); Paul I. Wellman, *Spawn of Evil: The Invisible Empire of Soulless Men which for a Generation Held the Nation in a Spell of Terror* (New York: Doubleday, 1964), 140, 141, 142. Larry McMurtry recalled that producer Alan Pakula asked him to write a treatment of the Murrell story based on Wellman's work. The film treatment, in McMurtry's recollection, ran more than five hundred pages, but the movie was never made. Given Wellman's leanings toward the purple, that may have been for the best. See Larry McMurtry, *Film Flam: Essays on Hollywood* (New York: Touchstone, 1987), 17–18.

46. William Faulkner, *Requiem for a Nun* (New York: Random House, 1951); William Faulkner, *Absalom! Absalom!* (New York: Random House, 1936); Jorge Luis Borges, "The Cruel Redeemer Lazarus Morell," in *Collected Fictions* (1935; reprint, New York: Penguin, 1998), 6–12; Eudora Welty, "A Still Moment," in *The Wide Net and Other Stories* (1941; reprint, New York: Harcourt Brace, 1971), 73–94; William Gilmore Simms, *Richard Hurdis; or, The Avenger of Blood: A Tale of Alabama* (Philadelphia, 1838); Mark Twain, *Life on the Mississippi* (1883; reprint, New York, 1901), 214–19; Smith, "Independence Day, 1835," 151–52.

47. Herbert A. Kellar, "A Journey through the South in 1836: Diary of James D. Davidson," *Journal of Southern History* 1, no. 3 (1935): 355; *Jackson Mississippian*, March 24, 1837.

48. Historians have long debated the causes of the Panic of 1837, and have particularly argued over whether the crisis resulted from foreign or domestic causes and about the role Andrew Jackson's banking and financial policies played. Varying perspectives on these arguments can be found in the literature on antebellum banking and finance cited in the prologue. The admittedly oversimplified summary

above attempts to place many of the factors scholars have identified in some kind of balance and draws most heavily on the work of Jessica Lepler, Peter Rousseau, and Peter Temin. See Jessica M. Lepler, "1837: Anatomy of a Panic" (Ph.D. diss., Brandeis University, 2008); Peter L. Rousseau, "Jacksonian Monetary Policy, Specie Flows, and the Panic of 1837," *Journal of Economic History* 62, no. 2 (2002): 457–88; and Peter Temin, *The Jacksonian Economy* (New York: W. W. Norton, 1969), esp. 113–37. Also see Edward J. Balleisen, *Navigating Failure: Bankruptcy and Commercial Society in Antebellum America* (Chapel Hill: University of North Carolina Press, 2001), 32–41.

49. *Niles' Weekly Register*, June 3, 1837. Jessica Lepler suggests that Americans in the era leading up to the Panic of 1837 had little sense of a business cycle and thus an extremely imperfect understanding of the likelihood of a crisis like the one they would experience. Even if Americans' comprehension of economics lacked maturity, however, many observers had expressed concern about the sustainability and substance of the speculative economy of the 1830s for years before it all came tumbling down. Lepler, "1837," 3–5.

50. John Hebron Moore, *Agriculture in Ante-Bellum Mississippi* (New York: Bookman Associates, 1958), 70–71; Mary Elizabeth Young, *Redskins, Ruffleshirts, and Rednecks: Indian Allotments in Alabama and Mississippi, 1830–1860* (Norman: University of Oklahoma Press, 1961), 177–78; J. A. Orr, "A Trip from Houston to Jackson, Miss., in 1845," *Publications of the Mississippi Historical Society* 9 (1906): 175 (quotation); Reginald Charles McGrane, *The Panic of 1837: Some Financial Problems of the Jacksonian Era* (New York, 1924), 118.

51. William H. Wills, "A Southern Traveler's Diary, 1840," *Southern History Association Publications* 8 (1904): 35–36; Franklin L. Riley, "Diary of a Mississippi Planter, January 1, 1840, to April, 1863," *Mississippi Historical Society Publications* 10 (1909): 311, 318. John Peters, a dry goods merchant from New York who made his way to Mississippi after a business failure in 1838, found conditions in the state so abysmal that he used the same language repeatedly to describe them: "business dull and money scarce" (Margaret L. Brown, "John Peters' Diary of 1838–1841," *Mississippi Valley Historical Review* 21, no. 4 [1935]: 532, 534, 536).

52. *Christian Secretary*, May 20, 1837; Wills, "A Southern Traveler's Diary," 35; Rev. J. R. Hutchison, *Reminiscences, Sketches and Addresses Selected from My Papers during a Ministry of Forty-five years in Mississippi, Louisiana and Texas* (Houston, 1874), 53.

53. McGrane, *Panic of 1837*, 117; Moore, *Agriculture in Ante-Bellum Mississippi*, 72–73; Orr, "A Trip from Houston to Jackson," 175–76; Wills, "A Southern Traveler's Diary," 35; Riley, "Diary of a Mississippi Planter," 317–18 (quotation).

54. Richard Holcombe Kilbourne Jr., *Slave Agriculture and Financial Markets in Antebellum America: The Bank of the United States in Mississippi, 1831–1852* (London:

Pickering and Chatto, 2006), 138–39; Moore, *Agriculture in Ante-Bellum Mississippi*, 72; Ulrich B. Phillips, *American Negro Slavery* (New York, 1918), chart opposite 370; *Jackson Mississippian*, May 5, 1837.

55. A state-supported institution in its origin, the Union Bank's reliance on the state escalated in 1838 when a supplemental law allowed the governor to use proceeds from the initial bond sales to purchase five million dollars of bank stock directly. See Bradley G. Bond, *Political Culture in the Nineteenth-Century South: Mississippi, 1830–1900* (Baton Rouge: Louisiana State University Press, 1995), 83–84; Edwin Arthur Miles, *Jacksonian Democracy in Mississippi* (Chapel Hill: University of North Carolina Press, 1960), 142–43; James Roger Sharp, *The Jacksonians versus the Banks: Politics in the States after the Panic of 1837* (New York: Columbia University Press, 1970), 63–64; Charles Hillman Brough, "The History of Banking in Mississippi," in *Publications of the Mississippi Historical Society*, vol. 3, ed. Franklin L. Riley, 327–29 (Oxford, Miss., 1901).

56. *Jackson Mississippian*, April 21 and May 19, 1837.

57. For some examples of Mississippi Supreme Court cases ruling against slave traders attempting to recover debts from resident Mississippians, see *Green* v. *Robinson*, 6 Miss. 80 (December 1840); *Glidewell et al.* v. *Hite et al.*, 6 Miss. 110 (December 1840); *Brien* v. *Williamson*, 8 Miss. 14 (1843); and *Thomas et al.* v. *Phillips*, 12 Miss. 358 (1845).

58. Lewis Cecil Gray, *History of Agriculture in the Southern United States to 1860*, vol. 2 (Washington, D.C., 1933), 1027; Sharp, *Jacksonians versus the Banks*, 60–88; Miles, *Jacksonian Democracy in Mississippi*, 146–59; Bond, *Political Culture in the Nineteenth-Century South*, 82–89; Larry Schweikart, *Banking in the American South from the Age of Jackson to Reconstruction* (Baton Rouge: Louisiana State University Press, 1987), 26–27, 180–82; *Groves* v. *Slaughter*, 40 U.S. 449 (1841).

59. Henry Ward Beecher, *Seven Lectures to Young Men, on Various Important Subjects; Delivered before the Young Men of Indianapolis, Indiana, during the Winter of 1843–4* (Indianapolis, 1844), 105, 53. For the observation that moral distinctions between "speculation" and "gambling" collapse especially during economic panics into a generalized suspicion of speculative economic activities, see Jackson Lears, *Something for Nothing: Luck in America* (New York: Viking, 2003), 100, 101, 128. On the rethinking of self-reliance, individual agency, and failure in the wake of the Panic of 1837, see Scott A. Sandage, *Born Losers: A History of Failure in America* (Cambridge: Harvard University Press, 2005), esp. 44–69.

60. *Fourth Annual Report of the American Anti-Slavery Society* (New York, 1837), 50–52.

61. "The Financial Power of Slavery," *Emancipator and Free American*, October 22, 1840. For more on abolitionists' use of the panic to draw attention to the economic distortions wrought by slavery and the significance of Leavitt's tract in

particular, see Julian P. Bretz, "The Economic Background of the Liberty Party," *American Historical Review* 34, no. 2 (1929), 252–56.

62. Even leading antislavery activists conceded there was propaganda value in drawing attention to slavery's role in the downturn. See *Fourth Annual Report of the American Anti-Slavery Society*, 55; Bretz, "Economic Background of the Liberty Party," 253.

63. *Fourth Annual Report of the American Anti-Slavery Society*, 56, 52.

64. Ibid., 51; "The Financial Power of Slavery."

65. Kilbourne, *Slave Agriculture and Financial Markets*, 2–3, 108–9, 127–40.

INDEX

~ ~

Race in the Atlantic World, 1700–1900

Missing Links:
The African and American Worlds of R. L. Garner, Primate Collector
by Jeremy Rich

Almost Free:
A Story about Family and Race in Antebellum Virginia
by Eva Sheppard Wolf

To Live an Antislavery Life:
Personal Politics and the Antebellum Black Middle Class
by Erica L. Ball

Flush Times and Fever Dreams:
A Story of Capitalism and Slavery in the Age of Jackson
by Joshua D. Rothman